THE CLASSICAL TEMPER

THE CLASSICAL TEMPER

A Study of James Joyce's
Ulysses

By
S. L. GOLDBERG

1961
CHATTO AND WINDUS
LONDON

Published by
Chatto & Windus Ltd
40-42 William IV Street
London W.C. 2

*

Clarke, Irwin & Co. Ltd
Toronto

Printed in Great Britain by
T. and A. Constable Ltd
Hopetoun Street, Edinburgh

For J

CONTENTS

ACKNOWLEDGMENTS

For permission to use material from the works of James Joyce, acknowledgment is gratefully made to The Society of Authors and to the following: for quotations from *Ulysses*, The Bodley Head and Random House, Inc; from *A Portrait of the Artist as a Young Man*, Jonathan Cape Ltd. and The Viking Press Inc; from *Stephen Hero*, Jonathan Cape Ltd. and New Directions.

Acknowledgments are also due to the following for material used: from St. Thomas Aquinas, *Summa Theologica* trans. by the Fathers of the English Dominican Province, to Burns Oates and Washbourne Ltd; from the translation of Aristotle edited by W. D. Ross (1928-52), to The Clarendon Press; from the article "The Jew in Search of a Son", to R. P. Blackmur and *The Virginia Quarterly Review* (Winter 1948); from Frank Budgen, *James Joyce and the Making of Ulysses* (1934, 1937), to Grayson and Grayson; from T. S. Eliot, *On Poetry and Poets* (1957), to Faber and Faber Ltd; from the article "Cormac's Ruined House", to D. J. Enright and *Scrutiny* (1943); from Stuart Gilbert, *James Joyce's Ulysses* (1930, 1952), to Faber and Faber Ltd; from Herbert Gorman, *James Joyce, a Definitive Biography* (1941, 1949), to The Bodley Head; from Charles Feidelson Jr., *Symbolism and American Literature* (1953), to The University of Chicago Press; from Robert Humphrey, *Stream of Consciousness in the Modern Novel* (1954), to The University of California Press; from Richard M. Kain, *Fabulous Voyager* (1947), to The University of Chicago Press; from Hugh Kenner, *Dublin's Joyce* (1955), to Chatto and Windus Ltd; from *Letters of James Joyce*, ed. by Stuart Gilbert (1957) and *The Critical Writings of James Joyce*, ed. by Ellsworth Mason and Richard Ellmann (1959), to Faber and Faber Ltd; from Stanislaus Joyce, *My Brother's Keeper* (1958), to Faber and Faber Ltd; from A. G. Lehmann, *The Symbolist Aesthetic in France*, 1885-1895 (1950), to Basil Blackwell; from Harry Levin, *James Joyce, a Critical Introduction* (1944), to Faber and Faber Ltd; from Wyndham Lewis, *Time and Western Man* (1927), to Chatto and Windus Ltd; from Percy Lubbock, *The Craft of Fiction* (1921 etc.), to Jonathan Cape Ltd; from Marvin Magalaner and Richard M. Kain, *James Joyce, The Man, the Work, the Reputation* (1956), to New York University Press; from William T. Noon, *Joyce and Aquinas* (1957), to Yale University Press; from W. B. Stanford, *The Ulysses Theme* (1954), to Basil Blackwell; from Allen Tate, *The Man of Letters in the Modern World* (1955), to Meridian Books, Charles Scribner's Sons, and Allen Tate; from W. Y. Tindall, *James Joyce, His Way of Interpreting the Modern World* (1950), to

A*

Charles Scribner's Sons; from Virginia Woolf, *The Common Reader, First Series* (1925 etc.), to The Hogarth Press.

Portions of this book have already appeared, in a rather different form, in *The Melbourne Critical Review, A Review of English Literature,* and *ELH.*

NOTES

PAGE REFERENCES to Joyce's works are placed in brackets in the text. The editions referred to are:

S.H. Stephen Hero, edited with an Introduction by Theodore Spencer, London, Jonathan Cape, 1944.

P. A Portrait of the Artist as a Young Man, London, Jonathan Cape, 1942.

U. Ulysses, London, The Bodley Head, 1937, *etc*. New York, Random House, Modern Library Edition, 1942, *etc*.

• N.B. References are given to each edition, the page of the English edition before the stroke, that of the American after. (There are a number of small differences between the two texts, which I have ignored.)

F.W. Finnegans Wake, New York, The Viking Press, 1945.

A CLASSICAL STYLE, he said, is the syllogism of art, the only legitimate process from one world to another. Classicism is not the manner of any fixed age or of any fixed country: it is a constant state of the artistic mind. It is a temper of security and satisfaction and patience. The romantic temper, so often and so grievously misinterpreted and not more by others than by its own, is an insecure, unsatisfied, impatient temper which sees no fit abode here for its ideals and chooses therefore to behold them under insensible figures. As a result of this choice it comes to disregard certain limitations. Its figures are blown to wild adventures, lacking the gravity of solid bodies, and the mind that has conceived them ends by disowning them. The classical temper on the other hand, ever mindful of limitations, chooses rather to bend upon these present things and so to work upon them and fashion them that the quick intelligence may go beyond them to their meaning which is still unuttered. In this method the sane and joyful spirit issues forth and achieves imperishable perfection, nature assisting with her goodwill and thanks. . . .

. . . The critic is he who is able, by means of the signs which the artist affords, to approach the temper which has made the work and to see what is well done therein and what it signifies.

Stephen Hero

Most books that live, live in spite of the author's laying it on thick.

D. H. LAWRENCE

Chapter I

INTRODUCTORY

PUBLISHED in 1922, after sixteen years of thought and seven years of writing, *Ulysses* was the third of James Joyce's creative explorations of Dublin—the Dublin in which his imagination dwelt all his life. He had voluntarily exiled himself in the flesh from the other, the "real" Dublin as early as 1904, returning only for occasional brief visits; his mind, on the other hand, never left its home, for there lived the people, the human experience, that had formed his imagination and that he knew in his very marrow. Time after time his memory and imagination turned back to it, lived in it, circled out from it, always seeking the fullest meaning of his knowledge. No spiritual exploration was finished before he was already meditating the next. The first was begun before he left Dublin in the flesh—the book of short stories, *Dubliners*, finally published in 1914, "a chapter", as Joyce called it, "of the moral history of my country". The second was made over the years 1904-14—*A Portrait of the Artist as a Young Man*, a chapter in the moral history of an exceptional individual born in that country. This was a much more difficult history to relate. At first it had seemed a simple matter of reporting events, thoughts, conversations, in order to explain his own personal case, of presenting his own life from within, perhaps, until he reached the stage where he was able to present it from without: rather like the old ballad of *Turpin Hero*, which begins in the first person and ends in the third person. But in 1906 this first attempt at a portrait, *Stephen Hero*, was put aside. The truth about his own case, he found, was not quite the deeper and more significant truth his hero, Stephen Dedalus, could embody; but to portray that required a maturer insight, a harder discipline of the imagination. Between *Stephen Hero* and the eventual *Portrait* Joyce learned both. Yet even while immersed in *Dubliners* he had conceived yet a third imaginative exploration of Dublin, and even before finishing the *Portrait* he had begun to plan it. The moral life of Dublin, the moral life of the isolated individual in it, contained a larger and more universal truth, although to

understand it and to portray it demanded yet a further experience, a further maturity and a further discipline: *Ulysses* would
be a chapter in the moral history of Europe. And beyond that
again lay the possibility of a still larger subject, an ultimate
history of mankind in its continual, endless death and resurrection—*Finnegans Wake*, which was published just as the world
plunged into war once again.[1]

*   *   *

This present study, let me say at once, is concerned only with
Ulysses, not with Joyce's work as a whole; and clearly the decision
to concentrate on this one novel—and at such length—calls for
some explanation.

The first and most important reason is simply that *Ulysses* is
Joyce's central achievement—the most important expression of
his imagination, the book on which, I believe, his reputation will
most firmly rest. Those that came before it—the volume of lyrics,
Chamber Music (1907) and the play, *Exiles* (1918), as well as
Dubliners and the *Portrait of the Artist*—exhibit an artistic assurance, an unusual subtlety and perceptivity, intensity, detachment, an unmistakable power—but they are not major works.
They are obviously the work of a man who took his art seriously,
who recognized that to practice it required intelligence and self-
knowledge as well as individual talent, and they show a sensibility in the process of real growth. Only with *Ulysses*, however,
did Joyce find the human experience, the objective themes, to
fulfil his possibilities. Whatever we think of its success, *Ulysses*
undoubtedly challenges the highest judgment. *Finnegans Wake* is
far more problematical. It displays a fluidity, an abstraction, a
hunger for the absolute, incompatible with the dramatic commitments of art, commitments that, as Joyce himself took pains to
insist, are not purely technical but, in the widest sense, moral or
spiritual. In this respect, *Finnegans Wake* seems to mark a shift in
Joyce's attitudes, a swing back to a view of life and of art like
those he had earlier rejected, and which the vast pretensions of
the work and its affinities with Mallarmé's *Un Coup de Dés* do
nothing to recommend. It certainly opens up possibilities in the
use of language; but art has deeper obligations than that, and
whether its experiments ever achieve any historical importance is
a question we may leave to the scholars of the future. But it is

precisely the virtue of *Ulysses* that it means too much to us now and here to escape our most responsive scrutiny, and for this reason I have focused my attention upon it, referring to Joyce's other works only where they might help to explain or to clarify.

I have tried therefore to define and account for my own enjoyment of the book—an enjoyment that is keen and deep but not consistently unflawed. Simply to do that, however, would be a much less elaborate matter were not *Ulysses* itself so elaborate. Into it Joyce put the imaginative labour of something over seven years, an amount of time and rather more than the amount of dedication most novelists spend on several books; and the intense concentration of his effort, the scale of his ambition, the diversity of his material, his integrity and originality, have given the book a more than proportionate complexity. We may hope that the time is past when it seemed impenetrably obscure (except, of course, for the "obscenity"). Many thousands have read it and, with or without the hundreds of commentators, have made out something of its design and meaning. Like *The Waste Land*, it has settled down as one of the central literary facts of the twentieth century. Everyone now knows that it is devoted to one day, 16 June 1904, in Dublin; that it exploits parallels with Homer's *Odyssey*; that it is very carefully constructed and that its odd techniques and pervasive symbolism represent a deliberate, serious exploration of modern life; that it concentrates on two figures who form a kind of composite protagonist: Leopold Bloom, a middle-aged Jew, canvasser for advertisements, and notoriously cuckolded by his wife, Molly—the commercial traveller who parallels the Homeric traveller, Ulysses; and Stephen Dedalus, a young Irishman, would-be artist, notorious rebel against his family, society and religion, in some ways representative of Joyce himself as a young man, and the counterpart of Telemachus, son of Ulysses. One can now assume the details of the story and the presence of some kind of "paternity theme" as common knowledge. What is less certain and still needs discussion is the meaning of the book as a whole and—even more—what are its real claims to distinction. These, at any rate, are the questions I have attempted to answer.

Not that *Ulysses* lacks interpretation and discussion already; indeed, there is probably too much of it to see the book itself very clearly. Countless reviews, essays, articles, dissertations, books, broadcasts, and even an entire periodical, have been devoted to it and Joyce's other works. Help is forthcoming from every side: biography, bibliography, linguistics, textual criticism, analysis of symbols, myths, techniques, formal aesthetics, comparative literature, history, social criticism, psychology, philosophy, theology—and so on. Joyce has been violently attacked and violently flattered; willing hands explicate and expound; his works have been related to every conceivable idea, ideology or aspect of modern times; mountains of commentary are even now being heaped o'er his head. Some of this commentary is such as no reader of his work can be ungrateful for, and certainly no one attempting a study of *Ulysses* can avoid acknowledging his inevitable debt to the perception and intelligence of Edmund Wilson, Harry Levin, R. P. Blackmur, William York Tindall, Hugh Kenner and a handful of other scholars and critics. But, as we might expect, most of the available commentary has little value or interest. Some of it is purely ephemeral, the casual assertion of opinion with no pretence of critical demonstration; some of it is pretentious nonsense, the idle chatter of the Joyce Cult; some of it is founded on disabling misconceptions about literary art in general (about the relevance of "ideas" or "beliefs", for example); some of it is the kind of scholarship—or the kind of recondite free-association that often passes for "explication"—to which questions of imaginative value are of no conceivable concern; and in total it is not merely depressingly unilluminating, but with its uncritical assertions, Alexandrian ingenuities, and grand generalizations, probably of more harm than good to its subject. Joyce deserves better than guilt by association with some of his critics.[2]

One fact worth remarking, however, is that the majority of these critics—and almost all the best of them—are American rather than English. Broadly speaking, the English have never shown the same assurance about Joyce's importance, and although this may be partly the result of dark suspicions about American enthusiasms and American "research", the causes obviously go deeper. Joyce's sensibility is Roman Catholic and Irish, the literary models to which he looked were Continental rather than English, while his art is more self-conscious, more abstract, more concerned with spiritual and social alienation, than is usual in the English novel. None of these characteristics is a disadvantage in America; on the contrary, American literature has always possessed many of them itself. As Richard Chase has pointed out in his study of *The American Novel and Its Tradition*, it has from its beginnings cultivated a kind of "Romance", a mode of the novel ambitiously symbolic and metaphysical rather than representational and social, more prepared to contemplate contradictions and disorder without trying to resolve them than to criticize life from a stable and traditional moral point of view. Again, American writers, over the last few generations especially, have looked to wider traditions than the English—to Continental literatures, to Catholicism, even to Eastern and primitive cultures—in pursuit of inclusive ideal "traditions" for themselves. When we recall how much they are concerned with themes of individual alienation, with a haunting sense of guilt and of destiny, with self-conscious experimentation, and with large, abstract symbols and concepts, then *Ulysses*, not to mention *Finnegans Wake*, clearly seems to fit both the mood and the methods of the American imagination. Where the best English critics have been able to receive Joyce with (on the whole) respectful indifference, the best American critics have received him with a warm and easy recognition. Yet this very hospitality of imagination has its dangers, of which the ready acceptance of *Ulysses* is an interesting example. Characteristically, and understandably, American criticism has concentrated on assimilating great works of art and on developing methods by which to possess them most fully. But in his anxiety to possess, the critic may overlook the need also to decide, to judge, to evaluate and order his responses, and to preserve his objectivity by making his decisions explicit—even if only to himself. The case of *Ulysses* suggests the risks of not doing so. Even some of the best analyses of the book tend to concentrate on its ambitiousness, its large use of symbol and myth, its universal suggestiveness, its general and abstract outlines, and in the process too often take the actual achievement of the work rather for granted, assuming reasons for its importance that are either unconvincing or eccentric. With some distinguished exceptions, the critics of *Ulysses* have been readier to talk about the general significance of its subject, its structure of intentions, its modernity, its "greatness", than to discriminate what is truly imagined, truly alive in it. "With our contemporaries," T. S. Eliot has advised, "we oughtn't to be so busy enquiring whether they are great or not; we ought to stick to the question: 'Are they *genuine*?' and leave the question whether they are great to the only tribunal which can decide: *time*." This was said of poetry, but it has its application to *Ulysses*. Criticism of the book needs to sharpen its edges and resume a certain modesty.

From its very first appearance, views of its nature and significance have varied enormously. Summing up three decades of interpretation, one recent scholar has come to the conclusion that Joyce still remains an enigma: "however much faith the critic may have in his own interpretation, an opposite reading has equally valid support".[3] Certainly, amid the mass of commentary the outlook does seem obscure, but it is not quite so hopeless as this suggests. If literary criticism does not admit of finality and exhaustiveness, it does admit of degrees of relevance, accuracy and intelligence; in any case, it is perhaps time that some of these interpretations were confronted with our critical sense of the text itself. In this present study I have tried to note my own debts, agreements and disagreements with other critics as far as seemed desirable. For the most part I have relegated these to notes at the back, but sometimes more important questions of approach and judgment are involved, and these I have ventured to treat in the course of the discussion. So common and pervasive are some misconceptions about Joyce's work, indeed, that in Chapter VI I have even diverged sharply from my main thread of exposition in order to explore them as best I can. I do not imagine that my opinions on such theoretical questions, or even my formulations of them, will always be found convincing (though that, I trust, does not invalidate my criticism of *Ulysses* itself), but I have offered them nevertheless as a tentative and preliminary attempt to clear the ground a little for the real critical issues Joyce's work does present.

Without attempting to summarize all the interpretations of *Ulysses* ever offered, we may select five main *kinds* of interpretation as most significant:

(1) The view that it is only a naturalistic Irish comedy, the apotheosis of the bar-room joke.

(2) The view that it expresses complete, cosmic indifference

to all moral values, reducing all experience to ultimate meaning-lessness either by its implicit nihilism or, what is much the same thing, its implicit relativity.

(3) The view that it expresses some important body of mystical, esoteric or metaphysical belief.

(4) The view that it is a pessimistic rejection of modern life, an encyclopædic satire on "the immense panorama of futility and anarchy which is contemporary history".[4]

(5) The view that it is an optimistic acceptance of life as it is, whether in a spirit of humorous relaxation, or tense tragic awareness, or quasi-mythic abstraction.

These are only general tendencies, of course, and each is capable of assuming very different colourings in different hands. For example, the view that *Ulysses* expresses a world of purely relative values has been offered as a reason both for its greatness and for its utter insignificance; all these views are compatible with the frequent objection that the book is over-elaborated, though the objection is usually offered in support of (1) and (2) and as a qualification to (5); some views merge easily into others —(1) and (2), for instance, or (3) and (4), or (3) and (5); while Joyce's attitude to Catholicism, his exile, his use of symbols and myths, have all been adduced in various proportions in support of each view in turn.

Each one of them seems to me true but limited. There is little point in trying deliberately to adjudicate between them, nor have I tried to do so except in so far as judgments are implicit in my reading of *Ulysses* as a whole. Nevertheless, since those judgments are important and unavoidable, it is probably as well to sketch out my views frankly from the start.

By and large, the first kind of interpretation—*Ulysses* as an elaborate Dublin joke—is hardly favoured anywhere outside Dublin itself,[5] and we could well leave it there, among those who have the misfortune to know too much about Jimmy Joyce to be able to take his work seriously, were there not a truth in it so obvious as to be often overlooked. For in one sense it hardly needs a full-scale volume to point out what is vividly alive in *Ulysses*; it stares one in the face: the crisp realization of Dublin itself, the comedy, the sharp satirical observation and a mastery (like Sean O'Casey's) of a rich and racy idiom both of speech and of character. What is wrong with the book is equally obvious: the enormous elaboration of the material, the rather pretentious parade of literary machinery, the encumbering and mortifying boredom. All this is so obviously true that it is almost always taken for granted, and it deserves to be said at the very beginning of any discussion of Joyce. Yet to assume it and to go on from there—as I would wish to do—is surely only to press one's primary response for its full significance. What larger interest, what moral interest, have Joyce's verbal facility, his vivacity, his self-conscious elaborations? Of what vision of life are they the medium?

The other four kinds of interpretation comprise the usual answers. The first of them (moral nihilism)—which has been offered by critics of very different persuasions[6]—points to Joyce's own aesthetic theories as expounded in the *Portrait*: did not Joyce himself object to art that attempted moral suasion and advocate that which produced only a calm, purely "aesthetic" contemplation? When we consider the jumbled *minutiae* of life he heaped together, the relativity and moral Naturalism of *Ulysses*, it seems that Joyce represents human existence as a vast and meaningless spectacle without room for moral values, a pointless (and so ultimately comic) flux. This again has an obvious truth. Joyce did object to what he called "kinetic" art and did advocate what he called "stasis" or contemplation; he does preserve an attitude of moral detachment towards life; and he does represent it as a flux. But this first interpretation of his theory of art as a kind of Aestheticism is ultimately a caricature, for the attitudes it ascribes to Joyce really belong to the callow Stephen Dedalus of the *Portrait* rather than to the author of *Ulysses*. More importantly, however, the whole interpretation is false to the facts of the book itself. Joyce's detachment is not indifference, his spectacle of flux is not meaningless, and his tricks with relative points of view and his occasionally "obscene" Naturalism are not altogether nasty and irresponsible trifling. But these are assertions that must await demonstration.

The third kind of interpretation rushes upon the opposite mistake. Fastening upon Joyce's wholesale employment of "symbols" and his interest in, and use of, such tenets as Theosophy or Thomism or the power of mythic Archetypes, some of his critics have tried to equate the significance of *Ulysses* with the significance of these doctrines themselves.[7] If we want impress-

ively profound values in Joyce's work, here we have them with a
vengeance. If we should hesitate about their actual informing
presence in *Ulysses*, we are assured that Joyce's art is of a special
kind and requires special methods of interpretation. It is all done
by Symbols—that is to say, by images, objects, words, that
somehow carry a burden of the mystery of another, spiritual,
timeless, more *real* world, of which this world and any representation of it are but shadowy emblems. This belief that art
should be a kind of metaphysical allegory or, alternatively,
should suggest as best it can "levels" of metaphysical reality, has
too venerable and complex a history to be examined here. It has
affected artists and critics of very different beliefs, not only those
who have held a formal religion or metaphysics quite outside art,
but also those who have looked to the artistic imagination as
itself the source of such spiritual intuitions. In either case, the
Symbolist tends to place the significance of poetry in the *things
referred to* in it, and in the relationships it suggests between things,
for he supposes these in some way to *correspond* with an invisible
order of Being. The Symbolist critic is thus led to seek as many
suggestions of meaning as he can, but in seeking them to admit
few, if any, limits to the potentialities of meaning that an object,
word, image or poem may be supposed to contain. In short, he
is liable to disregard the contexts in which the meaning of poetry
is created and by which that meaning is, if not defined, then
delimited. He is so impatient to discover high metaphysical
significances that he disdains the human and *dramatic* meaning of
what is before him, the "natural" or "literal" level of human
experience in which all other meanings are founded and cohere.
As Donne observed about similar tendencies in Biblical exegesis
in his day:

Though it be ever lawfull, and often times very usefull, for the raising
and exaltation of our devotion, and to present the plenty, and abund-
ance of the *holy Ghost* in the *Scriptures* . . . to induce the *diverse senses* that
the Scriptures doe admit, yet this may not be admitted, if there may
be danger thereby, to neglect or weaken the *literall* sense it selfe. For
there is no necessity of that *spirituall wantonnesse* of finding more than
necessary senses; for, the more *lights* there are, the more *shadows* are
also cast by those many lights . . . so when you have the *necessary sense*,
that is the meaning of the holy Ghost in that place, you have senses
enow, and not till then, though you have never so many, and never so
delightfull.[8]

The Symbolist is all too inclined to treat the poetic imagination as the Holy Ghost, and led by Joyce's own analogies between the two and his obtrusive use of symbols, some of his critics have made the same mistake as Donne criticizes. (Perhaps in *Finnegans Wake* Joyce finally made it himself.) It is easy to see that certain kinds of art can deliberately cultivate an ambiguity—indeed, a multiguity—of "metaphysical" meaning by avoiding any dramatic action, any human contexts, that might limit the subtlest and most far-reaching interpretations. Lyric poetry is an obviously exploitable mode, but a work like *Moby Dick*, which largely escapes the delimitations of social context and *human* drama, illustrates the possibilities even in the novel, and what Mr Chase calls "Romance" in American literature is very much of this same kind. Nevertheless, *Ulysses* does possess a densely specified "literal" or dramatic meaning, a *necessary sense* in Donne's phrase. To ignore it, out of "spiritual wantonness" or imaginative greed, is to induce a similar kind of uncritical acceptance, a similar undiscriminating generality, as that to which American criticism is also sometimes prone.[9] In any case, it is on the necessary sense of any passage and the dramatic meaning of the work as a whole that I have focused my attention. I have not conceived it as any part of my task to criticize in general terms the assumptions and reasoning behind this particular kind of Symbolist approach to literature; but the approach is so widespread among Joyce's critics (for it is not wholly confined to any one school of interpretation), and has so much affected the common view of his work, that it is impossible not to touch on some of the issues it raises. In particular, since Joyce himself is still sometimes thought to have believed in "formless spiritual essences" as the proper subject or end of art, I have underlined those elements in his symbolism—both in his theory and in his practice—that suggest he paid more attention to the dramatic necessities of his art than to such abstract, "metaphysical" and—for an artist—ultimately frivolous, profundities.

The fourth kind of interpretation (*Ulysses* as a moral and social satire) is the most popular of all and has been presented in many different versions.[10] We might summarize the general view thus: The subject of *Ulysses* is modern civilization in the West (Europe and equally, if not more so, America), a civilization in spiritual, cultural and moral disintegration. Every aspect of life, individual and social, exhibits this collapse of traditional order and values, and Joyce has set out to portray it with encyclopaedic thoroughness. Every chapter of *Ulysses* contains symbolic reference to some Art of human life—theology, economics, literature, politics, medicine, science, and so on; the book is full of references to Homer, Dante, Aquinas, Shakespeare and others, which are symbols of the traditional values whose decay is charted in the novel. Like Swift or Flaubert, Joyce sets out to castigate his age; his attitude is savagely ironic, for he portrays only to expose. To the institutions and values of industrial society Joyce responds with an uncompromising *No*. What "happens" in *Ulysses* is therefore nothing, since nothing of significance can happen in a world where the human spirit is paralysed and sterile. Bloom and Stephen meet and part, each divided from himself and from the other, and both futile. Instead of narrative and action, *Ulysses* has the organization of a symbolic poem. (So we return to Symbolism; and though this time the Symbol does not necessarily have a metaphysical meaning, interest in word, image or metaphor is still directed at its *abstract* significance.) Dublin is an Inferno; Bloom the citizen and Stephen the artist represent its essential loneliness or "exile". Bloom is a livelier Bouvard and Pécuchet, accepting everything in his environment, and so representing its crass materialism, unable to order it meaningfully or to judge it. Stephen is another lost soul, moved like Satan only by a destructive egoism and an impossible ambition, his conscience tortured by his rejection of faith and by his remorse ("ayenbite of inwit") at having refused to kneel and pray at his mother's death-bed. He is not Joyce himself nor is he held up for our admiration as a genius of any kind. He is a portrait of the would-be artist in modern society, his fatal dissociation within reflecting that without, a caricature of the really vital and creative being he cannot even imagine. Joyce does not say all this, he merely presents it; by his satirical techniques, his stylistic parodies, his symbolic patterning, he remains aloofly detached from his world and yet unmistakably reveals its true nature. He is a Realist, not in technique perhaps, but in moral outlook.

Where the "moral nihilist" school finds Joyce's picture of life directed by no values whatever, the "moral Realist" school claims, or certainly implies, that it is, though different critics offer different accounts of what those values are. Some do not raise the question explicitly at all, but (rather naïvely) suppose that "Realistic" moral criticism (like Flaubert's) bears its validity and imaginative power on its very face. Some critics point to Joyce's use of Homer, Aquinas, Blake and others, and speak, with more or less confidence, of his traditionalism; some, however, are inclined to find a certain confusion in Joyce himself as well as in his subject. Others again have seen him as a deliberate and consistent Christian—more specifically, as a kind of Thomist. But where all these critics find the value and importance of the book is in the depth and completeness of its critical rejections.

No one can deny that in very large measure *Ulysses* is what these critics say it is; the only question is the emphasis they place upon this aspect of the book. In the days when *Ulysses* was thought to be a meaningless chaos or an elaborate construction of esoteric symbols, it was necessary to insist upon its moral criticism of a chaos it seemed only to exploit. Today there can be no question that Joyce chose his material and his methods with the seriousness of a Flaubert and with perhaps an even deeper sense of the pervading rot in modern society. In fact, this is now so much the usual view of *Ulysses* that it hardly needs repeating. On the contrary, I believe, it needs correcting. To put it bluntly, the satirical and parodic aspects of the book, sharp and apposite as they are, seem to me to have been over-rated; certainly, to speak for at least one reader, they are not what I most admire and value about it, nor do they seem to me sufficient grounds for the importance usually ascribed to it. Joyce's art seems to me more significantly vital, far more positive and creative, than such an emphasis suggests; at its best, it invites precisely the observation the young Joyce made about Ibsen: "Life is not to be criticised, but to be faced and lived."[11] A criticism of modern life *Ulysses* certainly is, but it is much more than that. Or, to put it another way, it is a criticism of life in a larger and deeper sense than is always recognized.

Unfortunately, that sense has been sometimes obscured by the terms in which it is discussed. The fifth kind of interpretation (*Ulysses* as the "acceptance of life") is too often presented simply as the opposite of the fourth (*Ulysses* as the "rejection of life"), or with an infusion of false and sentimental optimism. Like the others, this version of the book is based on some important truths about it, and in my view is the most plausible of the lot. At the same time, one must add that it is difficult to find a convincing critical *demonstration* of Joyce's "acceptance of life" and what it means in proper imaginative terms. A number of more or less irrelevant issues seem to have got in the way. Edmund Wilson, for example, saw clearly enough that Joyce was no second Flaubert and that Bloom was no mere victim of social disintegration; but he emphasized that the outcome of the story was finally optimistic: as a result of the events of Bloomsday, Stephen will be stimulated to write *Ulysses* and the Blooms will live happily (or at least a little more happily) for at least some time after. Bloom makes the unprecedented demand that the unfaithful Molly bring him his breakfast on Friday, 17 June; and Molly, in admiring the intelligence and education of Stephen in the course of her final, silent, all-embracing monologue that begins and ends with the word "Yes", suggests the ever-upward striving of life itself.[12] As we have seen, the outcome of the story has looked very different in mood and meaning to others since, and its ambiguity continues to puzzle and disturb the commentators. As one of them sums it up, "if the position of *Ulysses* in modern letters be entrenched, as it now seems to be, the basic problem remains that of interpreting the narrative's resolution. How seriously must the meeting of Stephen and Bloom be considered in theory, when it remains so ineffectual in fact? Is the end result merely that of ineradicable loneliness, or does Molly's final 'Yes' indicate acceptance of the life force?"[13] There is even no certain indication that Molly will get Bloom his breakfast. Yet surely the basic issue is not that of the narrative's resolution at all, nor of Joyce's acceptance of the "life force". In fact, it is just because they see nothing more than this kind of indiscriminate "acceptance" that some critics have attacked Joyce for his nihilism. The meeting of Bloom and Stephen, and Molly's "yes", derive their meaning from the book as a whole, and if their dramatic significance is not effectually *realized*, then any theoretical significance Joyce may or may not have intended is hardly of much relevance. By the time Bloom and Stephen do meet in the penultimate chapter and Molly utters her "affirmation", *Joyce's* attitudes ought to be— and, I believe, are in fact—perfectly clear. These concluding events are not important in the same way plot usually is in a novel, for as we shall see, when we reach them we have been brought to a perception of the characters (and their situation) in which what they *do* seems less important than what they *are*. This does not mean, of course, that "nothing happens" in *Ulysses*; it means only that the narrative is resolved by *becoming* symbolic.

But to interpret Joyce's "affirmation", and particularly the final episodes, in purely symbolic terms seems to me equally fallacious. The main proponent of this reading is W. Y. Tindall, and although his generalizations about the book are usually convincingly perceptive, he is very much less convincing when it comes to supporting them with critical demonstration. He emphasizes Joyce's high estimation of comic "joy" in art and the serious comedy and equanimity of *Ulysses* itself. He sees Bloom as a figure who "emerges heroically in the end as one of the greatest representatives of human dignity", as the representative of the common humanity with which Stephen must come to terms in order to become the creative artist he wishes to become. He sums up Joyce's vision as "far less satiric than contemplative, less destructive or edifying than creative. Less concerned with what is wrong with man than with the nature of man and the power of creation. . . ."[14] All this seems to me penetrating and just, and precisely the emphasis to be made. What rather shakes our confidence is Mr Tindall's trust in abstract and mechanical "symbolism"—in particular, his surely excessive faith in cocoa. When Bloom and Stephen finally sit opposite each other in Bloom's kitchen, they drink a cup of cocoa ("Epps's massproduct"); this is briefly mentioned in the penultimate chapter, so briefly indeed that the not-very-attentive reader may well miss it altogether. Mr Tindall—and other critics too—see it as the climax of the book, the "symbolic celebration of Stephen's communion with man". *Massproduct* is the key-word to unlock the whole mystery: "the cocoa is mass-produced for the trade; as the product of a symbolic Mass, it is the sacrament; and it suggests the masses for whom it is produced. . . . Cocoa must have been a personal symbol for coming to terms with man and external reality. It was perhaps while living on cocoa in Paris that Joyce began to understand the world around him."[15] Even admitting the element of clean academic fun in this, one can hardly accept it as evidence of Joyce's greatness as an artist, or of the curiously matter-of-fact conclusion that the encounter with Bloom changes Stephen's egotism to humanity, and that having discovered what

INTRODUCTORY

charity really is, he leaves Bloom and "goes away to write
Ulysses"![16] To believe that—or to find such abstract symbolic
Masses significant "affirmations" of anything—is possible only
on the oddest assumptions about art and moral maturity; it is to
push what is really there in the book—a symbolic meaning—to
ridiculously naturalistic lengths. The confrontation of Bloom and
Stephen is, as a whole, indeed a climax, but a climax the meaning
of which only we and the author—but not the characters themselves—can understand. Part of its very point, I believe, is that
although Bloom and Stephen are in some sense aspects of Joyce
himself, neither of them can have more than an inkling of their
mutual significance. Both Edmund Wilson and Mr Tindall are
right in suggesting the writing of *Ulysses* as itself the event to
which the meeting of Bloom and Stephen points and in insisting
that both characters are in some way affirmed in the process; but
Bloom's almost unnoticeable (and problematical) demand for
breakfast, or Molly's "yes", or arbitrary "symbols" could not,
and do not, *enact* such a vital meaning. And the same must be
said of the analogous argument, that Joyce's "affirmation" is to
be found in his use of the Homeric and other myths since Myth
expresses the deepest activity of the human psyche. Once again,
we can only insist that art "affirms" or "accepts" life in ways
more difficult, and hence more important, than that.

Both these two latter kinds of interpretation, then—the satiric
and the affirmative—are illuminating only to the extent that
they are properly defined and not pushed beyond what is
imaginatively achieved in the book itself. On that condition they
are not really as incompatible as they seem at first sight, not at
any rate in the sense that they each mark one of the most important directions of Joyce's imagination. But they do require
discriminations and qualifications that are not always to be
found even in the most penetrating and solidest criticism of
Joyce; and it is for this reason that, in trying to place the critical
emphasis where I feel it ought to be, I have been led at times into
trying to shift it from where it currently is.

*   *   *

I cannot make any pretence in this study to academic completeness or of providing a rounded, synoptic account of *Ulysses*
which treats every aspect of it with equal deliberation. For one

thing, I have not discussed such very general questions as Joyce's place in the history of the novel, his technical experimentation, his development as an artist, or the various fields of scholarly enquiry (about sources, influences and the like) that have grown up around his work. Again, I have not stressed Joyce's attack on modern society as much as it may seem to deserve, partly because so much has been said about it already and partly because I wished to stress other aspects of the book. My aim has been to select, and to state as emphatically as possible, what I think is of central value—what is most firmly and richly *achieved*—in *Ulysses* and so in Joyce's work as a whole. Nor do I believe that *Ulysses* is a case requiring special methods or interpretation or special assumptions about Symbols or Myths or Art in general. What meaning is truly realized in it, what value it has, lies in its *dramatic* presentation and ordering of human experience, and nowhere else. In short, it is not "Romance", not a joke, not a spiritual guide, not even an encyclopaedia of social disintegration or a re-creation of Myth or a symbolist poem; it is a novel, and what is of permanent interest about it is what always interests us with the novel: its imaginative illumination of the moral—and ultimately, spiritual—experience of representative human beings. And though it is an unusual novel, and complicated with extraordinary elements, its importance is founded, in the last analysis, on that fact.

The complications are not gratuitous, however, although they may obscure our view of the essential structures of the book or even cause us to look for them in the wrong place. Certainly, they raise questions that with other novels and novelists can generally be taken for granted—questions not only about the nature of Symbolism and how it works in the novel, but also about aesthetic organization in general, about the significance of "stream-of-consciousness" writing, about the dramatic importance of aesthetic theory, and so on. The very comprehensiveness of Joyce's commitment to his book—his determination to say everything he wanted in its terms—provides difficulty enough in the intricate, meticulous and almost obsessively elaborated art to which it led. But his dramatic scrupulosity, his acceptance of the artistic discipline which permits the author to speak only in and through his action, techniques and style, provides even more. "Never trust the artist. Trust the tale", D. H. Lawrence advised;

but most people are only too ready to twist the tale in the direction they think the author wants. What baffles and dismays them is the author who never appears, a tale without explicit directions attached—in short, the cases where the author *becomes* the tale. The natural mistake is to suppose that because the tale has no explicit moral it has no meaning at all, that the author who is thoroughly assimilated into his art is simply not there. Thus Joyce's "impersonality" has been thought to consist in his avoidance of explicit commentary, and *Ulysses* has been both praised and blamed for its exact, "objective", impersonal representation of life "as it really is". As we shall see, such a conception of impersonality and such praise and blame are all equally beside the point. The relation of the artist to his tale may vary; T. S. Eliot's formula is all the more apposite in that it closely approximates to Joyce's own views. There are three voices of poetry, says Eliot:

The first voice is the voice of the poet talking to himself—or to nobody. The second is the voice of the poet addressing an audience, whether large or small. The third is the voice of the poet when he attempts to create a dramatic character . . .; when he is saying, not what he would say in his own person, but only what he can say within the limits of one imaginary character addressing another imaginary character.

But as Eliot rightly warns us, all three voices may be heard in a complex dramatic work. Sometimes the voice of a character seems to chime in unison with the author's, not like a dummy expounding the author's ideas or feelings, but expressing something that the author could also say for himself though perhaps with a different meaning to the words.[17] To distinguish where the voice of the author chimes with that of his characters is no easier with *Ulysses* than with Shakespeare, say, or Jane Austen. It demands the fullest and most sensitive response to the work as a whole, for to perceive the shaping activity of the author, the inner structures of his art, is, as Joyce himself understood, to distinguish the moral significance of the tale.

Joyce learned his artistic discipline from a variety of masters: Homer, Dante, Shakespeare, Ibsen and, in the novel, Flaubert. That discipline is a large part of what he called the *classical temper*. The meaning he gave to the phrase has nothing to do with academicism or plaster models from the Greek, nor is it to be

THE CLASSICAL TEMPER

confused with what T. E. Hulme and T. S. Eliot have meant by "Classicism". It is less definite and more complex than that, and to define its genuine presence in *Ulysses* is the main object of this study.

In very broad terms, we may say that, as Joyce understood the term, the classical temper is essentially dramatic. It accepts the ordinary world of humanity as the primary object of its attention, and endeavours to see it and present it steadily and whole. In order to do so, it seeks patiently for maturity, detachment, impersonality of judgment and an artistic method, that, while it begins with the local and the concrete as its foundation, enables it to penetrate beyond them. The classical temper thus involves a moral as well as an artistic ideal, an ideal of spiritual complete-ness and impersonal order. No one knew better than Joyce that to record life truly engaged the artist's whole sensibility in most complex, delicate moral perceptions and judgments. If he avoided dogmas and "beliefs"—all explicit systems of values—this does not mean he rejected all values whatever; it only means that he trusted to his dramatic imagination to discern and express them in life as he knew it. If in some ways he started his career from Aestheticism, "the romantic temper", he rejected it both in life and in art for exactly the same reasons. The classical temper displays itself as a responsive openness to life, a firm grasp on the centrally human, a respect for the present reality we all share, an allegiance to the objective, and a mistrust of meta-physical or naturalistic "realities" abstracted from the total complexity of human experience. This attitude is the ground of his finest inspiration.

Joyce quite rightly disclaimed any special depth or originality for his ideas: "if there is any difficulty in reading what I write it is because of the material I use. In my case the thought is always simple."[18] His work has nothing of Mann's massive deployment of abstract knowledge and theory, Gide's restless exploration of ethics, Lawrence's prophetic intensity, nor is his symbolism boldly, poetically speculative like that of Melville. All we can say is that his art turns upon certain focal themes, but themes which are finally inseparable from one another because finally insepar-able from their dramatic matrix. In no sense do they compose a "philosophy" or a doctrine. They are more like aspects of one organic whole or emphases within a continuous and complex rhythm, and in tracing the most important of them in *Ulysses* I have let them emerge as far as possible in the course of discussion without trying to enforce too rigid a scheme upon them.

I have chosen to begin (in Chapters II and III) with the only one about which Joyce himself developed any theory and which consequently requires theoretical understanding from his readers: namely, his personal conception of, and relations to, his art. The theme had a far more than theoretical interest for him, however. Coming to him as a sense of vocation—a duty laid upon him by the possession of a special gift, a fate in the acceptance of which lay his personal freedom and fulfilment—the rôle of artist had for Joyce a finality that turned its necessities into the very terms of his moral life. Once he saw, and accepted, and defended his destiny, his first task was to discover how he must fulfil it. The *Portrait of the Artist as a Young Man* is the record of his history—though a history conceived imaginatively and ironically —up to the point where, in his hero's theory of aesthetic beauty, he formulated his first conception of the task before him; but it also goes beyond that to the point where it becomes clear to us, if not to Stephen Dedalus, not simply that his first conception is inadequate but that with experience and growth Stephen will find it inadequate himself. The aesthetic theory in the *Portrait* is not *as it stands* to be taken as Joyce's own. It leaves out too much, and what it leaves out are precisely the moral responsibilities Stephen has still to learn that his vocation entails. No doubt Joyce himself had recognized them before Stephen is shown as doing so, for in the abortive *Stephen Hero* the hero is loud in proclaiming them.[19] But historical truth was not, as he came to realize, Joyce's real concern; poetic truth was more revealing. Stephen's militant Asetheticism and its collapse under the pressure of the social conditions and beliefs he had violently rejected, was a symbol such as Ibsen might have used, expressing a truth about more than the artist's own development or even about Art in the abstract: it could reflect the social and spiritual conditions that make Art possible and keep it flourishingly alive. So that Art in the *Portrait* became a symbol of those conditions, of the moral state of the artist and of his society.[20] In *Ulysses* Joyce takes up Stephen again at the stage where his earlier grandiose plans now seem to lie in ruins; in this sense, the two books rely on each other. Stephen, we discover, has had to return from Paris; he has written nothing significant (a little poetry, a few sketches and reviews); he feels the sharp discrepancy between his boasts and ambitions and his actual reputation; he lives in a Martello tower with an ambiguous "friend", isolated, bitter, and torn by remorse: the chickens have come home to roost. The question is whether his experience has taught him anything. It has; and the result is most clearly expressed in his theory about Shakespeare, *Hamlet*, and the relationship between father and son, maturity and immaturity. He has perceived what he had not before, that art "brings the whole soul of man into activity", as Coleridge puts it, and that no artist can achieve the heights Stephen aspires to, can never see his world truly, unless his own inner self be in order. The freedom and vitality of the artist depend on the "subordination of his faculties to each other according to their relative worth and dignity"—that is, on the same source as moral freedom and vitality.

All this lies implicit in Stephen's discussion of Shakespeare. In abstract aesthetics it necessitated a search for a way around the crude Romanticism that chained the artist either to his own personal emotions or to the very social values he wished to assess: subjectivism or naturalistic representation. The way Joyce adopted owed a good deal to the *Symbolistes* and could in some sense be called Symbolism; but in order to avoid some of the common connotations of that term I have rather preferred to call it symbolistic. For once he came to see Art as a symbol of moral and social vitality, the creation of art became largely the subject of the art itself. Attention now turns to the artist's understanding of his material—to the process by which the object becomes understood in being apprehended by a subject—rather than to any naturalistic or metaphysical world regarded as objectively real irrespective of any subject. In *Stephen Hero*, Joyce had expressed something of this central concern with the creative process and its significance in the celebrated notion of "epiphanies"— the acts of mind, moments of time, coincidences of matter, whereby anything becomes an object of understanding by being understood, or in somewhat different terms, becomes a *symbol* by being apprehended imaginatively. In *Ulysses*, Stephen puts this in a way more relevant to Shakespeare's case—and to Joyce's own. There is nothing mystical, supernatural, or anti-rational about his conception of the "epiphany" or aesthetic symbol, and

there is no urgent reason why we need buttress it with philosophical arguments when Joyce himself did not. Much more
important are its consequences in his work. Not only does
Ulysses become, in one aspect, a symbolistic "drama of meaning",
but since it is also a drama about its own birth, it necessarily
includes, as Stephen's argument unmistakably suggests, a hidden
character: *the author himself*. He is not the real Joyce, of course—
the Joyce who was known to his friends and died in 1941; not a
mere *persona* either; but Joyce the artistic or poetic personality
whose voice has completely passed into his work. In *Ulysses* he
lives in his characters, but beyond them. The events he narrates
are (in a soft and flexible sense) about himself as a young man,
but it is not the Stephen who goes out into the night who wrote
Ulysses. It is an older Stephen, a gayer and wiser man, seeing
more and understanding more. And once we see that *Ulysses*
insists both upon Joyce's presence in it *as a book*, yet outside it *as
an action* at a *real* place at a *real* time, we can see that it has a
temporal dimension of the utmost importance: the distance
between Dublin, 1904, and Trieste-Zurich-Paris, 1914-21, the
distance Stephen has to grow to become able to see himself as
he sits in the Dublin library talking of Shakespeare in the reflection of "that which then I shall be".

This theme thus assumes another aspect: the exploration of
moral order. As we should expect, self-knowledge, self-realization,
detachment, human completeness, balance, are Joyce's key-
concepts. He has nothing especially new to say about social or
ethical or religious values; in many ways he seems old fashioned,
humanistic, something of a Rationalist in ethics, with a strong
sense of the religious in life but without formal religion. His
obscurity, as he said, derives from his material, the complexity
of the world in which he sought these traditional virtues. Stephen
clearly lacks them, which is one of the essential points about him.
Bloom, who lacks the imaginative potentialities of Stephen and
yet so desperately needs them, is nevertheless the unexpected
figure who does possess something of the moral maturity Stephen
needs. Bloom is representative of an age of disintegrating values
and yet outside it, his "exile" partly exclusion and partly the
freedom of detachment, a man partly corrupted and yet deeply
innocent. Joyce's treatment of both his heroes is profoundly ironic,
and so important is it to understand that irony and the attitudes

35

from which it springs—especially, I should add, in the light of such recent interpretations as Mr Hugh Kenner's which seem to me to oversimplify them—that I have devoted the whole of Chapter IV to the subject. Joyce's irony is satirical, it is true, but it is complex with endorsement and (in the strictest sense) compassion as well—the attitudes, in fact, that distinguish Stephen from the author of *Ulysses*.

The distance between Stephen and Joyce, between Stephen and Bloom, between Bloom and his ideal fulfilment, between European society and its original values, between the events of Bloomsday and the understanding of those events, may be thought of as the gap of time, of history. For Joyce, time is the element of decay and disintegration, and of growth and fulfilment. *Ulysses* would be meaningless did not this sense of time pulsate through it—not, of course, as a mere matter of technical "structure", but as the rhythm of life and death in the characters' moral experience. To accept this ineluctable rhythm and yet to grasp what lives permanently in it and by it is for Joyce the end of human self-knowledge. That, at any rate, is as far as *Ulysses* goes as it moves from the partial self-knowledge of its characters, immersed as they are in the process of time, towards the final vision of human life in its completeness. It is a vision in which life is comprehended as in the *stasis* of religious, or perhaps mythic, contemplation; but it is the author's vision (and ours), not the characters', though it emerges inevitably out of the action of the book. As the ultimate source of the compassionate irony with which the characters and their world are ordered and "placed", it represents the maturity of insight to which the present nightmare of Stephen's history points as its end. In other words, the events of the book point towards the act by which the events themselves will finally be understood—an act completed by the "mythic" vision of the last episodes. In *formal* terms apart from the represented *events*, the author's understanding pervades the whole book, unobtrusively arranging and informing the material; but so important a character requires a more noticeable part. Delicately, tactfully, the author must draw attention to himself as outside the represented events. This, I believe, is one of the main functions of Joyce's unusual styles and techniques—and of the Homeric parallels too. These formal elements become part of a larger action. Paradoxical as it may seem, style, techniques and parallels are in some measure *meant* to obtrude on our attention, to remind us constantly but tactfully of the author, even though we are also meant finally to perceive that the various styles and techniques and the Homeric parallel *as a whole* are metaphors necessary to express the meaning of the material. Joyce's success is certainly not complete: the tact is not always adequate, the necessity not always visible, and both these criticisms are too serious to ignore. Nevertheless, both Homer and the "nightmare of history" are, in the ways I have tried to explore in Chapter V, integral to Joyce's symbolistic and moral vision.

After a preliminary digression in Chapter VI to clear the ground, I have touched on one last aspect of the book: the significance of its modes of organization, its formal structures. The kind of structure from which any discussion must start, however, is one that has been usually denied altogether and its absence used as the basis for critical attacks on Joyce. By apparently devoting himself to the realistic representation of the "stream of consciousness", Joyce has seemed to many of his readers to have surrendered completely to the formlessness of the reality he has so minutely imitated. The only meaning of his work apparently lies in the patterns of symbolic objects (or words) that recur in the otherwise chaotic flow. Neither Joyce's own theory nor a careful examination of his actual text will support this view in the least; and the fallacy is all the more serious in that it obscures one of the essential aspects of the book. For what links Bloom and Stephen and Joyce, the citizen and the artist (though Stephen is artist only potentially, not yet actually), the ground on which Joyce affirms the vitality and sanity of ordinary humanity as well as the possibility and importance of Art, is precisely the activity by which the formlessness of life is given shape and meaning as it is lived. In the last analysis, Joyce's streams-of-consciousness represent not the endless flux of subjective experience or the formless chaos of objective "reality", but the creative insight, the informing activity, that is the real subject of his aesthetic theories and the basis of his moral judgments.

* * *

Joyce's originality is probably deeper even than many of his critics have proclaimed, but it is of a sort hardly to be defined by generalizations about the Twentieth-Century Novel, or the

Individual and Society, or Realism and Symbolism, or Religious Values. No simple formula will express the relations between art and life, and certainly none will fit the particular case of a writer whose whole work was in one sense the exploration of these very relations. Joyce was not foolish enough to suppose that the artist must be, in the ordinary sense, a "good" man; on the other hand, he saw that the spiritual order and vitality implicit in the highest art is a moral condition which has a subtle, indirect but nevertheless very real connection with the actual life of the artist in all his personal and social relationships. A character like Stephen Dedalus, for example, or even Leopold Bloom, is both something of a self-portrait and not a self-portrait. As personal reminiscences of Joyce the man indicate, he was never the slightly unbalanced, conscience-stricken, frustrated young prig Stephen is, and certainly not so representative of the mass-world of advertisements and popular "culture" as Bloom. On the other hand, Stephen *is* a portrait of the artist, though as a young man. Joyce evidently had a similar consciousness of his talents, a similar cold and rather arrogant intellectuality, and a similarly ambiguous struggle with his native environment. What is more, as he grew older, he was also like Bloom in his extraordinary ordinariness as a family-man and citizen, in his humour, in his detached but insatiable curiosity. For all his critical irony towards his heroes, he never fails to recognize the imaginative potentiality of the young man and the essential virtue of the older one. So that the Joyce who is "all in all", who comprehends both his complementary protagonists but is larger and freer than either one of them or even the simple combination of the two—Joyce the *artist*—is not to be equated with Joyce the man nor utterly divorced from him. All we can say in general terms is that in his books he reworked situations and themes he found in his own experience, either actually or potentially—which is so obvious a truism that it is hardly of much profit.

Facile comparisons between Joyce and other modern novelists and poets are likewise of dubious profit. In our haste to generalize we may all too easily find only what we are predisposed to find, and miss what is truly unique and perhaps what is truly valuable. It is a mark of Joyce's originality in *Ulysses* that it requires a radical shift in our attitudes to the Novel to appreciate his art; but if we do adapt our view to what he offers it, we discover that what is important in his work is exactly what is important in any novel, however modified it is by his sense of, and responsibility to, the conditions in which the twentieth-century novelist finds himself. The artist's own experience, as Joyce insisted, is the artist's only material; his world is finally his own self, and fully to know that self is for him to know as much as he can of his world. At bottom this is a platitude, of course, but Joyce's way of putting it may lead to obvious dangers in practice: solipsism, egocentricity, or (in a world so complex and disjunct, among traditions and values so threatened by mass-society and its corrupting self-flattery) an art that is merely self-therapy or self-assertion. One of our main tasks is to distinguish where Joyce failed to avoid these dangers; at his best, however, he does see and maintain the necessary tension between the concrete conditions of life which are given and their significance which is created. It is for this reason that I have tried to shift the emphasis from his mechanical intricacies of design, the close and highly wrought texture of "symbols", the psychological subtleties of the "stream of consciousness", the passive manipulation of meanings supposedly already at the artist's disposal or inherent in his material—all matters of natural interest to Joyce as a slow and painful craftsman, but only irrelevant or misleading for the critical appreciation of his art—and to focus attention on the meanings he creatively revealed in his material, upon themes realized dramatically.

Although my method of discussion precludes taking the episodes of *Ulysses* one by one, each episode is, as Joyce pointed out, an integral dramatic unit. I have consequently tried to treat, however briefly, at least one episode as a whole in conjunction with each aspect of the book, and it may be convenient to note which they are. For convenience, I refer throughout to the episodes by the usual Homeric titles, the list of which is as follows:

Episode	*Scene*	*Discussed below in:*
1 Telemachus	Stephen and others at the Martello tower	
2 Nestor	Stephen, at Mr Deasy's school	
3 Proteus	Stephen, alone on the shore	chap. V
4 Calypso	Bloom, getting breakfast for Molly and himself at 7 Eccles Street	
5 Lotus-eaters	Bloom, peregrinating	
6 Hades	Bloom and others at the funeral of Paddy Dignam	chap. VII
7 Aeolus	At the office of the *Freeman's Journal*	
8 Lestrygonians	Bloom, peregrinating and at lunch	chap. IV
9 Scylla & Charybdis	Stephen, discussing Shakespeare in the Dublin National Library	chap. III
10 Wandering Rocks	Episodes in various parts of Dublin	chap. IV
11 Sirens	Bloom and others at the Ormond Restaurant	⎫
12 Cyclops	Bloom and others (incl. "the Citizen") at Barney Kiernan's pub	
13 Nausicaa	Gerty MacDowell and Bloom on the shore	⎬ chap. VII
14 Oxen of the Sun	Stephen, Bloom and others at the Holles Street Maternity Hospital	
15 Circe	Bloom, Stephen, and others at Bella Cohen's brothel	⎭ chap. V
16 Eumaeus	Bloom and Stephen at the cabman's shelter	
17 Ithaca	Bloom and Stephen at 7 Eccles Street	chap. V
18 Penelope	Molly Bloom alone	chap. VII

(A list of further details about the plan, including the symbolic organs, arts, colours, techniques, etc., may be found in Stuart Gilbert's *James Joyce's Ulysses*, p. 41.)

Chapter II

ART AND LIFE: THE AESTHETIC
OF THE *PORTRAIT*

TO approach Joyce's art theoretically, through his aesthetic, is not without its dangers. The commonest mistake is to take that aesthetic as a sort of criterion, a point of reference by which to measure Joyce's artistic success. Probably every reader of modern literature has met Stephen Dedalus's theory in the *Portrait* and his views on Shakespeare in *Ulysses*, and it seems only natural to apply Joyce's own aesthetic in the criticism of his books, if not of all literature. The fact is, however, that the real value of the aesthetic theories is of a different kind. For it is always dangerous to judge a writer's work by his own theories—we tend, only too easily, to beg the most relevant questions; and these dangers are particularly acute when, as in Joyce's case, the theories appear as an integral part of a complex work of art. But if they cannot supply us with a critical yardstick, or even a useful structure of the author's intentions, they *can* help us, I believe, in another way: if we are prepared to follow them patiently and critically, they lead us directly towards the preoccupations and the forms of his imagination.

The main interest of the aesthetic theory in the *Portrait* (and in *Ulysses* too) arises from the fact that it brings many of the themes of the novel itself to a convenient focus—in particular, both the kind of attitudes that subtly impel Stephen all through it and the limitations of those attitudes as well. The theory is primarily Stephen's, not Joyce's, even though Joyce used many of his own ideas in it, and to examine it is largely to examine Stephen as a dramatic character. The theory therefore offers a convenient starting-point for critical discussion of the art; yet even while it does so, it offers peculiar difficulties of its own.

One is simply the terminology that Joyce, and Stephen after him, adopted from his reading in Scholastic philosophy, and the rather elliptical and even crabbed style of his thought: its "scholastic stink", as one character puts it. This hardly makes for easy understanding or easy exposition—so much so, indeed, that to approach Joyce's work this way may seem (I confess) all too like struggling through a hedge instead of going in by the gate. But there are further difficulties still. The theory both in the *Portrait* and *Ulysses* raises problems of interpretation which are precisely equivalent to those raised by the novels themselves and which have no easy solution. No one could claim that the theory is always clear even when it is most explicit, and what Joyce has written about aesthetics in various places is still so scrappy that we can call it a full aesthetic theory only with a generous courtesy. But to increase the difficulty, it is not always very easy to distinguish between his own views and those of Stephen Dedalus. Joyce himself made some jottings on aesthetics in his notebooks in 1903-04; these are echoed both in *Stephen Hero* and the *Portrait*. He delivered two papers to his college Literary and Historical Society on "Drama and Life" (1900) and "James Clarence Mangan" (1902),[1] which are echoed in *Stephen Hero* and in *Ulysses*.* The term "epiphany", which is mentioned in *Stephen Hero*, not mentioned in the *Portrait* and then recalled in *Ulysses*, is one the young Joyce is known to have used himself for tiny sketches. However closely they resemble each other, none of these theories is exactly the same. Naturally enough, almost every critic of Joyce's work supports his view of it by an interpretation of what he takes to be Joyce's own aesthetic, even if the support is only that of a suggestive analogy; and it is clear that some interpretation at least is required. Yet the very fact that interpretations of the art and of the theory are so closely linked also requires us to make sure we view the latter as accurately as the former, and that we understand the full implications both of what Joyce has Stephen say in any particular context and, equally, of what he does not have him say. The basic problem of Joyce's aesthetic, in other words, is like that of his art—to detect where, and how, Joyce qualifies the attitudes of *the artist as a young man*. Critical probing as well as exposition is called for.

* The jottings in the notebooks are printed by Herbert Gorman in his *James Joyce: a Definitive Biography*, London (1941), 1949, the pages of which I have cited in brackets in the text. They are also reprinted in *The Critical Writings of James Joyce*, ed. Ellsworth Mason and Richard Ellmann, London, 1959. The latter volume also includes the two early papers by Joyce (which were used for the essay on "Art and Life" Stephen delivers to his college Society in *Stephen Hero*), together with Joyce's other essays and reviews—none of which, however, adds anything much of general theoretical value.

If we examine these various theories in relation to each other it quickly appears that those in the novels are more highly wrought, more developed, than anything that survives of Joyce's personal comments. It is understandable enough that Stephen's remarks in the *Portrait* should have led to an inflation of their value as a general aesthetic and some not very convincing applications of them to Joyce's work. But even on a casual reading, Stephen's character in the *Portrait* ought to provoke a certain caution about his theories. His emancipation from his society, for example, is clearly less assured than he supposes, and despite his citation of Aquinas in support of his aesthetic, the forms in which his imagination actually expresses itself seem more like those of a late nineteenth-century aesthete than a tough-minded, twentieth-century neo-Thomist. He is obviously not to be identified with the artist as an older man. If we look at Joyce's other novels, moreover, we also notice that Stephen is portrayed with far less irony in *Stephen Hero* and with a far more complex irony in *Ulysses*. This general difference is reflected in the differences between the theories he propounds in each work, differences important not only for their theoretical implications but also for their dramatic implications about the novel in which they appear. In other words, if we put the theory in the *Portrait* side by side with those in the notebooks and Joyce's other writings and *Stephen Hero*, and press certain problems they raise, we can hardly avoid concluding that the theory Stephen advances in the *Portrait* is not a satisfactory aesthetic in itself, that its force in the novel is not so much philosophical as dramatic, and that it awaits completion and rectification by the views he advances in *Ulysses*. The theory in the *Portrait* serves to reveal not so much the nature of art as the nature of Stephen Dedalus; and to miss this, or to attempt to assess Joyce's work by the theory as he there presents it, is inevitably to distort his artistic achievement.

Before examining the theory, however, it is probably as well to clarify right at the start two or three other common assumptions about it and about Joyce's art. The first is that, whatever difficulties we find in Stephen's views, Joyce's *own* theory is all of a piece, and was so from the very beginning, and that to discover what it is, all we need do is simply find the common denominators in his various formulations, supply the assumptions that will reconcile them together, and interpret the result to taste. The second

assumption is that this underlying aesthetic is specifically
Thomist, or neo-Thomist, and that what Stephen Dedalus says
in various places is "correctly" interpreted as what Aquinas
meant or what others have since constructed on a foundation of
his ideas. Both assumptions are highly questionable. To take only
one example: it is true, as any examination of the theories quickly
reveals, that the notion of what Joyce called "epiphanies", which
is touched on in *Stephen Hero* (but nowhere else, and never
explicitly developed), is essential to any aesthetic attributable
to Joyce himself. It is also true that the theory in the *Portrait* is
crippled by the omission of the concept (or something like it),
while the more satisfactory theory in *Ulysses* depends upon it.
But the concept as it is assumed in *Ulysses* is rather different
from the form in which it is mentioned in *Stephen Hero*, and if we
wish to understand Joyce's own views we ought to take that
difference into account. We may, for whatever reasons, prefer
the early formulation with its vaguely metaphysical flavour
(although personally I do not), but we cannot reasonably pre-
sume that it represents Joyce's own, real and always consistent
view. But the real importance of this is its bearing on the second
assumption. Although the notion of "epiphanies" is of central
importance, some critics have tried to add it to Joyce's other
aesthetic theories by supplying him with a gratuitous metaphysical system, and interpreting "epiphanies", as well as the
terms Stephen explicitly borrows from Aquinas, in a fully
Scholastic sense. Despite his Scholastic terminology, Joyce's
aesthetic is not strictly Thomist at all.[2] Nor is there any real
evidence whatever that he gave any of his aesthetic terms a
theological meaning, or that he intended at any stage to reveal
through art the ordered spiritual vision of Christianity. He may
never have cast off the effect of his religion even though he
rejected it, or escaped the influence of his Jesuit teachers; on the
other hand, his reading in Aquinas seems to have been private
and idiosyncratic, and certainly not undertaken in pursuit of a
Catholic philosophy.[3] Joyce was never a philosopher of any kind,
and we must not read too much into what he actually wrote for
the sake of making it consonant with what we perhaps feel he
ought to have written.

Another temptation, closely connected with this, is to over-
emphasize Stephen's theological analogies. In the course of his

discussion, both in the *Portrait* and again in *Ulysses*, he compares the artist with God; and though the insights his analogies are designed to illuminate are better postponed until later chapters, it is probably as well to insist at the beginning that his analogies are *only* analogies, not identifications. He is not arguing from art to religion, as is sometimes thought; he is advancing aesthetic doctrines, not metaphysics. When he compares the (limited) autonomy of art and of the human artist to the (unlimited) autonomy of God, we ought not suppose that his metaphor elevates the one to the place of the other or was meant to. Again, if he sometimes uses phrases or doctrines of doubtful religious orthodoxy, this may perhaps shock some people (as no doubt the aggressive young Stephen intended), but it does not necessarily invalidate his point about art. The foundations of his theory do not lie in his theological analogies, which are more expository devices than experiential premises, and we have to ask what purpose they serve, what point Stephen is really making, before assuming that his unorthodoxy is a dramatic hint from Joyce that his character's theory is completely wrong. The difficulty with Stephen's theories, indeed, is that they are not wrong in any simple, black-and-white sense at all; he is always at least partly right. The weaknesses are a matter of his emphasis—what he neglects, what he over-stresses, what he therefore distorts.

At bottom, both Joyce and Stephen are concerned with one main set of aesthetic problems: the relations between art and life, or (in slightly different terms) between the artist-as-man and the artist-as-artist. These are inevitably among the central problems of any aesthetic in our post-Romantic era, and they admit of no easy, universal solution. On the one hand, the desire to dissociate art and life has an obvious motive and an obvious validity—a work of art is not properly the direct expression of social or personal attitudes, and not therefore to be estimated simply as a social or psychological or moral epiphenomenon. It exists in its own right and demands a response in its own terms. On the other hand, the desire to relate art and life is no less necessary and no less valid—a work of art is a human artifact and it necessarily exists in a social context. Looking back over the various attempts of the last century and a half to satisfy these apparently conflicting impulses, we may at least say that either impulse alone is likely to emasculate art or to pervert its integrity unless checked

45

by the motives and insights that prompt the other. The difficulties of the artist himself in coming to terms with a society that all too crudely demands his service or all too easily provokes his rejection—difficulties from which perhaps no significant artist since Blake has been free—serve only to heighten the theoretical confusions.[4] Joyce himself offers a classical example of the issues, and all the more so since he was so conscious of them and tried, in the dramatic figure of Stephen Dedalus, at once to present them and to work out a solution. And although the terms in which he did so can be assessed only in a detailed analysis of his art, these issues constitute the broad underlying significance of Stephen's theorizing, and particularly of the most marked change of emphasis discernible between his views in the *Portrait* and those in *Ulysses*.

In the former novel, Stephen is intent on the dissociation of art and life, on the autonomy and integrity of the work of art in itself. In the course of his argument, however, he conspicuously underestimates the other side of the matter: the positive relations between the work of art and the life from which it springs, which it engages in others, and which it expresses in its own terms. The result is that what he says is largely disabled by what he omits. As it stands, his theory lapses all too readily into a barren formalism encouraging a purely internal analysis of works of art, a concentration on their patterns of organization to the exclusion of questions of imaginative depth and value. (Indeed, to view Joyce's own art through the theory in the *Portrait* would lead to just that kind of formalistic analysis and evasion of judgment it has received from some of its commentators.) Up to a point, Stephen's supplementary theory of aesthetic forms—"lyrical", "epical" and "dramatic"—is an attempt to fill this gap; but in so far as it is, it remains strikingly inconsistent with his more extended, and obviously more personally important, theory of beauty and art. The theory of forms really foreshadows what he attempts in *Ulysses*—and for this reason I have reserved treatment of it until Chapter III and (more thoroughly) Chapter VI: to understand it fully requires a context larger than that provided by the *Portrait* alone. But this being the case, it is also quite clear that the views in *Ulysses* make no complete break with the earlier ones. On the contrary, they partly assume them even while they reveal their inadequacy—just at the crucial points, indeed, where we might expect the immature and incautious Stephen to be inadequate. Consequently, although the theory in *Ulysses* is more adequate, it does not in itself form a completely satisfactory aesthetic either. Its greater strength lies rather in its correction of the earlier unbalance, its firmer grasp of the subtle, complex relations of art, artist and society—an insight that, theoretical though it is, nevertheless marks a significant shift from one book to the other.

There are three major, interrelated problems that Stephen fails to solve in his theory in the *Portrait*, problems that arise from and reflect his wider attitudes: the relation between aesthetic value and moral value; the difference between aesthetic beauty and natural beauty; and the relation between aesthetic form and aesthetic meaning. In each case, to follow out his ideas is to find ourselves reach the impasse of his immaturity.

I

Stephen, like Joyce himself, begins his theory not with art, but with beauty in general, and he makes the same assumptions and uses the same terminology about it as did his creator. In the first place, both assume that beauty lies not in the eye of the beholder but rather in the object beheld—it is an objective quality, though one that satisfies (as they argue) a special desire to behold it. This desire they call the "esthetic appetite"; the actual beholding "esthetic apprehension"; and they spend most of their time analysing what this latter consists in, for they both also assume that the phases or stages of the beholding correspond to the different characteristics in the object that together constitute its beauty.[5]

Before they turn to this, however, they have to distinguish the "esthetic appetite" from the various appetites that direct other human activities. Every action is directed by an "appetite" seeking to possess its particular end or "good", but the "esthetic appetite" can be distinguished from others very simply: its end, beauty, cannot be physically possessed. Like truth, it can only be "spiritually" possessed. What distinguishes beauty from truth is that the "intellectual appetite" seeks "the most satisfying relations of the *intelligible*", while the aesthetic appetite seeks "the most satisfying relations of the *sensible*". What distinguishes both appetites, however, is that all others are purely *physical*—mere "desire or loathing", the almost involuntary reaction of the flesh towards or away from anything.[6] These physical appetites (or reactions) they call *kinetic*. Beauty, on the other hand, raises the mind above desire and loathing, arousing only a spiritual *contemplation*: "Beauty . . . awakens, or ought to awaken, or induces, or ought to induce, an esthetic stasis . . . called forth, prolonged and at last dissolved by what I call the rhythm of beauty" (*Portrait*, pp. 233-4).

The most interesting thing about this distinction of appetites is the way Stephen applies it. He quotes a casual sentence from Aquinas on which he erects the elaborate structures of his argument: *Pulchra sunt quae visa placent*: that is beautiful the apprehension of which pleases. The word "visa", he says, can cover aesthetic apprehensions of all kinds, but vague as it is, it is nevertheless "clear enough to keep away good and evil which excite desire and loathing" (p. 236). In other words, the distinction between the spiritual and the kinetic appetites is used primarily to keep aesthetics and morals distinct: kinetic ends, he argues, are quite improper in the spiritual realm of beauty and art. The conclusion to be drawn from all this is simple but fundamental: didacticism, which is directly moral, and pornography, which is directly immoral, are equally invalid categories in aesthetics. Stephen, like the young Joyce, sweeps away both the praise and the criticism of the pious as equally irrelevant to the true business of art and of the artist. But we might well notice that the distinction here is extremely sharp—so sharp, indeed, that Stephen (like many other similar theorists) falls straight into the trap such distinctions may conceal. He manages at one stroke to cut art off from *all* "physical" responses—and by implication from *any* moral activity of the whole man. When the maturer Stephen talks about *kinesis* in *Ulysses*, this assumption is abandoned and the term takes on a rather different, and more satisfactory, meaning. In the *Portrait*, however, he is caught in a fallacy he does not perceive, in a way that (as we shall see) Joyce himself was not. Stephen makes no distinction between moral values and the values of morality, presumably because he cannot see any; he is, as we realize, too much in revolt against his society, too much concerned with his individual destiny. The result is hardly surprising: already, at the very outset of his theory, in trying to explain the activity for the sake of which he must reject his society, he fails to see that art is far more complex than his theory, and more complex because it necessarily engages human sympathies, rejections, feelings, thoughts and judgments, even as it gives them another value in ordering them.

We might illustrate the general point Stephen is concerned to make and also its limitations with two passages from *Ulysses*, for the point has an important bearing not only on *Joyce's* attitudes but also on how we read that book itself. When, for example, Mr Bloom dips into a work entitled *Sweets of Sin*, his response is portrayed as completely kinetic; it is a simple reaction to the kinetic prose he is reading:

Warmth showered gently over him, cowing his flesh. Flesh yielded amid rumpled clothes. Whites of eyes swooning up. His nostrils arched themselves for prey. Melting breast ointments (*for him! For Raoul!*) Armpits' oniony sweat. Fishgluey slime (*her heaving embonpoint!*). Feel! Press! Crushed! Sulphur dung of lions! (223/233)

On the other hand, when he listens later on to Simon Dedalus singing, the "mercy of beauty" achieves a very different result (260-2/269-71). The song induces in Bloom what seems to be an aesthetic *stasis*, prolonged and at last dissolved by the sheer beauty of the song:

—*Come!*
It soared, a bird, it held its flight, a swift pure cry, soar silver orb it leaped serene, speeding, sustained, to come, don't spin it out too long long breath he breath long life, soaring high, high resplendent, aflame, crowned, high in the effulgence symbolistic, high, of the ethereal bosom, high, of the high vast irradiation everywhere all soaring all around about the all, the endlessnessnessness . . .
—*To me!*
Siopold!
Consumed. (261-2/271)

This is the kind of result Stephen evidently has in mind when he speaks of "the luminous silent stasis of esthetic pleasure, a spiritual state very like to that cardiac condition which the Italian physiologist Luigi Galvani, using a phrase almost as beautiful as Shelley's, called the enchantment of the heart" (pp. 242-3).

Yet to suppose that *no* kinetic appetites were involved in a *stasis* like this is to miss the important fact that to Bloom the song has a deeply felt significance, and that its beauty to him derives from the way it arouses and orders his feelings and memories and lusts and judgments. It is the love-song from *Martha*, and so it quickens both his complex feelings about his pitiful flirtation with Martha Clifford and his memories about the first time he saw Molly, his wife, whose present infidelity is very much in his mind. His sense of frustration and of loneliness, his judgment of the singer—all these are carefully, and properly, interwoven by Joyce into the fabric of Bloom's experience of the song. It has a meaning and value that can only be called moral just because it effects a *statis* that is wider than Stephen's "spiritual" suggests. And the relevance of this truth becomes increasingly important as we go on with his theory in the *Portrait*, for it is something he nowhere properly recognizes.

II

The second problem—the difference between aesthetic and natural beauty—is very largely a development and a heightening of the first.

Having distinguished the "spiritual" appetites and ends from the "kinetic" ones, and having also distinguished truth from beauty, Stephen can now turn to the central act of "esthetic apprehension" itself. Here, both Stephen and the young Joyce follow (but only roughly) the Scholastics' three-fold analysis of any act of ordinary apprehension. Firstly, there is the stage where we perceive the physical presence and unity of an object—what Stephen calls its "wholeness" or *integritas*. Secondly—and of course these stages are more logical than chronological—our minds engage in analysis, perceiving the object in its conceptual or intelligible aspect: the process in which we reach an intellectual "recognition" of the object, seeing it as something shaped and informed by a "universal". This aspect is presumably what Stephen calls the object's *consonantia* or "harmony", but the way he describes it marks his first significant departure from the Scholastic analysis—one to which we shall have to return in a moment. But he also parts company with the Scholastics about the third stage as well, and, even more important, with both the formulations of the young Joyce himself (as we find them in the notebooks) and the formulations offered in *Stephen Hero*. To the Scholastic, the third stage of apprehension is the mind's expressing its perception of the object in a *concept* and ultimately in a *word*. But although this view is implied later on in *Ulysses*, it is not what Stephen thinks in the *Portrait* nor is it what the young Joyce himself thought. The differences are subtle and not immediately obvious; nevertheless, they are so significant of wider issues and wider attitudes that they have to be made clear from the outset.

We may start with Joyce's own remarks about "esthetic apprehension" in his notebooks. When he himself reached this third stage of his analysis, he recognized that he had to agree with the Scholastics that *any* object, if it could be perceived in the twofold way described so far, could also be called "beautiful"—but only in their general, transcendental sense of Beauty, the sense in which it can be regarded as a property of all Creation, like Truth or Unity. But of course this metaphysical or religious sense of Beauty is not what we mean by *aesthetic* beauty, which is not a property of all objects nor always necessarily perceived in those that do possess it. So, in his notebooks (Gorman, pp. 134-5), Joyce goes on to meet this problem by arguing that aesthetic beauty is perceived only in a special third stage of apprehension, a stage that is *specifically* aesthetic. He speaks of it as an "activity of satisfaction", and claims that in practice the words "beautiful" and "ugly" are "applied chiefly to the third activity, with regard, that is, to the nature, degree and duration of the satisfaction resultant from the apprehension of any sensible object." This is probably his first formal attempt to define what he himself was seeking in art, but clearly it could hardly do as it stands. For one thing, it is too vague really to explain anything about beauty; and for another, it puts the emphasis where Joyce was anxious not to put it—on a subjective response rather than the properties of the object itself.

Logically, therefore, the next formulation is that in *Stephen Hero* (p. 190), which attempts to get over this difficulty by introducing what is perhaps the best-known of all Joyce's terms: "epiphany". In a sense, this concept is central to all his subsequent thinking about art and its relations with life, his understanding of his own activity as an artist and his whole conception of its meaning and value. But although his art embodies his developing understanding of the term, and although the art of the *Portrait* implies a fully mature grasp of what it involves, it is not until *Ulysses* that he can show *Stephen* reaching even a proper theoretical grasp of it. In *Stephen Hero*, therefore, we find a far cruder conception of "epiphany" than in *Ulysses*, yet one that does, at least temporarily, get round the immediate problem Joyce found himself confronted with by his argument in the notebooks. By "epiphany", Stephen explains, he means a "sudden spiritual manifestation"; and he uses the term to explain what happens in the third stage of aesthetic apprehension:

After the analysis which discovers the second quality the mind makes the only logically possible synthesis and discovers the third quality. This is the moment which I call epiphany. First we recognize that the object is *one* integral thing, then we recognize that it is an organized composite structure, a *thing* in fact: finally, when the relation of the parts is exquisite, when the parts are adjusted to the special point, we recognize that it is *that* thing which it is. Its soul, its whatness, leaps to us from the vestment of its appearance. The soul of the commonest object, the structure of which is so adjusted, seems to us radiant. The object achieves its epiphany.

What this tries to do is obvious enough: firstly, to show how something in the object, its true inner nature, corresponds to a stage of its perception by a subject; and secondly, to show how this third stage follows from the other two. Having apprehended the physical presence of the object, its *integritas*, and the conceptual structure of the object, its *consonantia*, we now apprehend it as matter everywhere interpenetrated with intelligible structure, as the composition of matter and form that makes it the thing it is, so that it appears luminous, producing what Stephen calls *claritas*. Stephen also equates this with the Scholastic *quidditas* of an object, but the Scholastic term really applies to the universal form. What Stephen means is something like *haecceitas*, the individual this-ness of an object; he is closer to Hopkins, with his "inscape", than to Aquinas.[7] Unfortunately, he never clarifies the relation of the objective and the subjective aspects of the epiphany—the relation between the *self-revelation* of the object itself and the meaning that the beholder *gives* to it in beholding it. That question has to be left until *Ulysses* when it moves to the centre of the stage, for it is there seen to be a crucial one for the artist and the ordinary man alike: it involves the whole problem of the *values* we perceive in, or give to, our experience. At this stage, however, it is enough for Stephen to have worked out what it is we mean when we speak of the "beauty" of an object, and to have freed the artist—whose business is with beauty—from the encumbrance of both moralistic and merely conventional notions of beauty.

To turn from the notebooks and *Stephen Hero* to the *Portrait*, however, is to perceive a startling difference of emphasis—a difference in the way Stephen conceives *consonantia*, and closely connected with that, in the way he conceives *claritas*. In each case, the difference—subtle as it may seem—is of paramount importance, and in each case again it is a matter not of what he changes, but rather of what he leaves out: which is to say, what considerations he ignores, what factors limit his whole outlook.

At a first glance, the differences seem hardly to matter. With *consonantia*, for example, he seems only to restate what is said in *Stephen Hero:*

Stephen Hero:
Analysis then. The mind considers the object in whole and in part, *in relation to itself and to other objects*, examines the balance of its parts, contemplates the form of the object, traverses every cranny of the structure. (189; my italics)

Portrait:
you pass from point to point, led by its formal lines; you apprehend it as balanced part against part within its limits; you feel the rhythm of its structure. In other words, the synthesis of immediate perception is followed by the analysis of apprehension. Having first felt that it is *one* thing you feel now that it is a *thing*. You apprehend it as complex, multiple, divisible, separable, made up of its parts, the result of its parts and their sum, harmonious. That is *consonantia*. (241-2)

The crucial difference lies in the dropping of the phrase I have italicized in the former—or rather, in the dropping of any reference to *the world outside the object itself*. With *claritas* the difference is rather more obvious: it consists in the dropping of the whole notion of "epiphany"—and with it, once again, any reference to the spiritual insight, *the imaginative-moral activity*, of the beholder:

When you have apprehended [the object] . . . as one thing and have then analysed it according to its form and apprehended it as a thing

53

you make the only synthesis which is logically and esthetically permissible. You see that it is that thing which it is and no other thing. The radiance of which he [Aquinas] speaks is the scholastic *quidditas*, the *whatness* of a thing. (242)

Why these emphases in the *Portrait* do not seem to matter at a first glance is simply that at this point Stephen is talking about beauty in general, beauty as it may be found in *any* object. And if we think of the beauty of trees or oranges, for example, it is reasonable enough to limit our analysis to the qualities of the object itself. Whether we find it acceptable or not as an account of beauty, it provokes no immediate, fundamental objections as applied to natural objects. Applied to art, however, it most certainly does—and this is just where Stephen wants to apply it.

Art, says Stephen (and he is echoing Joyce's own definition), is "the human disposition of sensible or intelligible matter for an esthetic end" (*Portrait*, p. 235). What he means by an "esthetic end" is clearly the satisfaction of the three stages of "esthetic apprehension": the work of art must possess *integritas, consonantia* and *claritas*. Yet if we now apply Stephen's account of these terms to art, we can see how narrow his conception of it is. *Consonantia* amounts only to a purely formal relationship of parts; "structure" could be no more than pattern, any pattern; there is no real awareness of what the "harmony" of art is a harmony *of*. Even the phrase about "the disposition of sensible or intelligible matter" evades the problem, for since Stephen regards *all* objects of beauty as composed of sensible and intelligible matter, it hardly distinguishes the "matter" of art in any way. The truth is that Stephen's theory nowhere does; with the result that he does not, and cannot, suggest how one "harmony" can be deeper, more significant, than another. His definitions admit no possibility of perceiving a qualitative difference in the *consonantia* of (say) Poe's "The Bells" and Blake's "London". It is impossible to think that *Joyce* believed this, and the phrase in *Stephen Hero* about the mind considering the object "in relation to itself and to other objects" does at least make an attempt to meet the problem. But for Stephen in the *Portrait*, *consonantia* seems only a matter of mere organization rather than one of imaginative coherence. Once again, he cuts art off from the life which goes into it and from which its "harmony" derives significance.[8]

So, too, with *claritas*. The "whatness" of a poem, for example, is rather different from the "whatness" of a natural object. One thing they have in common may be, as *Stephen Hero* suggests, that to perceive either a spiritual activity on the part of the beholder is necessary, and certainly this is true of the poem, even if a good deal more has to be said about what the activity consists in and how it engages with the work. But to leave this activity of aesthetic apprehension out altogether, as Stephen does in the *Portrait*, is in effect to ignore what makes a *human* disposition of sensible or intelligible matter different from a natural disposition of sensible or intelligible matter: that is, the human (or, broadly, the moral) significance of art, its capacity to speak the language of human life in a way that natural objects do not.

Yet if we look at the *Portrait* as a whole, it is hardly very surprising that Stephen should fall into this confusion between nature and art. When he thinks of his own artistic ambitions, he can never clearly distinguish between what he feels is a natural and irresistible force in his life, his individual character and talent, and his own free choices as a moral agent. He feels himself impelled by his own nature to do what he must—rejecting the lesser claims of society, home and religion—and he feels it so strongly that he cannot conceive his inescapable moral responsibilities as a man very clearly. Thus art appears to him largely as the exercise of a natural talent, the product of a natural power in the individual (albeit a force disciplined by a conscious sense of formal craftsmanship); as yet he cannot see that it involves the matured feelings, values and choices of the artist as a man, and a far profounder discipline. His own callow poetry in the novel ("Are you not weary of ardent ways" and so on) is, as we perceive, an illustration of, and a critical judgment on, not only the theory but also on the underlying attitudes the theory expresses.

III

Thus the third problem raised by the theory—the relation between aesthetic form and aesthetic meaning—inevitably emerges from the other two, and Stephen's failure to solve this one is already implicit in his failure to solve them.[9] Yet it does also have a special importance in that it raises most acutely the difficulty of interpreting *Joyce's* attitude to art, and it is perhaps worth examining with particular care in order to avoid confusions about that. For this whole problem of aesthetic form and aesthetic meaning would never arise—or alternatively it could be regarded as solved—if only we could attribute to Stephen, and by implication to Joyce, some convenient set of metaphysical beliefs—like those of Aquinas, for example. This in fact is precisely what many of Joyce's critics have done. And yet if we look at what the relevant works actually say, we shall find that to do so is to miss the real point of Stephen's theorizing in both the *Portrait* and *Ulysses*.

We may begin with the question that has obviously been becoming increasingly urgent as we proceed with the theory: where in his argument does Stephen discuss—or even account for —the *meaningfulness* of art, those subtle relations with life that others have tried to explain with terms like "imitation", "universality", "revelation", "express", "symbol", and so on? Certainly the answer does not lie in his definition of art itself: as we have seen, the "esthetic end" involves no distinction between art and other kinds of beautiful things, nor does the term "sensible or intelligible matter". At a first glance, perhaps, this latter phrase may seem to include the possibility of *truth* as well as beauty in art (since truth is "the most satisfying relations of the intelligible"), but once we look at it more closely, we firstly begin to wonder whether the alternative of sensible *or* intelligible is really accurate, for if anything is "sensible" it is surely also "intelligible" in that it must embody a conceptual form that enables us to recognize what it is; and then we realize that, just because the phrase is so loose, it cannot help to distinguish a work of art from a chair (say) or even a tree.[10] All are "sensible or intelligible matter"; all may serve an "esthetic end" in that all may be "esthetically apprehended"; and logic-chopping about the rest of the definition— about "human disposition . . . for an esthetic end"—may be relevant to the attitudes proper to artists, but it tells us nothing about *art* except that it is made by human beings.[11] The kind of "truth" Stephen's definition includes in art, therefore, could only be (if anything) the transcendental "truth" that all objects have been said to possess because their "forms" or "essences" bring our minds into conformity with God's Intelligence (since all "forms" are His creation and also the metaphysical aspect of things that makes them "intelligible" to us). But like transcendental Beauty, this is not the kind of quality we mean if we speak of the "truth" of a work of art: that is a truth to human experience, a poetic truth, and one, moreover, that is capable of *qualitative* judgments. If, therefore (as some readers suppose), Stephen *is* trying to reconcile truth and beauty in art, his definition makes only the vaguest and most ineffectual gesture towards doing so.[12]

Nor does he do very much better with his manipulation of the term *stasis*. It emerges in the course of his exposition that *stasis*, as well as being the product of beauty, is also "the tragic emotion", a balanced combination of pity and terror. And of course pity and terror are responses to life:

Pity is the feeling which arrests the mind in the presence of whatsoever is grave and constant in human sufferings and unites it with the human sufferer. Terror is the feeling which arrests the mind in the presence of whatsoever is grave and constant in human sufferings and unites it with the secret cause. (232-3)

On this basis, only a genuinely serious art will produce *stasis*, and it is a seriousness that is capable of being judged as more or less profound: here, it would seem, is the relationship between art and life we are seeking. And significantly enough, the young Joyce himself used much these terms in his notebooks when he tried to define comedy as well as tragedy: the aim of comedy, he argues, is to produce the feeling of "joy"; this joy derives from the contemplation of "whatever is substantial or accidental in human fortunes"; and comedy is to be judged by whether the joy is excited by the more or the less "substantial" (Gorman, pp. 96-7).

Yet, as Joyce himself must have recognized, the problem is still there: the seriousness of art does not really depend on its *subject-matter*. Even Stephen himself seems dimly aware of this in the *Portrait*, and he tries to solve it by simply identifying the *stasis* that *all* beauty ought to produce with the *stasis* that serious subject-matter ought to produce:

Beauty . . . awakens, or ought to awaken, or induces, or ought to induce, an esthetic stasis, *an ideal pity or an ideal terror*, a stasis called forth, prolonged and at last dissolved by what I call the rhythm of beauty. (234)

Unfortunately, this simple identification of the two kinds of *stasis* solves nothing, for it leads Stephen straight into the same kind of fallacy as he fell into with *consonantia* and *claritas*: this

57

"ideal pity" and "ideal terror" may apply to the beauty of art, but they do not apply to the beauty of natural objects. We may perhaps speak in his fashion about some picture of an orange, for example, but we should hardly do so about an orange. Not that the difficulty with the theory has anything to do with representational art—that, except as a test case, is really beside the point. It is rather that Stephen explains nothing about the significance that art possesses *as* art, and how it is that we can in fact judge it; he scarcely recognizes that poetic meaning and imaginative truth are created in art, let alone offer any discussion of what these qualities are.

Once again the difference between the *Portrait* and Joyce's other early writings underlines how much of his own thinking Joyce deliberately refrained from here attributing to Stephen. The paper on "Drama and Life" that Joyce delivered at college, for instance, contains at least one passage that the Stephen of the *Portrait* could not have spoken. Art, Joyce maintained, became false to itself once it submitted to the demands of religion or morality or romantic idealism; it was equally falsified by submitting to the demands of the Aesthete, the critic who is concerned only with Beauty: "Beauty is the swerga of the aesthete; but truth has a more ascertainable and more real dominion. Art is true to itself when it deals with truth" (*Critical Writings*, pp. 43-4). This is to put the matter crudely, of course, but at least it does suggest an insight much wider than Stephen's in the *Portrait*, and it does point directly to the major assumption of the theory outlined in *Stephen Hero*.[13] In this work, the passage where Stephen expounds his theories to Cranly, which forms the basis for the passage in the *Portrait* where he expounds them to Lynch, is overshadowed by the longer and more striking argument of the paper he delivers at college—the argument for which Joyce drew on his own papers. Nothing of this argument remains in the *Portrait* and very little of the Stephen it represents; on the other hand, the same line of thought (though in different terms) does reappear in *Ulysses*. The reason is not hard to see: for all the traces of Aquinas in it, Stephen's paper owes far more to Shelley's *Defence of Poetry*, and it represents a Stephen, and a Joyce, who are Romantics no doubt, but Romantics really trying to meet their central problem—the relation of art and life—and reaching for a solution that will transcend the limitations of Romanticism without rejecting its genuine insights. The solution is only adumbrated here; like the concept of "epiphany", it was to take on a deeper meaning with greater experience. But already, as even a quick glance at the argument shows, Joyce had grasped what was far beyond a character like the Stephen of the *Portrait*: the need for "the classical temper".

The central theme of the argument is the same as Shelley's: art as the discovery and re-creation of values. Only the poet, Shelley had argued, can penetrate the outward circumstances of his society to the eternal truths about man and his universe, which it is the task of the mere "reasoners and mechanists" to apply to the current needs of the time. The fictions of Homer (to take a relevant example) are not mere representations of barbaric society now long outdated. Under the local customs and beliefs of the age, under the dress of a heroic society, are revelations of permanent value because of permanent validity. "Homer embodied the ideal perfection of his age in human character", inspiring his audience to become as like his heroes as they could by identification with figures that expressed "the truth and beauty of friendship, patriotism, and persevering devotion to an object". It makes no difference that the heroes are not quite perfect:

a poet considers the vices of his contemporaries as a temporary dress in which his creations must be arrayed, and which cover without concealing the eternal proportions of their beauty.

Indeed, the eternal truth and beauty the poet reveals are so dazzling that it is probably necessary for him to "temper this planetary music for mortal ears" by dressing his characters in the costume and customs of the time. The poet, then, has a double task—to represent the world around him, and to reveal through it the "unchangeable forms of human nature". Merely to catalogue the facts of the world about him is to write a "story" not a "poem".[14]

As soon as Stephen starts talking in his paper about the poet as the "mediator between the world of his experience and the world of his dreams" (*Stephen Hero*, p. 65), we recognize the characteristic Shelleyan flavour. It is absurd, says Stephen, for "a criticism itself established upon homilies to prohibit the elective courses of the artist in his *revelation* of the beautiful"—the emphasis is Stephen's. We are told that "every age must look for its sanction to its poets and philosophers"; that the poet is the "intense centre of the life of his age"; that "he alone is capable of absorbing in himself the life that surrounds him and of flinging it abroad again amid planetary music"; that critics must set their calculations by the "poetic phenomenon"—

It is time for them to acknowledge that here the imagination has contemplated intensely the truth of the being of the visible world and that beauty, the splendour of truth, has been born. The age, though it bury itself fathoms deep in formulas and machinery, has need of these realities which alone give and sustain life and it must await from those chosen centres of vivification the force to live, the security for life which can come to it only from them. Thus the spirit of man makes a continual affirmation.

Thus he also distinguishes between mere "literature" and "poetry", the one concerned with the "manners and customs of societies", the externals, and the other with the essential and "unalterable laws" of society.[15]

The artist has "twin faculties, a selective faculty and a reproductive faculty". He has to "disentangle the subtle soul of the image from its mesh of defining circumstances"—to catch what he elsewhere calls an "epiphany"—and to "re-embody" it in the most suitable artistic circumstances. This language is far from exact, of course, and the difficulties it raises are never discussed, but it is sufficient for Stephen's next major point—an attack on the "romantic temper". This is the artistic attitude that finds "no fit abode here for its ideals and chooses therefore to behold them under insensible figures"; the attitude, presumably, that damages a good deal of Shelley's own work and some of the French Symbolists', by producing remote, unsubstantial images whose feet never quite touch the ground. The dangers of the romantic temper, says Stephen, are to be remedied by the adoption of the "classical style". The classical temper, in opposition to the romantic, "chooses rather to bend upon these present things and so to work upon them and fashion them that the quick intelligence may go beyond them to their meaning which is still unuttered".

In other words, Stephen like the young Joyce himself is advocating art that combines an intense concern with values, so that it becomes an imaginative "criticism of life", with a technique firmly based upon a realistic fidelity to ordinary experience. "Life", as Joyce said in "Drama and Life", "we must accept as we see it before our eyes, men and women as we meet them in the real world, not as we apprehend them in the world of faery" (*Critical Writings*, p. 45). It is hardly surprising therefore that Joyce the Romantic rebel felt more at home with the art of Ibsen than with that of his Irish contemporaries at the turn of the century or with the kind of poetry that Stephen in the *Portrait* composes. The artist had to recognize the wider meaning and implications of his art; his devotion to it had to be in the interests of "spiritual truth" and "affirmation". A mere aesthete, as he said in *The Day of the Rabblement*, "has a floating will" (Gorman, p. 72). Ibsen combined the artist's "lofty impersonal power" with an admirably "classical" technique. In contrast, George Russell, as reported in *Ulysses*, advocates "formless spiritual essences" as the proper substance of art. Stephen's unspoken response to him there—"Hold to the now, the here, through which all future plunges to the past"—is in part a demand for the discipline of a technique committed to everyday life. But since Stephen has by that stage reached a rather maturer awareness of the same problems the young Joyce also had to face, it is also something more.

Returning to the *Portrait* with all this in mind, we find one of Stephen's remarks there particularly revealing. Speaking of his theory of beauty, he adds:

So far as this side of esthetic philosophy extends, Aquinas will carry me all along the line. When we come to the phenomena of artistic conception, artistic gestation and artistic reproduction I require a new terminology and a new personal experience. (238)

On the other hand, he obviously does not see the difficulties into which his "pennyworths of wisdom" from St Thomas have led him. Nor does he see how much more acute those difficulties are made by his adopting casual ideas from St Thomas without adopting the metaphysics that give the ideas coherence. Thus the problem of the poetic meaning and truth of art is capable of *some* kind of solution if we hold a philosophy that gives "intelligibility" a metaphysical range: if we believe, that is, that the intelligibility of art ought to reveal and reflect the intelligibility inherent in all things in the world. A Thomist aesthetic could be developed in this way (as Maritain, for one, shows[16]); and Hermeticism or Neo-Platonism or some kinds of Symbolism or Transcendentalism encourage the same approach too. But unless we foist a philosophy of this kind upon Stephen, or upon Joyce, the theory in the *Portrait* remains cripplingly limited.

The fact is, however, that neither Joyce nor Stephen accepts any such metaphysical philosophy. If there are vestigial traces of Shelleyan Platonism in the paper in *Stephen Hero* they are clearly out of place beside the arguments for "the classical temper", and in *Ulysses*, we find, the whole argument is reformulated precisely in order to avoid the slightest suggestion that art reflects some other metaphysical world. And even in the *Portrait* Stephen's attitude is perfectly clear and definite. He dismisses some possible interpretations of what Aquinas meant by *claritas* and (although he is probably wrong about Aquinas) his reasons for doing so are of the highest importance:

It would lead you to believe that he had in mind symbolism or idealism, the supreme quality of beauty being a light from some other world, the idea of which the matter is but the shadow, the reality of which it is but the symbol. I thought he might mean that *claritas* is the artistic discovery and representation of the divine purpose in anything or a force of generalization which would make the esthetic image a universal one, make it outshine its proper conditions. (242)

He rejects all these interpretations, and since he consistently stands by his rejection, since it is also the attitude of *Stephen Hero*, and since it is even elaborated still further in *Ulysses*, we must take it, I believe, as Joyce's rejection too. We could say, indeed, that it is a premise of the whole art of *Ulysses* itself, a corollary (though as put here, only a negative one) of "the classical temper". Joyce never believed that art represents ideas that can be extraneously formulated, or some supernatural "Reality". He is obviously at one with Stephen at least in trying to prevent art from disappearing altogether into any ethical or social or scientific or metaphysical Truth it is supposed to serve.

But if we can appreciate the force both of Stephen's rejection in the *Portrait* and of his contempt for the enormous pretensions, the "literary talk", of some of the Symbolist theories of the time, we have to admit that the mere rejection, however just it may be, is not enough. The basic problem still remains. Correct up to a point, but with a still limited insight into the issues he raises, he seems to suggest that if a work of art had *any* kind of universal meaning it would "outshine its proper conditions". The old term "universality" may be inadequate, but to put nothing in its place is again to cut art off from life altogether.

Of course, we could do what many of Joyce's critics do, and save Stephen's theory by interpreting it in the light of—or rather, by conflating it with—ideas from outside the *Portrait*. Some want to add the notion of "epiphany" from *Stephen Hero* to give a moral content to *claritas*[17]; some want to add emotions, attitudes, values, to give content to *consonantia* and *stasis*[18]; some want to add Aristotelian or Thomist metaphysics to give meaning to "intelligibility".[19] But whether these are acceptable as Joyce's views or not (and I hope that even so brief an examination of his writings will have suggested which are and which are not), all these interpretations import ideas *into* the *Portrait*, all add to what Joyce makes Stephen actually say. What is even more important, however, all such additions finally result in obscuring the crucial *dramatic* logic of the theory in both the *Portrait* and in *Ulysses* as well. For Joyce clearly limits Stephen's understanding of art just as he limits his understanding of life; what Stephen does not see about the one is what he does not know of the other. And his explicit rejection of any metaphysical view of art is significant just because it does lead him to an impasse, to a central problem he has to face as soon as he realizes what it is, just as Joyce himself had to face it: how does art have moral significance and of what kind? how, indeed, do *any* of our activities have moral significance, and of what kind? These are necessarily the questions he confronts in *Ulysses*.

To iron out the difficulties of his theory in the *Portrait*, therefore, is to miss the most important function it serves: its limitations focus exactly the limitations of Stephen's still "uncreated soul". At best, he can achieve an uneasy combination of "beauty" and "truth" as distinct and unrelated essentials, but it is precisely the lack of relation that robs them of significance and handicaps the theory as a whole. By ignoring the contexts of human experience in which art is created and apprehended, and the function of the language in which that experience is embodied, Stephen ignores the whole symbolic aspect of art. The result is, in a very pure sense, what has been called the "ontological fallacy"—the belief that "a work of art fulfils its purpose and achieves its value

63

simply by *being*, so that the critic becomes concerned only to demonstrate the mode of its being by descriptive analysis".[20] To ignore the meanings created in a work of art—and particularly to ignore the manner of their presence—is to come perilously close to pure Aestheticism, and this Stephen in effect does.[21] Subtly but inevitably, he suggests that as the artist is isolated from his society so art is isolated from life. His rejection of *kinesis* seems all too like a rejection of emotion rather than a demand for its purification, for a true impersonality; it hints at a fear of reality rather than a welcoming acceptance of it in order to transform it and express it in another mode. In the long run, Stephen extends the exile of the artist to the exile of art.

In short, both he and his theory lack real engagement with life. For all his desire and intention:

Yes! Yes! Yes! He would create proudly out of the freedom and power of his soul . . . a living thing (193)—

he has not yet achieved the necessary moral maturity, the necessary kind of power and freedom. His attitude towards his present circumstances of life is little more than a simple repudiation, a sharp, almost involuntary, reaction; in a word, a sort of personal *kinesis*. He uses the word "life", but only as an empty counter. He lacks the proper freedom that consists in mature understanding, a willingness to accept life as it is given as the necessary medium of one's own labour, even while one criticizes it at the same time. His alienation from his society and its values, though by no means irresponsible or unjustified, is not yet self-critical, impersonal detachment. What has to be left until *Ulysses* is a richer context of experience; the missing theory of artistic expression, which can explain how subject and object, meaning and quiddity, feeling and fact, are *fused* by the artist in his very medium, language; the recognition of how art, and the artist, achieve appropriate freedom and life; the healing of the split between "beauty" and "truth". There, the insights represented by the embryonic concept of "epiphanies", the callow essays on "Drama and Life", "James Clarence Mangan" and "Art and Life", and by other aspects of Joyce's own jottings in his notebooks, are developed, re-formulated and now redress the balance. In short, Stephen's aesthetic is made to grow and change as Stephen himself is made to grow and change.

It would seem, then, that although Stephen and the young Joyce shared a common desire to emphasize that quality of art Kant called "purposiveness without purpose", and to dissociate the ("static") appetites satisfied by beauty and art from the ("kinetic") ones of ordinary life,[22] Joyce himself did not fall into the same traps as Stephen: of supposing that human experience could really be divided in this way, or that, if the purposes of art are not in any crude sense moral, it therefore has no moral significance and its meaning is therefore negligible.[23] The mature artist obviously saw through his immature hero's theories well enough, and obviously arranged the elements of his own thinking to achieve the maximum dramatic effect. The importance of the theory in the *Portrait*—and in *Ulysses* too, for that matter—is not as a standard by which to appreciate or to judge Joyce's art. Rather, it is as a focus for the problems, which are fundamentally moral problems, with which both works are concerned as dramatic novels.

CHAPTER III

ART AND FREEDOM: THE AESTHETIC
OF *ULYSSES*

STEPHEN puts forward another theory of art in the library chapter of *Ulysses* ("Scylla and Charybdis")—this time in terms of *Hamlet*. Once again his argument is based on an Aristotelian and Scholastic foundation; again it is concerned with a theory of apprehension and knowledge; but apart from that, the difference from the theory in the *Portrait* is fundamental. Having developed in the meantime, Stephen now tackles those questions he had deliberately evaded in the earlier novel— artistic conception and artistic gestation—and through his theory of Shakespeare and *Hamlet* he discusses the "matter" of art, the conditions under which it is produced, and the relations of the artist to his art. He does this largely by means of his analogies between art and the divine Word, between the artist and God; and if his parallels are developed with a sometimes bewildering fancifulness, he does nevertheless restore art to its context in experience, and so restores meaningfulness and truth to art. The *stasis* of the artist's soul and the *stasis* of art are now related.

The result is that his new theory is one that the Stephen of the *Portrait* could never have conceived. Not only does he use Aristotle and Aquinas more accurately and to better effect, but also, as we might expect, he picks up and develops certain ideas that had found their first, unsatisfactory formulation in *Stephen Hero*. *Kinesis* and *stasis* are more properly seen as conditioning states of the whole man rather than separate and unrelated kinds of appetency; the notion of the epiphany is assumed but given a new solidity by the context of ideas in which it is assumed; and though Stephen talks mainly about Shakespeare's alienation and "sundering", it is the whole unstated axiom of his argument that these are significant only in relation to the "reconciliation" to which they point. Joyce's early remarks about art as the affirmation of life and of the spirit of man, about the stable, deep, "comic" joy of all perfect art, are given a richer meaning. Here, if anywhere, is something like a mature aesthetic of his own.

66

I

Stephen's theory is something of a parody of Shakespearian commentaries, but it is also something much more. Continually during the course of the discussion his reflections indicate how deeply he feels the connection with himself: "Elizabethan London lay as far from Stratford as corrupt Paris lies from virgin Dublin" (176/186). He is not seeking mere biographical parallels. What urges him is the need for explanation and understanding of his own situation. His theory is about Shakespeare, but it is also about himself and all other artists too. It is, as it were, a commentary on the myth of Shakespeare, the particular hero in whose story may be found the universal laws that hold for all his type, in whose deeds may be found a universal wisdom. Even though Stephen's theory seems a mere *tour de force* to his audience, it is a task of self-understanding imposed on him by necessity:

> What the hell are you driving at?
> I know. Shut up. Blast you! I have reasons.
> *Amplius. Adhuc. Iterum. Postea.*
> Are you condemned to do this? (196/205)

The answer to this unspoken question is clearly, yes. The theory itself explains the necessity. When he is challenged, Stephen promptly says he does not believe it, but the reply comes glibly. His silent reflections reveal more than his protective speech—"I believe, O Lord, help my unbelief" (202/211). Even if his theory is false in fact it is nevertheless, like the story of Odysseus, metaphysically true—"If we consider the matter well", says Vico, "poetic truth is metaphysical truth, and physical truth which is not in conformity with it should be considered false."[1] The case of *Hamlet* lies at the heart of *Ulysses*, and Stephen's argument about it as a work of art explains why. Although the aesthetic theory here is as dramatically "placed" as that in the *Portrait*, it is not as an ironic emphasis upon the action but as its intellectual principle.

The problem of the "matter" of art is introduced very early in the chapter. Russell cuts across the desultory conversation about *Hamlet*:

—All these questions are purely academic, Russell oracled out of his shadow. I mean, whether Hamlet is Shakespeare or James I or

Essex. Clergymen's discussions of the historicity of Jesus. Art has to reveal to us ideas, formless spiritual essences. The supreme question about a work of art is out of how deep a life does it spring. The painting of Gustave Moreau is the painting of ideas. The deepest poetry of Shelley, the words of Hamlet bring our minds into contact with the eternal wisdom, Plato's world of ideas. All the rest is the speculation of schoolboys for schoolboys. (173-4/183)

It is the "dreams and visions in a peasant's heart" that interest Russell; he is the Platonic Charybdis of the chapter to the Aristotelianism and Scholasticism of Stephen. Stephen does not contradict Russell explicitly or directly. His unspoken rejoinder is his real answer:

Unsheathe your dagger definitions. Horseness is the whatness of allhorse. Streams of tendency and eons they worship. God: noise in the street: very peripatetic. Space: what you damn well have to see. Through spaces smaller than red globules of man's blood they creepy-crawl after Blake's buttocks into eternity of which this vegetable world is but a shadow. Hold to the now, the here, through which all future plunges to the past. (174-5/184)

In other words, it is a disagreement about the substance of art and, with that, about Reality as well. To Russell art is a direct communication with a world more real than this, an ideal world of pure essences. Since the flesh and blood with which the artist may clothe his ideas are less real, they are inferior, not necessary, and therefore irrelevant to his main concerns. The aim of art is to bring the mind of the reader also into communication with the world of ideas, and this is done by a direct revelation of that world. The artist is only a medium, a middleman through whom the minds of other men may reach the world of Forms. The nature of the artist, his limitations, his name, are all irrelevant since these play no essential part in his artistic function. He is a kind of anonymous Aeolian lyre, visited by an inspiration he cannot understand but whose direction he must obey.

Much of this may seem to put words into Russell's mouth, but it is impossible not to recall the essay on "Art and Life" in *Stephen Hero* where Stephen, in adopting Shelley's views on the visionary rôle of the imagination—a romanticism that applied to the social function of art—had insisted at the same time on the discipline of the "classical temper", by which he had meant a deep and vital concern with the here and the now. Once again, after disappearing from the *Portrait*, where the whole tendency of the argument is to preserve art from subservience to distant "Realities", this line of thought appears in *Ulysses*, but in a more subtle and far-reaching form. Stephen's objections to "Platonism" now go further than to mere questions of style; they involve a different philosophical outlook. His earlier formula—that the artist is a "mediator between the world of his experience and the world of his dreams"—expresses something of his objection to Russell, but it is inadequate for all that he means. In the discussion on Shakespeare and *Hamlet* he attempts to make his deeper meaning clear—mainly to himself.

The course his argument takes is not designed to make the essentials stand out; it is dramatically presented, and we realize that the central points of the argument strike too close to Stephen's self for him to have given them open expression. In following the argument, therefore, we have to rearrange it and supply the connections between conclusions Stephen merely asserts. The real clues are his unspoken reflections, the odd phrases from Aristotle or Aquinas that indicate the drift of his thought. If once we catch that drift, however, his argument leads from this first disagreement with Russell to the nature of artistic freedom. And like a good Aristotelian, he drops the phrase about the artist's dreams. He assumes that the world the artist knows is the world of his experience—the macrocosm outside, and the microcosm within. And like a good Aristotelian again, he argues that the artist himself *is* his world, that macrocosm and microcosm are for the artist one and the same. The artist himself stands at the centre of Stephen's theory; art is for him personal expression and at the same time objective (though not necessarily representational) "truth".

Once again Stephen's point of departure is the same as in the *Portrait:* the Scholastic theory of knowledge. For Aquinas, as for Aristotle, man can have no direct intuition of forms or essences. He cannot know in the manner of God and the angels, whose knowledge is a direct apprehension of the proper nature (or quiddities) of things. Man forms concepts, reaches true knowledge of essences, only by the aid of his one direct contact with reality—his senses. The foundation of this theory of knowledge, and the foundation of Stephen's own treatment of aesthetic apprehension in the *Portrait*, is the principle, *Nihil est in intellectu nisi prius fuerit in sensu*. The first stage of human apprehension is the distinguishing and organizing of sense-impressions by the sensitive soul, the apprehension of the object as a sensible thing, "selfbounded and selfcontained", as Stephen magniloquently puts it, "upon the immeasurable background of space or time which is not it" (*Portrait*, p. 241). The second stage is the mind's action upon this sensible aspect of the object, and its abstraction from it of its intelligible structure: a stage that roughly corresponds with what Stephen describes as the perception of *consonantia*. But where Stephen had fumbled over the later stages of aesthetic apprehension in the *Portrait*, he now seems to revert to the more satisfactory, though still vaguely formulated, insight expressed in *Stephen Hero*. To understand what the notion of epiphany properly means—a meaning that Stephen now, but only now, tacitly assumes—we must turn to the remaining aspects of the Thomist theory of knowledge. For Aquinas, the whole act of knowledge concludes when the mind, which is both an active principle and also a potentiality of knowing all things, takes possession of the intelligible structure, apprehends the nature of the object, and now realizes and *expresses* its intellectual perception in a concept. It thus forms a *word*, and by this means it can communicate its understanding to others. Language is the product, or rather the expression, of the whole process of apprehension. Of course, only the concept that the mind *judges as true*— i.e. as exhibiting to the mind's self-conscious scrutiny a conformity between itself and the object—becomes *knowledge*, and it is this that Stephen takes as the material of art: the artist's knowledge of ordinary reality now and here.

Stephen's disagreement with Russell clearly cuts deeper than mere matters of style. He is maintaining that the particulars of experience can no more be ignored by the artist than by other men, for the mind apprehends truth only through contact with them. The forms of things can be known only in and through their sensible aspects. As Aquinas puts it,

the proper object of the human intellect, which is united to a body, is a quiddity or nature existing in corporeal matter; and through such natures of visible things it rises to a certain knowledge of things invisible. . . . For the intellect to understand actually its proper object, it must of necessity turn to the phantasms [i.e. images retained by the imagination and the memory] in order to perceive the universal nature existing in the individual. But if the proper object of our intellect were a separate form; or if, as the Platonists say, the natures of sensible things subsisted apart from the individual; there would be no need for the intellect to turn to the phantasms whenever it understands (Ia, lxxxiv, 7)*

The artist can have no direct knowledge of "spiritual essences", no intuition of the true nature of things apart from the things themselves. The world of here and now is itself the only door to its meaning. Stephen does not deny that the artist seeks to know and express what appear to him the essential natures of things; in this respect his argument is again closer to that in *Stephen Hero* than that in the *Portrait*. His difference with Russell is about what epiphanies are, and so about the conditions under which they may be apprehended and expressed in art. The contemplative philosopher strives to reach the rare, purely intellectual vision of the forms and principles of reality abstracted from all sensible particulars. But even if the artist—like all men—naturally strives to the same end, he cannot as artist neglect the very nature and material of his art. The knowledge he requires is not of abstractions but of things, of individuals. It is because he had dimly realized this that Stephen had defined art in the *Portrait* as the disposition of "*sensible* or intelligible matter" and had described it as the expression "from sound and shape and colour which are the prison gates of our soul, [of] an image of the beauty we have come to understand" (235). The artist tries to apprehend the nature, the meaning, of things—epiphanies—but not what Russell calls "*formless* spiritual essences". As a man he cannot think without recourse to images of sense; as an artist, endeavouring to impart knowledge of individual things and people, he is especially bound to use "sensible matter" to convey his "intelligible matter". The artist is like the lover; both must descend to particulars

> Which sense may reach and apprehend,
> Else a great Prince in prison lies.

Russell's attitude violates at once the nature of man and the nature of art. No one—and especially no artist—can rely on communications relayed through the "yogibogeybox".

* I have cited throughout from Aquinas's *Summa Theologica* in the translation by the Fathers of the English Dominican Province, 22 vols., London, n.d.; and Aristotle in the translation edited by W. D. Ross, 12 vols., Oxford, 1928-52.

But Stephen carries the argument further—from the nature of human knowledge in general to a special act of knowledge: knowledge of oneself. And this brings us not only to the reasons for his curious theory of *Hamlet* but also to the reasons why the argument is central to *Ulysses*—to the connection between art and freedom, between the *stasis* of the artist's work and the *stasis* of his spirit.

The clue to Stephen's direction is his unspoken reflection, which echoes his thoughts during the history lesson he had given earlier in the morning—"But I, entelechy, form of forms, am I by memory because under everchanging forms" 178:23/187: 26-7).[2] For Aristotle and his Scholastic followers, knowledge is the human soul in act, a realization of a potency, a perfecting. Man is distinguished from other creatures by the nature of his form or soul. In him it includes but transcends the sensitive soul of the animal; he alone is distinguished by his mind or intellect, his rational soul. Like all material things and creatures, he is composed of matter and form. To say that a thing is animate is to say that its matter is more highly informed than that of an inanimate thing. Man is so highly informed that he is self-determining. His soul—of a "slow and dark birth", as Stephen puts it in the *Portrait*, "more mysterious than the birth of the body"—is the principle of his individual being as a person. The sensitive soul of an animal can act only through the physical organs of the animal, which has no other life than that of the senses and appetites. The rational soul of man, however, although it needs the senses to provide it with the objects of its operation— i.e. the objects of its knowledge or understanding—nevertheless operates without their aid, for the intellect knows its objects as intelligibles. Moreover, since it is regarded as standing to its knowledge in the relation of potency to act, the human soul may be said to possess an infinite capacity for knowledge of the material universe. The soul is the principle of the human being; its proper end is knowledge; and in the act of knowledge the being fulfils itself—this is the heart of its life. To start with, of course, it knows nothing—it is like a blank page on which nothing is as yet written but on which is potentially written everything. The potentiality of the soul is successively actuated, progressively fulfilled in the achievement of knowledge. The record of our acts of understanding would thus be the record of the fulfilments of our soul. Our complete biography would have to include acts of perception perhaps, and certainly acts of will, habits and the like, but since the soul is most fully actuated in knowledge of truth it is acts of knowledge that form the most important aspect of a man's life.

On this view, knowledge is an activity that ends in a kind of possession. The mind reaches out and takes into its own life the form of the thing known, and in doing so it takes on that form itself. It *becomes* the form of the object, as it were. The subject and object are united in a single reality, a single form, which is at once the actualization of the object-as-knowable and of the subject-as-knower. The object cannot be known nor can the subject know except in relation to each other; the unity they achieve in the form of the object is the actual knowledge. Since the mind is capable of becoming all the forms in the material universe and in so doing actualizing its own potentialities, it may be said to be the form of forms. As Aristotle puts it, the soul

is in a way all existing things; for existing things are either sensible or thinkable, and knowledge is in a way what is knowable, and sensation is in a way what is sensible: in *what* way we must inquire.

Knowledge and sensation are divided to correspond with the realities, potential knowledge and sensation answering to potentialities, actual knowledge and sensation to actualities. Within the soul the faculties of knowledge and sensation are *potentially* these objects, the one what is knowable, the other what is sensible. They must be either the things themselves or their forms. The former alternative is of course impossible: it is not the stone which is present in the soul but its form.

It follows that the soul is analogous to the hand; for as the hand is a tool of tools, so the mind is the form of forms and sense the form of sensible things. (*De Anima*, 431^b-432^a)

What is known by the intellect is not the complete being of the object of course, but only its abstracted form. The intellect cannot know the form, again, without the phantasms of sense to aid it. What Aristotle says here must be read with the qualification that in the object itself the form is embodied in matter, that it is also a sensible object.

It is this passage that Stephen recalls in his reflections. During the history lesson earlier in the day he had mused on time as the process of actualizing the potential or possible—a thought that now recurs in the library scene (182/191). He had gone on to recall the moment in his own past when he sat reading in a Paris library, all the world he was to meet in the future lying in the darkness of his soul's potentiality—

in my mind's darkness a sloth of the underworld, reluctant, shy of brightness, shifting her dragon scaly folds. Thought is the thought of thought. Tranquil brightness. The soul is in a manner all that is: the soul is the form of forms. Tranquillity sudden, vast, candescent: form of forms. (23/26-7)

The idea is clear enough even in Aristotelian terms: a man's experience actualizes the potentialities of his soul as it joins with and takes on the forms of all the successive objects he comes to know. The development of the soul is thus the sequence of the epiphanies it discovers.

When he applies this line of thought to Shakespeare, Stephen begins, despite the unusual conclusions he draws out of his dialectical hat, with little more than a restatement of a commonplace, even if it is a restatement modified by his reading of Aristotle and Aquinas. We might restate his point by saying that the artist's self contains the forms or quiddities he portrays in art, or that an artist's material is the activity of his own soul; we might equally say that a man understands only what he has a capacity to understand, or that a Falstaff or an Ivan Karamazov represents both a form (or epiphany) of the artist's world and also something in himself. Thus Shakespeare's plays represent the world in which he lived—"All events brought grist to his mill" (193/202)—and also Shakespeare himself:

He found in the world without as actual what was in his world within as possible. Maeterlinck says: *If Socrates leave his house today he will find the sage seated on his doorstep. If Judas go forth tonight it is to Judas his steps will tend.* Every life is many days, day after day. We walk through ourselves, meeting robbers, ghosts, giants, old men, young men, wives, widows, brothers-in-love. But always meeting ourselves. (201/210)

Thus Shakespeare is all his characters, "he is all in all", and being a man of genius able to take advantage of his experience, he "makes no mistakes": "his errors are volitional and are the portals of discovery" (179/188). Stephen's manner is magniloquent, but he is presented nevertheless as having put a good deal of thought into his theory and as making a quite serious attempt to explain the relationship between the artist, his world and his art. And in order to carry the argument to the desired conclusion Stephen turns to the artist's understanding of his self.

To the Scholastic philosopher, inheriting as he did the arguments of St Augustine as well as Aristotle, self-knowledge was always important as a kind of *completion* of knowledge, a natural terminus of the most vital human activity: as Aquinas puts it, through this act "the intellect itself is known, the perfection of which is this act of understanding" (Ia, lxxxvii, 3). What he means by this is *philosophical* knowledge, of course, the abstract conception of what Man is and the principles of his own activity, not the knowledge of one's own particular, unique self; the intellect cannot "think" the particular matter in which a form is embodied. Even so, he is still faithful to his basic view of knowledge: the intellect can know itself in this way only by turning to its particular manifestations, its particular acts of knowledge, and considering these. To quote Gilson's account of his position, "our soul attains to knowledge of itself only in the measure in which it apprehends other things", which is to say, only to the extent that "it passes from potency to act".[3] Stephen is also faithful to this basic principle, but it is a different kind of self-knowledge that interests him—the knowledge of the *individual* self to be discovered in one's own acts and thoughts. Perhaps "self-understanding" is a better term, for it is not knowledge of the pure form of the object that he sees as the province of the artist, but of its form-in-this-particular-matter. He still sees self-understanding as a completion; he assumes that it can be found only by turning to the particular manifestations, the realizing acts of the self; but what he envisages is rather an autobiography than a treatise on Man. Or we might describe it more elaborately: he thinks of the individual soul understanding itself as it has been successively fulfilled in its acts of knowledge, in their sequence right up to the very point at which they are themselves understood. In other words, behind the Scholastic terminology, he is interested in the kind of self-knowledge to be found in *The Prelude*, for example, or *The Education of Henry Adams* perhaps, or—to take the case most relevant here—in *A Portrait of the Artist as a Young Man* and *Ulysses*. Such works are more than simple chronicles of the self—the past is not merely reported, but interpreted and formed by the imagination; and any aesthetic theory that seeks to explain and justify this process must concern itself above all with the artist's recollection and his self-development.

We might therefore put the drift of Stephen's thought in this way: A list or diary of the epiphanies a man apprehends, in the order he apprehends them, is a record of the successive fulfilments of his soul as well as a record of the knowledge upon which he has acted in the past and acts now. If the list were to begin in earliest childhood it would first record simple acts of understanding and correspondingly unreflective actions, since it is the extent of our understanding that enables us to reflect on ends and means and to make conscious choices. As the list extended, the acts of understanding would become more complex—i.e. the epiphanies more subtle and far-reaching—and the actions more conscious and deliberate. The individual's arrival at maturity may be understood as the progression of his understanding to the point where instead of regarding the things he perceives and knows in "kinetic" terms—as objects of subjective desire or repulsion, coloured by his own feelings and emotions—and consequently acting more or less unreflectingly, he is able to stand aside from himself and see the world more objectively. Being able to understand his own relations with the world, he is able to distinguish his kinetically distorted view of things from things as they are, and able therefore to act with a greater deliberateness. As we can see, the argument already involves a shift in the meaning of *kinesis* and *stasis*, turning them from different kinds of emotion (as in the *Portrait*) to different spiritual states of the whole man (the meaning characteristic of *Ulysses*). Thus the act of self-knowledge may be said to be a term in the process of maturation, to complete a spiritual pattern. For what such impersonal "standing aside" consists in is the apprehension of the pattern embodied in past knowledge and actions. It is the act that enables a man to make an autobiography out of a diary. It is to understand relationships that could not have been understood in any past act of understanding, to understand more fully what was known only partially, to see the limitations of past knowledge, to find the causal sequence in the succession of apprehended epiphanies, and to see the self extending backward in time, continuously if obscurely fulfilled, and forward, awaiting the actualizing of still unfathomed potentiality.

In the *Portrait* Joyce presents the sequence of Stephen's acts of understanding and his increasingly deliberate actions, but not to the point where Stephen reaches the maturity at which he could grasp and present this sequence himself. At the end of the book Stephen is still in a kinetic relation to the world—and he is meant to remain so even in *Ulysses*: Bloom listens to Stephen's "Pisgah Sight of Palestine", by which "potential narration was realised and kinetic temperament relieved" (646/669). He has not yet reached the point at which he knows enough about his world or himself to write objectively about either—which means, of course, about both as they have united in his experience. Joyce, as the title implies, had reached this point—though not when he wrote *Stephen Hero*. The major difference between the *Portrait* and *Stephen Hero* is precisely the degree of self-understanding they exhibit, or to put it in other terms, the degree of objectivity the author has achieved. Stephen sees something of this himself in the *Portrait* even though he cannot relate it to his other theories. His distinction between artistic "forms" is a distinction of degrees of objectivity or degrees of self-understanding. The "lyrical" is the "simplest verbal vesture of an instant of emotion", in which the artist is in a fully kinetic relation to the world, "more conscious of the instant of emotion than of himself as feeling emotion". The "epical" develops from this. The narrative is no longer "purely personal"; the author begins to distinguish between himself and his art, and his personality "passes into the narration itself, flowing round and round the persons and the action like a vital sea". The progress to objectivity is complete with the "dramatic". The artist is now capable of distinguishing and so separating his personality from his narration; he may refine his personality "out of existence". An impersonal, objective art stands free from kinetic stresses:

The artist, like the God of creation, remains within or behind or beyond or above his handiwork, invisible, refined out of existence, indifferent, paring his fingernails (*Portrait*, 244-5)*

It is a measure of Stephen's development between the *Portrait* and *Ulysses* that while in the former he had realized that he must free himself from the demands of family, country and religion in order to become an artist, he now realizes that he must also

* For a more detailed discussion of this distinction, see Chap. VI below (pp. 222 ff.).

77

achieve the objectivity of vision necessary for the highest art—
and that to do this he must understand himself. Seeking a pattern
of the artist's necessities in Shakespeare, he takes *Hamlet* as the
play in which Shakespeare records his self-understanding. His
theory about it is his explanation of why Shakespeare had to
write it—and why he himself will have to do the same in another
form. But only in the future. Time is also necessary: we may not
be able to understand our present actions or the limitations of the
knowledge on which they are based by tomorrow, nor perhaps
even in a year's time, but sooner or later the opportunity will
arrive.

—As we, or mother Dana, weave and unweave our bodies, Stephen
said, from day to day, their molecules shuttled to and fro, so does the
artist weave and unweave his image. And as the mole on my right
breast is where it was when I was born, though all my body has been
woven of new stuff time after time, so through the ghost of the unquiet
father the image of the unliving son looks forth. In the intense instant
of imagination, when the mind, Shelley says, is a fading coal, that
which I was is that which I am and that which in possibility I may
come to be. So in the future, the sister of the past, I may see myself as
I sit here now but by reflection from that which then I shall be.
(183/192)

The self one discovers in past epiphanies and actions is also an
epiphany, a quiddity that exists in and gives form to all its
sensible manifestations. Joyce sees himself and his experience
objectively from the point at which he writes the *Portrait* and,
we must add, *Ulysses*; Shakespeare from the point at which he
wrote *Hamlet*. Both Stephen and Hamlet are introspective, *lisant
au livre de lui-même*,[4] but trying vainly to understand themselves
before the time is ripe. For that very reason, however, they
cannot be identified with the author whose knowledge is so much
greater that he can present with far greater objectivity his
character (personal *and* dramatic) and the world in which he
moves. In the act of self-understanding the artist sees that which
he is, and was, and may even guess what still lies in the darkness
of his soul's potentiality.

Stephen realizes his own immaturity perfectly well; his whole
argument is founded upon that realization. Applying it to
Hamlet, he concludes that if Shakespeare is to be identified with
any character in the play it must be the older Hamlet, the Ghost,

and Hamlet himself with Shakespeare's son Hamnet. On the other hand, the argument that an artist's characters are also manifestations of his own soul results in the view that Shakespeare is to be identified with Hamlet too. Sabellius's heresy comes pat. The God-like self-knowledge of the artist, where knower and known are one and the same, permits the analogy with a greater relationship: as Stephen wittily puts it, the Father is His Own Son (196/205). Hamlet as a character has therefore a double aspect: he is Shakespeare's actual son and, being Shakespeare's creation, also expresses a form of Shakespeare's own soul—but only as a young man. So that instead of saying that Shakespeare found as actual in Hamnet what was possible in himself, we should rather say that he found in Hamnet as possible what had been actualized within himself. Hamlet is a portrait of the artist as a young man and also of the spiritual possibilities in Hamnet. Hamnet is more than a mere son of the flesh; he is also a spiritual successor, a son of the soul.

Aristotle and Aquinas agree in believing that the rational soul of man is not the result of natural generation. Aristotle's view is that it is not, like the nutritive and sensitive souls, generated by the semen, but is alone divine and comes from outside—"for no bodily activity has any connexion with the activity of reason" (*De Generatione Animalium*, 736b). As Aquinas puts it, the intellectual soul is created by God at the end of human generation, which so creates the matter that it is able to receive this form (Ia, cxviii, 2). Dante also explains the point in a passage that Joyce almost certainly knew:

> Apri alla verità che viene il petto,
> e sappi che, sì tosto come al feto
> l'articular del cerebro è perfetto,
>
> lo Motor primo a lui si volge lieto
> sopra tanta arte di natura, e spira
> spirito nuovo di virtù repleto,
>
> che ciò che trova attivo quivi tira
> in sua sustanzia, e fassi un' alma sola,
> che vive e sente, e sè in sè rigira.
> (*Purgatorio*, XXV, 67-78)

(Open thy breast to the truth which is coming, and know that so soon as the organization of the brain is perfect in the embryo, the First Mover turns him to it, rejoicing over such handiwork of nature, and

79

breathes into it a new spirit with virtue filled, which draws into its substance that which it finds active there, and [uniting with the nutritive and sensitive] becomes one single soul, that lives, and feels, and [completing its knowledge by self-knowledge] turns round upon itself.)

However tempting it would be to speculate on the exact point at which the rational soul enters—Stephen dates it precisely at the end of the second month (372/383)—the general principle is enough to indicate how paternity may be considered in two ways —paternity of the body and paternity of the soul. Stephen is careful to make this distinction. His own father, Dedalus senior, is the parent only of his body. But where, in the usual sense of the word, the father of the soul would be God, Stephen uses the word in a more metaphorical sense: "It is a mystical estate, an apostolic succession, from only begetter to only begotten" (195/204-5). In Stephen's sense—the metaphor that gives form to *Ulysses* itself—paternity of the soul is a succession of the spirit different and distinct from succession of the body, a handing on of spiritual power.

In Shakespeare's case, Stephen seems to argue, the two kinds of paternity coincided. Hamnet Shakespeare was son to his father in body, and in the figure of Hamlet, the image of the immature youth of Shakespeare the man, son also in soul. Shakespeare the man who has suffered and acted does not project himself directly and heroically in the play; he is there only as a pervasive presence, at most only

a ghost, a shadow now, the wind by Elsinore's rocks or what you will, the sea's voice, a voice heard only in the heart of him who is the substance of his shadow, the son consubstantial with the father. (185/194)

In his own case, Stephen sees only too well that the two do not coincide. A father is a necessary evil, he says, linked to his son only by "an instant of blind rut". Yet on the mystery of fatherhood in the spiritual sense the Church itself is founded—on the transference of a spiritual power from one man to another (195-6/205). The son is dependent on the father for this, his weakness needs the aid of that power. To be "no more a son", as Shakespeare was when he wrote *Hamlet*, means not merely that his own father was dead but that he no longer stood in spiritual dependence on another. He was himself a father, spiritually mature, handing that power, embodied in the art itself, on to his son.[5] All the power he had himself received, all that he would hand on, was concentrated in him as the mature, self-understanding, impersonal artist:

he was and felt himself the father of all his race, the father of his own grandfather, the father of his unborn grandson who, by the same token, never was born for nature, as Mr Magee understands her, abhors perfection. (196/205)

Thus the discussion about fatherhood comes back to the centre of the whole argument—the maturity of Shakespeare the artist, the spiritual power he possessed and in *Hamlet* passed on to his son. Stephen claims that we can guess at the events of Shakespeare's life, or at the main structure of it, from the evidence of the plays. What we must remember is that however true or false this claim, whatever the actual "biography" Stephen concocts, and indeed however absurdly its details are worked out, they are none of them of fundamental importance to the argument as a whole. It is easy to miss its essentials in the rather lurid accidents. The argument about the artist's knowledge and powers and the conditions necessary for the greatest art is central because it is this that concerns Stephen and Joyce himself; the story of Shakespeare's life is only a way of putting it, a myth in which a universal truth is enacted. The myth is itself important because of its relevance in twentieth-century Dublin; but it is the truth, not the particular myth, that is important to Stephen.

The main point Stephen makes about Shakespeare's life is that up to the writing of *Hamlet* he was in a kinetic relation to life, "sundered" from his fulfilment as a man. He had been seduced by the "boldfaced Stratford wench" who had then been unfaithful with his own brothers, and the inevitable result was that "belief in himself [had] been untimely killed". The spiritual wound rankles, fetters his mind, "darkening even his own understanding of himself".

—The soul has been before stricken mortally, a poison poured in the porch of a sleeping ear. But those who are done to death in sleep cannot know the manner of their quell unless their Creator endow their souls with that knowledge in the life to come. The poisoning and the beast with two backs that urged it king Hamlet's ghost could not know of were he not endowed with knowledge by his creator. (185/194)

Only the "life to come", the maturity of self-understanding, permits Shakespeare to understand the past truly. *Hamlet* is the record of such self-knowledge and objectivity as he could achieve. It is not quite perfect; kinetic strains still disturb the art; and he cannot make use of his power himself, Stephen argues. He feels, in the moment of its fulness, that he must hand it on to his son. His understanding came too late for his own life, the wound lay too deep, and the "note of banishment, banishment from the heart, banishment from home" sounds until the very end (200/209). Such reconciliation as he was able to effect—the love he felt for his daughter, his Marina—could not free him completely. The old note echoes when his daughter Susan, "chip of the old block", is accused of adultery. Though it was the "original sin that darkened his understanding" and "weakened his will" even the clearer understanding he achieved *as an artist* could not free him *as a man* from the pattern of actions that obsessed him. He could not achieve more than the partial freedom of his art.

It is freedom, as a man but even more as an artist, that Stephen ultimately desires—the freedom of spiritual power, the freedom of detached, impersonal objectivity. He concludes the argument about Shakespeare; then

He laughed to free his mind from his mind's bondage. (200/209)

The ineffectiveness of a laugh to free him, the failure of Shakespeare to free himself completely, the effort Stephen has made to free himself in his argument about Shakespeare, and Shakespeare's partial achievement of freedom in the art of *Hamlet*—all meet in the one line. The laugh and the motive for it and the argument it concludes cast reflections on each other.

The objective vision of one's experience is not a mere passive contemplation but a positive act. Certain conditions are necessary before it can be performed, but once a man's knowledge is complete enough, he may exercise his will and stand aside from the *kinesis* of life. The act frees him negatively: from the darkness of ignorance, from his former subjection to forces he did not understand. The burden of his environment, of obsessive ideas, of ruling emotions, can be shaken off if these things are known for what they are. In the act of self-understanding he may stand temporarily free of them; the mind contemplates its full content in freedom from the pressures it normally responds to. Again, the act frees positively: permits the will to act in the future, to determine the self more fully and more surely. Whether the burdens can ever be shaken off completely depends upon the man. Shakespeare could not manage it quite; Stephen can only try. The important thing for Stephen, however, is that the freedom wherein the mind is turned in contemplation upon its own experience is not only the proper aim of the artist but also lies within his power. What he is able to find in contemplation and to express in art is the measure of his genius; what he does with the further power his knowledge gives him is the measure of his will as a man. But this act is for him that which he must perform in order to write as greatly as he desires, in order to free himself of those "nets" rejected in the *Portrait*, and to awake from the "nightmare" of history (*Ulysses*, 31/35). The *Portrait* thus appears as Joyce's first necessary step as an artist; *Ulysses* is the consequent second step.

It is this freedom that gives meaning to the "apostolic succession" from Shakespeare to Hamnet; this is the power handed on by father to spiritual son. In the very writing of *Hamlet* Shakespeare won a self-understanding that is itself the gift he transfers. The knowledge the play provides is not simply of guilt and betrayal, an ineluctable pattern forever to be repeated, but of the nightmare of history from which Shakespeare the man partly awoke as Shakespeare the artist understood the causes and their pattern. The play, understood in Stephen's sense, is an act of creation about the conditions that had to be overcome before the act could take place. There is no need to underline the relevance of this to Stephen's rejection of the priesthood in the *Portrait* or the parallels with *Ulysses*. Like Stephen's *Hamlet*, it is a work of art about the nature and conditions of freedom. This is the theme realized in the references to Shakespeare and *Hamlet*, the symbolism of paternity, the relationship of Bloom and Stephen, and the irony that plays about Stephen, an irony that he himself is beginning to cultivate. Its theme, too, is the conditions that must be overcome before it itself can be conceived and written; but it is completed in self-understanding: a creation concerned with its own conception. But, as we can see, the conception and existence of art are presented as representative of *all* acts of human understanding and freedom. Stephen, in his slow growth from a "lyrical" to an "epical" relation to the world, with the "dramatic" foreshadowed in and actualized by *Ulysses*, becomes a universal symbol. Leopold Bloom stands as a kind of *terminus ad quem*. By this inter-dependence they form one figure: when they both look into Bella Cohen's mirror the one face of Shakespeare appears (536/553)[6]; they meet and depart—

> Both then were silent?
> Silent, each contemplating the other in both mirrors of the reci-
> procal flesh of theirhisnothis fellowfaces. (663/687)

In the course of the day Stephen begins to realize more fully what is necessary. The complement of his argument about *Hamlet* is his abrupt remark in the brothel—

> What went forth to the ends of the world to traverse not itself. God, the sun, Shakespeare, a commercial traveller, having itself traversed in reality itself, becomes that self. Wait a moment. Wait a second. Damn that fellow's noise in the street [a noise that is the "one great goal of history": see 32/35]. Self which it itself was ineluctably preconditioned to become. *Ecco!* (479/494)

Behind that sudden illumination of the processes by which the life of the individual fulfils itself lie Aristotle and Stephen's aesthetic theory.[7]

II

If Joyce's art seems centripetal (or as one critic has termed it, "cultic")[8], if the figure of the artist himself looms so large in all his novels, the theory he puts into Stephen's mouth in *Ulysses* suggests the reasons. It is a theory that views the artist as the focus, the symbol even, of a universal problem.

Despite the detailed biography Stephen concocts for Shake-speare, his attitude to his art is in some ways peculiarly modern.[9] For example, he emphasizes not only Shakespeare's immensely wide and subtle responsiveness to his age, but also the way in which his art combines "imitation" of the external world with the forms and values of his own spiritual life. His theory under-lines the relevance of Shakespeare's dramatic imagery or the imaginative relations between his works as much as historical influences or details of characterization. In other words, Stephen's interest is directed at the way the artist's imagination gives shape and meaning to life rather than his talent for holding the mirror up to nature. But although he treats Shakespeare's art—and by implication all art—as so markedly personal, we must be careful to distinguish the sense in which he does so, for he means it in no simple or obvious way.

To some of his readers, it is true, it seems as if he does.[10] To Fr. Noon, for example, who examines Joyce's theories in detail against the background of Scholastic philosophy, the fact that Stephen employs the Sabellian heresy reveals at once a basic and pervasive flaw both in the theory and in Stephen himself: specifically, an unconscious solipsism, which cripples his whole conception of art here no less than his Aestheticism had crippled that in *The Portrait*.[11]

The Sabellian reference arises from the analogy Stephen supposes between the relations of the Persons of the Trinity on the one hand and the relations of the artist and his work on the other. At various points he refers obliquely to Aquinas's discussion of the Trinity (and clearly Joyce knew that discussion very well: the terms *integritas, consonantia,* and *claritas,* for instance, occur in this section of the *Summa Theologica*).[12] The Divine Word, as Aquinas explains it, emanates from God as Intellect, and "the person Who proceeds in God, by way of emanation of the intellect, is called the Son; and this procession is called generation" (Ia, xxxiv, 2). Moreover, the Word is expressive of all creatures, "inasmuch as God, by understanding Himself, understands every creature; and so there is only one Word in God, and that a personal one" (*ibid.,* art. 3). But of course any analogy between the Trinity and the artist is no more than an analogy. We may call the artist's work his *word,* referring either to the "word" as spoken or written (i.e. the work itself) or the "inner word" (i.e. the artist's self-understanding) or, like Stephen, to either indiscriminately; but this does not establish, nor is Stephen even trying to establish, any real identity between the artist and God.[13] Nevertheless, there are clearly some opportune metaphorical puns for the taking, and Joyce (like Stephen) seized upon them for his own purposes in *Ulysses*: the Son, for instance, proceeding as the "Word" from the Divine Intellect in

85

its self-understanding, and proceeding moreover as "Image" or consubstantial likeness; or the third Person, proceeding from the Father and the Son as Holy Spirit or Love, in some sense deriving from the Divine Will.[14]

But where the orthodox theologian is careful to keep the three Persons of the Trinity distinct but consubstantial, Sabellius, viewing them entirely in terms of human experience, makes no fundamental distinction between them or between the world and God.[15] Stephen at one point deliberately invokes Sabellianism: "the Father", as he says, "is His Own Son", and it is this, as it applies to the artist, that provokes some sharp comments from Fr. Noon. By rejecting "the ultimate theological and metaphysical grounds for fatherhood", he argues, Stephen must ultimately deny the reality of the external world. Since the affinities of Sabellianism lie with Berkleyean and Romantic Idealism, Stephen's artist is reduced in every way to a mere isolated solipsist, and his heresy here still leaves him in the same trap as caught him in the *Portrait*.[16]

As an interpretation of Stephen's position as a whole, this has the plausibility of a half-truth. It is true that Stephen toys with Berkeley's formula that "esse est percipi"; it is likewise true that he uses the Sabellian heresy to formulate one of his points about *Hamlet* and another about the artist's experience; and it is true that his position can be understood only in the context of Romantic and post-Romantic theories of art. On the other hand, it is equally true that, despite his own imperfect understanding of the world he inhabits, he is at least aware that the maturity of the artist as a man and the maturity of his work as an artist are dependent on coming to terms with that world. If he flirts with Berkeley, he is finally content to rest on Aristotle: the modality of the visible and the audible, as he realizes in "Proteus", is *ineluctable*, and the "diaphane" limited *in* bodies; space, as he puts it in his unspoken rejoinder to Russell, is "what you damn well have to see". And as he points out in the course of the discussion, Shakespeare's art reflects external reality as much as it projects his own personal life:

. . . He drew Shylock out of his own long pocket. The son of a maltjobber and moneylender he was himself a cornjobber and moneylender with ten tods of corn hoarded in the famine riots. His borrowers are no doubt those divers of worship mentioned by Chettle Falstaff who reported his uprightness of dealing. He sued a fellowplayer for the price of a few bags of malt and exacted his pound of flesh in interest for every money lent. How else could Aubrey's ostler and callboy get rich quick? All events brought grist to his mill. Shylock chimes with the jewbaiting that followed the hanging and quartering of the queen's leech Lopez, his jew's heart being plucked forth while the sheeny was yet alive: *Hamlet* and *Macbeth* with the coming to the throne of a Scotch philosophaster with a turn for witchroasting. The lost armada is his jeer in *Love's Labour Lost*. His pageants, the histories, sail fullbellied on a tide of Mafeking enthusiasm. Warwickshire jesuits are tried and we have a porter's theory of equivocation. The *Sea Venture* comes home from Bermudas and the play Renan admired is written with Patsy Caliban, our American cousin. The sugared sonnets follow Sidney's. As for fay Elizabeth, otherwise carroty Bess, the gross virgin who inspired *The Merry Wives of Windsor*, let some meinherr from Almany grope his life long for deephid meanings in the depth of the buckbasket. (193/202)

Not merely does Shakespeare's art reflect a social reality, however. Stephen also insists that Hamlet is the image of Shakespeare's real son, Hamnet, who is consubstantial in both the physical and the moral sense, just as much as he is the image of Shakespeare himself—and it is only to illustrate the *latter* point that he calls upon Sabellius. Whether or not he assumes what Fr. Noon calls "ultimate theological and metaphysical grounds for fatherhood", he certainly recognizes that fatherhood exists and that the external world is "there all the time without you: and ever shall be, world without end" (34/38).

The basic difficulty in interpreting Stephen's argument is that he develops, by a series of flexible, unsystematic analogies, a number of paradoxes that he never explicitly declares. The paradoxes are hardly very startling in themselves—in fact, they are little more than commonplaces in modern aesthetics and criticism—but Stephen's application of them to Shakespeare permits him to extract the maximum effect from his quips and quiddities and his story of adultery, *kinesis*, and "sundering". At bottom, however, the ideas he exploits are easily recognizable and certainly far from absurd. To restate his argument by simply listing them is to sketch out an aesthetic position much less idiosyncratic, but considerably more important, than is always ascribed to Joyce.

 1. The artist is a man like any other, subject to the same moral predicaments and spiritual strains; nevertheless, the personality

that informs the world of his art, the *poetic* personality, is not to be equated with the ordinary personality of the man.

In the *Portrait*, Stephen had seemed aware only of the poetic personality, and it is this that he describes as God-like in the work of art. In *Ulysses* he explores the relations between the two in his own fanciful way.

The relevance of this paradox to Joyce's own works is obvious as soon as we ask the question, Are we to take Stephen (or Bloom) as James Joyce? The only possible answer is, in some ways, yes; in some ways, no. Stephen's theory of *Hamlet* points to Joyce's fundamental belief that as an artist he could have his cake and eat it too. His characters are projections of his self, but are not to be equated with him as he actually was at any stage. And just as Shakespeare's personality passed into the whole of *Hamlet* (not to mention his other works)—into all the details of the story, all the characters, his imagery, his whole dramatic world in fact —transmuted into the poetic personality that shapes, orders and objectifies that world, so Joyce himself is transmuted into the author of the *Portrait* and *Ulysses*. The artist-as-man becomes like God only as he achieves his impersonal creation. Joyce thus comprehends Stephen and Bloom and everything else that constitutes his total "word".

2. Art is both personal expression or projection *and* the impersonal, objective articulation ("imitation") of external reality: subject and object are united in the "written word" just as self-as-subject and self-as-object are united in the "inner word".

Stephen does not explain this paradox, except in so far as his citation of Aristotle and Aquinas on apprehension and the Word may be said to *suggest* an explanation; like Joyce, he nowhere engages in philosophical argument. His general position is clear enough, however: he refuses to reduce art to the mere representation of an objective reality or to the mere expression of subjective feeling or attitude. Even though he simply adopts and exploits ideas from Aristotle, these permit him to insist upon the co-presence of "truth" and "feeling" in the artist's work, for the co-presence of object and subject is assumed in the very act of apprehension in which language itself is born. As he interprets it, therefore, his remark that Shakespeare "found in the world without as actual what was in his world within as possible" is the cornerstone of his whole theory. Far from failing to ask himself Denis de Rougemont's question, "Do I project into the cosmos the forms of my spirit, or is it rather that I espouse by the spirit some of the objective forms of the real?"—a failure for which he has been severely criticized[17]—Stephen puts this question at the very centre of his speculations. His answer is not a metaphysical resolution of the issue; he performs his dialectical dance upon *both* horns of the dilemma, content simply to use and underline the paradox as it arises in literary criticism: in one sense, the shaped content of a work of art *represents* the objective forms of the real, which have (so to speak) been awaiting their release; in another sense, it is the creation of the individual artist, the *projection* of the forms of his spirit. As Stephen now sees, neither objective reality (in which the artist lives like other men) nor the artist's own creative spirit (which marks him off from other men) may properly be ignored in art, even though aesthetic theorists have tended to swing from one emphasis to the other (neo-Thomists usually favouring the former). To recognize both is the theoretic motive of his argument.

What he has reached with the aid of Aristotle and Aquinas is in effect a rather more mature notion of the epiphany. In *Stephen Hero* he could speak of the epiphany indifferently as "a sudden spiritual *manifestation*" in some external detail of behaviour, or as the *record* of such fragmentary revelations of inner significance. The observer, the subject, is largely ignored; the inner meaning is supposed to be objectively given; and the artist has only the task of recording the process of revelation as it actually occurred. The few examples of Joyce's early "Epiphanies" that have survived illustrate this early aesthetic.[18] The results are thin, lifeless and curiously subjective. The manifestations are certainly not manifest to anyone else, and whatever inner significance the epiphanies are supposed to possess, it has not been re-created. Nor have they the impersonal, imaginative validity that derives from the observer understanding and "placing" his own personal viewpoint: they are at the very bottom of the scale that rises through *Stephen Hero* to the *Portrait* and *Ulysses*. Their meaning is totally unrealized. Nor does Stephen's theoretical attempt to identify epiphany with *claritas* (or *haecceitas*) improve his conception of art. He does recognize that for the object to be understood requires an observer with the capacity to understand, but his recognition is so vague as to be useless. He is no nearer recognizing how the subject acts, and equally far from meeting the problems of artistic expression.

In *Ulysses*, the emphasis has altered radically. Stephen now sees that understanding is a personal act, an act in which both subject and object are realized, and which, since we may ask what and how deeply a man understands, also has a moral dimension. Such understanding is expressed in the "word", though for Stephen the artist's "word" is not only language as such but also the dramatic reality he projects by, yet in, his language. The world of art and the world of common reality are brought into relation in the medium of language and what is created by language. Thus the epiphany now becomes, at its first stage, the uttered word expressing any apprehension, and, by the extension of the same principle, at its second stage the created "word" of the artist, the shaped content of his creative act. The *aesthetic* epiphany, in fact, is the "dramatic" or (as it has sometimes been called) the "constitutive" symbol, the literary unit in which a meaning is realized. So long as we grasp Joyce's rejection of all theories that treat art as representative symbol, i.e. a sign standing *for* some reality other than it itself enacts, and understand the term "symbol" in this sense of a realizing or enacting unit of meaning (either within a work or, by extension, the work as a whole), we may accept Fr. Noon's summary definition: "The Joycean epiphany in literature may be described as a formulation through metaphor or symbol of some luminous aspect of individual human experience, some highly significant facet of most intimate and personal reality, some particularly radiant point to the meaning of existence."[19]

But of course this could be said equally of all literary art, and we ought not to take Joyce's theory as desiderating any special kind of literature. It is meant to have a general application to literature, and some of its further implications about Symbolism and Realism in *Ulysses* itself may be left to a later chapter. Nevertheless, Stephen's application of his basic insight is complicated by the kind of "objective" reality he takes *Hamlet* in particular to represent—namely, Shakespeare's own family history. The "subjective" life it projects is thus Shakespeare's understanding of that history. As his references to other elements in Shakespeare's other plays make perfectly clear, he is not claiming that all art is essentially personal in this peculiarly double way. He concentrates on the example of *Hamlet* only because he feels that his own personal case demands from him a similar reflexive scrutiny, and because Joyce, though for rather different reasons, obviously felt so too.

3. Those reasons are implicit in Stephen's emphasis on Shakespeare's membership of a society, cornjobber and moneylender and jingoist, a subject like any other of "the Scotch philosophaster with a turn for witchroasting". Stephen recognizes that, although Shakespeare's art embodies a world of its own, Shakespeare was nevertheless tied—as an artist *because* as a man—to a specific "now and here".

The failure to see this truth and to account for its effects in art was Stephen's major fallacy in the *Portrait*. His theoretical perception of it now leads him to take issue with Russell and it lies behind his notion of the aesthetic "word", but its full significance is made explicit only in the action of *Ulysses* itself. For what his argument implies is that while a work of art may be autonomous or autotelic, the activities engaged in its creation and appreciation are also a heightened mode of those engaged in ordinary life. While the artist must possess special talents in order to express his insights, and the perfection of his work is, as Aquinas puts it, "a perfection not of the maker, but of the thing made" (IIa, lvii, 5), nevertheless the way the artist understands his world, the imaginative maturity his work expresses, and the language in which his creative meaning is expressed, cannot be finally separated from the way other men understand their world, others' moral maturity, or the common language of society—in short, from the activities of the Leopold Blooms. Where Stephen was earlier inclined to divide kinetic and static emotions or appetites and assign only the latter to art, now in *Ulysses* he assumes a rather different distinction: he applies *kinesis* and *stasis* to the total state of the personality, recognizing that a man's perception of spiritual truth, whether he be an artist or not, is impossible while he is in a state of inner spiritual disorder.

The case of Shakespeare, the case of the artist in general, therefore becomes significant to Stephen, and even more to Joyce, because the artist represents for them, in a particularly clear and heightened way, the universal human effort to find genuine order and meaning in experience. The simplest human cry, the most primitive myth, the most ordinary gesture of articulation, though they are art only in the most rudimentary sense (if any), are still part of the same endeavour as the artist's. And in an age when the struggle to find order and meaning has become so much an individual concern, so urgent, and so beset with ignorance, conflict, sham, and a language that all too accurately reflects them, it is hardly surprising if the artist takes the creation of art as itself a theme for his art, exploring his own case as a subject of far wider import. It is for this reason that Joyce's art—in this perhaps like Gide's or Proust's—is in large part *about* the aesthetic theory, about its own creation of meaning in its author's experience of his world so that it may also represent the process and difficulties of every man's creation of meaning in his experience.

Ulysses in particular is so concerned with its own origins and creation, so explicit about its own gestation, that as a result its very existence and nature as a work of art (a "word") become essential elements of its total meaning. The experiences it records are significant, so it insists, inasmuch as they led to, and now point to, their own understanding and ordering in the imagination of the experiencing artist, Stephen-Joyce. Even its famous "stream-of-consciousness" technique attempts not so much to record the characters' passive registrations of external reality or the laws of human psychology, as to render the very process in which meaning is apprehended in life. Subject and object are conjoined in continual acts of perception or understanding, both actualized in the one epiphany. It is among the very humblest, most elemental acts of the moral being that Joyce seeks to trace the significance of human life.

The proof of Stephen's grasp of his theoretical insights therefore lies not in glorifying his own self as artist, but rather in what he can make of Bloom, if not now, then in the future. To translate his principle into personal terms, he must, as Joyce was to do, find Bloom in himself and part of himself in Bloom. No such deliberate process of discovery was required of Shakespeare, of course; it is a mark of the alienation of modern society and the modern artist that Stephen has to undertake it in full consciousness and that Joyce could make his undertaking the subject of his art. Bloom is the necessary centrifugal aspect of the work, the journey of the artist "to the ends of the world to traverse in reality himself"; but he is also the "not self", the ineluctable modality of "the now, the here". But if we grant Stephen's biographical interpretation of *Hamlet*, this one play does in a fashion represent the same problem as it might have appeared to Shakespeare: as an artist he did here have to discover himself as a man, and discover his kinship with his father and his son as well.

4. In his illuminating study of *Symbolism and American Literature*, Mr Charles Feidelson, Jr., has suggested that any symbolistic theory of literature, just because of its inherent self-consciousness about art, will find it doubly difficult to effect the reconciliation it attempts. And if we could not call Joyce's theory Symbolist without a good deal of qualification, nevertheless in the broad sense in which Mr Feidelson uses the term, it is pretty clearly symbolistic and caught up in the same problem. As he puts it,

The conscious symbolist will find himself in a curious position. He is committed to carrying out in an especially elaborate way what all writers, as he sees it, practice more or less. He must exploit his language where another would be content to take what language gives. In this lies his strength and his weakness. On the one hand, his *raison d'être* is the extent to which he inhabits the reality generated by words. What he finds and makes in his words will be at once himself and the world about him; the meaning that his words bring to birth will be a realization of his own being and of his environment. On the other hand, though the differentia of poetry may well be its peculiarly symbolic status—though science itself, in the largest view, may approach the status of poetry—the symbolic realm is definable only in the rational terms of subject and object. Poetic form presupposes the rational world at every point. And the more thoroughly the symbolist conceives of language as symbol, the more likely it is that he will lose touch with language as sign; to the extent that he attains his aim, it would seem that his sense of direction must waver, since he cannot locate his work with reference to himself or an external world. Deliberate symbolism is hazardous in its quest for a pure poetry, for poetry can be pure only by virtue of the impurities it assimilates. In the degree that the poem shakes loose from the poet himself and from the world of objects, in the degree that the poetic word is freed from logical bonds, poetry will be deprived of material; in performing its function, it will destroy its subject matter. At the same time every attempt to grapple once more with rational multiplicity can only lead the symbolist back to his starting point. It is the divisiveness of logic that occasions his effort to live in the unitive world of language. In practice the symbolist will be caught between the consequences and the necessity of his method—between a sort of pathless void, pregnant with significance, and a radically unknowable world of absolute distinctions.

And Mr Feidelson goes on to suggest the ambiguous attitude thus forced on the symbolist: he must combine "the passive reception and the active formation of meaning. To 'exploit' language is both to discover meaning and to create it". The very dichotomies he tries to overcome continually haunt his work.[20]

This not only provides a useful general commentary on Joyce's theory and art, but it also suggests a further paradox that Stephen exploits in his argument: namely, that although the artist must seek the impersonal aesthetic *stasis* in which his understanding of experience is embodied and therefore fixed, he cannot avoid being plunged back into the chaotic processes of experience itself. Stephen phrases his point in a way that applies to Shakespeare's human relationships but also, in another sense, to his relationships with his art:

—Where there is a reconciliation, Stephen said, there must have been first a sundering.
—Yes.
Christfox in leather trews, hiding, a runaway in blighted treeforks from hue and cry. Knowing no vixen, walking lonely in the chase. Women he won to him, tender people, a whore of Babylon, ladies of justices, bully tapsters' wives. Fox and geese. And in New place a slack dishonoured body that once was comely, once as sweet, as fresh as cinnamon, now her leaves falling, all, bare, frighted of the narrow grave and unforgiven. (182/191)

The application of this to the artist's relationships with his art is reinforced by Stephen's analogy with God:

He Who Himself begot, middler the Holy Ghost, and Himself sent Himself, Agenbuyer, between Himself and others, Who, put upon by His fiends, stripped and whipped, was nailed like bat to barndoor, starved on crosstree, Who let Him bury, stood up, harrowed hell, fared into heaven and there these nineteen hundred years sitteth on the right hand of His Own Self but yet shall come in the latter day to doom the quick and dead when all the quick shall be dead already. (186/195)

Here is the Sabellian heresy again, and we can see once more that Stephen must emphasize the unity of God for his analogy to make any sense at all on the human level. Inasmuch as he is really talking about Shakespeare or the artist generally, he cannot distinguish between the person who creates and the person who suffers and lives, the person who experiences and the person who comprehends that experience. Only one person is involved, even though as a man and as an artist he maintains different relationships with his experience. The only way in which different persons could be distinguished is metaphorically, as Stephen suggests Shakespeare did in *Hamlet* or as Joyce does in *Ulysses* when he hints at his own presence both within and also behind his dual-protagonists. But in so far as Stephen is talking of the artist's life, no real distinction is possible. The result, paradoxically, is the reverse of the situation noted above: the Sabellian analogy applies to the artist's relationship with his *art* in so far as that art is in any sense autobiographical; it applies to his relationship with his *experience* in so far as he attempts to rise above it, purifying and fixing it in the act of artistic creation. In both cases, though in different senses, Stephen insists on the identity of persons. To assent to his conclusions is not, of course, to approve either his theology or his super-subtle dialectics.

Stephen is here pointing, of course, to the conflict between the artist's necessary engagement in the processes of life, and his desire to detach his imagination from them in order to create a work of art with a life of its own, a life at once static and permanent. This was always one of the major problems hovering about the rhetoric of nineteenth-century aesthetics, issuing, for example, in the conception of the *poète maudit*, in Yeats's concern with the conflicting heroisms of art and action, in modern theories of Impersonality. To many writers, art and life seemed irreconcilably opposed. The artist was not merely alienated from his society in involuntary "exile", but he even felt himself obliged to undergo a voluntary "exile"—either from the taint of his world to a purer, detached inner life, or from his inner detachment and self-harmony to suffer the chaotic dissociation about him. The images of the rebellious Satan and the crucified Christ were inevitable, as was that of the *dio boia*, as Stephen calls him (201, 176/210, 185), the artist as the hangman god destroying life as he tries to wrest a meaning from it.

If Stephen in the *Portrait* feels oppressed by the need to exile himself from a life of action irretrievably committed to kinetic ends, and is only too ready to assume the double rôle of rebellious Satan and crucified artist,[21] this is very largely because Stephen did not write the book. The mature Joyce takes a rather more sophisticated view of the relations of art and life—the view

95

towards which Stephen is already groping in *Ulysses*. Stephen is still inclined to think of himself as "Christfox", the "sundered" artist, as "Hiesos Kristos, magician of the beautiful, the Logos who suffers in us at every moment" (174/183), as the hero who cries "Nothung!" and vainly tries to free himself of remorse and guilt by hitting at a chandelier with his stick, as the proud defier of God, whom he calls *dio boia* and tries to usurp. But his whole theory indicates a wisdom beyond this, a possible vision of himself as truly free in knowledge not only of himself but also of the ineluctable limitations in any human life. To this somewhat less futile Stephen, who can afford some irony for himself as "the sacrificial butter" (174/183), life and art are no longer opposed in a simple dichotomy; such "tragic" dilemmas seem less clear-cut and less desirable. The exile of the artist now appears as something other than a mere negative rejection of restrictive values; tentatively, but more truly, it seems to him the achievement of a positive, stable order of the spirit, an emotional balance rather than a mere disengagement. This alone, he is beginning to perceive, can effect a genuine impersonality of moral vision, a criticism of life which is something quite other than the mere assertion of an Ideal against the imperfections to which the now, the here is always subject. Though he seems at times to place art in sharp opposition to the natural world of the Vegetative eye, as in his remark in "Oxen of the Sun" (with its significant echoes of Blake and Yeats),

Know all men, he said, time's ruins build eternity's mansions. What means this? Desire's wind blasts the thorntree but after it becomes from a bramblebush to be a rose upon the rood of time. Mark me now. In woman's womb word is made flesh but in the spirit of the maker all flesh that passes becomes the word that shall not pass away; (374/385)—

even here Stephen is aware of the preconditions of the spirit necessary for this transmutation. The suggestion of becoming, of growth, is crucial: "we are the means to those small creatures within us and nature has other ends than we" (372/383).

Thus time moves towards its transformation in understanding, and hence in art; through the growth of the artist's spirit, art blossoms from life itself. They are different, but they are also intimately though not simply, connected. As Mr Bloom observes, listening to Mozart: "That's joyful I can feel. Never have written it. Why? My joy is other joy. But both are joys. Yes, joy it must be. Mere fact of music shows you are" (268/277). Art, as Joyce had observed in his early notebooks, is the expression of creative joy, an affirmation of life because its embodiment. As the representative of the "other joy" of ordinary humanity, Bloom stands in a more complex relation to Stephen than any simple opposition of Life and Art.

Between the *Portrait* and *Ulysses*, Stephen has come to realize (as was already foreshadowed in *Stephen Hero*) that for the highest artistic achievements the "artistic temperament", with its kinetic reactions to the world, is a handicap. As he put it in *Stephen Hero*, great art can spring only from "the classical temper", the "most stable mood of the mind" (182). In *Ulysses*, it is Bloom, once a "kinetic poet" himself (639/662), who now represents the "scientific temperament"—a stability, a detachment, an engagement with the external world—that Stephen, for all his knowledge and potential imagination, has yet to achieve (643/667). Bloom is the man "that is not passion's slave"; Hamlet-Stephen is still bound. Only time and patience will bring freedom, once he knows what it is he must achieve. The last paradox of his argument is the one most immediately useful to him: while he must *act* to free himself—as, indeed, he does act by deciding to leave the Martello tower and his job on Bloomsday—he must also rely on a kind of negative capability, a wise *passiveness* to the processes of time and growth. "Act", he tells himself. "Be acted on" (199/208). He must go forth to suffer experience and so become the person he is ineluctably preconditioned to become. He tells himself many times during the day that "evening will find itself in me, without me" (47/51); he knows he has no need of Mulligan—"Take all, keep all. My soul walks with me, form of forms" (41/45); and he realizes that as they depart from the library it is not the moment to free himself from external "nets" —"That lies in space which I in time must come to, ineluctably" (205-6/214). And as he decides this, Bloom passes by. Bloom, we must remember, is also compared with Christ, and it is he who, at a crucial moment, speaks out for Love. In short, Stephen must learn to accept the world outside him, and in accepting, to love: the Holy Ghost proceeds from the Son. Without that, the impersonal wisdom of maturity is impossible. Stephen, the bitterly critical Antisthenes, must grow to the maturity figured in Bloom. Time is with him, however, and the seed of freedom has begun to bud; after the self-knowledge of his theory he may

Cease to strive. Peace of the druid priests of Cymbeline, hierophantic: from wide earth an altar. (206/215)

For Stephen to accept "the now, the here" as the condition of life and so of art is to reject the "angelic" aspirations which he had once cherished himself and which Russell now defends: that "angelic" attitude Allen Tate has described as "the intellect moving in isolation from both love and the moral will" while the imagination "tries to disintegrate or to circumvent the image in the illusory pursuit of essence". Against this, Tate opposes the "symbolic imagination":

Perhaps the symbolic imagination is tragic in sentiment, if not always in form, in the degree of its development. Its every gain beyond the simple realism of experience imposes so great a strain upon the actuality of form as to set the ultimate limit of the gain as a defeat. The high order of the poetic insight that the final insight must elude us, is dramatic in the sense that its fullest image is an action in the shapes of this world: it does not reject, it includes; it sees not only with but through the natural world, to what may lie beyond it. Its humility is witnessed by its modesty. It never begins at the top; it carries the bottom along with it, however high it may climb.[22]

If Stephen and Joyce might have hesitated over the phrases about seeing through the natural world to what may lie "beyond" it, their general position is very much the same as this of Tate's. The only difference—and it is an important one—is that where Tate sees a tragic sentiment, Joyce saw a comic one. The ultimate limit of the gain appears as a defeat, it is true, but that was a source of irony to Joyce; if the dramatic, symbolic imagination climbs high, it carries the bottom with it still, and that to Joyce was a source of comic joy. Life for him was indivisible: Bloom, Stephen, Molly and himself. When we consider *Finnegans Wake*, it may seem perhaps that he never quite recognized the falsity of the angelic aspiration; but whatever we conclude about the later work, there is no doubt that in *Ulysses* at least Joyce was deliberately undertaking to guard and illuminate the sensible particulars of his now and here even as he carried them along within the movement of his poetic imagination. Bloom and Stephen had to be father and son: parallel, complementary, yet inevitably polarized.

All discussion about whether or not their relationship is "consummated" in "Ithaca" is consequently beside the point. Clearly it is not, nor could it be. "Ithaca" merely crystallizes all the earlier suggestions in the book of that far-off "divine" event, but it remains only an adumbration, a finger pointing to the future. Nor is it an imminent future. When Stephen is finally ushered by Bloom "from the house of bondage" to the unknown "wilderness of inhabitation" (658-9/682), he goes off not to write *Ulysses*, but to detach himself from his kinetic bondage by first writing *Dubliners* and then the crucial *Portrait of the Artist*, the self-scrutiny to which Stephen is already beginning to move. The controlling irony of *Ulysses* is that neither Stephen nor Bloom is capable of fully understanding himself or the other— Stephen needs Bloom's relative freedom, Bloom needs Stephen's knowledge and imagination. The only person who can understand and express them is Joyce. Their union is therefore impossible *within* the action of *Ulysses*. It takes place far beyond it—the end to which the life represented in the action moves as its "one great goal"—in that "intense instant of imagination" when "that which I was is that which I am and that which in possibility I may come to be". The "consummation" is the act whereby the artist, like God, by understanding himself, the Son, and all creatures, conceives and utters his Word, yet "remains within or behind or beyond or above his handiwork". The consummation of the action of *Ulysses* is *Ulysses* itself.

CHAPTER IV

THE MODES OF IRONY IN *ULYSSES*

JOYCE'S theoretical arguments are one thing, however; his actual art another. And it is already clear that central to any reading of *Ulysses* is the question of Joyce's attitude to his protagonists. How does he mean us to take them? Are they heroes, another Ulysses and another Telemachus, or merely the hapless victims of their age, pathetic and ridiculous mock-heroes? What values do they represent? And how are those values related to Joyce's? The possible answers, as we have seen, range from one extreme to the other, while to some critics the whole issue seems disturbingly obscure. As Mr D. J. Enright has put it, "it is not so much that Joyce over-emphasizes the lower instincts of humanity ('olla putrida'), as that he under-emphasizes the 'higher motives', the 'positive emotions' or whatever one chooses to call them. For while both Bloom and Stephen are proficient in their lusts and hatreds, they both tend to slip into vagueness when confronted with the opposing sets of values and emotions: Dedalus becomes cynical and mistrusting, and Bloom becomes sentimental. . . . But whether one considers this lack of balance just (i.e. genuine realism) depends on one's estimate of human nature." The result of this vagueness, he goes on to argue, is that we are left in real uncertainty at the end of the book about the final spiritual condition of its hero. It is possible that the Blooms will resume normal marital relations; there are other no less convincing possibilities. "I cannot but feel", he concludes, "that this indefiniteness (of which Joyce himself was well aware) is a blemish which cannot be lightly waved aside."[1]

Bloom and Stephen seem in truth very dubious heroes. The one is only too much a citizen of a seedy, vulgar, materialistic world; the other only too little the nobly creative artist he would like to be. Clearly, if Joyce offers them for our unqualified admiration, he was badly deluded by his own creatures. On the other hand, if they are heroes only in the most ironical sense of the word, as Mr Levin and others have insisted, we must ask what

THE MODES OF IRONY IN *ULYSSES*

values inspire that irony and how they emerge as the final meaning of the book.

Probably the most thorough attempt to do just this is Mr Kenner's study, *Dublin's Joyce*. The distinction of his work is not merely that he explores Joyce's symbols and techniques with uncommon subtlety but that he also relates them, with an uncommon consistency and rigour of mind, to the central issue, Joyce's moral vision. The result is one of the most detailed and suggestive readings of *Ulysses* yet offered; from now on any critical reader of Joyce must reckon with Mr Kenner. But although he asks most of the right questions, and often provides some of the right answers, he seems to me so unconvincing in general, and so unconvincing about Joyce's irony in particular, that it is worth examining his interpretation—the logical extreme, as it were, of a very widespread attitude to *Ulysses*—as a prelude to examining Joyce's work itself.*

I

Behind Mr Kenner's interpretation of Joyce, and giving it its critical edge, is the Sylla's ghost of Wyndham Lewis. In *Time and Western Man* (1927), Mr Lewis delivered his famous attack on the "time philosophy" he detected everywhere about him, including the works of Joyce. The enemy was the obsession with time for its own sake, the worship of process, the belief in the undifferentiating Unconscious, all of which he saw as productive of a mindless materialism or a romantic subjectivism equally destructive of conscious values. With something of the air of Dr Johnson, who did not care to establish the points of precedency between a flea and a louse, Mr Lewis waded in against a varied collection of

---

* Many of Mr Kenner's views and assumptions are already present in earlier studies of Joyce (some of which are very different in general tone and outlook, however). They include Ezra Pound's essays on Joyce, reprinted in *Polite Essays*, London, 1937, and *Literary Essays of Ezra Pound* (ed. T. S. Eliot), London, 1954; Harry Levin's *James Joyce, a Critical Introduction*, Norfolk, Conn., 1941, London, 1944; Richard M. Kain's *Fabulous Voyager*, Univ. of Chicago Press, 1947; Douglas Knight, "The Reading of *Ulysses*", *ELH*, xix, 1952, pp. 64-80. Two more recent studies also reflect Mr Kenner's interpretation: Wm. M. Schutte, *Joyce and Shakespeare*, and Wm. T. Noon, S. J., *Joyce and Aquinas*, both New Haven, 1957.

Since I shall be referring to many different parts of Mr Kenner's book in the following pages, for convenience I shall simply enclose in brackets in the text the relevant page numbers of the London edition of *Dublin's Joyce* (1955).

writers among whom he included Gertrude Steine and Joyce. One need not take his bracketing of these two together very seriously, of course, but his specific criticisms of *Ulysses* are quite another matter.[2] Joyce himself is reported to have replied, "Allowing that the whole of what Lewis says about my book is true, is it more than ten per cent of the truth?"[3] But if it is no more than a tenth of the whole story, it is a pretty crucial tenth.

Lewis's basic charge is that *Ulysses* exhibits "a certain *deadness*, a lack of nervous power, an aversion to anything suggesting animal vigour". Underneath its glittering surface it is merely an enormous accumulation of matter, a nightmare of the naturalistic method, an "immense *nature-morte*". The fault is more than a technical one, for the book not merely represents, it also unconsciously reflects, a mechanically conceived world. Joyce delights in hunting down verbal clichés "like fleas", but his characters are most of them mechanical "walking clichés" too—Bloom a stage Jew, Mulligan a stage Irishman, Haines a stage Anglo-Saxon, and Stephen an impossibly stagy "poet" whose affectations of superiority are ridiculous. Although he tells us so much about them, Joyce fails to bring them to life: "where a multitude of little details or some obvious idiosyncrasy are concerned, he may be said to be observant; but the secret of an *entire* organism escapes him". Lewis will have none of the usual formulas about Joyce's achievement. Claims for his impersonality in the presentation of the characters are absurd since "there are no persons to speak of for the author to be 'impersonal' about. . . . *Ulysses* is a highly romantic self-portrait of the mature Joyce (disguised as a Jew) and of his adolescent self"; luckily, Bloom-Joyce is a more likable fellow than Stephen-Joyce. Similarly, Lewis dismisses the claim that Bloom is a great portrait of *l'homme moyen sensuel*: *Ulysses* is simply a re-doing of *Bouvard et Pécuchet*. As for the Homeric framework, "that is only an entertaining structural device or conceit". Joyce's real distinction, when it is all boiled down, is merely his technical virtuosity—his brilliant parodies, his exploitation of clichés, his encyclopaedic resourcefulness in techniques of narration. He is, Lewis concludes, "essentially the craftsman", and it is the craftsman in him that is alone alive and progressive; as a *man* he is still "a 'young man' in some way embalmed".

This, we might say, is the classic case against *Ulysses* by those who take Bloom and Stephen as heroes without irony, and it is a formidable one. Mr Kenner sets out the classic reply. His tactics are those of judo: he adds momentum to Lewis's attack only to turn him neatly on his head. Very generally, Mr Kenner's case is that *Ulysses is* mechanical, the characters *are* clichés, it *is* an appalling *nature-morte*—but Joyce meant it so. It is all ironical.

He begins by assuming, quite rightly, what Wyndham Lewis might have realized—that Joyce's presentation of Dublin, although naturalistic in method, is ironic and critical in effect. Joyce does not merely hold the mirror up to nature; he tries to reveal the meaning of what he portrays, its significance to the spirit. In other words, his naturalism aims not at the "slice of life" but at the "epiphany". But in so far as he portrays twentieth-century Dublin truly, Mr Kenner argues, he portrays a society in which are incapsulated the traditional values of Christian humanism, though in a debased and well-nigh exhausted form. An objective picture of Dublin, 1904, must include those traces of eighteenth-century Dublin that still remain as mute symbols of the values by which the present corruption may be judged. In this regard, Dublin is not simply a representative European city; Mr Kenner insists that it is a special case. For Dublin, above all cities, he claims, exists most significantly in its love, and exploitation, of *language*; Dublin, we might say, *is* its language.

The rest of his argument is built on these two premises about the incapsulation of the past and the importance of language in Dublin. Dublin is really Mr Kenner's hero—it is Dublin's Joyce he sees. In one sense it is clearly true to say, as he does, that "every Dublin phrase has a double focus: the past meaning it locks away, the present vagueness it shapes. It is in language that the dead city is preserved; and it is language that maintains the citizens in deadness" (p. 9). It is always true that older values are preserved in the forms of language, and true, too, that many of our contemporary forms of language do express moral or spiritual confusion. It seems only a natural extension of this to claim, therefore, that the subject of *Ulysses* is "style" and "what style implies" (p. 17). But what this leads to is a defence of Joyce's exploitation of parody and cliché, on the grounds that his linguistic caricatures parody, and at the same time recall, the language of twentieth-century Dublin, which parodies and recalls the language of eighteenth-century Dublin, which in turn parodies and recalls the "true" language, based upon a knowledge of metaphysical essences, of unfallen man. Joyce's parodies are (somehow) designed to make their objects reveal themselves for the distortions they are; parody is (somehow) the means to spiritual objectivity.[4] In short, Mr Kenner has at one fell swoop answered the criticism that Joyce's art is excessively verbal by treating Joyce's obsession with language as the proper foundation of his ironic naturalism. This may not dispose of the criticism that if what Joyce was portraying *was* "Dublin's dead style" he might have done it more economically, but it does shift most of the critical issues on to other ground.

Ulysses, says Mr Kenner, is "an articulation of the city of the dead" (p. 16). The mechanical existence and the mechanistic ethos of Industrial Man are portrayed by means of mechanical organization, mechanical characters and the deliberate deployment of mechanical clichés of language: naturalism, but with an ironic intent. We should regard the book not as the expression of Joyce himself but of a *persona*—the god-like thinking-machine that is the real object of modern worship (pp. 165 ff.). It portrays a materialistic world entirely given over to the sterile dichotomies of the "time philosophy":

the body usurps the room of the soul, theology gives way to associationist psychology, visions become hallucinations, the metaphors of scripture receive bitterly literal realization in matter, in an inferno whose apotheosis is the debris-crammed brain of hapless Leopold Bloom. (p. 230)

The "prime symbol" of the book is matter (p. 247).

We must understand, therefore, that the characters are treated with a devastating irony. It is not an obvious or intrusive irony, of course, but an enormous repudiation. Bloom is the representative of the general spiritual death. He is hopelessly immersed in matter; his sensibility is shapeless and ineffectual. Mr Kenner grants that he has certain virtues: he is "humane, cautious, sympathetic" (p. 277), and the parallel with Homer's hero helps to define the Bloomesque *ethos*. Indeed, "much of Bloom's ignobility is a function of the ignoble materials with which his prudence, charity, temperance, fortitude, justice, etc. are engaged" (pp. 187, 189). But these are minor concessions; Bloom's virtues amount to very little in Mr Kenner's view because they are vitiated by his sentimentality, just as his values are vitiated by the "pathetic circumscription" of his spiritual insight (p. 199). Consequently, we must not think that his thoughts are simply transcribed naturalistically. They are always presented "in a matrix of irony", and so disposed as to produce "patterns of intelligibility", to bring Joyce's contemplation of his subject to a critical focus. Bloom's materialistically coloured thoughts are carefully adjusted not only to deflate the empty ideals haunting his environment and his own mind, but also to reveal the morphology of those ideals at the same time.

Stephen represents spiritual deficiencies complementary to those of Bloom: "ratiocinative violence", barren scorn and rejection, destructive anarchy. He is the Romantic aesthete-as-god. Mechanism and Romanticism are correlatives: "mind-as-machine enjoys peculiar rapport with Shelleyan art, a master-key to the sense in which Bloom turns out to be Stephen's spiritual father" (p. 168). Bloom vainly aspires to the artistic status of Stephen, Stephen to the status of the true artist, and the true artist to the status of unfallen man, who named things according to their true essences and enjoyed true freedom (p. 199). Stephen, in short, is in the *cul de sac* of idealistic Romanticism, and everyone these days knows what nameless horrors *that* involves. He is certainly not Joyce, at any rate. Rather, he is one of Joyce's *personae*, but one, Mr Kenner insists, that he sloughed off finally in *Exiles*. He is what Joyce was for a time—the aesthete who merely denies, who seeks only the freedom of isolation, irresponsibility and the arid "revolt" of Ibsen, whose gestures are still frozen in the mould of denial. There is no change from the Stephen of the *Portrait*. When he attempts a gesture of rejection in Bella Cohen's brothel, it is not only ineffectual, it also "makes for the night" (pp. 24, 38 f.). Even as early as *Stephen Hero* Joyce presented him with a certain irony; in the *Portrait* he could present him with complete detachment; in *Exiles* his "rebellious *superbia*" is reduced to absurdity as a theory of ethical freedom (p. 69 f.). If his potentialities as an artist are suggested in the *Portrait*, this is only a red herring: "an instant of promise on which the crushing ironies of *Ulysses* are to fall" (p. 119). In *Ulysses* Joyce's ironic repudiation of him is so complete that he can explore all the wider implications of his character and situation

(p. 42). He is a Romantic cliché, doomed to sterility by the nature of his Shelleyan revolt from life. He is not the artist, only the false idea of the artist misbegotten by an Industrial world.

Naturally, it is impossible to do justice to the weight and scope and detail of Mr Kenner's reading of Joyce in such a bald summary, but I hope that this represents his approach to *Ulysses* fairly enough. He sees it as a "dead-pan" parody of a world whose self-image is only too appropriately that of a vast clock. As the novel goes on the clock seems to run down; the tide of matter rises until it overwhelms everything in the mindless soliloquy of Molly Bloom. Where Stephen, in his unbalanced desire for the unconditioned, had rejected the limitations of the body, Molly accepts the body with "smug satisfaction" (p. 242): "the 'Yes' of consent that kills the soul has darkened the intellect and blunted the moral sense of all Dublin" (p. 262). With Molly's concluding "Yes", the divorce between body and spirit is complete; the epiphany of all that has taken place during the day is this final submergence in the sea of matter.

II

As a reply to such criticisms as those of Wyndham Lewis, Mr Kenner's reading of *Ulysses* is obviously on the right lines. Neither Bloom nor Stephen is presented to us for our unqualified admiration, and Joyce's attitude to the world he portrays is very far from uncritical. This, we might say, is almost commonplace, and if Ezra Pound and T. S. Eliot and Mr Levin have said it before, Mr Kenner says it again with unusual thoroughness and cogency. We may not take the alleged peculiarities of Dublin as seriously as he does perhaps, but at least it is hardly necessary after his analysis to demonstrate that *Ulysses* is a comprehensive portrait of modern civilization, a civilization that no longer vitally embodies the values to which it pays its nominal respects. As Homer portrayed an Heroic Age, so Joyce portrays a Humanistic Age in decay; *Ulysses* has Homeric dimensions as the definition of a society. The question is, however, whether Mr Kenner has read the definition—or the society—aright.

One remarkable thing about his interpretation is the extent to which it leaves Wyndham Lewis's criticisms intact. For one thing, on Mr Kenner's reading *Ulysses* is extraordinarily static.

Nothing whatever happens in it. It is only a machine; nothing more can emerge from it than is put in. It has no action in any sense but that used by watch-makers, only "rhythms"—the subtle placing and balancing of characters, symbols, techniques for critical effect. That is to say, it is a vast ideogram of symbolic meanings, with a kind of structure and verbal denseness closer to symbolistic poetry (*The Waste Land* or Pound's *Cantos*, for example) than to any novel. We read it to the end, presumably, only to gain the full encyclopaedic effect, to see the relentless clockwork release its spring, to make sure we miss no detail of this tour of the modern Inferno. It sounds—one must say— remarkably boring. And one wonders whether the natural objection to a clockwork book is really answered by the deistical claim that it has a Designer, even if he is an ironically critical one. The common assumption that *Ulysses* is a complex, symbolic poem, to which the ordinary interests and techniques of the novel are irrelevant, is justifiable only so long as we do not forget that it is also—and rather more obviously—a representational novel, and much, if not most, of its meaning is expressed in and through its representational mode. It contains "probable" and significant characters, in a "probable" and significant setting, doing and saying "probable" and significant things, so that it inevitably calls into play those expectations and assumptions we bring to the novel (as to each literary form) and which control the way we seek its meaning. Even if Wyndham Lewis misses the point of some of the characteristics he attacks, Mr Kenner seems equally to miss some of the point behind Lewis's attack itself.

Another interesting aspect of his interpretation is that, for all his insistence on the difference between the ironical Joyce and the destructive Stephen Dedalus, the two should emerge as so alike. He credits Joyce with an irony so comprehensive and so complete that it suggests an attitude towards modern life strikingly similar to Stephen's scornful rejection—and just about as arid. Joyce's criticism may be more personally detached, wider in range, deeper in penetration than Stephen's, yet it always seems to Mr Kenner to operate *against* his characters and all they represent. It implies a total repudiation of Industrial Man and everything he has spawned. It may be qualified by the recognition of the real values "parodied" by the present collapse, the ideas towards which the characters pathetically gesture, the insights that only serve to imprison them in their present rôles instead of freeing them. Yet as Mr Kenner interprets it, Joyce's attitude is a kind of Flaubertian, or rather, neo-Augustinian, recoil from modern man and his earthly city, which seems hardly more than another, more modern, variant of the Romanticism exposed in Stephen. One may call Stephen's attitude a barren isolation and Joyce's an ironic detachment, but as Mr Kenner presents them they come to pretty much the same thing. It is significant that he should take Joyce's aesthetic the wrong way—or, rather, interpret it in the light of what he feels Joyce ought to have said. He argues that Joyce's criticism of the contemporary world is regulated by the vision of a world metaphysically intelligible, of a language metaphysically "true", of an order supernaturally ordained—in short, that his aesthetic is founded upon Scholastic theology and, in seeking to direct the imaginative vision *through* his material to the spiritual world it parodies, he exhibits genuine and important affinities with the theoretical aims of some of the French Symbolists. But this is to take Joyce's Scholastic language and his flirtations with the pseudo-magical aspects of French Symbolism too seriously; as we have seen, there is no warrant for any such theological or metaphysical interpretation of what Joyce (or Stephen) actually says. One can use symbols without being a Symbolist, and Aristotelian or Scholastic language without being a Thomist. We must remember Stephen's explicit rejection in the *Portrait* of what he calls "symbolism or idealism" (p. 242), and what he says there, together with his argument in "Scylla and Charybdis", should make us at least wary of ascribing to Joyce the kind of attitude exhibited in, say, *The Waste Land* and *Four Quartets*. To criticize the deficiencies of men and institutions does not necessarily involve systematic theological or metaphysical beliefs, nor does it imply a total rejection of this world except as a symbol of another. To press these attitudes on to Joyce is not only to distort the fact of his break with Roman Catholicism, it is also to distort his work.

In fact, as one considers Mr Kenner's interpretation of Joyce further, it becomes difficult to resist the question, Just how ironical can you get? As he sees it, Joyce's irony is completely pervasive and totally comprehensive; like mock-heroic, it apparently multiplies all the values of *Ulysses* by -1. The result is like the critical analysis of the student who thought the poem, "A garden is a lovesome thing, God wot", was *intended* to be funny: one is spellbound at the perfectly possible vision of what the work might have been. And it has some curious critical consequences, for wherever Joyce's reader may think the characters or the writing not so impressive as they were intended to be, Mr Kenner is at hand with his irony to transubstantiate all. Sometimes he is clearly right in pointing to irony; on the other hand, he is sometimes merely puzzling. He does not seem to discriminate. Perhaps the most glaring puzzle is his interpretation of Molly Bloom's final silent soliloquy. Molly is one of Joyce's more doubtful successes. She has been acclaimed in terms similar to Joyce's own—"though probably more obscene than any preceding episode it seems to me perfectly sane full amoral fertilisable untrustworthy engaging shrewd limited prudent indifferent *Weib. Ich bin das Fleisch das stets bejaht.*"[5] Other readers have felt that Molly is too little realized, too neatly done to a formula, or too *fleischig*, to make affirmations of any great and convincing significance. But whatever his success with her, Joyce's intention is surely clear enough. If any reader felt that the final pages of her monologue can be "over-sentimentalized", one would expect him to raise some doubts about Joyce's success in artistically embodying his intention. Not so with Mr Kenner. The critical question is diverted by a piece of ingenious interpretation: "The 'Yes' of consent that kills the soul has darkened the intellect and blunted the moral sense of all Dublin. . . . Her 'Yes' is confident and exultant; it is the 'Yes' of authority: authority over this animal kingdom of the dead" (p. 262).[6] Joyce's irony is so comprehensive that it turns "Yes" into "No", and so fine that only one reader in ten thousand perceives the fact.

Stephen Dedalus is a more complicated case. Of course, Mr Kenner is certainly right in pointing to the irony with which Joyce views him in both the *Portrait* and *Ulysses*. He *is* something of a humourless and sterile young prig, uncertain of himself, cocksure, too ready to take his alienation as a virtue in itself, scornful, affected, rather absurd. One could make a similar list of Bloom's limitations and faults, though the list would not be quite so long for that more slippery character. But in perceiving the irony Joyce directs at his heroes, Mr Kenner concludes that he rejects the characters themselves. He assumes that such critical detachment *dissolves* the object. One need only state the assumption to see its extravagance. It is equally possible, and in Joyce's work is in fact the case, that irony is a qualifying criticism, which does not imply a total rejection of its object in the least. Irony and sympathetic understanding, or even love, are not necessarily incompatible, nor is there any reason why Stephen's potentialities as an artist should be dismissed because he is very immature and clearly portrayed as such. To think so is surely to miss Joyce's point, to ignore the process of growth upon which he insists. One of Mr Kenner's remarks about the *Portrait of the Artist* is very revealing of his critical difficulties. Noticing that the emergence of Stephen's artistic vocation is presented with a certain irony, he concludes that so unpleasant and aesthetic a young man could never have become a real artist. He is a *persona* Joyce necessarily rejected as futile. But this leaves the problem of what to make of the last section of the novel: "there remains a moral ambiguity (how seriously are we to take Stephen?) which makes the last forty pages painful reading" (p. 121). The assumption is that Joyce is repudiating Stephen *in toto*, that he dropped his *persona* like a pair of old socks, that it is merely the *Portrait of a Young Man*. We may admit that the irony is there, that Stephen's conception of freedom—"silence, exile, and cunning"—is limited and negative, "indigestibly Byronic" as Mr Kenner puts it (p. 132). On the other hand, however insufficient Stephen may be, and however limited his understanding, he surely must take the first steps. His ignorance may cripple the aesthetic theory he propounds, but at least he has an inkling that he is ignorant. If the word "life" which he constantly uses seems to mean nothing very definite to him, this does not mean that the immaturity and instability of a young man are necessarily fatal limitations to his development—or that Joyce thought they were. What is interesting and important about the last pages of the *Portrait* is, in fact, the first glimmering of Stephen's maturity—signs of the humour that Mr Kenner finds totally missing, and even a significant touch of *self*-irony:

April 15. Met her today point blank in Grafton Street. The crowd brought us together. We both stopped. She asked me why I never came, said she had heard all sorts of stories about me. This was only to gain time. Asked me was I writing poems? About whom? I asked her.

This confused her more and I felt sorry and mean. Turned off that valve at once and opened the spiritual-heroic refrigerating apparatus, invented and patented in all countries by Dante Alighieri. Talked rapidly of myself and my plans. In the midst of it unluckily I made a sudden gesture of a revolutionary nature. I must have looked like a fellow throwing a handful of peas into the air. People began to look at us. She shook hands a moment after and, in going away, said she hoped I would do what I said.

Now I call that friendly, don't you?

Yes, I liked her today. A little or much? Don't know. I liked her and it seems a new feeling to me. Then, in that case, all the rest, all that I thought I thought and all that I felt I felt, all the rest before now, in fact . . . O, give it up, old chap! Sleep it off! (287-8)

Perhaps such passages do not amount to much, just as Stephen's conception of freedom does not amount to much; but to think that Joyce's irony dissolves it away to nothing is to distort the portrait of a young man fumbling inevitably towards his proper stature as a human being. The irony points the false moves he makes, the "errors" whose successive unfolding forms the underlying structure of the novel. He does not triumph at the end of the novel, nor need we believe that Joyce thought he could. (At that stage Joyce himself did not.) But neither is Stephen necessarily lost forever like Icarus: he is flying high, he will suffer a fall, and in *Ulysses* will appear in the interesting condition of trying to do something about it. As Stephen says of Shakespeare, his "errors" are really "portals of discovery".

In much the same way, Mr Kenner seems to misinterpret the play, *Exiles*, which was written during the time the early parts of *Ulysses* were being composed. As he points out, it is certainly concerned with moral freedom—more explicitly, in fact, than any other of Joyce's works. On the other hand, it is probably the least successful of any. It seems to lack the personal detachment, the *objective* correlative, necessary to realize its meaning clearly and universally, and its flaws make it difficult to interpret. In particular, they make it very difficult to accept its hero, Richard Rowan, as the great and good man he is apparently intended to be. Inevitably we begin to suspect a deep irony on Joyce's part, a subtle, implicit rejection of his hero. This is Mr Kenner's view. He pounces on the idealistic "freedom" he takes Richard to represent—that is, mere unconditional impulse divorced from the limitations of fact and the recognition of moral law—and argues that Joyce is exposing its self-defeating sterility. No doubt the play would be profounder were this true; yet it is very doubtful if Joyce, in fact, does anything of the kind or even intended to.

It seems rather as if Richard were meant to embody, not a false ideal of perfect moral freedom, but the openness to experience and the self-determining "leap" of the will which are at least a necessary part of moral freedom. The play is more of a straightforward attack on the "morality" of mere habit and unexamined convention than Mr Kenner is prepared to allow. Richard invites—or rather, insists on—the possibility of his wife's unfaithfulness because without it, he feels, her faithfulness is meaningless. He will accept nothing less than an allegiance fully and freely given, nor will he accept beliefs and assurances to disguise the void in which such acts of choice must be made. The course of the play in effect is the purification and justification of his resolve to accept the void, and Joyce permits himself a certain irony about the masochistic pleasure his hero takes in contemplating the void, and even about the unconscious motives of his personal ruthlessness. The real trouble with the play, however, is not simply its stiff, factitious dialogue and action, but rather that Joyce's irony is never clearly and unambiguously directed, as it ought to be, at his hero's poisonous, self-absorbed wilfulness and his embarrassing self-pity. Richard thrusts freedom on his wife, Bertha, though she has all the freedom she wants or needs; yet the play never allows her to explode, as she naturally might and morally ought, about her husband's—and her unwanted lover's —view of her as a spiritual trophy. The reader can hardly avoid the suspicion that it is Richard himself who wrote the play; certainly, everyone else in it is only an instrument to his intense desire to reject the "darkness of belief" and achieve the pain of "restless living wounding doubt". As a work of art it is thus not only rather repulsive, lacking precisely a distancing irony, but its intention is perhaps all too clearly insisted upon. Richard is presented as bravely accepting the isolation of the heart, as seeking a genuine spiritual detachment; we are not meant to reverse his values. But granting Joyce's failure to realize his conception of moral choice, we may also allow that it is not altogether specious or absurd. It is not necessarily to be equated with the rejection of all moral law or a purely romantic subjectivism; imperfect though his treatment is, Joyce seems to be groping towards the freedom that lies at the very heart of moral life. Moreover, the fact that his hero is simply incredible as a creative genius does not necessarily mean that the freedom to which Joyce is pointing entails a purely negative ethic. To understand what he is getting at, I believe, we must remember that Richard's rejection was Joyce's rejection; both repudiated "nets" in order to create the conscience of the race. In a period that is a little bored or disillusioned with nineteenth-century "Revolt", and only too anxious to find certainty in the bosom of a common creed, we may sometimes forget how acute the individual conscience may find the need to choose and venture. At the centre of Joyce's play lies the perception that, wounding though doubt may be, without the capacity to accept the void, the creativity of freedom is impossible, that the moral imagination, which is in this perhaps one with the aesthetic imagination, requires a "negative capability".[7] Of course, there is a vast difference between possessing the capacity for "uncertainties, mysteries, doubts" or cultivating it, and Richard's deliberate creation of a situation where he can parade it: the touch of egotistical sublime in him, so uncriticized by Joyce as to suggest an imperfect awareness of it, is probably the central weakness of the play. But this is not to discredit Joyce's genuine basic intuition. All we can fairly criticize is his failure to express it without the distractions and confusions of not very relevant issues in his own domestic life.[8]

III

The nature of moral freedom is a central theme not only in *Exiles* and the *Portrait*, but also in *Ulysses*, and it is vitally important to understand the terms in which Joyce conceived it.

During the course of the *Portrait*, Stephen is brought to the point where he is at last able to grasp something of the meaning of freedom, but only to a limited extent: it seems to mean little more to him than revolt—escape or evasion from conventional "duties". But it is not merely that. It is important to notice that he rejects such "duties" for the sake of others that he considers higher and more compelling. What is at stake is not so much extraneous acts and conformities of behaviour as the allegiance of his whole personality to a group of values. He rejects the claims of family, church and state, not merely because of specific moral objections to them, but because they make, singly or together, exclusive claims to limit his moral perceptions, his moral imagination and his expression of what he perceives. They would inhibit, and therefore corrupt, the open responsiveness and creativity without which there can be no genuine moral life at all. What he rejects presents itself each time as an alternative vocation, but the sense of real vocation imposes for him a categorical moral demand that leads him to reject people and deeds that would conflict with its necessities. Very frequently he appears to have nothing but personal wilfulness to oppose to the clear-cut duties of his environment, for although he feels its presence, he discovers the nature of his vocation only gradually, by trial and error. Furthermore, once it is recognized and accepted, it seems less like a moral duty than a natural inevitability: his artistic calling is something he *has* to fulfil, both because he ought to, and also because, being the person he is, with the natural talents and moral values he possesses, he cannot avoid fulfilling it to some degree at least. That, in any case, is how he sees it; and it explains why, having rejected his religion (on other moral grounds), he uses the word "nature" instead of "God" to formulate his acceptance of a destined future. It is a moral decision, however. As early as *Stephen Hero*, Joyce explains that "he had come to the conclusion that nature had designed him for a man of letters and therefore he determined that, in spite of all influences, he would do as nature counselled" (p. 185).

The freedom he seeks is therefore not an unconditioned *self-expression*; his rejection of the "nets" flung out to catch the young Irish imagination is not simply lawless and irresponsible. Even in the *Portrait*, where he is at his most immature, Stephen does not champion the limitless, undisciplined individual will against all the claims of society and accepted moral values. He never seeks mere non-conformity. Rather, it is *self-fulfilment* that he desires— the satisfaction of a moral necessity laid upon him and him alone. His conception of how to satisfy it is still vague and uncertain, but he recognizes from the beginning that it involves renunciations and a discipline of its own, and that there are ordered and impersonal standards for its fulfilment, even if he fails as yet to perceive that these are not merely aesthetic standards. In *Ulysses*, however, he has come to understand that his aesthetic objectives depend upon the artist fulfilling himself as a moral being, that aesthetic *stasis* and *kinesis* originate in, and reflect, states of soul. And it is here that Joyce's conception of positive moral freedom, by animating the action of the novel, seems at once to continue and clarify the *Portrait*, and to cast a certain ironical light on Stephen's earlier immaturities.

In *Ulysses*, Stephen is still in constant opposition to his environing society. His actual criticisms may be postponed until the next chapter, but we can grasp something of his dramatic status from the interplay of ironies set up between him and Mulligan. There is no doubt that Joyce is fully aware of Stephen's bumptiousness—in fact, as we shall see, he insists on it. And one of his methods of emphasis is Mulligan's continual ironic mockery of Stephen's pretensions. Mulligan represents attitudes and values that Stephen rejects; his "needling" of Stephen helps us to understand that rejection and so helps crystallize Stephen's more serious feelings:

> —For a guinea, Stephen said, you can publish this interview.
> Buck Mulligan stood up from his laughing scribbling, laughing: and then gravely said, honeying malice:
> —I called upon the bard Kinch at his summer residence in upper Mecklenburgh street and found him deep in the study of the *Summa contra Gentiles* in the company of two gonorrheal ladies, Fresh Nelly and Rosalie, the coalquay whore.
> He broke away.
> —Come, Kinch. Come wandering Ængus of the birds.
> Come, Kinch, you have eaten all we left. Ay, I will serve you your orts and offals.
> Stephen rose.
> Life is many days. This will end. (202-3/211-2)

At the same time, however, Mulligan also serves as a comic chorus. Like the anonymous narrator of Bloom's adventure in "Cyclops", he provides a dash of ironic salt on Stephen's self-dedicated manner. We feel attracted towards Mulligan the more we feel that Stephen asks for what he gets:

> —Saint Thomas, Stephen began . . .
> —*Ora pro nobis*, Monk Mulligan groaned, sinking to a chair.
> There he keened a wailing rune.

115

—*Pogue mahone! Acushla machree!* It's destroyed we are from this day!
It's destroyed we are surely!
All smiled their smiles.
—Saint Thomas, Stephen, smiling, said, whose gorbellied works I
enjoy reading in the original . . . (194/203)

Although Mulligan is thus a means of focusing criticism upon
Stephen, Stephen focuses even more upon Mulligan. The
advantage seems to rest with the latter's wit and vivacity over
Stephen's guilt-ridden narcissism and ambition. In fact, the
advantage only serves to define Mulligan's limits more sharply—
his zenophobic provincialism, his corrosive scepticism, his essential conventionality and frivolity.[9] Despite the irony he directs at
Stephen, and however justified some of it is, the irony finally
rebounds on him:

—Ten years, he said, chewing and laughing. He is going to write
something in ten years. (236/246)

The irony is not that Mulligan is right to scoff, as Mr Kenner
thinks. Stephen is not forever fixed in his present mould. The real
irony is that the "impossible" Kinch ever becoming a serious
artist is, like so many things, beyond Mulligan's conception. (It is
interesting to recall that Mulligan's "original", Gogarty, always
thought *Ulysses* an enormous leg-pull.) Stephen as he appears is
certainly not a great artist—hardly an artist at all. But he is
protected by the sense Joyce conveys to us of potentialities still
in growth, of a future *stasis* already heralded by dawning self-
knowledge.

There is nothing odd or difficult about Joyce's conception of
freedom as *stasis*—except perhaps its classicality, since it probably
owes more to the ethical rationalism of Plato and Aristotle than
to anyone since. The discipline of the artist, "the most stable
mood of the mind", from which the most stable and impersonal
art emerges, is something Stephen, for all his theoretical knowledge of it, still lacks, and Leopold Bloom, for all his theoretical
ignorance of it, his frustrations, and his limited moral insight,
does possess: an inner balance, a measure of Justice in the soul.
Bloom, said Joyce, is "all-round" in two senses: he is seen from
all sides, like a sculptor's figure; "but he is a complete man as
well—a good man. At any rate, that is what I intend that he
shall be."[10] Virtue is human completeness; completeness is

harmony; harmony is freedom; only the just man is free; know thyself—the old, worn classical tags are still in some sense alive in Dublin, 1904. Stephen is bitter, divided against himself in the frustration of immaturity, and consequently incapable of the detachment that perceives truly and criticizes justly. Not all his judgments are invalid by any means, but his spiritual exile from society is still too much mere kinetic rejection, an almost involuntary recoil from what is alien to himself and the values he professes. Bloom's exile, on the other hand, while it is partly an involuntary exclusion from the society of his fellow-citizens, is also the detachment of a man free of many of their false values and giving allegiance to better ones. It is a positive detachment, deriving not from moral evasion and escape but from an active engagement with life in all its aspects. He perceives and feels more than his fellows, he judges further and more truly, and he triumphs, as a hero of Reason, over the temptations of the passions. His character analogously reflects the formal pattern of *Ulysses* itself. As each chapter of the book concentrates on some physical organ of man in order to compose a harmony of the whole, so Bloom exhibits the human combination of hopes, fears, virtues, passions, darkness and reason. Beneath his imperfections and the false ideals, however, there is a basic *stasis*, a sane and mature spirit. His is not meant to be the supernatural heroism of the saint, or even of Christ. His goodness is inclusive, not exclusive; he embodies an ideal other than that of spiritual specialization. He does not live by the passions, but he does not deny them either; he tries to guide them, to observe—without knowing he does so—the Mean. He is a moral being, not essentially as one who continually struggles with agonizing *cruces*, but as one who is committed to human rationality. His virtue is casual, habitual, without grandeur and without *arrière-pensée*. The one major problem with which he is faced is how he should take his wife's infidelity, and in the end he accepts it, as Richard Rowan accepts the possibility of Bertha's, not because he is a moral nonentity nor because of unconscious homosexuality or masochism, but because to abandon jealousy is the only rational thing to do. He cannot deny his own contribution to the situation and, more importantly, he cannot deny Molly's right to her own moral decisions. In compassionately accepting it, in fact, he establishes his own freedom both from vain sentimentality and from the passion of jealousy. In short, Bloom is a *moral* hero in his world. For Joyce, his brother tells us, only moral courage was truly virile[11]; Bloom is, properly enough, his "unconquered hero" (251/260).

Joyce's outlook is not a kind of *contemptus mundi*, nor a kind of perfectionism, nor a kind of Eastern spiritualism or pantheism. He does not dismiss the world for a higher spiritual vision, nor does he seek to amuse the world by painting its image. He has a rarer and more classical temper—a belief that man's desire will always reach beyond the limits of his imperfections but that even in the darkest places he may still proceed balanced between *hubris* and despair. Freedom is this *stasis* of mind, in which the world is held no cheaper nor dearer than it is truly worth. It is the attitude of mind towards which Stephen is struggling in *Ulysses*, out of his romantic, neo-Augustinian rejection of the earthly city towards a more balanced sense of it, which he supports by a remark from Augustine himself:

It was revealed to me that those things are good which yet are corrupted which neither if they were supremely good nor unless they were good could be corrupted. Ah, curse you! That's saint Augustine. (132/140)[12]

All things are made by God and He made "all things very good" in their degree—even, we should remember, Industrial Man. Joyce's outlook is neither exclusively tragic nor comic; it includes both, realizing itself in contemplation, in affirmation, and in a complex, compassionate irony.

IV

The most obvious mode of irony in *Ulysses* is the exposure of the protagonists' inadequacies and contradictions, the sharp, diagnostic irony that underlies Joyce's comparison of the noble and spacious world of Homer with the flaccid corruption of the present. Bloom and Stephen represent a disfigurement of the spirit for all to see, each, in his isolation, typical of a world in which everyone seems lost. Bloom's hopes and ambitions (like Stephen's pretentious egotism) are symbols of a universal decay. He is the suffering and excluded victim of a society he embodies in himself, and in "Circe" the two sides of his being arise and do battle within him. Stephen is also the victim of what he rejects. Guilt-ridden, sterile, conceited, kinetic, he embodies the very failures he so bitterly criticizes in the world around him. He seems to reject only because he is rejected. Together, the two men comprise the disintegration of "an age of whoredom groping for its god", their "heroism" a pathetic mockery of the firm, marvellous freshness of the Homeric dawn.

But there is another kind of irony, another side to the Homeric analogy. There are equally genuine parallels between the resourceful, insinuating, multi-faceted heroes of the *Odyssey* and *Ulysses*, between the common life of men and women in one age and the other, even between the gusto and vivacity of the two books; and these complicate and modify the mock-heroic perspective. The various effects of the Homeric parallels, as Mr Kenner's own excellent analysis of them shows, cannot be summed up in any one neat formula, for Joyce's irony is by no means directed simply at the shortcomings of the present age. By disregarding the conventional plaster draperies on the figure of Ulysses, by insisting on the absurd, vulgar confusion of life, Joyce's irony also cuts back on the supposed grandiosities of the past in order to reveal the living clay of humanity in every age. Hence the ambiguities of *Ulysses*, which seems at once a satirical caricature of the world and a clear-eyed, realistic portrait, a cry for the New Jerusalem and a tear for dear dirty Dublin. But Dublin is any city, Bloomsday any day—by concentrating on the ordinary Joyce makes his generalizations—and neither if they were supremely good nor unless they were good could they be corrupted. The citizens of his city are not saints, and not many even aspire to be. They are as good as they may be. They live and partly live; they perceive truth imperfectly; they realize their values in part; in all, they do no better nor worse than the citizens of any world, Homer's or Dante's. They are not all saved, nor are they irretrievably damned.

These two aspects of the Homeric parallel may serve to mark the extremes between which Joyce's irony maintains a poise far too little understood. Bloom does indeed represent the common man in modern society. Without religion, without friends, without a real community, even without a family, *déraciné*, cherishing the ideals of a mass "culture" composed of commerce, advertising, material comfort, scientific gadgetry and "progress", and

the fading memories of a traditional order, his social significance
is perfectly apparent:

I stand for the reform of municipal morals and the plain ten command-
ments. New worlds for old. Union of all, jew, moslem and gentile.
Three acres and a cow for all children of nature. Saloon motor
hearses. Compulsory manual labour for all. All parks open to the
public day and night. Electric dishscrubbers. Tuberculosis, lunacy,
war and mendicancy must now cease. General amnesty, weekly
carnival, with masked licence, bonuses for all, esperanto, the universal
brotherhood. No more patriotism of barspongers and dropsical
imposters. Free money, free love and a free lay church in a free lay
state. . . .

. . . the new nine muses [appear], Commerce, Operatic Music, Amor,
Publicity, Manufacture, Liberty of Speech, Plural Voting, Gastronomy, Private
Hygiene, Seaside Concert Entertainments, Painless Obstetrics and Astronomy
for the People. (465-6/480)

This is the figure against which Joyce directs an obvious satire.[13]

But since this view of Bloom has already received so much
emphasis from Joyce's critics—and from Mr Kenner perhaps
most of all—it seems worth recalling the other side of the matter.
For Bloom is not quite the hapless victim of his own ideals or his
society. On the contrary, his very isolation, his alertness, his
resource and his intelligence—in a word, his Odyssean virtues—
are precisely what preserve him from complete submergence and
make him, in fact, the main *vehicle* of Joyce's criticism. To ignore
Bloom's moral character when discussing his ideals is to distort
Joyce's whole meaning. Bloom's ideals are expressed just as much,
and perhaps more significantly, in the criticisms he continually
makes of his environment as in the petty frustrations he suffers
and in his formal declarations of belief; and it is just these
positive and active elements, limited as they are, wherein he is
representative of more than his own society. He becomes a
member of the partly realized, partly submerged, always
unsatisfactory human race.

The slippery ambiguities of the human condition may provoke
impatience or dismay, but in Joyce they provoked a kind of irony
—a richer and more stable irony, however, than he is usually
credited with, and one of which Bloom and Stephen are the
means as well as the object. Inasmuch as they represent genuine
values and aspirations—however imperfectly, however im-
maturely—they are the critics of the greater imperfections around

them, voicing the perennial objections of humanity against its constriction and waste. Indeed, to the extent that they represent modern society in its typical predicaments they also represent its capacity for self-consciousness and self-criticism; to the extent that we are shown the real limitations of their values—shown, that is, by the superior insight enacted by the art itself—they are placed by the fuller, encompassing outlook of the author. The tone of that ironic placing is not really Swiftian or Flaubertian, or a romantic alternation of acid and sugarwater, or aloofly indifferent to all moral values; it is far more complex and mature.

It would be both absurd and irrelevant to consider Bloom's a particularly penetrating critical consciousness. It is only a good fair average, and that is its primary significance. Sublimity and heroics are also quite out of his line, and in any case there is nothing in his society (apart from the high-flown rhetoric) that could support such noble postures. Joyce always adds a pinch of salt to his hero's most impressive moments. When he opposes "love" to the violence of "the Citizen" in "Cyclops", for example, he displays an admirable courage but also a complete inability to express his moral perceptions adequately or to know when to shut up (Bloom "the distinguished phenomenologist"); when he is in the murkiest depths of "Circe", it is the loss of a crucial trousers' button that helps save him; when he stands alone among his possessions and hopes in "Ithaca", their sentimental tawdriness is absurdly festooned about his dignity. Joyce never hesitates to joke about his hero, the Elijah who curses when a passing tramcar cuts off his appreciative regard of a lady's legs and whose love is so great that he lays down his wife for his friend.

Nevertheless we need only place a passage of Bloom's thoughts beside that of one or two other characters to see how far he is from a mere embodiment of social and moral corruption, a mere butt of Joyce's ruthless irony. To take a passage at random, near the end of "Lestrygonians" Bloom imagines what life must be like for the blind youth he passes:

Poor fellow! Quite a boy. Terrible. Really terrible. What dreams would he have, not seeing? Life a dream for him. Where is the justice being born that way? All those women and children excursion bean-feast burned and drowned in New York. Holocaust. Karma they call that transmigration for sins you did in a past life the reincarnation met him pikehoses. Dear, dear, dear. Pity of course: but somehow you can't cotton on to them someway. (171/179-80)

If this has a typically ironical application to Bloom himself ("not seeing"), it is also direct and honest: he does not pretend to feel more than he does, nor to understand the ways of Divine Justice. As his thoughts continue, he recognizes the similarities with human justice—at its worst a racket, hardly satisfying at its best. Compared to Bloom, however, the Very Reverend John Conmee, S.J., *is* a walking cliché and presented with a really hostile irony. His spiritual assurance fills him with a patronizing benevolence towards the whole universe:

Father Conmee began to walk along the North Strand road and was saluted by Mr William Gallagher who stood in the doorway of his shop. Father Conmee saluted Mr William Gallagher and perceived the odours that came from baconflitches and ample cools of butter. He passed Grogan's the tobacconist against which newsboards leaned and told of a dreadful catastrophe in New York. In America those things were continually happening. Unfortunate people to die like that, unprepared. Still, an act of perfect contrition. . . .

Moored under the trees of Charleville Mall Father Conmee saw a turfbarge, a towhorse with pendent head, a bargeman with a hat of dirty straw seated amidships, smoking and staring at a branch of poplar above him. It was idyllic: and Father Conmee reflected on the providence of the Creator who had made turf to be in bogs where men might dig it out and bring it to town and hamlet to make fires in the houses of poor people. . . . Father Conmee liked cheerful decorum. (209-10/218-9)[14]

Or we might compare Bloom's characteristic thoughts with those of another commercial traveller, Mr. Kernan:

Mr Kernan halted and preened himself before the sloping mirror of Peter Kennedy, hairdresser. Stylish coat, beyond a doubt. Scott of Dawson street. Well worth the half sovereign I gave Neary for it. Never built under three guineas. Fits me down to the ground. Some Kildare street club toff had it probably. John Mulligan, the manager of the Hibernian bank, gave me a very sharp eye yesterday on Carlisle bridge as if he remembered me.

Aham! Must dress the character for those fellows. Knight of the road. Gentleman. And now, Mr Crimmins, may we have the honour of your custom again, sir. The cup that cheers but not inebriates, as the old saying has it. (227/236)

To despise Bloom for his lack of true, deep understanding of Divine Providence seems to me unnecessary, but whether we do or not, he is hardly such a passive (and boring) reflection of his society as the crudely complacent Kernan. Mr Kenner (pp. 253-4) finds Kernan's interior monologue "almost indistinguishable" from Bloom's; it seems to me rather that beside this, Bloom's is characteristically responsive, intelligent and alive.

In some cases, of course, Bloom is an almost unconscious catalyst of Joyce's criticism. For example, Bloom's physical action while he reads Mr Beaufoy's short story unmistakably places the story (though Bloom's conscious admiration of it, we might notice, extends only to its cleverness): in any case, it moves him in only one way (61/68). But by far the greatest number of critical judgments arise in Bloom's own perceptions. If there is a second irony beyond these, which lies in his inability to grasp the fuller implications of his criticisms or of his own significance in his society—that is, the encompassing irony of the artist himself— Bloom is related to the artist in the very fact that it is his consciousness in which most of the criticisms are first formed. In our haste to endorse Joyce's condemnation of the evils of modern life we should not overlook the truth that Bloom, in his less sophisticated way, has condemned them too. By assuming *Ulysses* is "organized as a poem rather than as a naturalistic novel" and "its significance is not primarily to be discovered through a consideration of what its chief characters come to perceive",[15] we run the risk of supposing Joyce's characters to be mere flat, unconscious symbols like the figures in *The Waste Land* for instance. The truth is less simple. *Ulysses is* a novel, and what the characters perceive is as important as it is in most novels, and especially so since one of its central themes is the relationship between its characters and their creator, between the activity of the citizen and that of the artist. Even Mr Kenner has observed that Bloom, "as befits the Ulyssean wisdom, *polúmetis*, displays modes of sensibility haplessly inadequate to, but at least analogous with, genuine critical mobility" (p. 200). Others, too, have pointed out that Bloom is not unaware of the evil around him, though he never evaluates it properly.[16] All the emphasis, however, has been placed on Bloom as the hapless representative of general spiritual darkness, and far too little on his other function and significance, on the light he bears. For he is also

Joyce's direct spokesman very often; despite his habitual use of clichés it is also Bloom who initiates the critical rejection of cliché; and in the end, despite his victimization by life, he is still its active critic.

The first chapter in which he appears, "Calypso", does little more than introduce his characteristic circumstances and modes of behaviour. In "Lotus-eaters", however, his presentation begins to deepen with his casual but penetrating criticisms of his environment. Wandering through the streets, he notes the empty flabbiness of the life around him, and just as his world is revealed by his observations so it is measured by his moral activity. He does not simply reject the fleshpots and the evasions of lotus-eating; he judges and places them in a fuller context of human possibilities, a judgment none the less genuine for being often implicit in the turn of his thoughts. To cite a couple of typical examples:

They had a gay old time while it lasted. Healthy too chanting, regular hours, then brew liqueurs. Benedictine, Green Chartreuse. Still, having eunuchs in their choir that was coming it a bit thick. . . . Suppose they wouldn't feel anything after. Kind of a placid. No worry. Fall into flesh don't they? Gluttons, tall, long legs. Who knows? Eunuch. One way out of it. (74/81)

The chemist turned back page after page. Sandy shrivelled smell he seems to have. Shrunken skull. And old. Quest for the philosopher's stone. The alchemists. Drugs age you after mental excitement. Lethargy then. Why? Reaction. A lifetime in a night. Gradually changes your character. Living all the day among herbs, ointments, disinfectants. . . . (76/83)

Again, there is more to religion than the corruptions Bloom perceives about him—indulgence, evasion, mental opium, torpidity, and so on; but Bloom notes them truly enough and is clearly right in trying to stand beyond them. He is hardly very articulate about the ideal that is corrupted. The best he can do in abstract formulation is the sense that life is not "like that"; the idyllic weather ("cricket weather") "won't last"—"Always passing, the stream of life, which in the stream of life we trace is dearer than them all."

Enjoy a bath now: clean trough of water, cool enamel, the gentle tepid stream. This is my body.
He foresaw his pale body reclined in it at full, naked, in a womb of

warmth, oiled by scented melting soap, softly laved. He saw his trunk and limbs riprippled over and sustained, buoyed lightly upward, lemonyellow: his navel, bud of flesh: and saw the dark tangled curls of his bush floating, floating hair of the stream around the limp father of thousands, a languid floating flower. (79/85)

Yet with hardly more than an inarticulate conception of human complexity and moral activity, he is himself a symbol of them. His imaginary bath seems at first sight only another version of the indulgent resignations from life he has noted during the course of his wanderings. Seen in its dramatic context it is something rather different. Coming as it does at the very end of the chapter, it qualifies, and is qualified by, everything that has gone before. The physical and psychological relaxation, the temporary submergence, is less a moral evasion than a contemplative receptivity to *being*; Bloom's "wise passiveness" at the end, complementing his moral engagement with "the stream of life", seems to define the sense in which the lotus may be earned and eaten. Joyce's irony is more with Bloom than against him, though directed through him at the world in which he moves as the imperfect vessel of the spirit.

Similarly, it is Bloom's meditations on death in "Hades" that place the "Holy fields" and the funereal mummery, silently but firmly giving them such human significance as they have. I shall discuss this episode at greater length in Chapter VII in illustration of the dramatic art by which Joyce qualifies and endorses his hero, but even without lengthy analysis it is evident that Bloom's attitude to the customary clichés is far from uncritical. Throughout the book he is constantly sampling the attitudes of his fellows, his mind imaginatively informing itself with its object in acts of understanding, becoming part of all he meets. His clichés are very often the registration of his environment, a rapid sketching out of others' attitudes, so that to notice only the clichés without his turn of mind upon them is to miss Bloom and see only a dummy.

. . . Murderer's ground. It passed darkly. Shuttered, tenantless, unweeded garden. Whole place gone to hell. Wrongfully condemned. Murder. The murderer's image in the eye of the murdered. They love reading about it. Man's head found in a garden. Her clothing consisted of. How she met her death. Recent outrage. The weapon used. Murderer is still at large. Clues. A shoelace. The body to be exhumed. Murder will out. (92/99)

One might overlook the sentence that controls the tone and point of that passage—"They love reading about it"—just as one might miss the honesty and feeling that dignify death and give point to the whole chapter:

> Poor Dignam! His last lie on the earth in his box. . . . Only a mother and deadborn child ever buried in the one coffin. I see what it means. I see. To protect him as long as possible even in the earth. The Irishman's house is his coffin. Embalming in catacombs, mummies, the same idea. (102/108)

> Rusty wreaths hung on knobs, garlands of bronzefoil. Better value that for the money. Still, the flowers are more poetical. The other gets rather tiresome, never withering. Expresses nothing. Immortelles. (105/112)

During the whole episode Bloom preserves his usual sense of proportion, a mean between excesses, neither denying the significance of death as he apprehends it nor falling into hysterical horror. He has no formal religion, his outlook is naturalistic, but he is not despicable. And once again, at the very end of the chapter, Joyce clearly places him. The ridiculous episode of the dented hat sets Menton's snobbish pomposity and Bloom's goodwill and wounded feelings against the backdrop of the void—and it is Bloom who retains his human dignity.

"Lestrygonians" is one of the most frequently cited examples of Joyce's social criticism and of Bloom's materialism and spiritual blindness. As Mr Kenner perceptively notes (p. 232 ff.), Joyce's critical irony is directed at the brutal and bloody foundations of the modern social order, at the dark Satanic mills of priest, policeman and landlord that form a savage parody of the New Jerusalem. What is less frequently noticed, however, is the degree to which the irony is focused and directed by Bloom. To some extent he himself participates in the materialism he criticizes; to some extent the materialism is inevitable in any social order; but Bloom is also the voice of humanity against perversions of value. He stands apart from society, partly free of its illusions, involved in them, and yet deeply troubled by the bloody, chaotic flux it exhibits. He can find no spiritual refuge from it:

God wants blood victim. Birth, hymen, martyr, war, foundation of a building, sacrifice, kidney burntoffering, druid's altars. (140/149)[17]

He is given a throwaway offering religious salvation, but he places John Alexander Dowie, restorer of the church in Zion, in a phrase—"paying game". Similarly, he rejects the priestly injunction to increase and multiply: "Eat you out of house and home. No families themselves to feed." (We may disagree with his attitude and deplore his irreligion; what he points to are social realities, however sordidly "materialistic".) Yet he is also troubled by the fluidity of life, by the constant movement of matter, and by the vanity of *all* social institutions, which attempt to give it permanent shape: "How can you own water really? It's always flowing in a stream, never the same, which in the stream of life we trace. Because life is a stream" (142/151).

The thought of the "stream of life" recurs to him many times during the book, usually with the sombre colouring of his own problems ("Me. And me now"), but serving him as a kind of instinctive touchstone for the social phenomena about. His sense of the permanence of impermanence and of the basic realities of birth, growth and death, enables him to cut through cant, the "big words for ordinary things":

Sss. Dth, dth, dth! Three days imagine groaning on a bed with a vinegared handkerchief round her forehead, her belly swollen out! Phew! Dreadful simply! . . . They ought to invent something to stop that. Life with hard labour. . . . Time someone thought about it instead of gassing about the what was it the pensive bosom of the silver effulgence. Flapdoodle to feed fools on. . . . (150/159)

That he goes on to imagine the big hospitals "they" could have, and to sketch out a scheme for child endowments, will perhaps only cause some of his critics to shudder at his limited outlook. Joyce himself, as his brother tells us, liked to call himself a "socialist", which meant little enough, no doubt, to a man who always mistrusted "those big words that make us so unhappy", but at least suggests a certain minimal interest in the physical welfare of society.[18]

Bloom recognizes the "flapdoodle" for what it is and equally recognizes both the senseless violence embodied in the police force and the senseless violence it often has to check (151/160). But more than that, he perceives the dark realities of the Earthly City in which he walks:

His smile faded as he walked, a heavy cloud hiding the sun slowly, shadowing Trinity's surly front. Trams passed one another, ingoing, outgoing, clanging. Useless words. Things go on same; day after day: squads of police marching out, back: trams in, out. Those two loonies mooching about. Dignam carted off. Mina Purefoy swollen belly on a bed groaning to have a child tugged out of her. One born every second somewhere. Other dying every second. Since I fed the birds five minutes. Three hundred kicked the bucket. Other three hundred born, washing the blood off, all are washed in the blood of the lamb, bawling maaaaaa.

Cityful passing away, other cityful coming, passing away too: other coming on, passing on. Houses, lines of houses, streets, miles of pavements, piledup bricks, stones. Changing hands. This owner, that. Landlord never dies they say. Other steps into his shoes when he gets his notice to quit. They buy the place up with gold and still they have all the gold. Swindle in it somewhere. Piled up in cities, worn away age after age. Pyramids in sand. Built on bread and onions. Slaves. Chinese wall. Babylon. Big stones left. Round towers. Rest rubble, sprawling suburbs, jerrybuilt, Kerwan's mushroom houses, built of breeze. Shelter for the night.

No one is anything. (153/162)

This is one of the most powerfully realized passages in the book (the obvious comparison with *The Waste Land* suggests how much Joyce's irony gains from his more definite, more complex, dramatic context), and it is put, significantly, in Bloom's mind. Furthermore, his perception is tempered by his self-awareness, his capacity to see the horror, and his own participation in it, with a measure of proportion:

This is the very worst hour of the day. Vitality. Dull, gloomy: hate this hour. Feel as if I had been eaten and spewed. . . . Nature abhors a vacuum. (153/162)

Again, his personal pain over Molly's infidelity grows into a cosmic despair: "Waste of time. Gasballs spinning about, crossing each other, passing. Same old dingdong always." He remembers one occasion in particular, then breaks off: "Stop. Stop. If it was it was. Must." Yet far from calling upon Faith to criticize Bloom, Joyce offers an unobtrusive little comment of a different ironic significance altogether:

Mr Bloom, quick breathing, slowlier walking, passed Adam court. (155-6/164-5)

The whole chapter is pivoted on two small episodes in which Bloom tries to escape from the hard acceptance of life. He falls into an indulgent sensual languor in which his longing for love develops into a sentimental erotic fantasy:

> Useless to go back. Had to be. Tell me all.
> High voices. Sunwarm silk. Jingling harnesses. All for a woman, home and houses, silk webs, silver, rich fruits, spicy from Jaffa. . . .
> A warm human plumpness settled down on his brain. His brain yielded. Perfume of embraces all him assailed. With hungered flesh obscurely, he mutely craved to adore. . . .
> . . . Perfumed bodies, warm, full. All kissed, yielded. . . .
> —Jack, love!
> —Darling!
> —Kiss me, Reggy!
> —My boy!
> —Love! (157/166)

Woman, sex, becomes a substitute for the values he cannot grasp beyond the flux of time; he gropes for them, obscurely, craves to adore—and reality crashes through his makeshift refuge:

> His heart astir he pushed in the door of the Burton restaurant. Stink gripped his trembling breath: pungent meatjuice, slop of greens. See the animals feed.
> Men, men, men. (157/166)

The significant thing is that in his perception *he* is not an animal. He retains the fundamental capacity to know himself: "Bitten off more than he can chew. Am I like that? See ourselves as others see us. Hungry man is an angry man" (158/167). Love, as Richard says in *Exiles*, is not kinetic hunger; day-dreaming is not living; and in his isolation, cut off from everything except the acceptance of his situation, Bloom still retains his moral self. The passage that follows his exit from Burton's restaurant is an interesting example of how Joyce's irony derives from balancing in Bloom a legitimate rejection against an equally legitimate acceptance: "Eat or be eaten. Kill! Kill!" Bloom imagines the horrors of communal soup-kitchens ("all for number one"),[19] and those of the slaughter-house ("rawhead and bloody bones"); in short, the savage cannibalism of life. Beside the horror is the acceptance of the biological necessity: "Blood always needed. . . . Famished ghosts. Ah, I'm hungry" (159/168); even religious rituals express man's need to kill, to eat and to purify himself (160/169). Bloom cannot share the rituals; on the other hand, he is no vegetarian. He decides to eat cheese for lunch.

The second episode is foreshadowed while Bloom is at lunch. His memory suddenly overflows with the happiness he had once known with Molly, only to be painfully drained by the realization of what has happened since—"Me. And me now" (165/173). Two flies copulate on the window-pane: Molly's appointment with Boylan is for four o'clock. Bloom's glance falls to the veined oak in the bar counter:

Beauty: it curves: curves are beauty. Shapely goddesses, Venus, Juno: curves the world admires. . . . Lovely forms of woman sculped Junonian. Immortal lovely. And we stuffing food in one hole and out behind: food, chyle, blood, dung, earth, food: have to feed it like stoking an engine. They have no. Never looked. I'll look today. . . . (165/174)

(This is one of the problems he investigates at the Library in "Scylla and Charybdis", while Stephen is insisting on the bond between art and the human "now and here".)

The final episode of the chapter picks up Bloom's casual evasion here and presents it more explicitly. While meditating on the inscrutability of Divine Justice, if there is such a thing, he is suddenly startled by the sight of Boylan himself coming towards him. The present breaks in with a too violent irony: the world is all at once too much with him. He seeks a refuge from it:

The flutter of his breath came forth in short sighs. Quick. Cold statues: quiet there. Safe in a minute. . . .
His eyes beating looked steadfastly at cream curves of stone. Sir Thomas Deane was the Greek architecture. . . .
Afternoon she said. . . .
Hurry. Walk quietly. Moment more. My heart.
His hand looking for the where did I put found in his hip pocket soap lotion have to call tepid paper stuck. Ah, soap there! Yes. Gate. Safe! (172/180-1)

In both these pivotal episodes we feel the compassionate irony that, encompassing Bloom's perceptions, criticisms and predicaments, places them in larger contexts of significance. Bloom unwittingly flees for escape to what he really lacks, drawn by reasons he can only dimly understand to a spiritual order he could only partly possess. The "cold statues", like Keats's "cold pastoral", are symbols of a timeless world, beyond the imperfections of this and "all breathing human passion far above". Joyce's irony pierces through Bloom, revealing the incompleteness of his moral activity, the limitations of his self-understanding, the imperfections of his virtues—and, we should notice, his essential humanity. He is unmistakably judged, but the criticism is not mocking or sarcastic or patronizing. It never denies him. On the contrary, it respects, even while it delimits, his genuine intuitions, the honesty of his effort; it affirms both the representativeness of his predicaments and his fundamental sanity.

Obviously, Joyce's values are not simply Bloom's (or Stephen's). The central moral activity is the author's, expressing itself in the dramatic organizations of his material, enacting its values in the art. But the author's activity emerges out of Bloom's—qualifying his values, sometimes rejecting them, but always endorsing his responsiveness to life and the vitality that underlies even his false ideals. In other words, Joyce's attitudes to his protagonists cannot be reduced to any simple formula. Could they be, *Ulysses* would indeed be the static machine Mr Kenner supposes it, an ideogram with no dramatic, and hence with little moral, meaning as art. Joyce's attitudes (and his art) are more sensitively complex. The only valid generalization about them, I believe, is that he is related to his protagonists variably and ambiguously. Stephen's aesthetic theory looks forward to the growth of the artist's maturity out of his present immaturity; analogously, in Bloom's engagement with life are the shoots of the artist's moral outlook, though they are mixed in Bloom with a good deal of constricting rubbish. In both cases there is a gap between the artist and the character—with Stephen largely a gap of time, with Bloom of imaginative power—from which arises the complex irony of their presentation. But the implicit connection between creator and creatures is never denied. Rather, by means of the paternity metaphor, the Shakespeare theory, and the continually obtrusive commentary of the artist in extraneous parodies, parallels, and techniques, it is insisted upon as one of the central themes of the book. Bloom is no Bouvard or Pécuchet, nor Joyce an infinitely superior and aloof Flaubert: both are something larger and more admirable.

Only in this light can Bloom's social ideals and personal virtues be seen fairly. His beliefs are presented most explicitly in "Cyclops", "Circe" and "Ithaca". The weaknesses and limitations of his humanitarianism are glaringly obvious. To dismiss him for want of any genuine, positive ideals, or to suppose that Joyce

131

does, is to miss the point. For one thing, since his limitations are those of his society and age, entirely to despise him as some critics do, to see only hopeless corruption and blindness in him, is drastically to oversimplify the problem he represents. Joyce's main implication is that Bloom cannot be simply dismissed any more than the conditions he embodies can be cured by panaceas. The allegation that Joyce turned his back on life is very often the complaint of those who suppose that "life" leads an artist, and especially a novelist, to express clear-cut, explicit attitudes the reader can readily understand and the critic readily expound. Joyce's sense of the matter was different; and in Bloom he represented a state of affairs far too complex, and one in which we ourselves are far too involved, to be answerable to current political or religious programmes. The second thing to note, therefore, is that Joyce is too sensible to imagine that the limitations of Bloom's outlook are the whole truth about him, or even, by themselves, the major part of it. The limitations are the limitations of values, unconscious or inarticulate though they are very often, still appreciable and active—sufficiently so, at least, to offer genuine resistance to the world in which he finds himself. Bloom both represents his world and stands outside it. The young Stephen—especially in *Stephen Hero* and the *Portrait*—feels only disdain for the paralysis and ugliness of the modern world, unaware of his own participation in them and anxious only to reject. The mature Joyce, as Mr R. M. Kain, one of the few critics to understand something of Joyce's irony, observes, has no such disdain: "he has done more than merely to uncover ugliness; he has seen the soul of the little man beneath its mask. . . . It is not so much [Bloom's] ideal of good will that is ludicrous as it is its incompatibility with the values of the modern world."[20] That is one way of putting it, but we must also remember that Bloom is the modern world too. That is the central ambiguity Joyce seeks to express.

Bloom is most outspoken about his ideals in "Cyclops" and suffers there his most public indignity. Against "the Citizen's" bar-room *realpolitik* his attitude seems ridiculously inadequate. At the end of the chapter he is ignominiously hustled from the pub with a biscuit-box hurled after him by the Citizen, and bestowed with a comic metaphor by the author as the cab carries him away:

When, lo, there came about them all a great brightness and they
beheld the chariot wherein He stood ascend to heaven. And they
beheld Him in the chariot, clothed upon in the glory of the brightness,
having raiment as of the sun, fair as the moon and terrible that for
awe they durst not look upon Him. And there came a voice out of
heaven, calling: *Elijah! Elijah!* And he answered with a main cry:
Abba! Adonai! And they beheld Him even Him, ben Bloom Elijah,
amid clouds of angels ascend to the glory of the brightness at an angle
of fortyfive degrees over Donohoe's in Little Green Street like a shot
off a shovel. (329/339)

Bloom's objection to the Citizen's chauvinism, however, is not
to the Sinn Fein movement in itself: Bloom, like Joyce, supported
it and tried to further it (321/331).[21] Nor is he without some
admiration for the personal courage of the revolutionary (603-4/
626). His real objection is to violence, intolerance and exclusion
as self-destructive ingredients of any social ideal. He has been
called inconsistent and, against the Citizen's force, a helpless
an ineffectual humanitarian.[22] Quite apart from the fact that it is
the Citizen who is crippled and so ineffectual in throwing biscuit-
tins that he quite misses Bloom, the outlook Bloom opposes to
him is not simply humanitarian nor, as it is embodied in Bloom's
own character and actions, it is ineffectual. It does not overpower
the Citizen, but the force in the ordinary world of Bloom's
attitude is not of that kind:

—But it's no use, says he. Force, hatred, history, all that. That's not
life for men and women, insult and hatred. And everybody knows
that it's the very opposite of that that is really life.
—What? says Alf.
—Love, says Bloom. I mean the opposite of hatred. . . . (317/327)

Joyce follows this shortly afterwards by a parody, which has
sometimes been supposed to crush Bloom's position entirely:

Love loves to love love. Nurse loves the new chemist. Constable 14A
loves Mary Kelly. Gerty MacDowell loves the boy that has the
bicycle. . . . You love a certain person. And this person loves that other
person because everybody loves somebody but God loves everybody.
(317/327)

The object of the parody is only partly Bloom's genuine, if
stumbling, insight; it is directed much more obviously at the
debasement of the language he must use and at the false meaning

that is the only one the Citizen can understand—"That chap? says the citizen. Beggar my neighbour is his motto. Love, Moya! He's a nice pattern of a Romeo and Juliet." In himself, Bloom is clearly no Messiah or Elijah, and the final description of his departure does not offer him as such. But in his way, as the comic parallel suggests, he does represent the prophetic conscience of humanity in the world in which it must act. As he says, he is *not* talking about the New Jerusalem, he is talking about injustice (317/327): Joyce directs our attention to "the now, the here", to the limited grasp and imperfect action of values in our society— as in any.

The same ambiguity in Bloom is even more sharply defined in "Circe" and "Ithaca", where Joyce can portray him more from the outside and so with a fuller measure of his encompassing irony. Both episodes will have to be discussed further in the next chapter, but we may notice in both the complexity of Bloom's relations to his society. He plays all rôles: the representative of his age in its superficiality and disintegration, the "little father" of the "new Bloomusalem in the Nova Hibernia of the future" (461/475-6); the exile, outcast and criminal, attacked by his age as Judas Iscariot and "false Messiah" (448, 473/462, 487) despite his protestations: "Wait. Stop. Gulls. Good heart. I saw. Innocence . . ." (449/463). He is the critic of his world, attacking it even as it condemns him, and suffering from it even as he represents it. The "searching ordeal" of "Circe" expresses all the ironies of his position. Even his emergence from the ordeal is qualified by irony—he resists his gravest temptation, to resign all effort and desire in "the ethereal", largely because his back trousers' button snaps off (523/539). By turning his psyche inside out like this, Joyce portrays the moral dreams and nightmares that inevitably haunt Bloom. Yet the whole point of the episode is that Bloom is ultimately unable to acquiesce in *any* of his fantasies. Joyce's criticism goes beyond the actual values of his hero, beyond the particular society he represents, to the Circean drugs themselves—the complementary dreams of social messiah and social victim by which Bloom is tempted. Neither singly nor together, Joyce seems to imply, are such rôles adequate to the human condition, even in modern society. Bloom's moral strength lies in his failure to maintain them, to succumb to the passionate, violent chimeras that threaten his basic rationality—in other words, in the inarticulate, overlaid but vital core of human individuality in him that prevents his being swallowed up in *any* social or political ideal, and finally gives to his term "Love" a significance which, though abstractly unformulable, goes deeper than mere liberal humanitarianism. When the phantasmal Black Mass breaks over Stephen's head, and the whole of society seems split against itself in madness, Bloom remains sober (and loyal) amid the feast of unreason. In the end, it is his unconscious sanity that is vindicated, not any "ism"; the basic vitality of humanity rather than any of its beliefs.

In the anatomy of Bloom's *petit-bourgeois* values in "Ithaca", he once again seems to shrink to a mere embodiment of his society, a creature of estate-agents, stock-brokers, popular "culture" and spiritual vacuity (673 ff./697 ff.). Stephen and he find they have nothing to say to each other—or rather, nothing that they *can* say to each other—and must part. Their isolation seems all the more painful to contemplate in the pathetic setting of Bloom's most intimate dreams and the harsh light of the catechistic style. Yet even the harshest scrutiny cannot destroy him utterly. His home, as Joyce said of Ulysses, "gives him the pip"[23]; more relevantly, he retains the strength of his humility and self-knowledge. He recognizes "the irreparability of the past" and "the imprevidibility of the future", and the hard realities that limit his desire "to amend many social conditions, the product of inequality and avarice and international animosity". They are the permanent realities of human life, "the generic conditions imposed by natural, as distinct from human law, as integral parts of the human whole": "the necessity of destruction"; "the painful character of the ultimate functions of separate existence, the agonies of birth and death"; "monotonous menstruation"; "inevitable accidents"; "certain very painful maladies"; "catastrophic cataclysms which make terror the basis of human mentality"; and—significantly enough, since Stephen sits opposite him—the pain of growth, "the fact of vital growth, through convulsions of metamorphosis, from infancy through maturity to decay". In the possession of that knowledge, Bloom is no simple-minded perfectionist about human life. He desists from further speculation: "it was a task for a superior intelligence to substitute other more acceptable phenomena in place of the less acceptable phenomena to be removed". This is the final ground of the affirmation he shares ("not verbally. Substantially") with Stephen: "that as a competent keyless citizen he had proceeded energetically from the unknown to the known through the incertitude of the void" (657-8/681-2).

Bloom's personal virtues, then, are not to be reduced to a mere good-will which is continually and inevitably frustrated by the ignoble world in which he lives. The good-will is there, issuing in such actions as feeding the Liffey gulls, putting Menton's hat aright, arguing with the Citizen, or helping Stephen as far as he can; but with it go other, more unusual, qualities—tolerance, sympathy, generosity, prudence, fortitude, moderation and humour, and self-knowledge. He is rather more than "a decent quiet man" (166/175); "not one of your common or garden . . . you know. . . . There's a touch of the artist about old Bloom" (222/232). He would have understood the words Dante's Ulysses addresses to his companions, and echoes their sense in his own life:

> Considerate la vostra semenza:
>   fatti non foste a viver come bruti,
>   ma per seguir virtute e cognoscenza.   (*Inf.* xxvi)

(Consider your origin: ye were not formed to live like brutes, but to follow virtue and knowledge.)

In all his virtues lies an unselfconscious love of and reverence for life, which is the inarticulated meaning of his word "love" and the hidden cause that brings him, for instance, to visit a woman in labour and, from there, to follow, protect, and try to reach Stephen. If his limitations are partly those of his time and place, they are also those of ordinary humanity itself.

We therefore distort Joyce's meaning if we fail to discriminate between the kind of irony he directs at the accidents of his protagonists, their "now and here" as it were, and the kind he directs at their substance. To take one crucial case: when Bloom, at the end of "Circe", stands protectively over the homeless and unconscious Stephen, the physical situation of the two men forms an obvious symbol of the spiritual. Bloom imagines the figure of his dead, "unseeing" son, Rudy, resurrected, and dressed with a generously appalling sentimentality—"a fairy boy of eleven, a changeling, kidnapped, dressed in an Eton suit with glass shoes and a little bronze helmet. . . . A white lambkin peeps out of his waistcoat pocket" (574/593). The style of this clearly marks

Bloom's sensibility, but that is not the only, or even the major, point of the passage. The substance of his "wonderstruck" perception is genuine. The only irony that affects *it* is that which encompasses the paternity theme as a whole—the fact that neither Bloom nor Stephen can understand their relationship properly. In other words, despite Bloom's petty beliefs, his occasional sentimentality, his frustrations, his exile from other men and from clear ideals of spiritual relationship, it is probably more accurate to stress his moral stature (despite his limitations) than his limitations (despite his moral stature). The difference is only one of emphasis, and we must beware of pressing either side too far, for Joyce's ironies maintain a subtle and delicate balance. Bloom, as Mr R. P. Blackmur has put it, is the darkness shining in the light of the modern world.

Bloom is the wanderer, the movement and enterprise in man, the only thing immortal in society which persists from form to form. He is Everyman in exile, the exile in every man. A transigent man, easy, warm, kind, thinking, he makes up in little acts of imagination for frustrations not of his making. . . . Bloom is indeed bloom: he is the exemplar of Stephen's best phrases to Deasy—about the distrust of big words, the nightmare of history, the shout in the street. His soul walks with him, form of forms. . . . Stephen has somehow to become Bloom, or see the need of it; but Bloom has no need to become anybody, not though the world fall on him.[24]

This is well said, I think, and the various modes of Joyce's irony express just this poised comprehension of the opposite and discordant aspects of his hero—the stunted and unrealized possibilities that represent his bondage to his world, and the substantial human integrity that constitutes his freedom from it. His heroism is not revolutionary, apocalyptic, vitalistic; it lies in openness to life, self-knowledge, and the sober acceptance of what cannot be changed.

V

The basic attitude from which Joyce's most pervasive irony arises is not, therefore, one of moral nihilism or indifference. On the other hand, although he evades "beliefs", he certainly does not evade the moral exploration of life by retiring to some transcendental credo from which to condemn the whole industrialized world of the nineteenth and twentieth centuries. His ambition is quite different, I believe—to see life steadily and to see it whole, to grasp, without distorting or minimizing, its complexities and contradictions and to reconcile them, or rather properly to dispose them, within a stable and fruitful order of the spirit. His success is imperfect of course; much of the failure is the result of his attempt to explore more of life than he could really grasp; much is the result of inadequate critical insight. For the truth is that when the art does approximate to Mr Kenner's account of it, as it does at times, Joyce's purely hostile irony, compared with his maturer sense of qualifying complexities, is far less impressive, far less central to his real achievement.

Against the balanced ironies engaged by Bloom we may place three examples of Joyce at his most critical: "Wandering Rocks", "Eumaeus" and "Nausicaa". At its richest, Joyce's attitude emerges in a subtly responsive humour, a wit that is warm and positive as well as level-headed and alert. These three episodes illustrate his tendency to lapse into something more simple and more negative—in a word, *parody*.

"Wandering Rocks" parodies the fragmentation and mechanical "order" of modern society by its ostentatiously mechanical linking of nineteen fragmentary episodes in different parts of Dublin. The first and last provide a frame for the rest: Father Conmee's peregrinations represent the impotence of spiritual order, those of the Lord-lieutenant General and General Governor of Ireland, the impotence of political order. Into each episode is carefully inserted a reference to one or more exactly contemporaneous events, and in these insertions lurks Joyce's irony. Some of the juxtaposed events form deliberate criticisms of the actors. In the first episode, for example, Father Conmee's smug appreciation of "the ways of God which are not our ways", especially as they apply to "that tyrannous incontinence, needed however for men's race on earth" is juxtaposed with his evident unawareness of why the young man and the girl who come out of a field are flushed and embarrassed, while his complacent appreciation of his power over schoolboys ("He was their rector: his reign was mild") is juxtaposed with the tremendous words in his breviary about the reign of God (211-2/220-1). Another equally obvious case is the onelegged sailor, grimly singing about England, home and beauty, who passes two miserable children from the Dedalus home, and is finally flung a coin by the beauty at the home of Leopold Bloom (213/222). Again, while Boody Dedalus breaks out in bitterness at their hunger, destitution and feckless father, "Our father who art not in heaven", Bloom's crumpled throwaway, "Elijah is coming", rides lightly down the Liffey (214/223). Most of the juxtapositions, however, are ironical only in their deliberate meaninglessness:

> Corny Kelleher sped a silent jet of hayjuice arching from his mouth while a generous white arm from a window in Eccles street flung forth a coin. (212/222)

This, like the fact that the vice-regal procession leaves just as Mr M'Coy pushes a banana-skin off the footpath, or that Mr Kernan walks along James's street while Dilly Dedalus tries to get money from her father, amounts to no more than one of "life's little ironies", a casual or mechanical coincidence, of significance only to a mind devoid of moral depth. That is precisely what Joyce means, of course; the elaborate counter-pointing of events is a parody of moral sterility. But the chapter as a whole is hardly what it has often been supposed to be, a microcosm of the whole book. Although the parody is clever and the point well taken, the level of insight never reaches beyond the obvious. The art is inert, undramatic, so that with the significant exception of the episodes involving Bloom and Stephen (212-3/222; 222-4/232-3; 235-6/245-6), where implications elsewhere established dramatically are brought into play, the values implicit in the irony are entirely too superficial and quite negative. No amount of hidden transcendental values supposedly directing this imitation of mechanical order, no reference to Joyce's deliberate use of "symbols" of mechanics, can really deepen the actual level at which he has conceived his material. Beside the treatment of comparable issues in "Lestrygonians" and "Circe", this seems a triumph of fanciful artifice rather than of art.

Both "Eumaeus" and "Nausicaa" obviously invite the same objection—not to mention the notorious "Oxen of the Sun". In each case the level of critical insight seems insufficient to support the enormous construction raised upon it. There is a contra-diction between the verbal vivacity on the surface and the simplicity (in the limiting sense of that word) of the moral values ostensibly engaged. Beneath the surface the imagination is inert, the irony unsubtle. "Oxen of the Sun" is perhaps not so ironic in intention as the other two, apart from the suggestion at the end that English prose seems fated to degenerate into moronic chaos; but even as an attempt to express the growth of the human embryo by the parody or pastiche of historically important writers (a project pretty clearly doomed from the start, one would have thought), the chapter reveals Joyce's ineptitude as a literary critic. He admitted his limitations in that line himself, and we can feel a certain sympathy for the creative artist who gets on with his own job. It is a significant limitation nevertheless, and even putting aside the self-criticism that might have prevented the whole enterprise, one of the least convincing features of the chapter is the mechanical conception of literary history it rests upon, a conception of what literary history *is* hardly more sensible than that of a conventional text-book of "Eng. Lit.". The wide and powerful intelligence exhibited in *The Sacred Wood* or *Studies in Classic American Literature* is clearly outside Joyce's range.[25]

"Eumaeus" again has complex functions in the work as a whole, but again it also seems to embody a too simple sense of its critical object. The skill lies all in the hostile observation and the verbal display. The chapter captures well enough the clichés jibbering in Bloom's mind and in his society at large; what is less convincing is the meticulous industry with which they are exhibited in parody. So too, I would suggest, is the view of Bloom the parody implies. By the last three chapters, as we shall see, the work does shift us to a more distant, more comprehensive, and hence in some ways apparently simplifying view of its whole world. Yet to present Bloom as though the jaded and jumbled clichés of his tired mind were somehow revealingly characteristic involves too drastic a simplification. It forms an acrid comment that applies only to some aspects of the society he represents, for he too has criticized that society, explicitly or implicitly, all through the book; by the time we reach "Eumaeus" we surely know him well enough to be surprised that he thinks like this—even at one o'clock in the morning. The tendency to caricature is an index of the mechanical superficiality of the artistic organization.

The final example, Gerty MacDowell in "Nausicaa", is often

praised as an illustration of Joyce's ironical criticism of modern society. There is of course a sharp comment on the "innocent" *jeune fille* of the age in the satirical juxtaposition of the Virgin, and the clear freshness of the Homeric episode, with the viciously sentimental sexiness of Gerty, rendered as she is in Joyce's parody of a "namby-pamby jammy marmalady drawsery (alto la!) style with effects of incense, mariolatry, masturbation, stewed cockles, painter's palette, chit-chat, circumlocution, etc. etc.".[26] Yet all the same limitations are apparent. As Joyce conceives her, Gerty and all she represents are surely, for all the comedy, no very difficult target for the social critic. Besides some of Lawrence's women characters, or even Emma Bovary, Gerty is hardly a large enough creation by which to explore the nature and meaning of feminine eroticism in modern society at any depth. She is too simple, too static; her formula, so to speak, once again provokes the adjective, mechanical. So hostile and so extended is Joyce's satirical attack, indeed, that we may wonder if she is quite worth twenty pages of his powder and shot. As Arnold said of Flaubert, "he is cruel, with the cruelty of petrified feeling, to his poor heroine; he pursues her without pity or pause, as with malignity; he is harder upon her himself than any reader even, I think, will be inclined to be".[27] If we once think of Gerty with any compassion as a human being during those twenty pages (as Bloom does afterwards), we may conclude that Joyce's ironic parody is breaking a butterfly on its wheel. It is always a danger with extended parody that the joke will wear thin. "Cyclops" avoids it, largely because of its dramatic structure, but not "Nausicaa".

It seems as if Joyce's imagination always tended to drift towards the simple—either the elemental or the monolithic—and sometimes grounded there in elaborate but mechanical complication, in the monotonous repetition of a single formula—the quality, in fact, wherein Mr Kenner would place the real value of *Ulysses*. The parodies of "Cyclops", "Nausicaa" or "Eumaeus", and the parodic structure of "Wandering Rocks" or "Oxen of the Sun", like the so-called encyclopaedic range of Joyce's verbal "symbolism", are remarkable more for the infinite pains with which Joyce develops a basically simple attitude than for subtle and comprehensive criticism. The kind of art they exhibit is like that he lavished on the physical setting of the action, the time-scheme, the Homeric parallels, and occasionally even on the characters (Molly is a case in point), where his meticulous ingenuity may remind one of the lady who devoted herself to making artificial flowers out of fish-bones. Even at their most elaborate, the details fulfil comparatively superficial purposes, and one begins to suspect Joyce's grasp of the difference between means and ends.

At his best, however, his attraction towards simplification is balanced and given meaning by a deep attachment to the richness, the complexity of life, "the now, the here", and to an art *dramatic* in the sense that it is fully responsive to the human situation. Without that, Bloom would never come alive nor *Ulysses* amount to more than a massive but lifeless encyclopaedia of decay. Despite those aspects of his work that Ezra Pound and others since have very properly admired—the brilliant verbal resource, the comic verve, and the ruthlessly efficient destructiveness of his parodies (a destructiveness that suggests the obvious comparisons with Swift and, with rather more reason, Flaubert) —these qualities have tended to overshadow the deeper and more valuable vitality of the work. Joyce's imaginative strength is not really the energy of his rejection of life. On the contrary, *Ulysses* is most impressive as a criticism of life in its creation of Bloom, in its comprehensive and uncensorious vision of humanity, and its irony richest when it includes and balances, when it responds to the complexity of its object, rather than in its sharp hostilities and rejections. It is not easy to think of another novelist who would have taken Bloom for his protagonist without turning him into a Babbitt, or a Kipps, or a self-consciously pathetic and comic Little Man, or some other simplified text for social commentary. Joyce's distinction was to penetrate beyond the social epiphenomena and to discover, in the intense examination of them, the permanent realities of human life. The result is a comment on the age far more mature, because far more dramatic in this sense, than that of *Bouvard et Pécuchet* or *The Waste Land*— the works with which it is most often compared, the general attitude to which Joyce's is most often assimilated.[28] The drama of the book derives from Bloom's ambiguous relations to his society, from the interplay between his limited values, his social exile, and his underlying sanity. More specifically, as we shall see, it lies in the gradual unfolding of his significance. In its fullest sense, the action of the book comprises not only the physical and mental acts of its protagonists but also the acts whereby the artist, looking back over his world within, evaluates theirs by shaping them; that is to say, it includes Joyce's manipulation of narrative techniques, his parodies, his intrusive parallels. Plot, we should notice, becomes an almost irrelevant concept to apply to the book unless we are prepared to extend its application to the development of *our* point of view, our understanding, rather than (or as well as) that of the characters'. Similarly, the characters cannot, in the ordinary sense, develop over one day. Although they are displayed and scrutinized, and perform acts upon which the meaning of the work depends, ultimately, as their wider meanings are progressively revealed, *their* acts, however crucial, become subordinated to those of the artist himself. But this is a theme for another chapter.

The truth is that the real achievement of *Ulysses* lies as little in its parodic irony as in its representational accuracy or the ingenious reticulation of its verbal symbols. Nor is every part of it as vital or profound as every other. Its value lies in its underlying and over-arching vision of human life, a vision both more humane and more complex than is always perceived. When all is said and done, the book rests upon the firmly realized figures of Bloom and Stephen (Molly, I think, is a much less important and a much less convincing figure). Their relations to each other are explored in a very simple action—they only meet and part—but superimposed upon that is another action in which we, with the artist, are the real actors. As the day goes on, our understanding of its events grows fuller as we too participate in them, until, finally, we are projected, as none of the characters is, beyond them. Unlike the characters, we become freed from involvement in process; and as we do, we become able to view them as representatives not merely of our age but of humanity itself, and to see the ordinary adventures of the day—its common accidents, comedies, pains, judgments, fulfilments and potentialities—as the perennial condition of humanity. We reach this point by "Ithaca", I believe, and as we do so, we share most fully in Joyce's comprehensive, ironical vision of life. But in fact, as we may perceive even at this stage, it pervades the book all along. For the heart of Joyce's irony—the source and end of his treatment of Bloom and Stephen, and the attitude they each grope towards—is the detachment of the artist who imaginatively comprehends his world, his own experience, because he contemplates it in spiritual *stasis*: accepting it, as he must, as the element in which he lives ("the now, the here"), but also, in his mature self-knowledge, free from complete bondage to its values.

CHAPTER V

HOMER AND THE NIGHTMARE
OF HISTORY

PARALLEL to, and often bound up with, the critical uncertainty about Joyce's attitude to his hero and the nature of his irony is the uncertainty about his use of Homer's *Odyssey*. Although everybody now knows that *Ulysses* is in some sense founded upon the *Odyssey*, there is rather less agreement about why it is. In what is still the most detailed exploration of the Homeric parallels in *Ulysses*, Mr Stuart Gilbert tries to explain them by theories about Metempsychosis, Temporal Recurrence, and historical connections between ancient Greece, Ireland and the Jews. Others, as we have seen, take them as mock-heroic, exposing the sordid darkness of the modern world by contrasting it to the bright gleams of an Heroic age. Others again, tempted by the dubious theory of Archetypal Patterns and seizing upon what they take as Bloom's "identification" not only with Ulysses but also Christ, King Hamlet, the Wandering Jew, Sinbad the Sailor, the Ancient Mariner, Robinson Crusoe, a Solar Hero, and so on, see the book as the re-expression of some deep generic Myth—which naturally requires a correspondingly profound interpretation.

Even in the face of all this, the ordinary reader may well wonder if the parallels as he meets them are of any real significance at all, whether they really arise from and imaginatively illuminate the basic action. The more parallels he is told of, the less they seem like deeply meaningful organic metaphors and the more like curious, even witty, but quite extraneous analogies. Obviously, Joyce handles Homer's story very freely, picking and choosing among its episodes as he pleases, and obviously, too, despite all the carefully intervowen parallels with the *Odyssey*, the structure of *Ulysses* is completely its own.[1] And, in fact, as one discovers the way in which Joyce translated some of the details, Dr Johnson's criticism of the pointless ramification of Cowley's conceits seems only too appropriate: "what is little . . . by claiming dignity becomes ridiculous".

The most sensible account of the Homeric parallel as a whole is still that of Mr Harry Levin in his critical introduction to Joyce. He indicates three reasons for it. In the first place, since the *Odyssey* "embodies everything" and its hero is all-embracing, it offers an archetype for modern man. Its relation to *Ulysses*, however, is that of "parallels that never meet"; the gap between Heroic and modern values generates a critical irony. In the second place, the parallel is a cognitive device for the reader: "by giving him something to take for granted and showing him something to look for, by helping him to control an overwhelming flux of impressions, it justifies its existence". The third reason is in terms of a quite different effect. The Homeric—and the other "mythic" parallels as well—provide the action with a special depth and meaning: Joyce's intention is to "attach a universal significance to the most minute particulars", to project into *Ulysses* a sense, which the characters themselves partly possess, of the continuities and permanent patterns of human experience. But, Mr Levin concludes, apart from its help to the reader, the Homeric parallel as a whole "seems more important to Joyce than it could possibly be to any reader".[2] As a reaction from Joyce's excessive ingenuities, not to mention those of some of his commentators, such a conclusion seems the voice of common sense. The detailed analogies are, as Mr Levin says, too various in effect and too extrinsic for the parallel as a whole to seem convincingly part of the subject itself. True though this is, however, it is not the whole truth. The Homeric parallel, I believe, *is* centrally important in *Ulysses*, and very much in the way Mr Levin himself has suggested: in so far as the parallel worlds do not meet, the result is a kind of mock-epic irony, an oblique criticism of the Bloomworld; in so far as they do, the result is a kind of *stasis*, a universalized vision of the life of modern man. The central question is therefore *how* the parallel is related to the dramatic action and what effect it really achieves.

I

The first point to be made is a very obvious one but one too often overlooked: not all the various historical and mythical parallels are of the same kind or function in the same way. Some are in fact organic metaphors, others like a chorus of extraneous

146

footnotes, and we do well to distinguish the two kinds.[3] At one extreme, the parallels emerge naturally and inevitably from the action. An obvious example is that at the end of "Cyclops", after Bloom has affirmed Love against the Citizen.

—By Jesus, says he, I'll brain that bloody jewman for using the holy name. By Jesus, I'll crucify him so I will. Give us that biscuitbox here. (326/336)

Bloom's departure in the waiting carriage is described in terms of Elijah's ascent in a chariot of fire:

When, lo, there came about them all a great brightness and they beheld the chariot wherein He stood ascend to heaven. And they beheld Him in the chariot, clothed upon in the glory of the brightness, having raiment as of the sun, fair as the moon and terrible that for awe they durst not look upon Him. And there came a voice out of heaven, calling: *Elijah! Elijah!* And he answered with a main cry: *Abba! Adonai!* And they beheld Him even Him, ben Bloom Elijah, amid clouds of angels ascend to the glory of the brightness at an angle of fortyfive degrees over Donohoe's in Little Green Street like a shot off a shovel. (329/339)

This is live, realized metaphor, and its effect, like that of all metaphor, is to cast its component elements into a new, unexpected but significant relationship. Its critical or ironical effect is as inevitable as its universalizing effect, just because it cannot be simply reduced either to "Bloom *is* Elijah" or to "Bloom is *not* Elijah".

At the other extreme from this are those parallels imposed on the action: one might cite Bloom's "knockmedown" cigar (Ulysses' club) in the same chapter (290/300), or any number of the details mentioned by Mr Gilbert. Perhaps a more significant example is that at the end of "Ithaca":

Womb? Weary?
He rests. He has travelled.

With?
Sinbad the Sailor and Tinbad the Tailor and Jinbad the Jailer and Whinbad the Whaler and Ninbad the Nailer and Finbad the Failer and Binbad the Bailer and Pinbad the Pailer and Minbad the Mailer and Hinbad the Hailer and Rinbad the Railer and Dinbad the Kailer and Vinbad the Quailer and Linbad the Yailer and Xinbad the Phthailer.

When?

147

Going to dark bed there was a square round Sinbad the Sailor roc's auk's egg in the night of the bed of all the auks of the rocs of Darkinbad the Brightdayler.

Where?

●   (697-8/722)

The parallel here with Sinbad no more arises naturally from the action than does, say, a parallel with Alice back from the Looking-glass. The Sinbad conceit is funny in its way, and Joyce elaborates it as far as it will go; nevertheless, it remains fanciful, extrinsic in origin and effect. At best it illustrates, not illuminates. It does not add meaning to the material, it merely adds material. Where the Elijah passage says in effect that we must see Bloom as Elijah in order to see him truly at this moment, and *shows* him to us so, the Sinbad passage says in effect "compare Sinbad", drawing our attention to the analogy but not asking us to see, much less attempting to show, the meaning of the analogue as the meaning of Bloom. To suppose that every time Joyce draws our attention to an analogy in this way he is "identifying" values or meanings is a naïve slide from the belief that imaginative analogy is a mode of apprehension to the belief that every analogy is imaginative. Unfortunately, only too many of Joyce's commentators do treat every detail and analogy as of equal symbolic importance.

That at least some of the parallels do serve to "universalize" the action is generally agreed; but there are two senses in which this may be meant, depending on which kind of parallel we have in mind. At first sight, it seems rather odd to suggest that explicit parallels, either metaphorical or analogical, are necessary to the universality of a work of art. Many a work without them succeeds in becoming *itself* a metaphor (or, as some would prefer to call it, a "symbol" or "myth") whose meaning, though it strikes a note in us that makes other stories, other experience, vibrate in sympathetic harmony, reaches, as does all metaphor, beyond the limits or jurisdiction of explicit analysis, discursive philosophy or factual history. But the universality of metaphor, whether it be a whole work or Joyce's Bloom-Elijah parallel, is an aspect of its imaginative coherence and truth, a universal *effectiveness*. Nevertheless, discourse and fact have their universality as well—a universality or comprehensiveness of *reference*. Applied to a work of art, this is the sense in which we might speak of the range of its material as distinct from the force of its meaning—*War and Peace* as "more universal" than *Pride and Prejudice*, or of *Finnegans Wake* as "all-including: universal".[4] In the former sense, we should probably judge *Faust I* more universal than *Faust II*; in this latter sense, the position would probably be reversed. If, then, we mean merely that Joyce *indicates* the recurrence of a similar situation elsewhere, merely increases the range of his material, as it were, we might say that the Sinbad passage "universalizes" Bloom's experience as much as the Elijah parallel. It is like the Epilogue to Shaw's *St Joan*: in each case, it is a *historical* universality consciously added to the work, but not necessarily affecting such *artistic* universality as it possesses. But the remark of one critic (typical of a common formula), that the effect of Joyce's parallels is to make us feel the "oneness of the ages", ambiguously straddles this distinction.[5] Since the Elijah passage is cited in illustration, the comment may suggest that *Ulysses* would be crippled as a symbol without the metaphorical parallels, unable to speak "not for an age but for all time"; when we consider the more mechanical and extrinsic parallels, and the range of Joyce's analogies, the phrase takes on another meaning altogether. This is the confusion behind the extraordinary conclusion of another critic that "the parallels of Telemachus and Hamlet helped Joyce to make the individual more general. . . . Stephen, while literally young Joyce, is symbolically every young man in search of maturity and adjustment."[6] One recalls other writers who have managed to portray "every young man" without recourse to Homer, Shakespeare, Dante and the rest.

The effects of the Homeric parallels vary from place to place: sometimes purely funny, sometimes critical, sometimes clever technical virtuosities, sometimes opportune metaphors for Joyce's action, sometimes more serious structural analogies with the Shakespeare-*Hamlet* analogy.[7] Yet even these broader analogies between Bloom and Ulysses, Stephen and Telemachus, Molly and Penelope do not, I think, strike the reader as really establishing that sense of deep, abiding imaginative truth in which *artistic* universality consists. Unlike the Shakespeare parallel, or even the Christ parallel, the Homeric parallel nowhere seems to emerge *of necessity*, dramatically realized in, and an integral part of, the action. Where the others, as we have seen, are essential expressions of the moral and aesthetic themes of the work, the Homeric parallel seems merely to hover over the action like a mesh whose finest wires are all but invisible. Even were the forms of classical civilization still present in Dublin as in no other European city, as Mr Kenner suggests, this remains a piece of extraneous social information as far as the book itself is concerned —the talk in "Aeolus" and elsewhere about the superiority of Greece and Ireland to their imperial masters, Rome and England, is hardly the kind of artistic realization necessary to make the hundreds of detailed parallels with Homer more than "capricious" and "mechanical". Joyce himself may have loved the *Odyssey* (and Lamb's version of it) from his early youth and always been fascinated by its "complete hero"; he may have thought Homeric epic encyclopaedic in its range; he may have found Ulysses a rich, time-honoured symbol for the adventuring spirit of man[8]; but in *Ulysses* the main effect of his particular employment of the Homeric stories is not artistic, but historical universality. And that, I believe, is the prime reason, though not the final reason, why the Homeric parallel is there.

Whether we emphasize the differences between the parallel worlds of Bloom and Ulysses or the broader similarities of situation and character, Joyce's superimposition of a map of another society over a map of our own has at least one important result— it helps sharpen and define a world only too familiar to us and only too chaotic. The other society Joyce chose is generally regarded as being better than our own, and perhaps in some ways it was. But in any case we are continually being forced to discriminate it from our own. We recognize that Bloom has certain values and virtues—justice, love, charity, resignation and so on—that are only partly Homeric values and virtues. He represents a society very different—even in its ideal form—from the Heroic Age of the *Odyssey*. And one thing, perhaps the crucial thing, that distinguishes Bloom's and Stephen's world very sharply from Ulysses' is precisely what Mr Kenner calls its "letch towards the forms of classical culture"[9]: its more reflective values, its greater knowledge of its own history, and its acutely self-conscious attitude towards its own history. The deliberate urge towards self-awareness—especially historical self-awareness—not only distinguishes Joyce's civilization from Homer's; it is this same urge that underlies the whole enterprise of a work like

Ulysses or *Finnegans Wake*,[10] exhibiting itself in just those ironical juxtapositions of different ages that delight the critics—as in the critics' own delight. The characters of *Ulysses* naturally and properly possess a sense of the past, of the "recurrence and continuity of human experience",[11] a sensitivity to time which is the peculiar burden of the modern consciousness.

The superimposed analogy of the Homeric world thus adds to the material, the range of reference, of the action. It helps define modern values and the particular ways in which the modern individual is related to his society, by offering the contrast with another age, while at the same time it draws our attention to the recurrences and continuities of human experience. The actions of the duo-protagonists of *Ulysses* express, like all actions imaginatively shaped and realized, a meaning wider than that of their immediate case: this is their artistic universality. But it is the peculiar nature of these protagonists to possess a partial understanding of the temporal circumstances in which they act. They become aware of themselves and the significance of their personal situations in their consciousness of time. The critical attitudes of both Bloom and Stephen towards their society, no less than their efforts towards personal freedom from inner disharmonies, force them to consider the positions they occupy in history—the history of their society and their own—because the past, as they fully realize, produced what is and conditions what may be. The Homeric parallel does little more than provide a sense of temporal perspectives, but though they are longer perspectives than the characters possess, they are nevertheless projected from the concerns and predicaments of the characters. The difference between the two worlds of the parallel is not the simple gap between noble Ideal and sordid Reality; it is the gap of time, which brings recurrence and change, fruition as well as decay.

The reader's perception of these temporal perspectives is greater than that of the characters to the extent to which he is more aware than they of the various parallels and analogies—indeed, one might say to the extent to which the parallels are external to the action. As we have already noticed, some of the parallels other than the Homeric one occur to the characters themselves; even so, the reader is much more aware of their implications; *and the Homeric parallel is outside the characters' con-*

sciousness altogether. The result of this is that the various parallels also change and add to the material by cumulatively and gradually transmuting our view of it into another mode. They "universalize" the action by making all ages, all history, its subject-matter. The action becomes a "myth" (with a universal imaginative meaning) about "heroes" in a universal spatio-temporal setting—ancient Greece, Calvary, Elizabethan England, the War in Heaven, ancient Ireland, Crete, the world of the Wandering Jew, of Sinbad, of Don Giovanni, the solar system, and Dublin, 1904.[12] All ages become as one. But here, again, the effect of the parallels can only be understood by understanding the dramatic action, for this "mythical" vision also originates in, and is projected from, the characters' acts and their own vision of themselves and their world. As they reach the limits of their self-understanding, we are led beyond them, not rejecting their vision but transcending it—transcending, indeed, the limitations of all process, of all human activity in the flux of history.

II

Both to Bloom and to Stephen the past wears a Janus face. They are both exiles from the traditions of their respective races, yet both are inextricably bound to those traditions. Both are in bondage to a personal past, but only in the understanding and acceptance of that past lies freedom from it. Time is the gap between potentiality and actuality, separating each from his past, from himself as he seeks to become, and from the other. It is also the dimension in which the possibility of reconciliation may be realized. Within these broad similarities, however, their individual consciousness of the past is markedly different. They are juxtaposed, counterposed, complementing each other in this as in temperament and talents. As it presents itself to Stephen, his relationship to time is one of conflict—a conflict between the necessitating conditions of the past and the no less necessitating demands of his future as an artist. His sense of this conflict largely defines his consciousness of his present self. He feels himself at a crisis of his destiny, and his continual awareness of this points to, and helps define, the significance of his actions on Bloomsday. Bloom also exhibits a conflict in his consciousness of time, but it is more a conflict of emotions. For him, only the past represents hope, beauty, happiness; the future seems a blank. His only son is dead; his daughter, possibly about to follow in Molly's footsteps, has left home; his marriage seems to have foundered on his psychological impotence, and the distance between him and Molly is only increasing. The present is the point of intersection for all this emotional traffic. The expected, inevitable act of adultery between Molly and Blazes Boylan at four o'clock in the afternoon sharpens, as it represents, Bloom's personal predicament; his developing attitude towards it focuses his attitude to life as a whole. But his attitude is best understood in contrast to Stephen's.

Stephen's sense of vocation and his search for self-realization as a man and an artist involves certain rejections—personal and social no less than aesthetic, Mulligan and Irish nationalism as well as "Platonic" romanticism. The violence of these negative attitudes in him reveals an element of fear—both of the dead hand of the past and of the uncertainty of the future. Yet if there is an obvious instability about him, a nervous explosiveness, it is properly to be seen as the price of his struggle towards a positive, stable, free and fruitful maturity of spirit. To achieve that *stasis* he must achieve the necessary insight into his own nature as it has been conditioned and grown. The self must be understood in depth: hence the meaning he gives to "parallax", an idea that also haunts Bloom during the day:

Lynx eye. Must get glasses. Broke them yesterday. Sixteen years ago. Distance. The eye sees all flat. . . . Brain thinks. Near: far. Ineluctable modality of the visible. . . . (529/546)

More than that, he must also, as he realizes, understand the proper relationship between art and life, the way an impersonal art may grow, through the maturation of the author, out of the very process of life itself. He tries to express this conception in a teleological theory of history, according to which life moves towards its own static epiphany in art.[13] His belief in such a process seems tentative as yet, merely notional, but it is nevertheless the real basis of his trust in the future and his one positive weapon against his difficulties, uncertainties, even dangers.

The continuous dramatic interaction of these issues is established in the first three chapters (the "Telemachia"), which are closely linked by this common theme and develop its implications.

At the beginning, Stephen's crisis is portrayed in terms of his rejection of Mulligan, or rather of the image of him that Mulligan wishes to impose. Against Mulligan's easy compromises with the material values he affects to despise, and his possessiveness and aesthetic provinciality—both of which are neatly exemplified in *his* naming of the tower in which they live the *omphalos* (5, 15/9, 19)—Stephen opposes his scorn in return, a scrupulous evasion of commitment, and a contemptuous compliance with Mulligan's desire for the key to the Martello tower. When Mulligan (and the peasant milk-woman whose respect for him identifies the nature of his power) usurp what Stephen regards as his place, he is ready to go. The key is, of course, a symbol of his attachment to a centre; he is willing enough to give it up when he feels the centre (home and country) usurped, but he goes with the burden of bitterness. And as Wyndham Lewis and Mr Kenner have pointed out, his emotional attitudes do seem rather theatrical. In this first chapter he gives the impression of posturing—an impression only the more heightened by the contrast with his more private attitudes as they are revealed in the third chapter ("Proteus"): the rigid and somewhat operatic posture largely dissolves once we see him from the inside. Here, in "Telemachus", he is presenting an image of himself to the world; but he is presenting it in deliberate opposition to those Mulligan and others wish him to adopt. His own image may be false and immature; theirs, he feels, would involve a fundamental lie to his true nature and vocation. "To discover the mode of life or of art whereby [his] spirit could express itself in unfettered freedom" (*Portrait*, p. 280): his own youthful image, inadequate as it is already beginning to appear to him, at least offers a negative ideal, and he uses it as a shield. If he cannot be much more positive, he does know what he does not want.[14]

The waves of his personal crisis spread wider than the immediate struggle with Mulligan, however. For one thing, he is entangled with a kinetic remorse, a sense of guilt arising from his rejection of Roman Catholicism and the fear that his rejection may have contributed to his mother's death. This, it must be said, is an aspect of his character that does seem wholly theatrical, an unpleasant combination of self-accusation, self-pity and pride. He can evidently see through the current "romantic" and pretentious twaddle about Ireland, as his speculations about the milk-woman suggest (12/15). But although he savours that sentimentality with a dry irony, it is in fact very like many of his own thoughts about his mother:

In a dream, silently, she had come to him, her wasted body within its loose graveclothes giving off an odour of wax and rosewood, her breath bent over him with mute secret words, a faint odour of wetted ashes.

Her glazing eyes, staring out of death, to shake and bend my soul. On me alone. The ghostcandle to light her agony. Ghostly light on the tortured face. Her hoarse loud breath rattling in horror, while all prayed on their knees. Her eyes on me to strike me down. *Liliata rutilantium te confessorum turma circumdet: iubilantium te virginum chorus excipiat.* (8/12)

Yet it is worth noticing that, even despite the self-pity, the unfortunately Gothic horrors, and the over-elaborate cadences (which it is hard to be quite sure whether to ascribe to Stephen or to Joyce), the passage does conclude with an instinctive, and significantly direct, cry for freedom and life:

Ghoul! Chewer of corpses!
No, mother. Let me be and let me live.

It is hardly a conscious critical response, an appeal to ideals positively held; Stephen is too divided for that. It is still a kinetic reaction, but it is very much in the right direction.

Similarly with the other false images of himself: he regards them, as he had regarded them in the *Portrait*, as nets to be avoided. The Englishman, Haines, comments,

—After all, I should think you are able to free yourself. You are your own master, it seems to me.
—I am the servant of two masters, Stephen said, an English and an Italian. . . .
—And a third, Stephen said, there is who wants me for odd jobs. (18/22)

As Haines replies, "It seems history is to blame". To Stephen the past does seem almost overwhelmingly determinant. He sees tradition not as a liberating force but (with a more intimate knowledge of some traditions than has every *laudator temporis acti*) as constricting and deadening. Yet again, although his freedom seems little more than the minimum of mere escape, he is shown groping towards something more. Carefully placed beside this conversation with Haines is a passage about a man drowned in the bay, which reinforces the point already implicit in Stephen's rejection of possible masters. Throughout *Ulysses* the sea appears as a symbol of the chaotic flux of experience, the element[15]; drowning is defeat, submergence, the death of the spirit in the overwhelming flood of kinetic appetencies. Stephen fears death by water. The drowned man objectifies his fear of suffocation, his need to rise above the waves, to swim in the element—in other words, to achieve a free *stasis* of spirit by understanding and accepting himself, his predicament, and his necessities. He must, as he clearly realizes, launch out. When the chapter ends, he is literally homeless. We do not know where he is going, nor does he.

The second chapter explores the historical aspects of his situation further. It begins by crystallizing our feeling, and Stephen's too, about his "victory" over Mulligan and his other potential masters: it is not enough, not decisive, indeed Pyrrhic. And the main theme of the chapter is Stephen's hostility to, and fear of, the past. Time seems to him only to repeat itself in "the same room and hour, the same wisdom. . . . Three nooses round me here" (27/31), or in the repeated experience of the Jews:

Time surely would scatter all. A hoard heaped by the roadside: plundered and passing on. Their eyes knew the years of wandering and, patient, knew the dishonours of their flesh.
—Who has not? Stephen said. (31/35)

In short, "history was a tale like any other too often heard" (22/26). The individual seems helplessly bound to the pattern; the "dear might of Him that walked the waves" does not exist for Stephen (23/27). He can see as little in the present as he can see in Elizabethan England—"an age of exhausted whoredom groping for its god" (195/204). The ages, as John Eglinton puts it, seem only to "succeed one another" without change or hope. So conceived, history must seem a nightmare.

—History, Stephen said, is a nightmare from which I am trying to awake.
From the playfield the boys raised a shout. A whirring whistle: goal. What if that nightmare gave you a back kick?
—The ways of the Creator are not our ways, Mr Deasy said. All history moves towards one great goal, the manifestation of God.

Stephen jerked his thumb towards the window, saying:
—That is God.
Hooray! Ay! Whrrwhee!
—What? Mr Deasy asked.
—A shout in the street, Stephen answered, shrugging his shoulders.
(31-2/35)

Stephen cannot accept that history moves to any supernatural end outside itself. If God exists, He manifests Himself here and now, in all life however pointless or trivial it may seem. History is not like a detective story; there are no comforting revelations to follow. When Stephen uses teleological arguments himself later on, he does so only analogously for another and very different conclusion.

His obsessive fear of the past is partly balanced, however, by a different strain of thought about history. If past events limit the present and the future, they also, as acts of will, liberate possibilities into the world of fact. Stephen ponders this dual aspect of history in Aristotelian terms:

Had Pyrrhus not fallen by a beldam's hand in Argos or Julius Caesar not been knifed to death. They are not to be thought away. Time has branded them and fettered they are lodged in the room of the infinite possibilities they have ousted. But can those have been possible seeing that they never were? Or was that only possible which came to pass? Weave, weaver of the wind. (22: cf. 182/26: cf. 191)

And during the schoolboys' reading of *Lycidas*, the grounds of hope occur to him: time is not only a burden, it is also a means to the fruition and fulfilment of the soul in action. As he tells himself a little later, he could, if he willed it, break free of his present nooses (27/31)—and in fact he does. History involves more than the ossification of life; it is also dynamic:

It must be a movement then, an actuality of the possible as possible. Aristotle's phrase formed itself within the gabbled verses and floated out into the studious silence of the library of Sainte Geneviève where he had read, sheltered from the sin of Paris, night by night. By his elbow a delicate Siamese conned a handbook of strategy. Fed and feeding brains about me: under glowlamps, impaled, with faintly beating feelers: and in my mind's darkness a sloth of the underworld, reluctant, shy of brightness, shifting her dragon scaly folds. Thought is the thought of thought. Tranquil brightness. The soul is in a manner all that is: the soul is the form of forms. Tranquillity sudden, vast, candescent: form of forms. (23/26-7)

157

The relevance of this (even the Siamese student) to his moral problems as an artist, his desire to mature and freely and creatively to act, requires no emphasis. Mr Deasy's ambiguous wisdom confirms the implications of Stephen's drift: "to learn one must be humble. But life is the great teacher" (32/36). For Stephen's situation, that cliché is the wisdom of Nestor.

"Proteus" develops these implications still further, both in Stephen's reflections about them and in the dramatic presentation of the way his reflections themselves progress. Joyce's writing here has often been praised for its sensitive delicacy, but it is not always realized how much more it is than that, how finely and firmly the chapter is organized as a poetic, dramatic unit. Generally speaking, the chapter explores the Protean transformations of matter in time—matter, as we should expect from Stephen's aesthetic theory, both as object, the "ineluctable modality of the visible and audible", apprehensible only in the condition of flux,[16] and as subject, Stephen himself. In the one aspect, Stephen is seeking the principles of change and the underlying substance of sensory experience; in the other, he is seeking his self among its temporal manifestations. Consequently, he seems narcissistic, self-conscious, *lisant au livre de lui-même* like Hamlet. Yet, although he is still egocentric and still in uneasy kinetic relationship to his environment and himself, he exhibits in this chapter more of the incipient irony he had displayed at the end of the *Portrait*, a dawning capacity to stand off from himself and criticize what he sees, and concomitantly, to observe external reality with a certain detachment. His potentiality of growth is perhaps here most clearly visible. The humourless and priggish aesthete appears much less certain about his poses; he has after all, we discover, some sense of the ridiculous and some glimmerings of maturer values. "Proteus", in fact, is the crucial chapter for our conception of him. Without it, his other appearances in the book would hardly convince us of his solidity or interest as a protagonist; as it is, they are all enriched and qualified by his presentation here.

The setting on the sea-shore has an obvious metaphorical significance. Stephen speculates at the edge of life about the meanings in, and beyond, the immediate sensible world—his material as an artist. Bloom, who finds himself on the same shore in the evening, can make nothing of it:

All these rocks with lines and scars and letters. O, those transparent! Besides they don't know. What is the meaning of that other world. I called you naughty boy because I do not like.
[He draws with a stick: I. AM. A.]
No room. Let it go.
Mr Bloom effaced the letters with his slow boot. Hopeless thing sand. Nothing grows in it. All fades. . . . (364/375)

But Stephen has the intellectual and imaginative capacity to read the "signatures of all things", to penetrate the diaphanous sensible world and the ineluctable *nacheinander* and *nebeneinander* placed before the individual consciousness, the world that is "there all the time without you: and ever shall be, world without end" (33-4/38).

His thoughts turn to the permanent patterns of change—in particular, to the pattern of the life-cycle within which the individual's destiny is played out (35/39). He scorns theosophical hocus-pocus about the navelcord, but he acknowledges the common bond of continuity it represents. For him—and for Bloom, too—womankind represents the permanent force and pattern of biological history: birth, copulation, family and death. Indeed, when we recall the figure of Molly Bloom, it is true to say that this is one of the constant symbolic values of the book as a whole. Women do not figure in it as people but as biological symbols. And the polarity some of Joyce's critics have observed between Stephen ("intellectual life") and Molly ("biological life") already exists in Stephen's own point of view—especially in the rather abstractly "deep" speculations about Woman in which both he and Bloom sometimes indulge.

The first transformation of "matter" lies in the changing substance of Stephen's thoughts from the life-cycle in general towards his family and its particular life (35-6/39-40), and equally in his rejection of their "paralysis": "Houses of decay, mine, his and all. . . . Come out of them, Stephen. Beauty is not there." His father, as he says to Bloom later, is "all too Irish" (585/607), and his criticism here includes the whole "hundred-headed rabble of the cathedral close" (36/40), the general state of Ireland.

Swift provides the link to the second transformation—Stephen's "temptation" to enter the priesthood, or, more generally, to achieve and exercise magical powers; and, correspondingly, in

159

"subjective" terms, his rejection of the possibility in both its religious and aesthetic aspects:

> Cousin Stephen, you will never be a saint. . . . You were awfully holy, weren't you? . . . On the top of the Howth tram alone crying to the rain: *naked women*! What about that, eh?
> What about what? What else were they invented for?
> . . . You bowed to yourself in the mirror, stepping forward to applaud earnestly, striking face. . . . No-one saw: tell no-one. Books you were going to write with letters for titles. . . . Remember your epiphanies on green oval leaves, deeply deep. . . . Someone was to read them there after a few thousand years, a mahamanvantara. Pico della Mirandola like. Ay, very like a whale. When one reads these strange pages of one long gone one feels that one is at one with one who once . . . (37/41)

The sharp juxtaposition of this mystico-Symbolist nonsense with the "grainy sand" in the following line adds Joyce's endorsement to Stephen's self-criticism; clearly, we are not invited to take the aesthetic attitude Stephen parodies very seriously. Nor, for that matter, are we Stephen's third transformation, which begins with the sight of a "maze of dark cunning nets" (38/42). He himself punctures the attitude of the *esprit libre* he had adopted on his flight to Paris: "My latin quarter hat. God, we simply must dress the character" (38/42).

With his latest transformation—failed missionary to Europe, bedraggled Icarus—he is naturally less detached and less critical. He recognizes his failure, but the recognition is qualified by his sense of undefeated pride:

> His feet marched in sudden proud rhythm over the sand furrows, along by the boulders of the south wall. He stared at them proudly, piled stone mammoth skulls. Gold light on sea, on sand, on boulders. The sun is there, the slender trees, the lemon houses. (39/43)

Despite the earlier *débâcle*, Paris still represents something of value to him, though he also recognizes the meaning for himself in Kevin Egan, exiled revolutionary in Paris, forgotten, remembering Sion. But all his retrospection leads him finally to a crucial decision which involves a crucial perception:

> He has the key. I will not sleep there when this night comes. . . . Take all, keep all. My soul walks with me, form of forms. (41/45)

The decision to leave again is more than a recognition that he has been forced out; it is based on a firmer knowledge of what his nature positively seeks—the discovery of itself in a deeper experience of ordinary life.

His self-identification with the introspectively heroic Hamlet is the last transformation of matter portrayed. The significance of the parallel is mainly suggested and dramatically qualified by Stephen's theory in "Scylla and Charybdis", but it is also partly qualified (and naturally it can only be partly) by his own self-critical reflections here. The significant point emerges from his fear of attack by a dog on the beach: "Respect his liberty. You will not be master of others or their slave" (42/46). He rejects all violence. The nightmare of history is within him—

Famine, plague and slaughter. Their blood is in me, their lusts my waves. I moved among them on the frozen Liffey, that I, a changeling, among the spluttering resin fires. I spoke to no-one: none to me (42/46)

As he says at the end of "Circe", it is *within* that he must kill the king and the priest, symbols of spiritual tyranny and slavery. His means to freedom are still silence, exile, and cunning—the evasion of action and violence—but they also seem like cowardice. He wonders if he too is not another "pretender": he fears drowning, he is not a strong swimmer; he hates water; life may well overwhelm him. In short, ironic self-scrutiny has begun to temper his will.

His reflections now turn reflectively upon themselves. He identifies himself with the sniffing dog, "tatters", "poor dogsbody", fox who has buried his mother under a hollybush (24/28); he sees himself "vulturing the dead", "looking for something lost in a past life"—

Dogskull, dogsniff, eyes on the ground, moves to one great goal. (43/47)

His search for the self beneath the protean flux of life concludes with such partial knowledge as he is capable of discovering and with a recognition of the nature of his search. The future can be only prefigured: in a symbolic dream ("That man led me, spoke. I was not afraid"); in his adolescent longing for contact with the female tides of life[17]; in his continual effort to find his self in reality yet avoid the sterility of solipsism, to grasp the significance

F   161

of the sensible world, where subject and object unite by "parallax":

Hold hard. Coloured on a flat: yes, that's right. Flat I see, then think distance, near, far, flat I see, east, back. Ah, see now. Falls back suddenly, frozen in stereoscope. Click does the trick. (45/49)

The scribbled note for his poem is part of the action of the chapter, a transformation that transcends all those that precede it, an emblem of the "great goal" of his process of self-scrutiny, a symbol in little of *Ulysses* itself. History, understood, moves towards the goal of art, but art is itself a symbol of the wider spiritual life it ideally embodies. The phrase from Yeats that Stephen quotes—"and no more turn aside and brood"[18]— signalizes his progress to a precarious *stasis*, or at least to a less kinetic frame of mind, in which he tries to express the sound and unending movement of water, his sense of the life into which he must plunge (46/50). That his present *stasis* is precariously unstable is implicit in the way he tries to accept his fear and the necessary rôle of death in life; the language reflects an intention, an effort, more than achieved assurance:

God becomes man becomes fish becomes barnacle goose becomes featherbed mountain. Dead breaths I living breathe, tread dead dust, devour a urinous offal from all dead. Hauled stark over the gunwale he breathes upward the stench of his green grave, his leprous nosehole snoring to the sun.
A seachange this, brown eyes saltblue. . . . Just you give it a fair trial. . . .
. . . Evening will find itself.
. . . Yes, evening will find itself in me, without me. All days make their end. . . . (47/51)

This is a passage less important for the symbolic relationships it suggests (father—sea—life, urine—death, etc.) than for the dramatic significance of its tone. Stephen's trust in the future is no mere involuntary drifting with the stream. As the rest of the chapter has established, he has some appreciation of the direction he must take and of the importance of growing towards it as well as simply willing it. His attitude still remains tentative, largely a passive, but watchful, waiting. In order to crystallize its positive value, Joyce must direct us outside Stephen's consciousness, and this he does with the "objectively" rendered episode of the ship

at the very end of the chapter. Revealed to Stephen's significantly "rere regardant" gaze, her sails "brailed up on the
crosstrees, homing, upstream, silently moving, a silent ship"
(47/51). With the final hint that he too is silently moving home-
ward, Stephen is dismissed, and the stage is set for Bloom.

We do not meet Stephen again until his brief appearance at
the *Freeman's* office ("Aeolus") and the more important scene in
the library ("Scylla and Charybdis"). In the latter, the significances established by his earlier appearances, together with
those established around Bloom, are combined and woven
together by Stephen's theory about Shakespeare and *Hamlet*.
The protagonists are thus brought together precisely in the
argument of art, an argument which is also the first major
projection, as we have seen, of the historical and mythical
dimension of the action. But even in the earlier scene at the
newspaper office, where Bloom and Stephen merely pass each
other, this is already adumbrated in different terms. History and
art are again the main themes of Stephen's thoughts. To a lesser
extent, they are the main themes of everyone else's thoughts too,
but the chapter places Stephen's *against* those of the others. They
see history as the conflict of Irish-Catholic ideals with English-
imperial ideals, of Greek with Roman, of Light with Darkness,
of Right with Wrong. To them, Pyrrhus was the last champion
of the ancient world, "loyal to a lost cause" (124/132). The turn
of the conversation from history to assassination and murder
serves to underline their assumption of unending violence. So
does Bloom's earlier reflection on the Old Testament conception
of Justice: "Justice it means but it's everybody eating everyone
else. That's what life is after all" (114/121); but Bloom in the
chapter as a whole is placed against the group of Dubliners
rather by personal exclusion than by conscious opposition to their
values. And Stephen's opposition emerges only when the
Dubliners' assumptions about art emerge. To them art means
primarily rhetoric, at best an art committed to kinetic ends;
Stephen reflects on Dante's rhymes (129/136-7).[19] "We make out
of the quarrel with others rhetoric," as Yeats observed, "but
out of the quarrel with ourselves, poetry." Stephen's conception
of the proper relation between art and history is different even
from that the sympathetic MacHugh ascribes to him. After
reciting a famous speech comparing the Irish with the Jews

exiled in Egypt and glorifying the heroism of Moses, MacHugh turns to Stephen:

—Come along, Stephen, the professor said. That is fine, isn't it? It has the prophetic vision. *Fuit Ilium!* The sack of windy Troy. King-doms of this world. The masters of the Mediterranean are fellaheen today.
The first newsboy came pattering down the stairs at their heels and rushed out into the street, yelling:
—Racing special!
Dublin. I have much, much to learn. (134/142)

Nevertheless, it is to MacHugh that Stephen "dares" recite his bitterly ironical "Pisgah Sight of Palestine or the Parable of the Plums", and it is MacHugh who perceives Stephen's own kinetic state: "none could tell if he were bitterer against others or against himself" (138/147). For all his rejection of an art that serves the violent, ambiguous, corrupted world of history, and that dies when its purpose is performed, and despite his own determination to create only out of the inmost depths of experience, he is still, as he realizes himself, far from the capacities of the true artist.

In fact the portrait of Stephen in the rest of the book charts the tension between his present *kinesis* and his potentialities for the future. He is in an uneasy, chrysalid state between two worlds. The whole of "Scylla and Charybdis", as we have seen, reveals his condition, and when we catch a glimpse of him next in "The Wandering Rocks", his inner confusion and bondage lead to a momentary suicidal impulse. He feels himself caught uncertainly by his vocation—"you who wrest old images from the burial earth!"—by bitterness at the sterility of his present world, by the unceasing conflict between the mechanical dynamo without and the heart throbbing within:

I between them. Where? Between two roaring worlds where they swirl, I. Shatter them, one and both. But stun myself too in the blow.

As Mr Kenner points out, Hamlet is an ambiguous hero.[20] But Stephen's impulse is significantly qualified and succeeded:

Shatter me you who can. Bawd and butcher, were the words. I say! Not yet awhile. A look around. (229/238)

The artist capable of detaching himself from his world sufficiently to write *Dubliners* is still in growth; the freedom of the *Portrait* is ten years off; the mature artist capable of perceiving the life even in the apparent sterility of Dublin is even more distant. Mulligan and Haines are partly right, but essentially wrong, about Stephen (235-6/244-6). He does lack balance; his wits were driven astray by visions of hell. But Mulligan's remark that "he will never capture the Attic note. The note of Swinburne, of all poets, the white death and the ruddy birth", that "he can never be a poet. The joy of creation", is only a shrewdhead's guess, not the truth. Neither he nor Haines realizes that Stephen's fixed idea is not quite the sense of retribution, but rather the sense of destiny, the burden of vocation. Once again Joyce uses the symbol of the homing ship (this time in conjunction with a symbol involving Bloom as well), together with the more ordinary means of comic satire, in order to place the two young men:

. . . Buck Mulligan slit a steaming scone in two and plastered butter over its smoking pith. He bit off a soft piece hungrily.
—Ten years, he said, chewing and laughing. He is going to write something in ten years.
—Seems along way off, Haines said, thoughtfully lifting his spoon. Still, I shouldn't wonder if he did after all.
He tasted a spoonful from the creamy cone of his cup.
—This is real Irish cream I take it, he said with forbearance. I don't want to be imposed on.
Elijah, skiff, light crumpled throwaway, sailed eastward by flanks of ships and trawlers, amid an archipelago of corks beyond new Wapping street past Benson's ferry, and by the threemasted schooner *Rosevean* from Bridgwater with bricks. (236/245-6)

We are thus prepared for the desertion of Stephen by these "friends" at the end of "Oxen of the Sun". During the drinking party in that chapter, Stephen's thoughts revert to the conversation with Deasy in "Nestor" and also, indirectly, to the central aesthetic theory in "Scylla and Charybdis". Joyce's narrative technique—suited at least to render the obfuscation of drunkenness if not the development of the human embryo—makes it difficult to tell exactly what is going on, but what Stephen seems to be trying to express is his conception of art as the final cause of history, the growth of a timeless world of meaning out of the process of life. His objection to contraception—the "sin against the Holy Ghost", upon which the chapter is supposed to be constructed[21]—is apparently the orthodox Catholic one,

except that he significantly refers to Nature instead of God: "we
are means to those small creatures within us and nature has other
ends than we" (372/383). A little later, however, it becomes clear
that this teleological notion has another significance for Stephen:
it is art to which life moves as its end—"in the spirit of the maker
all flesh that passes becomes the word that shall not pass away"
(374/385). God is once again his symbol for the artist in the
maturity of imaginative insight. And once again his sense of
vocation is qualified by his sense of immaturity. His self is still
hidden from him in the dark backward of time; he cannot
discern "from what region of remoteness the whatness of our
whoness hath fetched his whenceness" (376/388). As his fearful
reaction to the crack of thunder reveals, he has still "in his bosom
a spike named Bitterness" which all of Bloom's calm rationality
cannot assuage. He still goes in fear of the religion he has
renounced (377-8/388-9); the only Word he can apparently utter
as yet is—"Burke's!" (404/415). In his drunken daze at the end
of the chapter, the noise in the street of a firecart seems a warning
that God may well have a "coughmixture with a punch in it for
you, my friend, in his backpocket" (409/421). The obscurity of
the future holds a threat no less than that of the past.

In "Circe", Stephen plays a subordinate rôle to Bloom, for the
chapter is to Bloom very much what "Proteus" is to Stephen.
But for both equally it is a descent and a purgation. With
Stephen it also represents a break in the pattern of his presentation in the earlier chapters. He enters with an echo of the very
beginning of the book, an echo of the Mass, but here its significance is almost the opposite of Mulligan's version in the first
chapter. Mulligan's was a perversion, and at the end of "Circe"
he and Haines appear appropriately celebrating a full-scale
Black Mass.[22] Stephen's version recalls Easter, resurrection,
rebirth (412/424); the gesture that is "the universal language",
the "first entelechy", is the beckoning invitation to love—
though here it is made by the whores (412-3/425). In this place
at this time it is an invitation to unreason, degradation, death of
the spirit; but out of that death finally emerges life of the spirit.
As Stephen instinctively perceives, the altars of life are varied:
"David's that is Circe's or what am I saying Ceres' altar" (478/
493). Although his sense of the cycles of life is much less assured
than Bloom's, it underlies his consciousness nevertheless, in

characteristically intellectual and uncertainly ironic terms: 'Jew-greek is greekjew. Extremes meet. Death is the highest form of life. Bah!" (479/493). (Stephen's irony, significantly, is directed at his *own* way of putting his perception.) And it is at this point that he becomes dimly aware of the relevance of Bloom to his aesthetic theory, aware that he is not so negligible as he seems and that art is the meeting-place of different kinds of heroism:

What went forth to the ends of the world to traverse not itself. God, the sun, Shakespeare, a commercial traveller, having itself traversed in reality itself, becomes that self. Wait a moment. Wait a second. Damn that fellow's noise in the street. Self which it itself was ineluctably preconditioned to become. *Ecco!* (479/494)

The bonds of kinship between himself and Bloom now begin to emerge more clearly, even in his own mind. He ponders the relation of fundamental and dominant (479/494), of his and Bloom's ages (533/549); as they both gaze into the mirror the face of Shakespeare seems to appear—a young man ("beardless"), in kinetic bondage ("rigid . . . in paralysis"), yet triumphant ("crowned") in the (artistic) "reflection" of the antlers of his dishonour (536/553); and he remembers again his dream of the future (540/557).

As his bondage is tight, so his affirmations of freedom are correspondingly violent. His first cry of affirmation in "Circe" echoes the pride and wilful determination of "Proteus"—his Paris flight was not in vain: "No, I flew. My foes beneath me. And ever shall be. World without end. . . . *Pater!* Free!" (540/557). His second is equally a mere kinetic assertion—his rejection of his mother's religion and of the agony of remorse he has tried to reject all day. He joins in a frenzied dance of fantastic symbols (542 ff./559 ff.), a dance of life that has become in this place and to Stephen a "dance of death" (546/564). His mother's shade appears, appeals to him: "Repent! O, the fire of hell!" (549/566). He cries a "heroic" reply, "*Nothung!*", smashes at the chandelier, and rushes, frenzied, out of the brothel. But this is not the real climax of the chapter, much less of the book; it is merely Stephen's most violent act. As an act it solves nothing and reveals nothing except Stephen's determination—and failure—to get clear of his obsessions. Nor is the real climax his subsequent encounter with the two soldiers who knock him down, and the visionary struggle

167

between Reason and Unreason, non-violence and suicidal strife, that culminates in the Black Mass (564-6/582-4). This episode does restore Stephen to something like sobriety; he does explicitly recognize that his struggle is a spiritual one: "Struggle for life is the law of existence. . . . (*He taps his brow.*) But in here it is I must kill the priest and the king" (556/574). Moreover, he recognizes the necessary limits of his anti-nationalism: "But I say: Let my country die for me. Up to the present it has done so. I don't want it to die. Damn death. Long live life!" (558/576). He recognizes violence for what it is, "this feast of pure reason" (566/585). But, as we have seen, he has felt these things all along; it does not need the whole of "Circe" to reveal them. The climax of the chapter is not in Stephen's actions or thoughts at all—it is in Bloom's. Stephen's purification consists merely of being shocked into a proper recognition of his own extravagant and blundering *kinesis*, a restoration of human dignity, but a restoration limited by his generally kinetic state. He is not a changed man at the end of the chapter, only a rather soberer one. But he has gained one thing—an unconscious, instinctive sense of kinship with Bloom.

Part of their kinship is their common attitude to history and the patterns of time. During the fight in which Stephen is knocked down, Bloom, with phrases more appropriate to Stephen, appeals to the whore standing by, "Speak you! Are you struck dumb? You are the link between nations and generations. Speak, woman, sacred lifegiver!" (563/582) Though the ironies are pointed, Bloom, like Stephen, sees all the agitations of history contained by the larger patterns of biological necessity; as Stephen says, "*amor matris*, subjective and objective genitive, may be the only true thing in life" (196/205). As the two sit later in the coffee-stall, Bloom recounts to Stephen his argument about history with the Citizen:

I resent violence or intolerance in any shape or form. It never reaches anything or stops anything. A revolution must come on the due instalments plan. It's a patent absurdity on the face of it to hate people because they live round the corner and speak another verna-cular, so to speak. (605/627)

Again, although this is clearly not the wisdom of this world, Stephen finds no difficulty in agreeing. He sees in Bloom a victim of the nightmare of history, and his perception crystallizes one of the major parallels established by the action:

> —*Ex quibus*, Stephen mumbled in a noncommittal accent, their two or four eyes conversing, *Christus* or Bloom his name is, or, after all, any other, *secundum carnem*. (604/627)

When, in "Ithaca", Bloom chants a scrap of the Jewish anthem, Stephen hears "in a profound ancient male unfamiliar melody the accumulation of the past", and he senses in his companion the concealed identity of the substance of God (650/673-4). The figure of the Sufferer, the victim of history, unites them. They are identical in their effort to free themselves from violence, unreason, mere kinetic reaction to external forces, and to live truly as themselves. Each has his own particular problem, each his particular kind of solution—Stephen in art, Bloom in responsively living life as it is. But Stephen's depends on Bloom's as its precondition, and for all his crudity in intellectual and aesthetic matters, Bloom, in his concern for Stephen, does fasten on the dangers his present bitterness and self-division hold for his future. Where Stephen sees in him merely a representative and victim of the past, a view of him that is only a part of the truth, he sees in Stephen a son, "the predestination of a future", and hears "the traditional accent of the ecstasy of catastrophe" (650/674). It is not their disagreement over politics that worries him in the cabmen's shelter; it is his knowledge of "cultured fellows that promised so brilliantly, nipped in the bud of premature decay, and nobody to blame but themselves" (607/629). His freedom and maturity stand as actuality to Stephen's mere potentiality; his wisdom to Stephen's knowledge; his love to Stephen's bitterness; his acceptance of life to Stephen's uneasy division; his *stasis* to Stephen's *kinesis*; his waking to Stephen's nightmare.

Stephen remains split: bitter at the world that resists not only his vocation in art, but also his *conception* of art; bitter at the necessity for struggle; bitter at his own sterility. His goal seems clear enough to him, yet there is one crucial vagueness about it— he wants to meet and master "life" but he has no real idea of what the word means. His bitterness and immaturity shield him from it, and so increase his frustration. He feels himself at the mercy of a hostile world, conditioned by a past he wants only to reject. But he at least partly realizes that until he understands and, in understanding, accepts it, he cannot be free of it. His preoccupation with history is thus not merely a pretentious irrelevance, nor does Joyce develop it for the sake of modish aesthetic effects with Time. History, for Stephen, focuses on himself—it is his own history, his own self, that is the nightmare; his groping speculations about it are his means to the freedom of self-knowledge. That our knowledge of his history is greater than his, that we perceive historical and mythic parallels (such as Telemachus) that he cannot, or take his parallels (such as Hamlet) in a sense rather different from his, means only that, as he recognizes in his soberer moments, he cannot yet know himself. When he does, he is the author of *Ulysses*, who points out (though undoubtedly with an excessive zeal) the parallels to us from his position above and beyond his handiwork.

III

If we should wonder what Stephen means by "life", the figure of Bloom provides a large part of the answer. Unlike Stephen, Bloom is not much aware of his own individual character nor is he concerned with establishing any special relationship between himself and "life". He *is* alive. Of course, as we have seen, we cannot take him as fully alive, an unqualified hero, but his common humanity does represent that "life" against which Stephen is placed.

Bloom engages with everyday life at many points—that is the primary and obvious significance of the Odyssean parallel: he is an "allroundman" (222/231). More important, however, is the way in which he engages—the sense in which his completeness is a sign of moral vitality and his consciousness the expression of a man truly, if not ideally, alive. For all his comparative un-selfconsciousness he is not unreflective; for all his absorption in everyday matters, he is far from completely absorbed by them. His active consciousness is the clearest basis of his moral stature and his dramatic significance; he is a modern Odysseus, express-ing himself less in outward action than in inward awareness. Much of his pathos, much of the dramatic irony, derives from this limitation of his capacity for physical action, but neither this, nor the limitations of his intelligence and sensibility, destroy his fundamental dignity. This dignity, however, lies ultimately in his un-selfconscious being, in what he *is* unknown to himself, which it is one of Joyce's prime intentions to reveal to us in "Circe" and "Ithaca". The most important difference between Bloom and Stephen is that while Stephen aspires to a special dignity of his own as an artist, he has not achieved it, where Bloom does possess his dignity, and all the more securely because he is never for one moment aware that he does—or that he possesses heroic dimensions.

His first appearance places him in careful *contrast* to Stephen. The first fact we learn about him is his liking for the inner organs of beasts and fowls: "most of all he liked grilled mutton kidneys which gave to his palate a fine tang of faintly scented urine" (48/55). We recall Stephen's reflection on the previous page, at the end of "Proteus": "dead breaths I living breathe, tread dead dust, devour a urinous offal from all dead" (47/51). Where Stephen can slip free of the dead hand of the past and accept the necessity of death only fitfully and with difficulty, Bloom accepts death easily and transforms it into life.[23] One need not solemnly trace the symbolism of offal and urine through the whole book—though it is important to remember that Stephen and Bloom urinate together before they part (663-4/687)—in order to perceive this major difference between the attitude of the two men to the dead past.[24] But so far this is not a realized difference, only the symbol of one dramatically established in the acts and consciousness of Bloom as the action proceeds.

In "Calypso", where Bloom's racial and familial relationships are first outlined, his awareness of them is inevitably his awareness of time. He considers a prospectus for recultivating Palestine; his mind turns to a sudden vision of the Holy Land as barren, exhausted, dead: "Grey horror seared his flesh. . . . Cold oils slid along his veins, chilling his blood: age crusting him with a salt cloak. Well, I am here now." From the horror of the past he turns to the living flesh of the present: "to smell the gentle smoke of tea, fume of the pan, sizzling butter. Be near her ample bedwarmed flesh. Yes, yes" (54/61). This does not represent the whole of his attitude to the past, of course, but already it is clear that he does not agonize in the manner of Stephen.[25] Even when he is immediately reminded that the ample bedwarmed flesh is waiting for Blazes Boylan, and the thought of the future chills him like the thought of the dead Promised Land, he does not remain fixed in his pain. His mind constantly shifts between past, present and future. The little discussion about "metempsychosis" establishes one of the verbal symbols of this movement: they say we have forgotten the lives we are supposed to have lived in the past, Bloom tells Molly; "some say they remember their past lives" (57/64). Bloom himself forgets and remembers as a human being active in the present. If he recalls his ghosts, he salutes them and passes on. Where Stephen fights and struggles and has suicidal impulses, Bloom wears the past, and hence the present, more easily. At the end of "Hades", after he has faced the shadow of death, his thoughts "turn aside and no more brood": "Back to the world again. Enough of this place. . . . Plenty to see and hear and feel yet. Feel live warm beings near you. Let them sleep in their maggoty beds. They are not going to get me this innings. Warm beds: warm fullblooded life" (107/113). He recognizes the savagery of life, the necessity even of killing ("Eat or be eaten. Kill! Kill!" (159/168)), but, unlike Stephen, he can accept this without the knowledge corrupting the springs of action. He moves on always, rejecting the false *stasis* of imprisoning frustration: "Life those chaps out there must have, stuck in the same spot. Irish Lights board. Penance for their sins" (362/372). To Bloom, life presents itself as an inescapable activity, the moral exigencies of which control the influence of the past as much as the influence of the past controls them.

Like Stephen, he recognizes the general patterns that circumscribe the life of the individual, though his awareness has a very different tone: "It's the blood sinking in the earth gives new life. Same idea those jews they said killed the christian boy. Every man his price" (100/107). He preserves the same tone in his reflections about himself too:

June that was too I wooed. The year returns. History repeats itself. . . . Life, love, voyage round your own little world. And now? . . .
All quiet on Howth now. The distant hills seem. Where we. The rhododendrons. I am a fool perhaps. He gets the plums and I the plumstones. Where I come in. All that old hill has seen. Names change: that's all. Lovers: yum yum.
. . . She kissed me. My youth. Never again. Only once it comes. Or hers. Take the train there tomorrow. No. Returning not the same. . . . The new I want. Nothing new under the sun. . . . Think you're

escaping and run into yourself. Longest way round is the shortest way home. . . . All changed. Forgotten. The young are old. . . . (359-60/370-1)

Bloom's pathos here arises from his helpless recognition of ineluctability; it is the helplessness of humanity itself. As the contrasting echoes of Stephen's parable of the plums and of his speculations about the actualization of the self in experience suggest, Bloom's recognition is an experiential one, not a merely theoretical acceptance like Stephen's. For him, the life-cycle, the biological limits of the individual's experience, are a felt part of his actual life. He accepts the universe not because he has found any intellectual formula into which he can fit it, but for the more compelling reason that he simply has to. Inasmuch as he does so, moreover, he represents one of the values *Joyce* expresses in the work. Bloom's simple awareness of these natural patterns is not offered as stupidity or moral surrender, but as a kind of unthinking wisdom. Thus, when Bloom hears of Mrs Purefoy's difficult lying-in, "his heavy pitying gaze absorbed her news. His tongue clacked in compassion. Dth! Dth!" (147/156)—the suggestion of the life-cycle is Joyce's as much as, if not more than, Bloom's. Or again, when Bloom actually visits the hospital and hears of the death of a friend, he stands silent "in wanhope", whereupon the narrative comments in general terms on the inevitability of death (368/379-80). Even though Joyce makes no unqualified endorsement of Bloom, he does in this endorse his characteristic attitude. So that when Bloom's attitude to time and Stephen's are finally juxtaposed in "Ithaca", we should recognize the sense in which the former's is a criticism of the latter's. Standing beneath the stars and ready to part, they hear, as Bloom had heard among his thoughts of Dignam's death in the morning, the bells of St George's church striking the passage of time:

What echoes of that sound were by both and each heard?

By Stephen, an echo of his unpurged remorse:

Liliata rutilantium. Turma circumdet.
Iubilantium te virginum. Chorus excipiat.

By Bloom, an echo of death, and yet also an incipient turn from it:

Heigho, heigho,
Heigho, heigho. (665/688-9)

His attitude can be easily mistaken for a completely passive resignation. In fact, it is something rather different, an *active* resignation, so to speak. Certainly, Bloom does not do obvious battle with his world, though we should remember that he has lost one job "for giving lip" (299/309) and stands up to the Citizen where no one else does.[26] He does occasionally surrender to a sentimental and uselessly nostalgic acceptance of things as they are—his daughter, Milly, usually provokes this reaction: "A soft qualm, regret, flowed down his backbone, increasing. Will happen, yes. Prevent. Useless: can't move . . ." (60/67). He submits without overt protest or resistance to the petty indignities that mark his social exclusion. On the other hand, his important acceptances are made with an awareness of the complexities; they are not easy resignations by any means. His proposals to Stephen for future meetings—meetings that William Empson has argued are to be regarded as having really taken place and to be the real point of the book[27]—are the product of his deep and pathetic desire for friendship. The proposals are, in fact, accepted by Stephen. Bloom, however, knows more than to take the arrangement at face-value:

What rendered problematic for Bloom the realisation of these mutually selfexcluding propositions?

The irreparability of the past: once at a performance of Albert Hengler's circus . . . an intuitive particoloured clown . . . had publicly declared that he (Bloom) was his (the clown's) papa. The imprevidibility of the future: once in the summer of 1898 he (Bloom) had marked a florin . . . for possible, circuitous or direct, return.

Was the clown Bloom's son?
No.

Had Bloom's coin returned?
Never. (657/680-1)

In short, if Bloom accepts the past as it has been and life as it is, it is not because he does not also desire them otherwise.

Probably the most important illustration of his whole general attitude is provided by his feelings about Molly's adultery. These change, or rather crystallize, during the course of the book, and in fact this crystallization is one of the central threads of the action. Bloom's first reactions are distress and emotional flight; when he sees Boylan in the street, for example, he meets the insupportable by escaping into the Museum, turning to the

174

refuge of "cold statues" and "the Greek architecture" (172/180-1). When he does allow his mind to dwell on the situation, it is with a certain self-pity and nostalgia: "Me. And me now" (165/173). Later on, the art of song in the "Sirens" chapter induces another mood, more reflective, more detached, in which he is able to generalize his situation:

> Thou lost one. All songs on that theme. Yet more Bloom stretched his string. Cruel it seems. Let people get fond of each other: lure them on. Then tear asunder. . . . Human life. . . .
> Yet too much happy bores. He stretched more, more. Are you not happy in your? Twang. It snapped. (263/273)

His personal isolation is heavily emphasized in this chapter, of course, but it is an isolation which is partly an active movement of his mind towards a fuller understanding of his past and present situation (that the chapter is focused upon an *art*, and that Bloom's capacity to comprehend his situation is as limited as the elasticity of his string, are equally significant). But understanding of a sort he does achieve:

> I too, last my race. Milly young student. Well, my fault perhaps. No son. Rudy. Too late now. Or if not? If not? If still?
> He bore no hate.
> Hate. Love. Those are names. Rudy. Soon I am old. (270/280)

By evening ("Nausicaa"), he has begun to see Molly's behaviour in an even wider context as only one more illustration of the laws of attraction, of a universal natural process (357/367; 360/370). And his reconciliation to her proposed tour with Boylan is significantly juxtaposed with his charitable thoughts about the Citizen who had abused and assaulted him (363/374). His mood is not quite a surrender to mere amoral natural processes; it includes a positive charity, a compassionate realization of the common human lot. The mocking sound of the cuckoo that concludes the chapter seems cheap, almost irrelevant, by comparison; its irony leaves his substance untouched. Still further, in "Circe" and "Eumaeus", he comes to recognize that his own sexual failure has a good deal to do with Molly's infidelity (533 f./550 f.; 612 f./635 f.). Gradually he moves from *kinesis* to "a silent contemplation", which is summed up in "Ithaca":

> With what antagonistic sentiments were his subsequent reflections affected?
> Envy, jealousy, abnegation, equanimity.

175

Envy of Boylan, jealousy of Molly, abnegation for complicated
motives, and equanimity because, finally, Molly's act is "more
than inevitable, irreparable".

Why more abnegation than jealousy, less envy than equanimity?
From outrage (matrimony) to outrage (adultery) there arose
nought but outrage (copulation) yet the matrimonial violator of the
matrimonially violated had not been outraged by the adulterous
violator of the adulterously violated. . . .

By what reflections did he, a conscious reactor against the void of
incertitude, justify to himself his sentiments?
[The naturalness of the attraction and the act]: the futility of
triumph or protest of vindication: the inanity of extolled virtue: the
lethargy of nescient matter: the apathy of the stars.

The equanimity results in a final satisfaction in the warmth and
beauty of Molly's female "mute immutable mature animality"—
the eternally given, but never to be possessed, richness of the
flesh.

The visible signs of antesatisfaction?
An approximate erection: a solicitous adversion: a gradual eleva-
tion: a tentative revelation: a silent contemplation.

Then?
He kissed the plump mellow yellow smellow melons of her rump,
on each plump melonous hemisphere, in their mellow yellow furrow,
with obscure prolonged provocative melonsmellonous osculation.

The visible signs of postsatisfaction?
A silent contemplation: a tentative velation: a gradual abasement:
a solicitous aversion: a proximate erection. (692-5/717-9)

That Bloom's silent contemplative *stasis* is followed by a kind of
kinesis (characteristically weak and ambiguous, we might notice)
marks the difference between the continuing process of life and
the fixity of art. If Bloom's slaying of the suitors by a victory over
himself seems paltry or despicable by contrast with Ulysses' more
conclusive methods, we must not therefore suppose that Joyce
is being simply ironical at Bloom's expense.[28] He rarely supports
his characters in postures of moral violence; his notion of true
moral activity is less overtly militant. Bloom kills his enemies, as
Stephen hopes to do, within, and they are not Molly's suitors so
much as his own inner frustrating imbalance of envy, jealousy
and excessive abnegation. He wins a temporary equanimity, but

clearly no final victory. Life, Joyce implies, is not art; there is nothing concluded, no absolute command possible.

Bloom's comparative freedom from guilt, remorse, nostalgia, jealousy, egotistic assertion and other nightmares of history is to be contrasted with Stephen's bondage. Similarly, his curiosity and openness to experience, unlike Stephen's search for "life", express a desire to place the past at the disposal of the future. Where Stephen is a novice, incapable as yet of using the past and so in search of a spiritual father, Bloom is oppressed by the complementary frustration that, as the last of his race, he has no one to whom he can hand on his spiritual gift.

The problem haunts him all through the book, emerging perhaps most explicitly as he sits with the young men in the hospital ("Oxen of the Sun") where he has been drawn by his compassion for Mrs Purefoy and kept by his half-conscious attraction to Stephen. After a passage in which Mulligan mocks Stephen's divine analogies ("the black panther was himself the ghost of his own father"),[29] Bloom, contemplating the label on a bottle of Bass, passes to the "incorruptible eon of the gods" (393-6, 398/405-7, 409). "What is the age of the soul of man?" Bloom relives his own youth—"he is young Leopold, as in a retrospective arrangement, a mirror within a mirror (hey, presto!), he beholdeth himself". But the mirror clouds; "now he is himself paternal and these about him might be his sons. Who can say? The wise father knows his own child." His intense regret that he has not fathered a living man-child, his unwilled frustration, reflects mirror-wise the deliberate contraception that forms the abstract theme of the chapter:

No, Leopold! Name and memory solace thee not. That youthful illusion of thy strength was taken from thee and in vain. No son of thy loins is by thee. There is none now to be for Leopold, what Leopold was for Rudolph. (395/406-7)

For Bloom, as his "soul is wafted over regions of cycles of cycles of generations that have lived", the past is barren, "Agendath is a waste land", horrible and damned. But womankind, "link between nations and generations . . . sacred life-giver" (563/582), still remains, with her potentialities for the future—"And, lo, wonder of metempsychosis, it is she, the everlasting bride, harbinger of the daystar, the bride, ever virgin. It is she, Martha, thou lost one, Millicent, the young, the dear, the radiant" (396/407).

Bloom cannot understand, any more than Stephen, what he can offer the younger man. It is certainly not his good advice, nor anything he could formulate consciously; the essence of his gift is that he is unconscious of it—it is what he represents and is. Partly, of course, he is Stephen's possible "material" as an artist, the City against which Stephen reacts and which is therefore the necessary subject of his self-reflective art. More, however, he represents a relationship to the history of his own people that is analogous to Stephen's and yet unlike it. It is part of Bloom's relevance that, like Stephen, he also embodies a racial tradition (which is also a spiritual tradition), even though it is consciously present to him only in fragments.[30] His "defective mnemotechnic" (649/673) links him with attitudes and patterns of life that he unwittingly re-experiences in his own circumstances. They are not Jewish in the narrowest sense; they have a wider reference, which emerges in "Circe", and to Bloom himself Christ is a symbol both of his values and the mixed tradition whence they derive: "Well, his uncle was a jew, says he. Your God was a jew. Christ was a jew like me" (326/336). The racial parallel with Stephen is explicitly drawn in "Ithaca": both inherit a long and rich tradition, both are conscious only of fragments of it (649/ 672). Yet the contrast between the two men is equally explicit and equally important. Where Stephen consciously (and uneasily) rejects, Bloom accepts. Once, earlier, Bloom had impatiently criticized his father's beliefs and practices; now, they appear to him "not more rational than they had then appeared, not less rational than other beliefs and practices now appeared" (685, cf. 361/709, cf. 372). As we shall see, this detachment is by no means the whole of Bloom's attitude, for much else in it is, as it should be, quite unconscious; his significance, nevertheless, is as an example, parallel to but contrasting with Stephen's case, of an involuntary involvement, an involuntary exile, but a real if unemphatic freedom.

Such contrasts between Bloom and Stephen would have little point without the relationship that lies at the centre of the whole book: they are here, as always, complementary counterparts, "fundamental and dominant" (479/494), actuality and potentiality. The father-son theme is one metaphor for this; the theory about Shakespeare another; the figure of Christ, in whom are expressed the dichotomies of crucified citizen (Man) and crucified artist (God), of action and passion, of involvement and freedom, is yet a third. By its different aspects, the symbol of Christ links the diverse facts of the situation Joyce explores, but the meaning of Joyce's *symbol* lies in the facts it orders. Unless the values it relates and expresses are themselves realized, imaginatively established as denotations, the symbol remains empty and inert. Stephen cannot be portrayed as the suffering and crucified Artist redeeming the world; in the very terms of the book, he lacks the freedom, the love, and the capacity, and has only the desire to become an artist and the uneasy realization of what is involved. For the most part, he rejects. He is Christ as the "black panther", and the very incompleteness of his state provokes the metaphor of Lucifer. Stephen as Christ often passes over into Stephen as Satan: it is a sign of his immaturity that he is ready to adopt either rôle at any time. He is not quite *der Geist, der stets verneint,* of course; it is rather that his affirmations seem only velleities, or at best unachieved intentions. Bloom, therefore, must carry the heavier burden of significance—be not merely passive but active, not merely involved but free, not merely representative of, but crucified by, his world, the scapegoat and redeemer, and tied all the while by close analogy and parallel with Stephen, so that the reader may perceive what Stephen must learn to perceive: the values Bloom represents and the deep similarity between the two of them. Bloom's ambiguous position, his example, his love, his freedom, if only he could understand them, are what Stephen must come to. For the parallels between the two men are fundamental: Bloom's exclusion from society reflects Stephen's spiritual exile from it (a situation neatly portrayed early in the book when they are both at the newspaper office). Each is an alien in the life of Dublin. They are both isolated by "parallax", each in his personal world, and only a full spiritual outgoing—or its symbol, art—can alleviate their condition. They both reject violence and the senseless agitations of the mob as incompatible with the freedom and order they seek. They are both keyless, citizen and artist, yet both "born adventurers" (588/610) and committed to the essential isolation of their individuality (628-9/651-2). They both have personal courage, one in his pride, the other in his humility. Both strive to awake from the nightmare of history, though Stephen cannot yet realize what values he seeks, and Bloom cannot express what he means. But his attempts are the justification for the Christ metaphor—his positive courage in "Cyclops" for example, but more especially his unalienated integrity in "Circe". The most important structural parallel between the two protagonists, in fact, is that between Stephen's self-examination of the past, which is conducted consciously, and Bloom's, which is necessarily much less conscious; between "Proteus" and "Circe". The connections between these two chapters, with all that is implied by those connections, is what really establishes the metaphor of paternity.

The "Circe" chapter has often been compared to Goethe's *Walpurgisnacht* and Flaubert's *Tentation de Saint Antoine*. It is Bloom's—and to a much lesser extent, Stephen's—descent into the maelstrom of the Unconscious, the unpermitted. Its function, however, is not to explore the Unconscious for its own sake, nor to express modern psychological discoveries in literary terms, but rather to explore and express the material of *Ulysses*. It is a temptation and purgation of human dignity. The temptation is the traditional one—to abandon Reason, the powers of the spirit, the moral sense, the conscious will, and to relapse into animality, mere appetency, illusion and compulsion: in a word, to revert to simple *kinesis*. The City, modern society, no less than the individual, assumes its most grotesque and horrifying aspects, emptied of meaning to the extent that it is swayed by the most violent, chaotic irrationality. The objective world unites with disturbed and driven subjects in an epiphany of delirium and collapse. From all of this Bloom is at last preserved by the fragments of his racial inheritance, his inalienable Reason, and sheer chance; Stephen is preserved in turn by Bloom.

Early in Bloom's descent the ghosts of his parents warn him of his dangers—"What are you making down this place? Have you no soul?" (418/430)—and later on his memories of their traditional attitudes come to his rescue. But the first of the two major, interrelated aspects of his descent—the sexual and the social—is introduced as the phantasm of his mother modulates into that of his wife, Molly, and his masochistic pleasure in her sexual vigour mingles with his fantasies about other women (419-20/431-42). The other aspect, the social, develops out of these fantasies, once again combining his ambivalent feelings of guilt and persecution. Society begins its phantasmagorical pursuit of him—for imputed cruelty, lack of money and position, his sexual adventures, and so on (432 ff./445 ff.). His appeals go unheeded—"I am a man misunderstood. I am being made a scapegoat of" (436/449). Against the laws of society he proposes his "artistic" pretensions as a defence; he is promptly branded "plagiarist". His attempt to seduce a former servant becomes an instrument to plague him. He cannot persuade the world of his complete respectability. His defence attempts pathos:

There have been cases of shipwreck and somnambulism in my client's family. If the accused could speak he could a tale unfold one of the strangest that have ever been narrated between the covers of a book. . . . I shall call rebutting evidence to prove up to the hilt that the hidden hand is again at its old game. When in doubt persecute Bloom. (441-2/455)

The defence is true, of course, but so is the guilt—or at least it exists at a level of personality where its truth is in one sense irrelevant, and in another guaranteed. Bloom is the victim of society and its scapegoat. His sexual fantasies are all largely masochistic (even including a degree of satisfaction in Molly's adultery); they are also anarchic, destructive of the accepted social order. The spiritual conflict here implied rises to its first climax in a composite charge—

Whereas Leopold Bloom of no fixed abode is a wellknown dynamitard, forger, bigamist, bawd and cuckold and a public nuisance to the citizens of Dublin. . . .
  Who'll hang Judas Iscariot? (448/462)

But Bloom's acceptance of guilt and of the values of the society that condemns him is counterbalanced by the implicit criticism of that society—its hypocrisy, treachery, injustice—and by his consciousness of an innocence however ambiguous—"Wait. Stop. Gulls. Good heart. I saw. Innocence" (449/463). The visionary trial finally dissolves in his remembrance of death and of the honour he had paid it at Dignam's funeral. This is his saving alibi (449-50/463-4), the tribute of his innocence and of his social right to live.

A little later he stands swayed by his lusts "smiling desirously, twirling his thumbs" at Bella Cohen's whores (485/500). At this point, another crisis of spirit, his father appears to his inner consciousness with criticism and admonition: "Stop twirling your thumbs and have a good old thunk. See, you have forgotten. Exercise your mnemotechnic" (488/503). This time it is the past, like the thought of death, that comes to his aid in the predicament of the present; as Bloom says (using a phrase Stephen would not even understand), "the touch of a deadhand cures". The reminder of his own detached ("scientific") and moral traditions changes his lust to self-insight. In a moment of vision like that Stephen had described in his theory, he sees himself as he was by the light of what he now is and what in possibility he may come to be:

I wanted them to have now concluded. Nightdress was never. Hence this. But tomorrow is a new day will be. Past was is today. What now is will then tomorrow as now was be past yester. (489/504)

From this moment, the tradition of rational, critical detachment represented by the weird, dispossessed ghost of Virag enables Bloom to disengage himself from lust. He becomes able once again to generalize about his situation and is saved from it: "Instinct", he observes, "rules the world. In life. In death" (490/505), and in the very thought his own example proves differently.

Against the most insidious sexual temptation of all, however, it is chance that preserves him. This is not the temptation offered by the fantasy he weaves about the whoremistress herself, in which his masochism is given its fullest (and most sensational) expression and his surrender to it revealed as the temptation to resign his own activity, to become merely the passive sufferer, a Rip Van Winkle whom life passes by:

BELLO

... Too late. You have made your secondbest bed and others must lie in it. Your epitaph is written. You are down and out and don't you forget it, old bean.

BLOOM

Justice! All Ireland versus one! Has nobody ...? ... (*Clasps his head.*) My will power! Memory! I have sinned! I have suff ...

(*He weeps tearlessly.*) (515/531)

The climactic temptation is more subtle. It is finally that of the
Nymph, the Virgin, to whom Bloom directs a "spiritualized"
lust. She offers him the lure of a false repose, a false resolution of
conflict:

THE NYMPH

(*Eyeless, in nun's white habit, coif and huge winged wimple, softly, with remote
eyes.*) Tranquilla convent. Sister Agatha. Mount Carmel, the appari-
tions of Knock and Lourdes. No more desire. (*She reclines her head,
sighing.*) Only the ethereal. Where dreamy creamy gull waves o'er
the waters dull. (523/539)

At this supreme crisis, as Bloom half rises to follow her ("*Verweile
doch! du bist so schön!*"), his back trousers' button snaps off. The
temptation, clearly enough, is yet another version of the "Platonic" ethereal, that "other world" where mere absence of desire
masquerades as equanimity, where humanity is degraded by
"spirituality", religiosity, a self-indulgent "art". It is the ideal
of "an age of exhausted whoredom groping for its god", the
product of frustration rather than fulfilment, a self-deluded
kinesis rather than the plenitude of real *stasis*. Its relation to the
"Platonism" Stephen rejects in his theory is obvious. At first,
Bloom is indignant at his own salvation; in a moment, however,
he perceives for himself the falsity of the ideal he had contemplated, and for the first time in the whole chapter recovers his
capacity to act. He now stands before the whoremistress "composed" (524/541) and critical; he resumes his proper activity
and dignity, winning even admiration from her as he quietly
takes charge of Stephen as best he can. The popping of his button
restores his measure of freedom. The wounds of his dishonour still
rankle: the face of Shakespeare that appears as he and Stephen
look in the mirror is crowned by the reflection of antlers (534-6/
550-3). But if he is still separated from a full humanity, and even
from his later equanimity, he is no longer merely a victim of his
own compulsions, but the active-passive citizen we had known
before. (Which is why, perhaps, we may feel a certain inconsistency in his characterization in "Eumaeus", where he seems
more the mere butt of Joyce's critical irony than he really
deserves.)

The same purgation has already partly emerged in another
way, however, from the long fantasy about social ideals (455-75/
469-89) that Bloom weaves in evident compensation for his social

exclusion and his sense of guilt. In this vision he sees himself as a social messiah instead of a victim.[31] Beginning with a stump speech as a working-man, and passing through the stages of Lord Mayor, the "famous Bloom, the world's greatest reformer", the founder of "Bloomusalem", and "little father", he carries the ideals of his society to their logical conclusion: "Free money, free love and a free lay church in a free lay state" (466/480). He assumes an heroic, divine status as a parody of Christ Triumphant wielding the power and the glory in a world refashioned nearer its own material desires. They are partly his own desires, too, in so far as he shares its present ideals, but they are not altogether so. He accepts his martyrdom as necessary to his status as the hero god—"Lynch him! Roast him! He's as bad as Parnell was" (468/482), and as the vision continues both his enjoyment of the rôle and its foundation in a basic nihilism become apparent in the devastating parody:

BLOOM

(*In caubeen with clay pipe stuck in the band, dusty brogues, an emigrant's red handkerchief bundle in his hand, leading a black bogoak pig by a sugaun, with a smile in his eye.*) Let me be going now, woman of the house, for by all the goats in Connemara I'm after having the father and mother of a bating. (*With a tear in his eye.*) All insanity. Patriotism, sorrow for the dead, music, future of the race. To be or not to be. Life's dream is o'er. End it peacefully. They can live on. (*He gazes far away mournfully.*) I am ruined. A few pastilles of aconite. The blinds drawn. A letter. Then lie back to rest. (*He breathes softly.*) No more. I have lived. Fare. Farewell. (474/489)

The sceptical resignation into which messianic materialism so readily passes over is perfectly caught; and Bloom's father's suicide is revealed as the other side of his helping hand from the past. But what follows this fantasy is the most important comment on it. Zoe, the whore standing by Bloom's side, interrupts his thoughts, and still under the influence of them, Bloom—most uncharacteristically—turns on her "bitterly":

Man and woman, love, what is it? A cork and bottle.

ZOE

(*In sudden sulks.*) I hate a rotter that's insincere. Give a bleeding whore a chance.

BLOOM

(*Repentantly.*) I am very disagreeable. You are a necessary evil. Where
are you from? London? (475/489)

The point made here is continually repeated throughout
"Circe": Bloom is finally unable to sustain any of his visions
because none of them is finally adequate to his real character.
In the end, he is not a bitterly disillusioned materialistic utopian,
nor yet satisfied to resign social criticism and action altogether.
His characteristic sanity always preserves him from the temptation of such extremes. His innocence is thus not a matter of his
willing assent to his guilt or to his victimization by society, nor
even of his humanitarian good-will. He realizes well enough the
connection between scapegoat and messiah, and his visions
dramatically enact the truth Joyce first formulated in *Stephen
Hero*:

Satan, really, is the romantic youth of Jesus re-appearing for a
moment. I had a romantic youth, too, when I thought it must be a
grand thing to be a material Messias: that was the will of my father
who will never be in heaven. But now such a thought arises in my
mind *only in moments of great physical weakness.* So I regard that view of
life as the abnormal view—for me. . . . [*The*] *seat of the spiritual principle
of a man is not transferable to a material object.* (198-9; my italics)

What is true for Stephen is equally true for Bloom. He is not a
material Messias, nor on the other hand a complete sceptic; he
is not a pure victim of others, nor capable of the indulgence of the
fake "ethereal". Being committed to the world in which he lives,
but not wholly committed to it, always forced back to being
himself, he represents a problem deeper and more complex than
his unsatisfying fantasies can answer. What Joyce portrays is a
man whose genuine impulse is towards Love but who cannot
discover any adequate image of himself as a social being practis-
ing it. As each fantasy arises and fades away, the man himself
still remains, further and further purged of the illusory rôles his
society seems to him to offer. To himself it would seem a purely
negative process; to us, however, aware of his moral activity as a
citizen all through the book, the process points to his essential
humanity as well as to the absence of any available ideal of social
or personal relationships adequate to it. And it is this humanity—
to which *any* ideal is perhaps inadequate—that is the pivot of

the whole phantasmagoria of "Circe". The brilliant dramatisa-
tion of a spiritual crisis in modern life, the sure, swift art of the
chapter with its violently comic juxtapositions of various planes
of reality, offers more than the surface excitement of a ruthless
satirical anatomy. The negative force of rejection and withdrawal
is—as with "Proteus", as, indeed, with the book as a whole—
counterbalanced by the positive force of what is affirmed. The
virtue of Bloom is that he never really succumbs to the nightmare
of what his depressing history (that of his race, his society, or his
own) would make him. He emerges from his trials and temptations clearly enough for us to understand, even if he cannot, the
nature of his superiority to Stephen. Where Stephen still flounders
in his paralytic *kinesis*, Bloom can be said, without irony, to live.
Preserved by good luck and his unconscious core of innocence
and integrity, he affirms in effect his dignity as a "competent
keyless citizen" proceeding "energetically from the unknown to
the known through the incertitude of the void" (658/682).

The climax of the chapter is therefore where we should expect
it to be: in the last vision of all, as Bloom, standing over the
unconscious Stephen, who has come violently in contact with
the solid reality of a drunken soldier's fist, sees (though in
characteristically sentimental terms) the ghost of his dead son,
Rudy. At this moment, Bloom is probably as close as he ever
gets to understanding the significance Stephen has for him and,
by the same token, the significance of his own position and values
in his world. Generally speaking, Bloom's self-knowledge is short-
circuited: he never understands himself, as Stephen tries to do,
mainly because he lacks the capacity (and the inclination) to
grasp the nature and process of such insight. On the other hand,
he has less need of any reflexive understanding of the process
because, unlike Stephen, he already possesses himself. His
impersonal, mature sanity is almost instinctive, or more accurately, habitual; his self is continually and objectively realized in
virtuous action. "Circe" thus reflects, focuses, and places
"Proteus", but in another key. The first section of the book is
concerned with Stephen, and reaches its climax in its last
chapter, "Proteus", which is later explained in more theoretical
terms by "Scylla and Charybdis"; the second section of the book
is concerned with Bloom, is also explained in a different sense
by "Scylla and Charybdis", and reaches its climax in the climax

of its last chapter, "Circe". Bloom's last long speech in it, therefore, appropriately echoes Stephen's broken phrases from Yeats's "Who will drive with Fergus now?", the song that Stephen's mother had loved, and which combines his unpurged remorse with his desire for freedom:

> And no more turn aside and brood
> Upon love's bitter mystery;
> For Fergus rules the brazen cars,
> And rules the shadows of the wood,
> And the white breast of the dim sea
> And all dishevelled wandering stars.

Echoing this, and Stephen's fear of the waters of life, Bloom adds to them the oath of freemasonry, and gropes towards his moment of insight:

... (*He murmurs.*) ... swear that I will always hail, ever conceal, never reveal, any part or parts, art or arts ... (*He murmurs.*) in the rough sands of the sea ... a cabletow's length from the shore ... where the tide ebbs ... and flows ...
(*Silent, thoughtful, alert, he stands on guard, his fingers at his lips in the attitude of secret master. ...*) (574/593)

"Proteus" presents Stephen the groping novice, "Circe" Bloom the mature master. The son-father relationship of Stephen's theory is thus established in Bloom's "wonderstruck", inaudible cry, "Rudy!"

Of course, no simple formula can express the total meaning of the father-son metaphor. It involves similarities and differences between Bloom and Stephen, parallel and complementary predicaments and significances. Exclusion from society, alienation, exile and free detachment are ranged to reflect and set off one another. Paralytic *kinesis* stands in contrast to active *stasis*; potentiality and actuality point to each other. Both adventurers move to related but different goals. Each is redeemer and redeemed. The paradoxes and ambiguities of their individual selves and of their relationship—a relationship of the metaphorical meanings they unconsciously embody and enact for us—are fully expressed only by the total action. Nevertheless, in the Shakespeare theory of "Scylla and Charybdis" Joyce attempts to explore them more explicitly, and he does so again in "Ithaca". In the former, the exploration is also Stephen's own attempt at self-understanding, but it serves us as a kind of preliminary guide to the nature and development of the action of which it forms a part. As yet the paternity metaphor does not seem to arise inevitably from the action itself; it appears so far only as a hint, a possibility. "Ithaca" on the other hand comes at the end of the action—at any rate, that part of it solely concerned with Bloom and Stephen—and it explores their relationship in a different way. It turns back on the action and forms an abstract, choric commentary on it as a whole. Stephen's own limited grasp of his situation is now very clearly part of the *res gestae*. At this stage all the suggestions and fragments of meaning can be brought together and crystallized. In "Ithaca" the action may be said to reach towards a conscious statement of itself.

Seen in this light, the chapter that lies between the climax of "Circe" and the moment when the two men really confront one another in Bloom's kitchen—the dreary lassitude of "Eumaeus" —produces a sort of suspense. While Bloom flounders in the clichés of communication to reach common ground with Stephen, as one false start after another comes to nothing, we await the possibility that they may yet reach something of our understanding of their kinship. As they finally approach mutual recognition the dramatic irony becomes acuter. They do seem to discover a few attitudes in common, Stephen accepts Bloom's invitation home, and as they walk Stephen describes variations on an air significantly called "Youth here has end." He sings a ballad about "sirens, sweet murderers of men"—especially poets, and the conversation finally turns to "sirens, enemies of man's reason, mingled with a number of other topics of the same category, usurpers, historical cases of the kind . . ." (624, 626/647, 649). The links between them—*kinesis-stasis*, Mulligan-Boylan, their attitudes to past, present, and future—seem about to emerge into conscious discourse. Yet, as is hinted by the ballad with which the chapter ends ("The Lowbacked Car"—concerning a marriage that notoriously does not take place),[32] there is no real chance they will understand one another. When "Ithaca" anatomizes the significance each has for the other, it is, we realize, a significance that neither can fully perceive for himself. Since Bloom lacks the imaginative capacity and Stephen the moral capacity, *we* are left isolated as well as they, sharing our understanding only with the author, who combines in himself the capacities his divided counterparts lack.

The result of this, the technical registration of the deeply ironical situation and of the isolation of everyone in it, is that the narrative must now move outside the consciousness of the characters altogether—not merely outside the "stream-of-consciousness" (which disappears between "Nausicaa" and "Penelope", and is used only intermittently in any case), but even outside any reflecting consciousness in Henry James's sense. In "Ithaca", for the first time in the book, the material is no longer focused by a "reflector". Even in "Wandering Rocks", where the material is so fragmented, Dublin is still portrayed in the actions, relationships and consciousness of its characters. Now the "reflector" is replaced by an intelligence utterly superior to the whole action, an ironic *persona* directing us from beyond or above it. But because the technique remains within the terms of an impersonal dramatic art, it is more than merely a device. It is part of the action, a development from, and of, the material. As Joyce himself put it,

I am writing *Ithaca* in the form of a mathematical catechism. All events are resolved into their cosmic, physical, psychical etc. equivalents, e.g. Bloom jumping down the area, drawing water from the tap, the micturating in the garden, the cone of incense, lighted candle and statue so that the reader will know everything and know it in the baldest and coldest way, but Bloom and Stephen thereby become heavenly bodies, wanderers like the stars at which they gaze.[33]

Not enough attention has been paid to Joyce's achievement of the end he outlines in the last few phrases of this. The cold, catechistic, "objective" style is indeed a parodic mask, as for example Mr Kenner has so pertinently shown. But the point of the chapter is the difference between what the mask represents and its actual dramatic *effect*. The mask proceeds with its ruthless vivisection of the "scientific" facts of modern society and of the sensibility characteristic of that society—a sensibility, of course, that Bloom largely shares. This vivisection, however, is not the final comment on Bloomsworld; it is only one term in the dialectic of the chapter. For its effect is again like that of the pervading irony of the whole work, not to demolish Bloom and Stephen into scattered, fragmentary "facts", but rather to show their ultimate invulnerability to this view of them. The author's sympathetic understanding of the two men, and the feeling it generates, are intense in this chapter, though the sympathetic feeling is not direct, spontaneous, unchecked. On the contrary; it is challenged by, and has to meet, the attack of critical "thought", its rejection by the naked intelligence, which is represented by the depersonalized catechism. The deeper affirmation does emerge nevertheless. The supreme irony of the chapter is that of the whole work: that the artist accepts, but ultimately transcends, the terms in which his purely *critical* intelligence challenges his protagonists. In the event, the "scientific" perspective only heightens our sense of an imperishable dignity and vitality in the two characters; it sharpens the compassion that underlies the mask; and it points to what it cannot reduce to its terms. The artist's assumption of an absurdly cold, implacable superiority (which is always parodying itself) is meant to recall to us, by reaction, the artist's continual activity *within* his creation. Taken in the total context of the work, it parodies the method and outlook of naturalistic Realism in order to suggest what lies beyond its grasp. Thus "Ithaca" is like the final test of human life: it survives its own cold pride of "intellect".

The first question of the chapter describes the "parallel course" of the protagonists returning to Bloom's home; the second, the subjects of their talk; the third, the similarities between "their respective like and unlike" attitudes that Bloom discovers; the fourth draws the line sharply between the citizen and the artist, though both, we discern, are partly right and partly wrong:

Stephen dissented openly from Bloom's views on the importance of dietary and civic selfhelp while Bloom dissented tacitly from Stephen's views on the eternal affirmation of the spirit of man in literature. . . . (627/650)

Bloom himself is conscious of four forces separating them—name, age, race, creed (638/662), and a good deal of the chapter is concerned with the effects of these on their views about history and themselves. As well as these, however, there are differences that neither really understands. Thus Bloom admires water—"neverchanging everchanging water", the symbol of life itself—

while Stephen fears it (632-3/655-7). Even the difference between citizen and artist—

What two temperaments did they individually represent?
The scientific. The artistic. (643/667)—

does not, in the light of the whole work, mean the same to them as it does to the reader. Bloom's equanimity seems without significance to either of them: he bears his humiliations with tranquility, content to have sustained no positive loss, to have brought gain to others, light to the gentiles (637/660); his vision has always been detached from the "round precipitous globe" (641/665); he has learned to look on his father's beliefs without "immature impatience" (684/708); he has recognized the inescapable limitations of social improvement and is prepared to accept them humbly (658/681-2).

Although these qualities have meaning only for the reader, who can contrast them with Stephen's, the differences between the two men are nevertheless clear enough for both to appreciate the gulf between them. They know quite well that their futures lie apart, even though they do not know that in another sense they do not. As we have seen, Stephen evidently has little intention to return, and Bloom is too wise to count on his acceptance (657-8/680-1). Once again, the superior position in time of the author and reader provides an ironical depth to the characters' own understanding of themselves. It is not that they are quite mistaken about themselves, but neither is capable of that imaginative insight whereby past, present and future may be all contemplated together, and which alone could reveal them to themselves. As yet it is only a possibility in Stephen's future; for the artist, and for us, it is already present at this moment.

And from our position the similarities and parallels between Bloom and Stephen appear more significant than the differences. Like Stephen, Bloom hates violence; like Stephen, he too has been a "kinetic poet" (639/662); like Stephen, he is an exile from his race; and, most importantly, like Stephen he also, in his way, asserts his human dignity. As Bloom's thoughts wander from the unlikelihood of meeting Stephen again to the humble acceptance of the necessity of destruction, accident, disease, the pain of birth and death, the "convulsions of metamorphosis, from infancy through maturity to decay", he sits dejected. Stephen provides

the necessary comment, and we may note the fact that it is he
who, expressing a meaning beyond the other's formulation,
already speaks *for* Bloom:

Did Stephen participate in his dejection?
He affirmed his significance as a conscious rational animal proceeding syllogistically from the known to the unknown and a conscious
rational reagent between a micro- and a macrocosm ineluctably
constructed upon the incertitude of the void.

Was this affirmation apprehended by Bloom?
Not verbally. Substantially.

What comforted his misapprehension?
That as a competent keyless citizen he had proceeded energetically
from the unknown to the known through the incertitude of the void.
(658/682)

With that, Stephen departs, intoning to himself the psalm
commemorating the Israelites' departure from Egyptian bondage: "In exitu Israel de Egypto: domus Jacob de populo
barbaro." Once again there is an ironical gap between Stephen's
view of the situation and ours. If he regards Bloom as representing his bondage, or even his shelter and sympathy as the
sanctuary of Judah, he cannot realize as yet that Bloom is also
his dominion. It is we, not Stephen, who catch the symbolic
echoes when Bloom, light in hand, earlier stands *inside* his door
beckoning Stephen to enter (630/653), or when he serves him
"Epps's massproduct, the creature cocoa" (637/661)—the
symbol of the sad, real, but unconscious kinship between the
two men. Their meagre awareness of their mutual relations is
now restated in the explicit, abstract terms of this chapter. When
Bloom sings a few bars of the Jewish anthem (breaking off
because of "defective mnemotechnic"), Stephen hears "in a
profound ancient male unfamiliar melody the accumulation of
the past". Bloom sees in Stephen "a quick young male familiar
form the predestination of a future".

What were Stephen's and Bloom's quasisimultaneous volitional
quasisensations of concealed identities?
Visually, Stephen's: The traditional figure of hypostasis. . . .
Auditively, Bloom's: The traditional accent of the ecstasy of
catastrophe. (650/673-4)

Yet this is no more than a "quasisensation", and as the catechism
explores their complementary significance further, we again pass

beyond their understanding altogether. Neither is aware that
both are victims predestined, reluctant and unresisting (653/676).
Neither is aware of Stephen's departure as yet another manifestation of a dynamic power that moves the spirit of man to adventure no less than it moves the material universe (659-60/683-4).
Neither perceives the similarities in difference between them,
"centripetal remainer" and "centrifugal departer" (664/688), as
they stand together at the last beneath the "visible splendid sign"
of Molly in the bedroom above:

> Both then were silent?
> Silent, each contemplating the other in both mirrors of the reci-
> procal flesh of theirhisnothis fellowfaces. (663/687)

Their consequent act—urinating together—is not really (as
"making water") a symbol of the life they embody, seek and
master, so much as a farewell to what is done, a much less
significant gesture of elimination. The grim comedy derives from
the diminutive size of the gesture, its suggestion of futility.
Despite our awareness of their mutual relationship, despite the
symbols of their kinship, each still remains alone, cut off in
isolation beneath "the cold of interstellar space", each hearing
his own message in the bells of St George's (665/688). Father
and son have become representatives of humanity in general—
impelled by desire yet seeking a wisdom beyond desire, drawn
together by inklings of a kinship they cannot grasp, and in the
last analysis separated by the ineluctable isolation of every
individual soul. Only the mature wisdom of the Imagination
can trace true connection and meaning. As Bloom considers the
silent constellations, his conclusions about them apply equally to
Ulysses itself. As Mallarmé (and others) have also suggested,
Man confronting the stars and Artist confronting the chaos of
experience are parallel symbols of the human spirit (instances,
we might say, of Coleridge's Primary and Secondary Imagination): each projecting yet finding meaning in what is given. The
sight of the heavens, Bloom concludes,

was not a heaventree, not a heavengrot, not a heavenbeast, not a
heavenman. That it was a Utopia, there being no known method from
the known to the unknown: an infinity, renderable equally finite by
the suppositous probable apposition of one or more bodies equally of
the same and of different magnitudes: a mobility of illusory forms

immobilized in space, remobilized in air: *a past which possibly had
ceased to exist as a present before its future spectators had entered actual present
existence.* (662/686; my italics)

Stephen's departure leaves Bloom alone once more; in fact,
since we are now quite detached from his consciousness and view
him from our vantage-point of complete knowledge, he seems
more isolated than ever before. And yet at this very point—
where, standing alone in the cold of interstellar space, listening
to Stephen's footsteps retreat, and remembering the dead, he still
remains to salute "the apparition of a new solar disk"—his
universality at last emerges clearly. We begin here to see him
completely objectively and representatively; the narrative moves
us away from all sympathetic identification *with* him towards a
more abstract, depersonalized perception *of* him. He becomes
less himself and more a symbol, now consciously and explicitly
abstracted from the action. Only his most general outlines—or
rather, his most essential qualities—now remain. We examine
him as a symbol of his society and its material ideals; then
reduced, "by cross multiplication of reverses of fortune, from
which these supports protected him, and by elimination of all
positive values to a negligible negative irrational unreal quan-
tity" (668-686 ff./692-710 ff.); then as a prospective wanderer
and exile from his home, "assumed by any or known to none.
Everyman or Noman", with tributes of "honour and gifts of
strangers, the friends of Everyman. A nymph immortal, beauty,
the bride of Noman"—become at last an interstellar wanderer,
returning at last "an estranged avenger, a wreaker of justice on
malefactors, a dark crusader, a sleeper awakened", with untold
financial resources (688/712).

What would render such return irrational?
An unsatisfactory equation between an exodus and return in time
through reversible space and an exodus and return in space through
irreversible time. (688/713)

Bloom, though Ulysses, remains himself, attached to the conditions of his world; yet the nature of his attachment is that of
mankind in every age, and his activities during the day are now
seen as a comic, but genuine re-enactment of the now dim, but
immemorial, rituals that always shape the life of Everyman:

The preparation of breakfast (burnt offering): intestinal congestion and premeditative defecation (holy of holies): the bath (rite of John): the funeral (rite of Samuel): the advertisement of Alexander Keyes (Urim and Thummin): unsubstantial lunch (rite of Melchisedek): the visit to museum and national library (holy place): the bookhunt along Bedford row, Merchants' Arch, Wellington Quay (Simchath Torah): the music in the Ormond Hotel (Shira Shirim): the altercation with a truculent troglodyte in Bernard Kiernan's premises (holocaust): a blank period of time including a cardrive, a visit to a house of mourning, a leavetaking (wilderness): the eroticism produced by feminine exhibitionism (rite of Onan): the prolonged delivery of Mrs Mina Purefoy (heave offering): the visit to the disorderly house of Mrs Bella Cohen, 82 Tyrone street, lower, and subsequent brawl and chance medley in Beaver street (Armageddon): nocturnal perambulation to and from the cabman's shelter, Butt Bridge (atonement). (689/713-4)

And so, with his equanimity regained and his final salute to Molly, he disappears from view with Sinbad the Sailor, Tinbad the Tailor, and the rest, "in the night of the bed of all the auks of the rocs of Darkinbad the Brightdayler" (698/722). To the question, *Where?* the only answer is a large full-stop: his whereabouts are now irrelevant to his significance.

* * *

Three processes take place at once here in "Ithaca", and especially in this last section of it, which must be distinguished from each other. In the first place, the action of the preceding chapters comes to a close as Bloom most clearly becomes his isolated self. We behold him, as he beholds himself, "a solitary (ipsorelative) mutable (aliorelative) man", turning his "obscure tranquil profound motionless compassionated gaze" upon his most intimate environment (668/692); his few possessions, material and spiritual, are laid out for us in the bleak jargon of his commercialized world; his tranquility of mind about Molly at last achieved.

In the second place, as the images of day recede and he is thus left for our contemplation, he assumes a universal significance as an image of the human condition. "Luminously apprehended as selfbounded and selfcontained upon the immeasurable background of space or time which is not it", the image of Bloom contains all the ambiguous elements of Modern Man, which are also in part the elements of Everyman: all the futility, pathos, and heroism interfuse in a universal symbol whose meaning is imaginatively defined only by the whole book.

To these processes Joyce adds a third: the juxtaposition of this image of Bloom with others of a similar meaning—most notably, of course, that of Ulysses. In so doing, he provides a historical and critical comment on his own imaginative work. "Ithaca" is the stage at which the Homeric and other parallels brought in from outside are seen to coincide in outline with the outlines of *Ulysses*, and where we perceive, paradoxically, the *imaginative* propriety of such apparently non-imaginative commentary. For what happens here is that different but equally valid images of the human condition throw reflections on each other, and hint in their similarity at the more distant, broader (and vaguer) structures of human life in all times and places. (Whether these structures lie in the "objective" world as recurrent patterns of experience (like Vico's cycles, for example), or in the "subjective" imagination as Archetypal Patterns by which the artist apprehends experience, is irrelevant; subject and object coincide in the apprehended form.) Consequently, although the temporal perspective of *Ulysses* arises out of the characters' immediate situations and reflections, and is always directed by them, it ultimately becomes longer and wider as we move away from the characters. We come to perceive their acts, thoughts, history and potentialities in a spatio-temporal setting far larger than they could hope to command, for we see them as a completed *action*, which is fulfilled both by the book itself to which it points as its goal and in the silent luminous *stasis* wherein all men appear as adventurers, all adventurers appear as one, and all adventure, all process, a simultaneous, static, eternal pattern—the entelechy of all history, existing (like the self) "by memory under ever-changing forms"[34]. It is thus that Stephen and Bloom achieve their apotheosis, "wanderers like the stars at which they gaze".

It is necessary to distinguish these three aspects of the chapter because the third, to which so much critical attention has been given, can be too easily confused with the second. The two sorts of universality, poetic and referential, apparently coincide in the book, but really one depends upon the other. The intellectual and imaginative vision of life as eternal pattern depends on the imaginative assent we give to Joyce's art, on the truth and power of Bloom and Stephen as images of genuine human predicaments.

It certainly does not derive from casually or mechanically elaborated parallels scattered through the book, sometimes invisible to the uninitiated reader or merely witty when discerned—which is why I have paid them so little attention in themselves. The final vision of life-as-a-whole is a result, not a cause, of the truth and effectiveness of the art, a universality of application or reference that is superadded, as it were, to the aesthetic universality of the action. This is to oversimplify, of course. One must add that this reach, and mode, of abstract application is *part* of the book, for the action of *Ulysses*—which includes past, present and future, Joyce as well as Stephen and Bloom—reaches its climactic self-understanding in the last two chapters. Such an abstracting, "mythic" vision could only be reached dynamically, through the development of the action (in this case, development in *reading* time), to the point where its general outlines emerge from flux and apparent unorder. *Finnegans Wake* is Joyce's most thorough-going presentation of such a static vision of the vast, composite pattern of all ages, all life, and Vico's cycles and Archetypal Patterns play a correspondingly larger and more obvious rôle. But the vision is no longer realized by a dynamic, dramatic unfolding. The later book suffers from the disadvantage—a crippling disadvantage, I think —of dissolving the conditions of time and place, the gritty, resistant, representational *facts* that the imagination requires for the apprehension of epiphanies. It starts from the point where *Ulysses* concludes; it seeks what Allen Tate calls the "angelic" vision; life seems too readily subsumed by the artist's generic categories; and his work thereby offends against the very conditions of art Stephen had rightly opposed to George Russell's "Platonism". The result of its extreme fluidity is that it seems to express merely *"formless* spiritual essences".[35] In *Ulysses* the spiritual essences are revealed in the world as we experience it, not as we may imagine it to be; the creative imagination and its instrument, language, are still committed to what they must subdue, not released into an ambiguous, self-subsistent empyrean of meaning.[36] Our apprehension of a universe ceaselessly moving in its living patterns, of Stephen moving towards his distant goal, of Bloom (Everyman—"Noman"—Christ—Shakespeare—Sinbad, and so on) lying in bed with Molly (Everywoman— Penelope — Nausicaa — Anne Hathaway— Beatrice — Mother

Mistress, and so on), finally "at rest relatively to themselves and to each other" but "in motion being each and both carried westward, forward and rearward respectively, by the proper perpetual motion of the earth through everchanging tracks of neverchanging space" (697/721)—this transcendence of the nightmare of history is not simply assumed or given. In itself, divorced from the drama in which it is realized, it would be a flat, inert banality of the intellect. But it is not given, it is gained, emerging from the imaginative truth, the poetic universality, of the characters' history and bestowing upon it in return a fuller meaning.

IV

Ulysses may be said, then, both to use myth and to achieve the condition of myth. In deploying the imaginative symbols of Homeric myth around his material, Joyce develops a critical irony that mediates between the world of heroic ideals and the world of present fact. The differences between the two sharpen the edge of his action as a critical definition of a particular society at a particular time, but in turn the action also subjects the high and "poetic" Homeric ideals to the scrutiny of commonplace reality. On the other hand, while the differences help Joyce define his hero more specifically, the similarities between the two worlds—and particularly between the individual human experience typical of each—contribute to the referential universality of his hero, and so help project his "trans-temporal montage", his "mythic" vision of Man. Joyce's purposes thus comprehend all the possible ambiguities of effect. Indeed, to speak of *Ulysses'* double relationship with myth is only another way of expressing its characteristic tensions of direction and feeling: its impulse toward fact *vs* its impulse toward ideal; Naturalism *vs* Symbolism; criticism *vs* affirmation; comic irony *vs* tragic irony; centrifugal diversity and elaboration *vs* centripetal simplicity and self-containment.

Despite claims that the details of the Homeric parallel are never disposed without point,[37] probably no reader of *Ulysses* has really thought every single detail is fully justified. The devotion with which Mr Stuart Gilbert reveals them[38] seems only to increase our misgivings as our astonishment recedes, but less because the details are imposed on the action from outside—as I have tried to show, they serve a rather different purpose from organic metaphor—than because they often seem incommensurate with, or even irrelevant to, any purpose. When we discover that there are many allusions in "Cyclops" to the *eye*, the singular form being "precise homage to the monocular Polypheme", or that "Oxen of the Sun" includes a mock-Mandeville description of a tin of sardines because the companions of Ulysses were driven by hunger to catch and eat fish,[39] we can only agree with such critics as Mr Levin and Mr Kain that many of the detailed parallels are idiosyncratic and irrelevant fancies.[40] Evidently Joyce felt he could indulge himself a little by elaborating his basic idea with virtuoso arabesques; he himself compared his art with that of the Book of Kells, and we might well question the adequacy of such a manner in literature.[41] Again, although the ironical or mock-heroic effect of the parallels is more discussed than any other, it is probably less noticeable in actual reading than in the hindsight afforded by commentaries on it. Irony derives from a *felt* disparity between juxtaposed ideas or facts, and it is a fundamental objection to some of the alleged ironies produced by the Homeric parallels that the disparity is not felt—either because the parallel is not visible, or alternatively, because it lacks any important critical implications in itself, depending rather for its point on our total retrospective knowledge of the book. For example, there is surely not much ironic criticism involved in enclosing an interpolation in the narrative with the same line before and after as Homer does[42]; or in having Bloom return to the *Freeman's* office at the end of "Aeolus" because Ulysses had to return; or in including popular phrases about "raising the wind" and the like in the same chapter; or in describing the tattoo marks on a strange sailor because returning pretenders have often relied on birthmarks.[43] In fact, it is hard to see any purpose whatever in such details. Furthermore, to take only the most obvious examples of the other kind of case, the Molly-Penelope parallel has only the simplest and slightest critical effects during the book because we do not meet her until the end—though by then, of course, the effect of the parallel as a whole is considerably deepened and modified in retrospect by her appearance.

Nevertheless, as this implies, the Homeric parallel does make its presence felt as its meanings accumulate and develop through the book until they are discharged in the illumination of "Ithaca". The action is gradually, though not equally and evenly, infused with another temporal dimension, the imaginative effect of which is not fully realized until we look back on the process from its point of completion. To put it in its simplest terms, we need to know Bloom and Stephen fully—that is to say, we need to know what happens—before we can appreciate truly the parallels in the "Telemachia", for example, or in "Aeolus", or "Scylla and Charybdis", or indeed anywhere. From about the end of "Nausicaa", I believe, the Homeric parallel begins to establish itself, to be *felt*, more definitely, as Joyce's narrative techniques begin to distance and objectify his action; but until the relationships between Bloom and Stephen are fully explored, we cannot know them fully; until we do, we cannot see their relationship to their Homeric analogues in all its ironic ambiguity. (*Re*-reading the book is a different matter, of course.) "Ithaca" (and "Penelope") complete our sense of an order that has pervaded the whole of our imaginative experience of Blooms-world and yet transcends it. Our imagination is finally held fascinated in the aesthetic *stasis* of "myth". It is Joyce's myth, however—the *mythos*, the action, that unfolds Bloom and Stephen to their full symbolic status and is, finally, their full symbolic meaning. But by extraneous juxtaposing, by deliberately exploiting his position outside the action, Joyce has also revealed its alignments with other myths, older, more public and imper-sonal, and richer in diffused emotional power.

It is easy to see why *Ulysses* should appear to some readers as a re-enactment of these older myths, and why its meaning and the source of its emotional power should seem to lie in the outlines it shares with them—the "archetypes" of experience they embody in common. The exploration of Myth and Archetype has become a popular preoccupation with literary critics (especially in America, where Jung's theories have permeated most widely), even though the meaning of the terms themselves and their precise relevance to works of literary art are no more settled than their foundations in anthropology and psychology. But in his search for the furthest possible meaning of a work of art, the mythologist-critic is often prepared to use any speculative instrument (sometimes, one is tempted to say, jump to any conclusion); and since the possibilities of analogous application grow proportionally larger as the pattern to be interpreted becomes more abstract, such Archetypes and Myths as can be abstracted from works of art provide a ready way to "deep", multiple interpretation. And so the critic proceeds, most commonly on the assumption that in the patterns of myths, rituals, dreams, lie the permanent configurations of the human mind, and that in these configurations lie the ultimate meanings of works of art—stimulating our deepest emotional responses, and adumbrating a vision of life, mysterious, exciting, numinous, in which all may participate by virtue of their common humanity, but which is apprehensible only by the imagination and emotions, and explorable only through the flexible use of analogy among the various imaginative activities of the mind. Whatever the validity of these assumptions, it is probably inevitable that the results of their application to literature should often seem subjective, speculative, pretentious, or simply platitudinous. Works that express what we may perhaps call a "religious" consciousness seem particularly to attract this kind of treatment (it is, in some ways, a kind of Natural Theology); and works, like *Ulysses*, that deliberately exploit myth seem almost to demand it.[44]

Understandable as this approach may be, however, it seems to me a mistake to consider *Ulysses* a re-enactment of any myth. The kind of mistake involved is like (and sometimes is even a version of) the belief that the structure of the book is modelled on that of the *Odyssey* or of some other myth.[45] The truth is, of course, that the structure of *Ulysses*, like that of most great books, grows by an inner necessity, and is no more a re-enactment of the *Odyssey* (or of other myths) than it is a fictionalized guide to Dublin. A serious artist would waste his time as little on the one project as on the other. Properly speaking, it may be called a re-creation of a myth, though it is that only in part (far less so, for instance, than Mann's Joseph tetralogy or his *Dr Faustus*). It is a work of art in which certain myths are re-imagined, and in re-imagining them the artist has re-formed them and re-created their meaning. Put so baldly, this may seem either a truism or a quibble, but to mistake re-creation for re-enactment (with its suggestions of ritual and belief) is to be led away into exploring the possible significances the myths used may be thought to possess in themselves, into infinite speculations about their archetypal patterns and analogies, instead of the realized meanings of the work itself—the meanings the work bestows upon the myths.

The great dominating myths of our culture have been so powerful, and perhaps still are, partly because they escape restriction within any specific interpretation; they are stories, patterns of human experience (and human experience remains their focus even while they infuse it with the supernatural) that dominate our apprehension of life by enfolding it in a matrix of everpresent wonder and order. They "explain" so much because they seem to comprehend and unite in one symbol all the possible rationalizations we might extract from experience; their power is partly their inherent ambiguity. Once divorced from their origin in implicit, pious belief—and that is the only condition under which we now know the myths of Greece and, for most of us, the myths of Christianity as well—their meanings are perpetually created in our experience, are the colouring they take on from the material into which we project them. The myth is like a potentiality of meaning awaiting actualization in the world we recognize as real, in a specific "now and here". The myth of Oedipus becomes the re-created myth of the Oedipus-complex; Homer's Ulysses becomes Dante's symbol of guile and adventurous pride: the myth is reshaped as its present meaning is created. While we cannot exhaust its potentialities in discursive terms, we can re-experience the myth in the context of our beliefs. Placed among the scattered fragments of our experience, it draws them into the patterns of its own magnetic field; but its meaning is this universal potential power exercised within these given fragments. For the fragments have their own power too. The myth does not remain static and unchanged, but is modified under the pressure of its present actuality. Whether the psycho-analyst can explore its purely potential power or not, its only ascertainable meanings arise in a realizing context, in the process of what Jung calls its "animation" and "shaping".[46] In other words, for the literary critic (I do not speak of the psychoanalyst or anthropologist, whose aims and material are different) the significance of myth lies primarily in the text before him, in the imaginative meanings the artist has realized in his work: the relevant shape, meaning and force of any myth or archetype re-created by the artist are there. And to return to *Ulysses*, the vital meaning of the Homeric and other parallels—the point from which Joyce is enabled to bring the culture of Europe within his range, the source of the mystery to be felt in his apparently anatomized heroes, the centre of the impersonally "mythical" vision towards which the action moves—is to be found not in Homer or in Aquinas or in Buddhist thought or in Dr Jung, but in *Ulysses* itself. Joyce said that his intention was "to transpose the myth *sub specie temporis nostri*".[47] By transposing, he has re-created it (and all the other myths he has adduced) by creating Bloom. The whole existing order, as Eliot has said, is altered by the imagination that renews it.[48] In short, as Bloom becomes Ulysses, Ulysses becomes Bloom.

To define, or even summarily to describe, the mythic vision of *Ulysses* is to define the whole book; at most, one can only point here to certain broad characteristics.

Perhaps the first thing to notice is that, whatever the rôle and effect of mythic Archetypes in *Finnegans Wake*, what we actually feel in *Ulysses*, and especially in "Ithaca", is its force of affirmation, and affirmation not of any doctrine superhuman or supernatural, but of *the mythopoeic imagination itself*. It is as if we come to apprehend in and through Bloom and Stephen—which is to say, in and through the total action—the vital truth of the myths of Ulysses and Christ and the Wandering Jew and Sinbad and so on. We perceive man forever the victor-victim in his world, forever at war with his gods yet unwittingly preserved by them, always seeking adventure homewards, always coming, separated from himself, towards himself, and we perceive and feel these things immediately and together. Our participating experience in the action testifies not only to the cultural disintegration of the world Bloom represents but to its underlying unity and vitality as well. We are thus made to experience what Bloom cannot and Stephen not yet: the validity of our common myths, the present, living truth in Homer, Shakespeare, the Gospels, Dante, and in all the other imaginative matrices of our culture that Joyce includes. And to that extent, of course, our common culture, with its imaginative patterns manifest in so many different forms, also becomes Joyce's subject—but only to that extent. By his periodic but insistent hinting at these parallels, the action becomes, not an encyclopaedia of fixed and definite archetypes or myths,[49] but a living articulation of some (not all) of the cardinal patterns of European experience. Nevertheless, it assumes such a range of reference only because these forms or patterns, abstracted from so large a human experience, are introduced into, and are consonant with, an action we accept as imaginatively valid in itself.

If the action affirms the validity of the myths, the myths also help affirm the validity of the action. They cast upon it their enriching glow of mystery and wonder, and with that all the connotations, the different metamorphoses, they have assumed over the centuries of their life. Joyce, as we know, read widely in Aristotle and Aquinas, in Homer and Odyssean literature,[50] in Shakespeare and Shakespearean criticism, in Dante, in Blake, and in the literature of Buddhism and of popular American evangelism; and each contributes something to the significance of Joyce's myths. The relevance of these writings is not the opportunities they offer for tracing patterns and analogies, nor do they provide us with the key to *Ulysses*. Rather, they help Joyce, and therefore help us, to define, to *specify* the mythic perspective in which the action is finally apprehended. We can appreciate the Homeric parallel more truly if we know how Dante and Shakespeare and Tennyson and others saw Ulysses; we can appreciate the Christ parallel (the total analogy, that is, as it emerges from the work as a whole) more truly if we know how Aquinas saw the Trinity; we can appreciate the Shakespeare parallel more truly if we know something of Romantic and post-Romantic literary theories; and so on. Joyce uses such theories, in the dramatic terms proper to his art, as a critical commentary on his parallels. But the more we comment on and rationalize myth, the greater seems the mystery at its centre. No interpretation or use, no detailed application, ever exhausts its potentialities of meaning, and the only effect of such critical commentaries as Joyce employs especially in "Scylla and Charybdis" and "Ithaca" is to heighten our sense of this. By the same token, the genuine re-creation of myth, especially by such means of cultural montage as Joyce's, serves to heighten our sense of what myths were originally created for: to express, as the artist tries to express in his way, wonder, awe, delight and human kinship, in the face of life and its manifold destinies. In different ways, therefore, both the theoretical commentaries on Shakespeare, Christ, and Ulysses and the mythical parallels themselves point towards the inexpressible centre from which they arise: in the one case, to what in imaginative symbol theoretical commentary cannot reach, and in the other to what imaginative symbol cannot reach in life itself.

This, then, is yet another aspect and effect of "Ithaca"; it is the apex, as it were, of such pointing. After the strain of application, denotation, detail, intellection, in the earlier chapters, "Ithaca" releases something of the *feeling* of myth to enfold the action. The intense regard, the effort of self-knowledge, the critical cerebration of the book as a whole, would lie hard and barren without this mollifying, modifying sense of compassion and wonder at the inexhaustible mystery of man—even twentieth century man. It suggests the link with the divine, or at least the numinous, that makes Bloom man, and makes *Ulysses* more than an irritable scratching in barren sand.

To characterize the process that takes place towards the end of *Ulysses* simply as the achievement of myth or the mythic vision, however, requires the qualification implicit in the context and the conditions of the achievement. The same applies, and more clearly perhaps, to another term which has sometimes been applied to the book, though with rather less justice, I believe— epic. We could say that Joyce, in borrowing from Homer elements he wanted to use for his own different purposes (just as Virgil and Milton and others borrowed what they wanted), was implicitly adopting the long tradition of European epic. We might even go further and, taking "epic" in a loosely generic sense like that used by Ortega y Gasset for example, say that Joyce releases epic elements overlaid in the later tradition of the novel: that his imagination finally shifts away from the prosaic, the ordinary, the representative, the drama of moral experience, which form the characteristic realm of the novel, towards the purity of the ideal, the unique, the marvellous, which form the characteristic realm of the epic; from an art critical and programmatic to an art "neither sad nor gay . . . an Olympian, indifferent art full of forms of eternal ageless objects; . . . an extrinsic, invulnerable art". Senor Ortega, whose phrases these are, argues that the epic perspective, viewing events from the vantage-point of myths whose plastic vitality has been liberated from cosmogonic and historic belief, has always formed the ideal poetic and cultural order against which the novel has deployed the ironical critique of harsh, mute, inert, material fact.[51] We might thus describe the characteristic tensions of *Ulysses* as those Senor Ortega finds typical of the novel as a *genre*: the texture of ironic comedy, the oscillation of criticism between ideal and reality, the ambiguity of the hero who is at once conditioned by the world of fact he inhabits and yet strives, by remoulding it, to become truly and ideally himself. But where Senor Ortega argues that for the novelist there are only two possible attitudes towards the fact of such heroism—"either we rush with it towards sorrow, because we consider that the heroic life has 'meaning', or we give reality the slight push which is enough to destroy all heroism, as a dream is shattered by waking the sleeper"—Joyce seems to transcend the characteristics of the novel by releasing once again the epic perspective from within it and presenting it anew. Thus, although his critics sometimes rush towards sorrow with Bloom's (or Stephen's) heroism, or, more frequently, give reality the slight push that shatters it, Joyce himself does neither—or rather, seems to do both. By holding the two tendencies in balance, and suggesting thereby the perspective in which they are equally possible but equally incomplete, he seems to achieve an Olympian detachment and finality. In "Ithaca" (and, we must add, "Penelope", though severe qualifications will have to be made about it in a later chapter), the events of the book derive their meaning not from their relation to anything in the world in which they are enacted, nor from the mere exhibition of heroic will to transform that world, but from the plenitude of the vision that beholds them. If we do use the term "epic", therefore, it cannot be in reference to the epic *form*, nor is it the same mode as Stephen calls "epical" in the *Portrait*. *Ulysses* is clearly not an epic in the same sense as the *Odyssey* or even as the *Aeneid* or *Paradise Lost*. Joyce does not borrow from Homer literary elements or methods that have a traditional, accepted, recognizable significance for their implicit tone or mood or outlook; by abandoning the epic form or *genre* he really abandons epic as a living mode of apprehending and expressing contemporary experience. *Ulysses* remains a novel, even though in its mood and outlook it is high, aloof, so impersonal that its shifts back towards something like the objective universality of myth.

We must finally recognize that even in a loose sense "epic" does not quite meet the case. Joyce's shift is not back to any un-selfconscious, social, accepted vision of life; he does not share the direct impulse of a community that seizes the human and the divine together in a totality of belief. As Hegel says, "what fails us . . . is the *primitive* world-condition as poetically conceived, which is the source of the genuine Epos".[52] In our age, myth can be meaningfully approached only by the individual and through art, deliberately sought and re-created so that it affords a valuable commentary on the present. The very common urge towards "epic" or myth in the last few decades is very largely directed at the *idea* of "epic" or myth, almost apart from its putative content, for the supernatural crosslight it apparently throws on the spiritual decay in ordinary prosaic reality. Nevertheless, the truth about the individual acting and reacting in his world is no longer expressible in genuine epic or myth. The mythopoeic Heroic Age has long been corroded away by reason, by philosophy, science, and historical self-consciousness, and a simple retreat is cut off except at the price of deliberate self-mutilation of the spirit. The way through, as artists so different as Yeats, Eliot, Lawrence, Mann and Joyce have discovered, is harder and full of traps. But equally, the conventions of the realistic novel have also seemed to be corroding away. Like the musical conventions Mann's Dr Faustus repudiates, once directly expressive because they did not seem conventions at all, the methods of the nineteenth-century novelist, in narrative and plot, character and motivation, have seemed less and less adequate to explore what has happened to the individual and his world. The characteristic result in the literature of this century has been to press beyond individual feelings and "conventional" truth towards some common and impersonal grounds of vision and communication. In one aspect, this appears as an imaginative drive towards the original, primitive sources of spiritual wholeness and vitality—through the gasworks to the Fisher-king, so to speak; in another aspect, it appears as a movement towards the one apparent objective basis of human unity, the impersonal symbol of myth, in which all individual significances may be accommodated—through the rose-garden, as it were, to the Rose. But since this movement towards myth is from, as well as through, subjective experience, starting from but also carrying along with it the intuitions of the individual, it is necessarily (and perhaps fatally) self-conscious. And in that fact, obvious but often overlooked, lies the most important inadequacy of "epic", in any sense, as a term for the imaginative process undertaken, and also the necessary quali-fication even to the description of Joyce's final vision in *Ulysses* as "mythic".

Since Joyce's use of myth (like his use of parodies and changing narrative techniques) is a means of suggesting obliquely what lies beyond accepted beliefs and attitudes and thus beyond con-ventions so thoroughly accepted as to be invisible, it must, like his theoretical commentaries too, draw attention to itself *as* technique in order to urge the reader to look beyond it.[53] The extraneous, choric parallels serve the various purposes of social definition, of historical inclusion and reference, of suggesting the heart of darkness in the protagonists, but, like the narrative techniques, they also frankly declare themselves as a device towards the end of the book—specifically, of course, when the Odyssean and other parallels are explicitly elaborated in "Ithaca". The shift back from the predominant conventions of naturalism to myth is revealed as self-consciously and demon-stratively undertaken to reach what could not be expressed through the consciousness or imagination of the characters. In its effects, the shift actually serves to define their limitations, for the temporal perspective it creates enables us to perceive that *Ulysses* is the future dimly prefigured to Stephen; that time, projected out of the characters' immediate concerns with it, is also one of the actors; and that the action fulfils itself only in the self-knowledge and freedom of the artist contemplating his world and aware of the unknown that surrounds and inhabits it.

For beyond the freedom of the artist who creates *Ulysses* we glimpse the freedom of the life he contemplates—that is to say, the achieved liberation of its possibilities of being apprehended and, more than that, its self-contained fulness of potentiality. The last pitch of Joyce's achievement is to see around and beyond the realms of social and of moral life, even though his attention remains focused there and he accepts no doctrine about what transcends them. In resorting to mythic parallels and theoretical commentary, he points not only to the radical deficiencies of his protagonists and the world they represent (which is all that many of his critics see), but also to their still more radical vitality. Bloom is no Ulysses or Christ, yet in truth he is; the modern world manifests itself in any one day, but so does the world in any age, and Bloomsday exhibits as well as the social contours of today the permanent contours of human life. The parallels are made to point to the gap between *Ulysses* as an action and *Ulysses* as a fact, a deed; by that means the action (which we must now therefore understand as including all the points of view developed by the artist himself) is made to point to the synthesis of Bloom and Stephen in the comprehension of the artist; and in and by that comprehension, we behold the process of human life, now and here, in its perennial condition. This, I believe, is the imaginative truth that most deeply moves the book—and most deeply moves the reader. It is what underlies Joyce's impersonal, comprehensive irony, and if we do not feel that quality of irony animating the book we cannot be moved by it ourselves. We may agree that *Ulysses* is a magnificent indictment of modern society, a profound and subtle analysis of Christian-Humanist civilization in decay, a superb construction of inter-related symbols; but as well as, or perhaps in spite of, its Flaubertian facets, it is a book that attracts readers, holds them, moves them, and brings them back to re-experience it. It engages more than our historical or cultural ideas and our critical insight. It draws our participating sympathies and refashions them into an original, felt apprehension of life at a deeper and more inclusive level.

The work itself, the artist, and the material, all become analogues of each other. Not only does the work achieve the completion and freedom of a universal imaginative symbol, but the dramatic action of Stephen-Bloom-Joyce achieves completion in the *stasis* of the "mythic" contemplation of life. And finally life is also revealed in its fulness of potentiality: in and yet behind the critical tensions of its ironies, in the interplay and in the collapse of accepted distinctions, and in the sense Joyce creates of the mysterious, inexhaustible processes that move in time but only towards the one great goal of their own manifold efflorescence.

Joyce's outlook is sometimes described as coldly aloof from human life, cosmically indifferent to all moral values. On that view of it, as we have seen, *Ulysses* has been both implicitly praised and, with more justification, vehemently attacked. Yet it is not really an adequate description at all. How far it may apply to "Penelope" is a question I shall take up in Chapter VII, but the wider question of its adequacy is not answerable from any one chapter. The only relevant outlook worth discussing, the only valid one, is that expressed by the book as a whole. And if Joyce's "mythic" vision, as I have tried to suggest, transcends the moral life of "now and here", it is never detached from it. It neither places different values side by side with a shrug of relativistic indifference, nor denies the validity of human effort and concern. On the contrary, just as the vision itself emerges out of the closest engagement with daily life, so it finally expresses and affirms the values partly realized in it. As Joyce sees it, art neither denies life nor provides a substitute for it. Art is continuous with life, but capable, by understanding, directing and shaping, of clarifying and deepening it. This, indeed, is what constitutes the real achievement of *Ulysses* itself. But to explore its values further, and especially to assay them in the actual organizations of the work, involves a preliminary glance at some critical preconceptions about Joyce's art that seem to stand in the way of its proper appraisal.

CHAPTER VI

SYMBOLISM AND REALISM:
A DIGRESSION

PERHAPS no aspect of *Ulysses* has provoked so much commentary and exegesis as Joyce's linguistic and technical
virtuosity—in particular, his use of metaphorical analogy and
allusion, of verbal association, of ambiguities of phrase and
syntax, musical suggestiveness, indirect evocation, and other
devices more common in Symbolist poetry than in the novel.[1]
But if the day is past when this virtuosity quite obscured the
more fundamental aspects of the book, it has nevertheless led
Joyce's critics to explore the meaning and value of his art along
two different (though related) paths, both of which, I believe,
lead away from its central interest and tend to darken the central
critical issues.

On the one hand, as we have seen, some have tried to read
Ulysses as a poem. All the events and objects in it seem to be
connected, and connected in ways well beyond the view of any
of the characters. Objects, thoughts, images recur again and
again, sometimes mentioned explicitly, sometimes suggested by
metaphorical association, so that they finally seem to form
meaningful patterns or "themes" in themselves, patterns whose
significance is quite different from the contexts or purposes of
objects and events in the ordinary world the novel represents.
It is a significance that apparently stands over and above the
represented action. Thus "omphalos", for example, or "parallax", water, paternity, the Mass, *Hamlet*, Bloom's potato talisman
and that whole elaborate "symbolic" structure of arts, organs,
colours and techniques on which Joyce evidently organized each
chapter and, through the chapters, the whole book, are all taken
as "symbolic themes". and the meaning of the book, like the
meaning of a poem, sought in the totality of meanings the
"symbols" may be said to possess in themselves. It is hardly
surprising that the significance of *Ulysses* should seem richer than
that of any other novel (*Finnegans Wake* excepted) and yet more

intangible and obscure to the reader who attempts it without
benefit of critics.

Unfortunately there seem to be as many meanings as there are
critics. This would not signify, of course (for what complex work
of art has a simple meaning? what two people respond to it in the
same way?), were the interpretations not so wildly different.
There seems little general agreement even about the fundamental
question of how to set about deciding what are the important
"themes"—a problem that arises very largely from the fact that
Ulysses is not a poem. Probably the first major attempt to interpret the book thematically was Mr Stuart Gilbert's, and we can
see the problem implicit in the method and nature of his interpretation. It seemed to him "impossible to grasp the meaning
of *Ulysses*, its symbolism and the significance of its *leitmotifs*
without an understanding of the esoteric theories which underlie
the work".[2] Under his intense regard every detail became
significant, and significant of theosophical and other esoteric
doctrines about the Soul. All subsequent readers of Joyce are in
Mr Gilbert's debt for his analyses; very few readers, however,
have been prepared to accept his interpretation. Yet it is a
perfectly possible one—granted, that is, his assumptions about
how to interpret symbols. There is no denying the dense symbolic
organization he was one of the first to point out, nor the references
scattered through the book to various Symbolist writers;
undoubtedly Joyce's symbolism has to be considered as part of
the total meaning of the work. But if Mr Gilbert's way of interpreting it is generally felt to be wrong, what is the right way,
and why?

The other direction in which Joyce's verbal techniques have
led critical discussion is towards *psychological* analysis, the
examination of how his devices enable him not so much to create
"thematic" patterns as to explore the depths of the human mind.
The natural end of this critical direction is another body of
complex exegetical commentary: comparisons with other
"psychological" novelists like Dorothy Richardson, Virginia
Woolf or William Faulkner, discussions of Bergson on Time,
William James on "the stream of thought", Freud, Jung,
multiple consciousness and Symbolism once more. Apparently
Joyce's aim is to delve into the subtle and irrational recesses of
mental life; how better, then, can we grasp the significance of

his work than by referring to what philosophers and psychologists have discovered about the mind? Once again the reader is faced with the intimidating suggestion that he requires elaborate special knowledge before he can properly understand the book at all.

There is no need to deny that critical and exegetical scholarship can throw new and valuable light on a work of art, or that Joyce's symbolism and narrative techniques have seriously to be explored as part of his total meaning. On the other hand it is important not to confuse new light with the only light, and important likewise to grasp what are the relevant critical problems facing reader and critic alike, even if no one can claim to give final and exhaustive answers to them. For instance, it is perhaps the most surprising aspect of both the critical approaches I have mentioned that each seems frequently to issue in a crudely realistic interpretation of *Ulysses*. The book is taken as the representation of some predetermined kind of Reality—either the naturalistic reality of social and psychological facts, or the metaphysical reality of some spiritual world assumed to be revealed elsewhere—so that the meaning and value of the book are sought in its embodiment of that Reality. Most of Joyce's critics would very properly repudiate any blatant correspondence theory of art if it were presented to them in so many words; the odd thing is how many seem to accept and apply a glossier version of the same belief when explaining his techniques or his symbolic structures.

Before turning to a necessarily brief and tentative examination of these in the new chapter, therefore, it may be a helpful preliminary to digress a little from the book itself and, looking again at the aesthetic theories outlined in Chapters II and III, enquire how Joyce himself conceived the nature of symbolism in art and thought about technique in the novel. Doing so, I believe, may help clear away some of the simplistic assumptions about his Realism—an endeavour perhaps marginal to the actual achievement of *Ulysses* but certainly not to the present view of it; and since Joyce's theory is sometimes more convincing than his practice, it may also enable us to use the one as a point of vantage from which to explore the other.

I

As we have seen, there are certain uses of symbolism that Stephen (or Joyce) deliberately rejected from art. In particular, he would have nothing to do with "Platonism" or any doctrine of metaphysics by which the work of art became a mere reflection of a transcendental Absolute. His fundamental concept—the epiphany—involves a conjunction of subject and object. The latter reveals its inner form, a meaning; the subject's mind also takes on that form in apprehension; in doing so, it partly realizes itself; and it finally expresses the meaning it apprehends in a "word". The expressive medium is not necessarily verbal language, of course; Stephen makes a point especially familiar to Symbolist aestheticians when in "Circe" he remarks that "gesture, not music, not odours, would be a universal language, the gift of tongues rendering visible not the lay sense but the first entelechy, the structural rhythm" (413/425). But he never imputes any metaphysical status to that structural rhythm. The epiphany is the object as the subject apprehends it in the context of his total experience, not a subjective idealization of the object, nor some supposed metaphysical "essence" of the object, nor the object turned into a symbol of some other object or of some higher Reality. His rejection of any supernatural world or Ideal Intelligibility revealed by art is quite explicit in the *Portrait* and obviously implied in the conception of the "classical temper" expounded in *Stephen Hero*. It is by working upon the present reality that "the sane and joyful spirit issues forth and achieves imperishable perfection, nature assisting with her goodwill and thanks" (*S.H.* 66). And whatever Stephen's changes of formulation and emphasis, in this his general attitude is perfectly clear and perfectly consistent with his more considered, if apparently more paradoxical, assumptions in *Ulysses*. Art is not the expression of "formless spiritual essences", nor the revelation of an Ideal world, nor the representation and deployment of natural objects considered as "signatures" or allegories or emblems of a system of metaphysical abstractions. Art does not fulfil, nor is fulfilled by, metaphysical commitments; the artist's words and images are not especially meaningful before he *makes* them so.

For Joyce, then, the way in which art is symbolic has no

necessary connection with the systematic employment of "symbols" in the ordinary sense, of images or words whose meanings are to be discovered only outside the work of art and then to be attributed as meanings of the work itself. The meanings of which a work (or an incident in it, or an image) is the symbol are created in, and by, the art itself; they are the relationships, or "forms", or "rhythms", it establishes among the meanings of the words of which it is composed. Its raw material is the ordinary language—and hence what is embodied in it, the common life—of all men, not a private or esoteric language available to initiates with separate means of access to another "order of Being". In other words, art is inevitably tied to "the now, the here", the ordinary reality of this world, which is open to all, and whose limiting resistance to the ordering of the artist's vision is to be accepted with the "security and satisfaction and patience" of "the classical temper". If art re-forms life by re-forming language, charging it with meaning to the utmost degree, it charges it from within, as it were; it continues the same process by which ordinary language is created. For just as the word expresses the apprehension of the object by the subject in an act of apprehension, so, at a higher level, does art. And because art expresses a "spiritual" meaning—a moral meaning, in the widest sense of that term—which is ideally born from the harmonious order within the artist himself, and because his order includes the acceptance of the world he shares with others—its problems, its language, its traditions—the meaning of that art becomes a universal one and capable of critical judgment. In short, while an artist believes in a transcendental world in which his readers do not, he cannot express it directly except at the cost of artistic impoverishment. The natural world is only his starting-point, his material, but as an artist he must work upon and refashion that. To try to by-pass it by relying on any philosophy or esoteric tradition to furnish his work with significance is to mistake the nature of art just as much as to suppose that artistic significance could consist in direct *reportage* or kinetic effectiveness.

In themselves, the ideas developed in Joyce's various works are by no means either very original or complete. It seems obvious enough today that aesthetic symbolism has little to do with allegory however dilute—though it was perhaps not quite so clear in 1900[3]—but Joyce never developed an explicit theory of symbols or language beyond what he felt necessary to his immediate purposes. Furthermore, it would be absurd to suppose that his practice is exhausted by his theory or even entirely at one with it. But whatever their limitations, his views are clear and sensible enough to see what he meant and why, and to see, too, why certain aspects of his own art themselves demand criticism. At the least, his theory serves to warn us against certain ways of interpreting his symbolism and to direct us towards others.

In the first place, in Joyce's view the artist creates the significance ordinary objects may have for the human spirit by re-creating them in aesthetic images. There is no suggestion that the objects do not exist in their own right as observable and interpretable by each man in his own way and as material facts to reckon with in human action. What Joyce does deny is that they possess *a* spiritual significance which it is the artist's function to discover and express. A bird, a tree, a tin of potted meat, may be so worked on and fashioned by the artist in his appropriate language as to express very complex states of soul; nevertheless they are not in themselves already or merely symbols of Ideas or of what Plato or Plotinus or Aquinas or Blake or Mme. Blavatsky says about the Soul. They are not "signatures" the artist merely presents to the reader's attention. Thus, whatever Joyce's symbols do signify, we can at least assert that his aesthetic theories do not encourage an allegorical interpretation of his work as the expression of esoteric or other metaphysical "Realities". The allusions in the course of *Ulysses* to Hermetic writers, like the allusions to other kinds of speculative theories, are Stephen's, and must be read in the context of the novel as a whole. They are not hints of Joyce's "angelic" aspirations nor guides to the "proper" interpretation of *Ulysses*. As one critic has truly remarked, when Joyce toyed with such metaphysical notions he did so as an artist, not a magician.[4]

Joyce's conception of the aesthetic symbol also suggests another danger: a too easy and superficial distinction between Naturalism and Symbolism in his art. For Joyce the aesthetic symbol expresses both the "naturalistic" world of external reality and the activity of the individual at the same time. On his basis, symbolism is simply the method of all art, though a method open to abuse as a result of misunderstanding its nature and necessity. In the context of other Symbolist theories of the nineteenth century, Joyce's appears as an early attempt to justify the aesthetic symbol without the encumbrance of mystical or occult doctrines to support the meaningfulness of art and without relapsing into a solipsistic Narcissism. His gropings towards a theory of knowledge and of language are an inevitable consequence of that attempt. But to say that he pressed Naturalism into the service of Symbolism is too simple a description of his aims and his art. It would be just as true, and just as misleading, to say that he tied Symbolism to the discipline of Naturalism. In fact, his mature theorizing was designed to avoid the dichotomy altogether. And he saw the further implications of his attitude quite clearly. If art must accept the ordinary world of common language in order to refashion it, and if the meaning of art is the further insight the refashioning affords into that world, this has its application to other human activities besides art. For as Stephen's early phrases about "the classical temper" already suggest, it is only a particular case—one relevant to his own vocation as an artist—of a moral truth he believed to apply to *all* men. The central theme of *Ulysses* is consequently figured in its artistic theory: the spiritual kinship of citizen and artist, and their common need to accept, as the medium of their transforming activity, the present reality they share with all other human beings—not, of course, as messianic materialists, or in the spirit of "whatever is, is right", but with a temper of "security and satisfaction and patience". Bloom is a mature and profound gloss on those early phrases in *Stephen Hero*. As for Stephen, his tendency to retreat into purely idealistic and speculative realms is really an index of what is crippling him; it is his instinctive love and grip of the ordinary material world in which men think, feel, act, apprehend and create meaning and beauty, that preserves him from utter defeat. Though he is drawn towards the whirlpools of speculative metaphysics, perhaps even towards the artistic dead-end of solipsism at times, the question he asks himself at the beginning of "Proteus" indicates the force that keeps him from succumbing, and, tentative as it seems, really underpins his whole discussion of Shakespeare:

Ineluctable modality of the visible: at least that if no more, thought through my eyes. Signatures of all things I am here to read, seaspawn and seawrack, the nearing tide, that rusty boot. Snotgreen, bluesilver, rust: coloured signs. Limits of the diaphane. But he adds: in bodies. . . . *Why in?* (33-4/38; my italics)[5]

Whether we like it or not, there is a real and important sense in which Bloom speaks for his creator as he stands among the graves of the dead:

There is another world after death named hell. I do not like that other world she wrote. No more do I. Plenty to see and hear and feel yet. Feel live warm beings near you. Let them sleep in their maggoty beds. They are not going to get me this innings. Warm beds: warm fullblooded life. (107/113)[6]

Joyce's symbolism has been variously compared to that of the Hermeticists,[7] Dante, Boehme, Phineas Fletcher, Swedenborg, Blake, Flaubert, the French Symbolists, Freud and Jung—and we might easily add another analogue in Bruno. Stephen's allusions certainly suggest that Joyce had read in most of these authors (though how deeply in each case is another question), and his aesthetic theories clearly belong in the tradition of symbolist speculation. *Ulysses* itself testifies to his intense interest in the possibilities of symbolic expression both in art and in other activities; in correspondences between the different senses and between macrocosm and microcosm; in the value of the non-rational, symbolizing capacities of the mind; in the possibility of an eternal realm of Being beyond the categories of time and space; in the techniques of the *Symbolistes*—musical evocation, suggestion, metaphorical ellipsis, implication and other means to express intangible complexities of meaning; in the creation of "myth"; in the conception of artistic impersonality; and in the conception of art as a self-contained symbol. But before we can trace the influence of any of these writers or ideas upon him, we must understand his own ideas, aims and practice.

Actually to trace and estimate such influences obviously demands a series of accurate, sensitive and thorough-going studies in itself, and this is not the place to attempt it. All that need be done here, however, is to suggest a few of the considerations that emerge even from so brief a summary as this. We must realize, for example, that as the evidence up to and including *Ulysses* indicates, Joyce's Symbolism, if it can be called that, involved no Idealist or mystical doctrines, nor any real, magical correspondences between microcosm and macrocosm. Again, despite the important debt he owes to Mallarmé—both in his art and (very probably) in his aesthetic theory as well—he was very much less concerned with the complex ontological issues of artistic creation, and much more alert to the danger both of sterility for the self-conscious artist and of impenetrable obscurity for art too heavily committed to the *lyric* impulse.[8] Moreover, he firmly rejects any suggestion that art is merely the evocation of personal mood or emotion. On the other hand, he does not, like Blake, believe that it reveals any unitary world of spirit in which everything exists more or less: despite the similarity between some of his views and Blake's—on the *aesthetic* symbol, for instance, and even on such moral issues as repression and jealousy—he does not share Blake's tendencies to universal spiritual prophecy (though perhaps *Finnegans Wake* might invite a qualification to this). As Stephen puts it to himself, people like Russell "creepycrawl after Blake's buttocks into eternity of which this vegetable world is but a shadow. Hold to the now, the here . . ." (175/184).[9] Nor does Joyce pretend to the religious beliefs that gave Dante and Phineas Fletcher an elaborate system of meaningful symbolism they shared with their age. The collapse of any such common belief (not to mention Joyce's own rejection of Catholicism) deprived him, as any modern artist, of any such accepted, exoteric *language*; if he uses it, it is as any other esoteric language which must be given meaning in his art. And finally, there is no evidence to suggest that, whatever scraps of psychological insight Joyce picked up from the Freudians or Jungians, he shared their belief in the primary importance of the Unconscious, or their rational, unitary interpretation of what they regard as symbols.

When we look for real artistic affinities rather than influences on his symbolic techniques, I think the closest analogue is not Dante, or Mallarmé, or Blake, or Flaubert, or even Ibsen, but Shakespeare. Despite the rigorous cast of mind and the vast, encyclopaedic aspirations he shared with Dante, despite the aesthetic principles and linguistic resources he partly inherited from the French Symbolists, despite even the naturalistic "classicism" (in Stephen's sense of the word) he partly inherited from Flaubert and Ibsen, Joyce's outlook is finally less intense, less absolute, more comic, more humane, than any of theirs.

Of course, there were deeper motives for his attraction to Symbolist writers than mere technical curiosity. All of them, from Blake to Mallarmé, and even (in another kind) Dante too, were "exiles" deeply critical of the material reality of their times, and most of them, on one ground or another, rejected it for another kind of reality in their art. That the status of spiritual activity, the reality of values, presented acute philosophical and aesthetic problems to the writers of the nineteenth century only exacerbated the tone in which they rejected the apparently meaningless reality of an industrial and bourgeois world. There is no denying that Stephen's allusions to them represent important tendencies in Joyce himself; as we have seen, *Ulysses* is also in part a similar rejection of the same chaotic world. Yet this was only one side of Joyce's reading, and only one side of his outlook and art. To speak only of living presences in *Ulysses*, we might point to Defoe, and Sterne, and Rabelais perhaps; certainly there is Homer; above all there is Shakespeare. These seem to come closer to the "sane and joyful spirit", and they remind us of the elements of "affirmation" Joyce valued in Ibsen and presumably in Blake and Dante too. They suggest another outlook on human life and aspiration, another tone of voice, which in *Ulysses* balances and finally outweighs criticism, "parody", spiritual intensities and rejection.

They also suggest two major questions for the critic of *Ulysses*. The first is whether there is anything in Joyce's view of reality that supports the values by which he criticizes or rejects it. If he denies Ideal Realities of all kinds, where *in the world he portrays* is there anything more than the mechanical bodies and subjective emotion that Mr Kenner sees there? Dante's values, Shakespeare's values, are securely founded in the world as they exhibit it; on what are founded the values Joyce implies in his criticism of life? The second question is closely connected with this and concerns the range of *Ulysses*, its claim to encyclopaedic authority as a critical survey of reality. Can such a claim be established by a vast range of closely interlocking "symbols" such as those arts, organs, colours, techniques, objects and phrases—the "themes" to the analysis and interpretation of which so much commentary has been devoted? Does it not rather depend on the range of *aesthetic* symbols (or epiphanies), the created units of imaginative meaning? In the course of his discussion of French

Symbolist theories, Mr A. G. Lehmann brings the issue out very clearly. One of the dreams that haunted the Symbolists, as he says, was that of the universal poem, "a work of art of epic dimensions in which the entire experience of Man is set out, ordered, and subordinated to a general interpretation of Life", on the model of *The Divine Comedy* or *Faust* or, Joyce might have added, the plays of Shakespeare considered as a whole. In some ways, *Ulysses* can be regarded as the fulfilment of this dream. But in suggesting why the fulfilment did not come from the Symbolists themselves, Mr Lehmann incidentally illuminates the reasons why Joyce went to Aristotle and Aquinas for his terminology, why he took Shakespeare for his illustration, and why the range of his work needs closer scrutiny. For a poem of such epic scale, Mr Lehmann goes on, "every line is needed that is there" even though it is also true that "a greater span of structural —formal—problems must be taken in hand". The problems are not essentially different from those of a work on a smaller scale. The Symbolists thought that they were.

The symbolists, once again, attempted to draw a demarcation line between simple poetry and *l'Œuvre*, something entirely different in kind; for Mallarmé an absolutely unconditioned masterpiece; for others, a *summum opus* of special and indeed religious attributes. Only with poetry in its actual state, no such achievement. Hours might be spent speculating on the possible claimant to the succession of Dante and Goethe; but they would be wasted hours; for where among the symbolists was the poet with that familiarity with his age, its affairs and problems, to write the poem of industrial and colonizing France? Symbolist tradition, for all its claims to be a new religion, to give unequalled insight into deep truths, was too narrowly-based to carry the weight of an epic.

The encyclopaedic ambition demands the assimilation of an encyclopaedic range of experience, and probably the aid of rich and vital traditions and conventions is indispensable to the individual effort. Yet, as Mr Lehmann says, "in place of—say— the solid and immense body of symbolism and experience offered by a mediaeval Christianity, as pressed into service by Dante, the symbolists had nothing but some pseudo-philosophical scraps, some new developments of metaphor, a museum-knowledge of some myth, and a powerful dislike for middle-class life in an industrial state. No place here for 'total art'."[10] The question with Joyce is to what extent he triumphed over these same creative handicaps in pursuit of the same ideal.

II

Turning from these general considerations about Joyce's aesthetic to their relevance to the Novel in particular, the first thing to notice is that just as Stephen's conception of the epiphany has sometimes been misinterpreted as a special theory of Symbolism, so his distinction in the *Portrait* (243-5) between the lyrical, epical and dramatic "forms" has sometimes been misinterpreted as a special theory of Realism in the novel—either a Realism of critical attitude on the part of the novelist or a Realism of technique. Although I have already suggested (in Chapter III) what I think Stephen does mean by his distinction, it is worth re-examining it at this stage in the context of the assumptions of *Ulysses*, to which it really points, if only to see how these misconceptions about Joyce's approach to art have arisen. For the truth is, I believe, that while Stephen himself confuses several different issues in his discussion, with the result that his key terms—"dramatic" and "impersonal"—function with several senses at once, his confusion has been the worse confounded by the various efforts of Joyce's critics to fit his novels into Stephen's scheme.[11]

Stephen's distinction may be regarded in any of three ways, but in no one of them consistently: (*a*) as a *descriptive* distinction between literary "forms" or *genres*; (*b*) as a *critical* distinction between the self-subsistent aesthetic symbol (or work) and that which is imperfect because not self-subsistent; and, connected with this, (*c*) a *demand* that the novelist render his subject dramatically.

The first is the most obvious and the one from which the discussion actually starts. Stephen's initial account of his forms is completely without critical overtones. The lyrical, as he defines it, is that "wherein the artist presents his image in immediate relation to himself"; the epical is that wherein "he presents his image in immediate relation to himself and to others"; the dramatic that wherein "he presents his image in immediate relation to others" (243). At first sight this seems only a differentiation of obvious *genres*, but as Stephen elaborates it it becomes something rather different. To follow his elaboration, however, we must first grasp his underlying conception of the aesthetic "image", even though, as we have seen, his own grasp of it in the *Portrait* is anything but secure.

We have seen in Chapter III that Joyce encourages us to consider the poetic process, the formation of the "epiphany", under several aspects. It is a constructive act, a creative *making*. It is also the *expression* of a personal attitude on the part of the maker. It is also, in so far as the thing made has signification, the expression of an intuition, *an act of understanding* or apprehension. Or we may place the emphasis differently and think of the structure of the work itself as objectifying and thus *revealing* a structure, a meaning, *in reality*. These are not separable elements or functions, but simply different aspects of the one complex activity. In "Scylla and Charybdis" that fact provides the ground for some of Stephen's paradoxes about Shakespeare. In the *Portrait*, his account of *consonantia* and *claritas* exhibits no very perfect understanding of the two latter aspects of the process. In his theory of "forms", however, he does to some extent assume that the constructive activity of the imagination both expresses a personal attitude and at the same time projects a "reality" which is the object—or, rather, the content—of that attitude. We can phrase his assumption more clearly perhaps in the terms Joyce gives him in *Ulysses* (413/425): an "epiphany" (or work of art) is basically a "gesture", an act of the total personality of the maker, which "renders visible" what is there to be revealed in reality—"an entelechy"—by and in the medium of a constructed "structural rhythm".

He begins his elaboration from the obvious fact that although these aspects belong to any work of art, the relations between them differ in different kinds or forms. In a lyric, for example, personal expressiveness predominates over objective revelation. The lyric is the most subjective of poetic gestures, its "structural rhythm" expressing primarily a mood or, as Stephen puts it, an "instant of emotion". We can see what he means readily enough if we consider a poem like "O western wind". The personal gesture of the poem does, to a certain extent, reveal a structure or meaning in reality: a connection between "small rain" and the intimacy of lovers for example. But the emphasis is all on the personal gesture rather than on any vision of life it bodies forth; the poem, we might say, is concerned with an attitude to reality rather than with reality itself. No world we can recognize or imaginatively live in ourselves is objectified, no conception of life created, more than is necessary as the simple correlative (to adapt Eliot's term) of the simple emotion. The poem has force and its meaning is quite public; the point is that we are not inclined to make judgments about the *moral* sensibility of the artist. "Dramatic" art, with its greater impersonality, finally develops out of this mode, not quite as an "escape from emotion" or an "escape from personality" as Eliot puts it, but as a development of emotion and of personality.[12] The attitude expressed in the work becomes more elaborate, more conscious of itself *as* an attitude, and so more conscious of the world as its object. Consequently it expresses itself in a more complex and specific sense of "reality". Stephen calls the first stage of this process "epical" presumably by analogy with the heroic epic, in the most primitive forms of which a society unconsciously projects its ethos as a vision of reality, although from the further inspection of that reality it may eventually become conscious of itself as possessing a specific ethos and in doing so achieve philosophic self-understanding. This seems to be what is in Stephen's mind when he speaks of the "lyrical" artist uttering his cry while "more conscious of the instant of emotion than of himself as feeling emotion", and of the "epical" artist as one who "prolongs and broods upon himself as the centre of an epical event" while his personality "passes into the narration itself, flowing round and round the persons and the action like a vital sea. This progress", he continues, "you will see easily in that old English ballad *Turpin Hero* which begins in the first person and ends in the third person" (244). The "dramatic" mode is reached when the development of self-awareness is complete, when the personality of the artist reaches maturity. The content of its poetic gesture can now be a complex, mature understanding of "reality"—"life purified in and reprojected from the human imagination", in Stephen's phrase. The personality of the artist indeed now hardly seems to matter—it "impersonalises itself, so to speak"—because its expression is no longer that of a relatively simple and, because unconscious, relatively private attitude (desire or dream, for instance), but something more adequately described as a vision of *life*. The artistic attitude is so complex that it demands the most specific and searching image of reality for its expression; and the artist in his maturity becomes an impersonally sensitive catalyst of the spiritual condition of his society and age. Again Stephen evidently names this mode of art "dramatic" by analogy, for drama is the *genre* wherein the author never formally appears but expresses his meaning in a convention that is (to some degree at least) an image (or "imitation") of the objective world. But of course the dramatic conventions are not essential to Stephen's mode: a work in any form could fit his description. Some poems we call lyrics, for instance, reach a degree of impersonal complexity and self-awareness that might well entitle them to Stephen's term "dramatic". Clearly "O western wind" does not, but what of "Dejection: An Ode" or "Sailing to Byzantium"?

All this is a matter of descriptive terminology, however, and clearly of more importance to Joyce himself—and to Stephen's situation and rôle in the *Portrait*—than to the critic of his works. If we wished to place those works within this scheme the result would be more obvious than informative: *Chamber Music*— "lyrical"; *Stephen Hero*—"epical"; with the three later novels all "dramatic". The one work that would give us trouble, interestingly enough, is *Exiles*, for here, despite the use of the dramatic conventions, we feel the artist present as a man, prolonging and brooding on himself as the centre of the action, rather than an impersonal artistic presence, with the man refined out of existence. And this, we also feel, is an imperfection, just as we feel that *Stephen Hero* is imperfect beside the *Portrait*. At this point we can perceive another distinction in Stephen's remarks as well as the purely descriptive one.

It emerges most clearly in his suggestion that the "dramatic" mode is the best, or is at least more perfect than the "epical". As he describes "dramatic" art his language grows eloquent: "the mystery", he says, "of esthetic, like that of material creation, is accomplished"—a conclusion hardly implicit in his definition of the mode as that wherein the artist presents his image "in immediate relation to others". More importantly, although he does not say it in so many words, nor would it bear examination if he did, he implies that in some sense all other art is lower in status than the dramatic. In other words, he is making a distinction of value. Such a distinction cannot apply simply to works in the particular forms—plays as against lyrics or epics. What it can apply to, however, is the complexity of the artistic activity involved in any work, the comparative richness and maturity of the artist's moral and spiritual attitudes as they are realized in the work itself. That is the first evaluative implication of Stephen's distinction and, though he does not grasp it himself until *Ulysses*, the most important. But there is also another, connected with this, which he does see a little more clearly in the *Portrait* because it is closely related to his conception of *kinesis*. Once again his use of the word "form" partly obscures his meaning. When he speaks of the "epical" passing over into the "dramatic" he can hardly mean that narrative forms develop into dramatic forms—even if only because he speaks of the development as that of the artist himself. Rather he seems to imply that the "epical" artist really expresses a personal attitude in a *quasi*-dramatic mode, that the vitality expressed in the "epical" is only an incomplete version of that expressed in the "dramatic". It merely flows "round and round the persons and the action" without giving them a *"proper and intangible* esthetic life". If we think of *Exiles*, or of *Stephen Hero* in comparison with the *Portrait*, we can see why he puts it this way. Like *The Way of All Flesh* or perhaps (on another level) some of Blake or some of the last plays of Ibsen, *Exiles* and *Stephen Hero* are uneasy works of art whose lack of perfect objectivity seems to mark the presence of unassimilated personal issues of the author's. They are not self-subsistent, integral, *impersonally* meaningful in themselves without reference to the peculiar situation and characteristics of their maker. They are disturbed by having to serve, partly at least, personal kinetic ends rather than achieving a proper and intangible aesthetic life of their own. This, as we find in *Ulysses*, is the basis on which Stephen traces the presence and resolution of Shakespeare's kinesis in his works. It is also, incidentally, like (though it is not the same as) the conception of aesthetic impersonality upon which Eliot's celebrated criticism of *Hamlet* rests.

When we try to fit Joyce's own works into this scheme, the latter two categories present no difficulty, but the "lyrical" does. The crucial issue is now the distortion that the artist's bondage to physical or emotional desires, whether for possession or rejection, effects upon the truth and stability of his vision of life. Creative ordering is impossible without a spiritual harmony in the artist, the proper engagement of his whole sensibility—the activity of "the whole soul of man with the subordination of its faculties to each other according to their relative worth and dignity". To take this distinction to its logical conclusion, however, would reduce Stephen's scheme to absurdity. "Lyrical" would then have to refer to *completely* kinetic art, that is, art wholly under the domination of the artist's spiritual disharmonies and a poem like Joyce's own "The Holy Office" would become even more lyrical than "O western wind", and *Childe Harold* one of the major lyrical works in the language. Obviously Stephen does not mean that by the lyrical mode; at this point his distinction rapidly shifts back to its descriptive sense.

Most of the further confusion has been the result of the way Stephen talks about "dramatic" art, and of two of his sentences in particular:

The personality of the artist, at first a cry or a cadence or a mood and then a fluid and lambent narrative, finally refines itself out of existence, impersonalises itself, so to speak. . . . The artist, like the God of creation, remains within or behind or beyond or above his handiwork, invisible, refined out of existence, indifferent, paring his fingernails. (244-5)

To some commentators, this—together with Stephen's rejection of kinetic art—has suggested that Joyce was hostile to the expression of any moral attitudes in art, believing rather that it should retain a God-like neutrality; in other words, that he was a moral "Realist" undertaking to examine human behaviour in a spirit of detached, scientific indifference.[13] Others have taken Stephen to be distinguishing progressively larger, more impersonal *subjects* in art, and have illustrated his point by the widening inclusiveness of the *Portrait, Ulysses* and *Finnegans Wake*.[14] To others, Stephen's term "impersonality" seems to imply, like Eliot's, the expression of an impersonal, i.e. an "external", system of beliefs and values, which also forms the ultimate sanction of all aesthetic value; in other words, they regard Joyce as what we might call a Metaphysical Realist.[15] To others, yet again, Stephen is apparently advocating a God-like dramatic *technique* for the novelist, a technique by which he can present his characters and action completely detached not only from any authorial commentary but from any narration at all; in other words, they regard Joyce as here adumbrating the ultimate naturalistic realism of the stream-of-consciousness.[16]

None of these seems to me a justifiable inference from Stephen's or Joyce's actual statements, and none of them affords an adequate approach to his works. Undoubtedly Joyce's novels are all realistic in some sense, and each perhaps realistic in a rather different sense from the others. *Ulysses*, for example, does seem to reach the limits of representational realism possible in the novel, so much so indeed that many people have felt it signalized the end of the novel altogether. Realism of setting can apparently go no further than Joyce's rendering of Dublin or the mass of "scientific" facts shovelled (exquisitely and lovingly shovelled) into "Ithaca"; psychological realism can apparently go no further than the moment-by-moment record of his characters' lives; while the realistic vivisection and deflation of all bourgeois values can apparently go no further than its dispassionate critical anatomy of individual isolation and frustration, social collapse, and spiritual cliché. Yet this is far from an exhaustive account of the meaning or methods of the book, and to suppose this is what Stephen's theory really means is surely to mistake his intentions and development.

Even with *Dubliners*, Joyce made no bones about the moral and social judgments implicit in the book, for all its naturalistic realism. It was not his fault, he wrote to Grant Richards, that "the odour of ashpits and old weeds and offal hangs round my stories. I seriously believe that [by suppressing the book] you will retard the course of civilisation in Ireland by preventing the Irish people from having one good look at themselves in my nicely polished looking-glass."[17] *Dubliners*, in fact, is the book that really does fit the parodic-realism view of his work, and it is apparent from *Stephen Hero* that the young Joyce did start off with a similar conception of his art in mind. His realism, though never to become subservient to moral ends, was ultimately to have a moral effect. Dissociating himself from the paralytic, priest-ridden materialism of Ireland, he proclaimed he would (in the characteristic spirit of modern literature) "vivisect" its decay (165); he would reveal his world as an Inferno that parodied Dante's (141); and in some way, he felt, by expressing his own nature freely and fully, he would "bring to the world the spiritual renewal which the poet brings to it" (171)—or, as he put it at the end of the *Portrait*, he would create the conscience of his race. Of course, it is a callow enough conception, but it is important to recognize that Stephen (or Joyce) never *tried* to remain morally neutral or indifferent as an artist, even while his immaturity blinded him to the sterility both of his purely negative reaction to his society and of his quasi-Thomist account of art and beauty. For all his proclamations about the moral force of art and the freedom of the artist, he was still far from the complex, positive maturity of *Ulysses*. Stephen does not see this himself in the *Portrait* (much less in *Stephen Hero*) except as the purely theoretical, and confused, perception that the moral maturity of art represents a development in the artist. Nor does he realize how fundamentally that perception strikes at the rest of his aesthetic. The result is that in the *Portrait* he is, as we should expect of him, inconsistent, at once disengaging art from life altogether and at the same time trying to explain how they are related. But although he is inconsistent and confused, he is not really advocating the implacable indifference of a machine as the proper, or even a possible, moral stance for the artist *as artist* and, as we have seen, by *Ulysses* he himself has come to realize more fully what his position entails. Nor are Joyce's own objections to kinetic art, or his avoidance of various personal commitments, reason to suppose that he tried to avoid the engagement and endorsement of moral values in his art. If kinetic art is that which merely asserts *one* of the values it engages, static art is not that which regards all as equal and so denies validity to any. In the light of what Joyce says about positive "affirmation" in art and the kind of "joy" he believed the highest art expressed,[18] it becomes obvious—although it is even more obvious in the art of *Ulysses* itself—that by static art he meant that which affirms all the moral values it engages and orders them as it does so. *Stasis* is a balance of moral attitudes, not their absence.

As for the second misinterpretation of Stephen's scheme—the progress of wider and more abstract subjects—this also neglects the moral development he clearly implies; while the third—the progressive "surrender" to "impersonal" values—imputes to Joyce the wrong kind of moral outlook. Although he used systems of theology and philosophy as metaphors, he remained independent of all systematic and dogmatic beliefs. As far as I can see, such "impersonal" beliefs are implied neither in his aesthetic nor his art, and we may perhaps leave it to the Theosophists, Thomists, Marxists, Naturalists, Relativists, Freudians, Jungians, Surrealists, and others, to decide among themselves just which God they think the artist should imitate and which truths he should surrender to. Joyce's moral attitudes are always worked out dramatically, presented for our inspection only in the proper and tangible life of his art and never reducible to doctrines or "ideas". Certainly, the kind of mind that inspects life from the distant refuge of an ideal Truth—with its tendencies to spiritual absolutism and transcendental disgust, its deep hostility to *dramatic* expression—was precisely the attitude of Stephen in *Stephen Hero*, and precisely what in his hero Joyce came most sharply to criticize.

As for the last misinterpretation, which places the emphasis on the "impersonality" of the stream-of-consciousness technique in the novel, this seems to be based on an elementary confusion between the conventions of the dramatic *genre* and the principle involved in the demand that the novelist render his subject dramatically. In some degree Stephen's remarks do refer to technique in the novel, but it is the latter—dramatic rendering— to which he points. We might compare his phrases with Coleridge's famous description of Shakespeare's dramatic imagination in *Venus and Adonis*: "It is throughout as if a superior spirit more intuitive, more intimately conscious, even than the characters themselves, not only of every outward look and act, but of the flux and reflux of the mind in all its subtlest thoughts and feelings, were placing the whole before our view; himself meanwhile unparticipating in the passions, and actuated only by that pleasurable excitement, which had resulted from the energetic fervour of his own spirit in so vividly exhibiting what it had so accurately and profoundly contemplated." That could equally well be said of Joyce's dramatic impersonality in the *Portrait* or *Ulysses*, and it expresses what I take to be the point at which Stephen is driving in his theory. Like Henry James, Joyce was one of the first to see that for the novelist this was the great lesson of Flaubert; and this (more than any hankering for moral Realism) is the reason why Stephen echoes Flaubert's famous remarks about *Madame Bovary*:

Madame Bovary n'a rien de vrai. C'est une histoire *totalement inventée*; je n'y ai rien mis ni de mes sentiments ni de mon existence. L'illusion (s'il y en a une) vient au contraire de *l'impersonnalité* de l'oeuvre. C'est un de mes principes, qu'il faut pas *s'écrire*. L'artiste doit être dans son oeuvre comme Dieu dans la création, invisible et tout-puissant; qu'on le sente partout, mais qu'on ne le voie pas.

Et puis, l'Art doit s'élever au-dessus des affections personnelles et des susceptibilités nerveuses! Il est temps de lui donner, par une méthode impitoyable, la précision des sciences physiques! La difficulté capitale, pour moi, n'en reste pas moins le style, la forme, le Beau indéfinissable *résultant de la conception même* et qui est la splendeur du Vrai comme disait Plato.[19]

Joyce may equally well have used another remark of Flaubert's: "Mme Bovary, c'est moi". But he no more adopts Flaubert's whole outlook than at other points he adopts Aquinas's or Blake's. Similarly, Stephen's remark in *Ulysses*, "Hold to the now, the here, through which all future plunges to the past" may echo a phrase at the beginning of Edouard Dujardin's novel, *Les lauriers sont coupés*,

Car sous le chaos des apparences, parmi les durées et les sites, dans l'illusion des choses qui s'engendrent et qui s'enfantent, un parmi les autres, un comme les autres, distinct des autres, semblable aux autres, un même et un de plus, de l'infini des possibles existences, je surgis; et voici que le temps et le lieu se précisent; c'est l'aujourd' hui; c'est l'ici; l'heure qui sonne; et, autour de moi, la vie . . .

and it may also recall a phrase of Bergson's about the "invisible progress of the past, which gnaws into the future".[20] ?On the other hand, it also echoes St Augustine and Aristotle.[21] Joyce said he derived the stream-of-consciousness from Dujardin, and Bergson may have been one of the philosophical patrons of the technique, but it would be very rash to take Stephen's phrase as desiderating merely a special technique to transcend the limitations of the reported narrative and mental analyses of the conventional novel.

This very common misconception about Joyce's "dramatic" techniques is worth dwelling on a little further, for it has obscured not only his theory, but, much more importantly, his actual use of narrative "point-of-view" and of the stream-of-consciousness. I shall postpone any detailed examination of these until the next chapter, but even at this stage it is perhaps worth recalling some obvious facts. For one thing, if the impersonal dramatic novel were merely that which presented its story without narrative, or merely that which established a basis in the story itself for the narrator's knowledge of the story, what some critics have called "reader-confidence", how "dramatic" is *Ulysses*? Despite all the stream-of-consciousness writing, it is full of "omniscient" narrative, which is presented (so we must conclude if we consider the matter) by a narrator who has not (*pace* Mr Kenner) any clearly defined limitations of position and view. In fact, as I have noted already, the narrative is often deliberately and significantly "omniscient". At one stage it ostentatiously withdraws from the action in order to comment upon it at great length; at another it even draws attention to the fact that *Ulysses* is a book— "this chaffering allincluding most farraginous chronicle" (405/ 416), and that, if anything did, would certainly give "reader-confidence" a shrewd blow. But of course there is no one order of objective reality that the book simply *represents*. Techniques of narration are part of the total aesthetic activity which creates its own relevant sense of reality. Techniques are impersonal not when there is no narrative voice, or when the voice clearly belongs to a character in the story, but when they help realize the projected "reality" of the work so fully that we are not provoked to question their mediation at all or the adequacy of the "omniscient" view they present.

The problem of the dramatist and novelist alike is to present an image of life, an action apparently as free and spontaneous as life itself appears to us, while at the same time preserving the sense that his image is ordered, constructed, significant. As the history of the novel shows, one of the novelist's problems from the first was to establish his "reality" as authentic—by making his report of it circumstantial, immediate, apparently unselective, and as morally objective as possible—while yet retaining his necessary power to show that reality as, in fact, the content of *his* creative gesture, projected from and the medium of his understanding of life. The difficulties of his task are notorious. It is useless for him to impose comment or a moral on his story, or to assert a significant order where no sense of it arises for others from his action itself. Equally, it is useless for him to embody values in his formal devices, in his style or narrative technique for example, where no such values are to be felt in the "reality" they help create. It is perhaps just as dangerous for him to concentrate on ordering his "reality" too much, wringing too much significance out of it: the risk here is the stifling hint of premeditation (like that Wells and Forster criticized in James, for instance), or, in Stephen's sense, a too "lyrical", too simplifying, use of the novel. Each of these represents a failure of integration, a failure in the novel's *impersonal* significance. The artist's shaping activity, the "rhythm" of his poetic gesture, so to speak, is the aesthetic form of his "reality", and it must seem like a Providence moving behind, yet within, the "reality" it projects. What this means is that the "structural rhythm", the artist's *poetic* personality, not his ordinary personality as a man or that of an assumed narrator, is what is God-like. Confusion sometimes arises in attacks on novelists (Fielding or Thackeray or Trollope are cases in point) who exploited their position as "omniscient authors". These attacks often suggest that editorial comment and analysis are in themselves an aesthetic betrayal of the novel because they compromise "reader-confidence", destroying the illusion of a represented reality by implying a narrator who intrudes upon the action and knows what no one could know.[22] This is surely naturalistic naïvety. The novel as a *genre*, by its very nature, cannot avoid narration; furthermore, it is a work of art, not a quasi-report of "real life". Dr Johnson's objections to the unities in the drama have their relevance to the novel, too: the artist must balance our sense of the reality of his world (however naturalistic or unnaturalistic it may be) against our sense of it as an artifact. Our objection to the "omniscient author" is justified only when we feel that the voice of the author asserts what the impersonal voice of the action itself does not. But the same principle, we should remember, is a premise of the drama too: indeed, it is so much more firmly established there than it seems to be with the novel, that this is probably why it is so often phrased as a demand for "dramatic" presentation in the novel. Yet in the end it is only a special application to these relatively objective *genres* of a formal principle that applies to all art.

In short, we require of these *genres* truth to life, the imaginative projection of experience understood or "purified", not merely the naturalistic representation of life. Actually, Stephen's description of "dramatic" art is a more sensible variation of the Symbolist formula that all art aspires to the condition of music. Stephen has modified it by his recognition and welcome of the power of literature to specify and elaborate its content, to deal with moral life, and he has so translated it into terms that include the drama and the novel as well as the lyric. As it affects the novel, the proper conclusion to be drawn from it is simply that style and technique must be organically related to the "subject" so that all form one total and impersonal articulation. Poetic form (or "structural rhythm") is the means by which "reality" is created as immediate, objective and meaningful. Thus there is no other suggestion in Joyce's aesthetic but that narrative "point-of-view" is the medium of moral point-of-view. When we turn to examine how he deploys it in *Ulysses*, we shall find that he does so in the same way as any properly competent novelist does. He exploits his characters' point-of-view, and when he needs to he leaves it.

The seeing eye is with somebody in the book, but its vision is reinforced; the picture contains more, becomes richer and fuller, because it is the author's as well as his creature's, both at once. Nobody notices, but in fact there are now two brains behind that eye; and one of them is the author's, who adopts and shares the *position* of his creature, and at the same time supplements his wit. If you analyse the picture that is now presented, you find that it is not all the work of the personage whose vision the author has adopted. There are touches in it that go beyond any sensation of his, and indicate that someone else is looking over his shoulder—seeing things from the same angle, but seeing more, bringing another mind to bear upon the scene. It is an easy and natural extension of the personage's power of observation. The impression of the scene may be deepened as much as need be; it is not confined to the scope of one mind, and yet there is no blurring of the focus by a double point of view.[23]

Percy Lubbock's description of "dramatic" technique in the novel is as accurate for Joyce's practice as for James's or that of anyone else. He is in his characters, but he can, and does, also move out of them as he wishes. Yet far from disguising this movement, he increasingly insists upon it through the book. He exploits his—and hence our—position more and more, so that the action includes and finally establishes that position in all its complex relations to the characters'.

III

The confusions over Joyce's Realism, however, have also obscured the essential truth about his use of the stream-of-consciousness, and hence about the characters whose streams they are—namely, that he employs it as an artistic *convention* and not simply for the sake of accurately representing psychological processes. Once again, before we can understand the convention and its significance in *Ulysses*, it may be worth trying to clarify some of the misconceptions about it.

Although it is true that the novel no more needs to create the illusion of ordinary, everyday life than the drama, it has nevertheless usually tried to lessen the disparity between its conventions and what has been commonly understood as "reality" in its society at large. As a *genre* it has characteristically cultivated an easy recognition of the material it explores, even though various novelists from Fielding onwards have also had to insist (with more or less artistic tact) on the novel as a poetic gesture, a thing made to express a meaning *in* the life it represents. But just because artistic conventions when they first arise seem less conventions than direct means of access to a "deeper" or "truer" reality, they are often attacked and defended for their realism without regard to what is made of the realism by the individual artist. This has been the fate of the various conventions of the novel usually labelled together as "stream-of-consciousness".

An interesting example of the terms in which stream-of-consciousness fiction has been discussed is Virginia Woolf's celebrated essay on "Modern Fiction".[24] Not unlike Dorothy Richardson, who sought what she calls a "feminine equivalent of the current masculine realism" of Bennett, Wells and Galsworthy,[25] Virginia Woolf was led to attack these three writers for what seemed to her the misrepresentation of life entailed in the naturalistic conventions of their novels. "Is life like this?" she asked.

Look within and life, it seems, is very far from being "like this". Examine for a moment an ordinary mind on an ordinary day. The mind receives a myriad impressions—trivial, fantastic, evanescent, or engraved with the sharpness of steel. From all sides they come, an incessant shower of innumerable atoms; and as they fall, and as they shape themselves into the life of Monday or Tuesday, the accent falls differently from of old; the moment of importance came not here but there; so that, if a writer were a free man and not a slave, if he could write what he chose, not what he must, if he could base his work upon his own feeling and not upon convention, there would be no plot, no comedy, no tragedy, no love interest or catastrophe in the accepted style, and perhaps not a single button sewn on as the Bond

Street tailors would have it. Life is not a series of gig-lamps sym-
metrically arranged; life is a luminous halo, a semi-transparent
envelope surrounding us from the beginning of consciousness to the
end. Is it not the task of the novelist to convey this varying, this
unknown and uncircumscribed spirit, whatever aberration or complexity it may display, with as little mixture of the alien and external
as possible? . . . Let us record the atoms as they fall upon the mind in
the order in which they fall, let us trace the pattern, however dis-
connected and incoherent in appearance, which each sight or incident
scores upon the consciousness.

She went on to discuss Joyce, and suggested that any reader of
the *Portrait* and of the instalments of *Ulysses* then appearing
(1919) in the *Little Review* "will have hazarded some theory of
this nature as to Mr. Joyce's intention". Unlike Wells, Bennett
and Galsworthy, who are "materialists", Mr Joyce is "spiritual";
he is concerned with mental impressions and is prepared to
sacrifice the conventional signposts of probability and coherence
to achieve his end. "The scene in the cemetery, for instance, with
its brilliancy, its sordidity, its incoherence, its sudden lightning
flashes of significance, does undoubtedly come so close to the
quick of the mind that, on a first reading at any rate, it is difficult
not to acclaim a masterpiece. If we want life itself, here surely
we have it."

While it would be unfair to represent this as a considered
judgment of Joyce's work, I have quoted it at such length
because it exemplifies the underlying assumptions of most
subsequent discussions of stream-of-consciousness fiction. Such
novels have usually been approached by way of their psychological realism, or the "Symbolist" devices employed to express
it, or their avoidance of "alien and external" narrative that
might compromise "reader-confidence".[26] Few critics are so
naïve as to suppose that such novels merely report reality, of
course; rather, they "render mental experience" or "capture . . .
the atmosphere of the mind" by creating the illusion of direct
contact with the apparently unselected thoughts of the characters.[27] Some critics emphasize the simple mental processes so
illustrated: association and non-verbal juxtaposition, for example;
others emphasize the more recondite processes analyzed by
Bergson, William James, Freud, and Jung; but in the end the
common assumption is that stream-of-consciousness fiction is
justified by its realism, that the relevant critical formulae to

apply to such novels is "here surely we have life itself" or "here surely we have a truly dramatic novel".[28] Put as baldly as that, however, the critical inadequacy of the psychological approach becomes obvious. We may admit the realism straight off—undoubtedly the conventions of interior monologue, sensory impressionism, symbolic suggestion and the rest, do express something of "the actual texture of consciousness" as we know it from personal introspection and the psychology text-books.[29] But then so do other conventions express other aspects of consciousness; the human mind was not invented in the early years of the twentieth century.

One of the most significant features of Virginia Woolf's essay is the *kind* of "reality" she supposes most real. Not the outward object but its subjective "impression" is the real thing; not the organizations of social conventions (in which, as she suggests elsewhere, we have lost belief),[30] but the "pattern" of the individual consciousness; not public arrangements of gig-lamps but a private halo surrounding each of us from birth. What is significant at the moment is less the wider cultural implications of her views, or the fact that she was insisting, quite rightly, on realities too often ignored by naturalistic novelists, than the strangely sharp dichotomy she assumes between "outer" and "inner", public and private, object and impression. As her critics have sometimes pointed out, this is very much the same assumption made by the "materialists" she is attacking; her own view (and even more clearly, that of Dorothy Richardson) simply inverts their value signs and is, in fact, in subjection to the very materialism she deplores.[31]

Unfortunately, similar confusions all too often ensnare others as well who emphasize the "realism" of the stream-of-consciousness novel. In one sense, such critics are clearly right to value techniques that enable the novelist to explore areas of experience "beneath" the surfaces of ordinary social intercourse (though stream-of-consciousness techniques are not, we might remember, the only ones that do). Similarly, there is also a broad, obvious truth in the claim that the stream-of-consciousness novel characteristically gives a greater weight to the private, "inner" life of the individual as against his public, "outer" life. Joyce's use of the stream-of-consciousness techniques, for example, unmistakably has this effect: Bloom's and Stephen's isolation, their alienation from their society, and their inability to enact their deepest values in outward deeds and institutions shared with others, are impressed upon us by the very mode in which they are so largely (though by no means entirely) portrayed. But as we have seen, this is only part of the truth about them, and to take it for the whole is seriously to distort Joyce's meaning and achievement. They are also shown to be related in their common humanity, to participate in their society, and, though limited and confined, to enact their deepest values nevertheless, in their critical engagement with each other, with their fellow-citizens, and with the institutions they share with them. In other words, the stream-of-consciousness techniques also enable Joyce to render the continual activity of his characters as representative individuals, and to define the nature and quality of that activity.

Once we realize this, the common distinction between "inner" and "outer" begins to seem less secure and less satisfactory, and the emphasis on psychological realism less relevant. We begin to raise questions of a rather different kind: why does this writer or that use stream-of-consciousness techniques in this particular novel? is his art "lyrical" (in Stephen's sense) or does it transcend the purely personal, and how? why does he present "reality" as he does?—in short, what meaning does he express by these conventions? Simply to hypostatize the "inner" life, and to suppose it more "real" than any other, and then to diverge into amateur Psychology or Philosophy, is inevitably to obscure the real differences between one novelist's vision of life and another's, and to obscure in turn—if not entirely to ignore—the artistic significance of a particular novelist's concentration on certain aspects of his characters' experience. The so-called "stream-of-consciousness" novelists are not necessarily comparable in their purposes or vision just because they employ certain roughly similar techniques. It is obvious enough, for instance, that Dorothy Richardson's conception of "reality" is profoundly different from (say) William Faulkner's; but what is more, that conception *is* intimately connected with the nature and the weaknesses of her novels, and it is to this connection the critic must first devote his attention before generalizing about the stream-of-consciousness. The same applies to the novels of Virginia Woolf too. Her world does often seem split between a confusedly related "inner" and "outer", her characters' consciousness does often seem passive and associative, and though this is hardly an adequate criticism of her novels in itself, it is enough perhaps to suggest that her conception of life imposes limitations no less rigorous than those of the "materialism" she attacked. But is her conception Joyce's? Is her account of his psychological realism adequate? If we do surely have life itself in *Ulysses*, is this enough to claim it a masterpiece, and is it "life" as she supposes it—a world of "spiritual" subjective impressions through which we may glimpse, if we wish, a world of meaningless "material" objects, conventions and actions?

Comparable to Virginia Woolf's theory of "impressions" is Joyce's theory of "epiphanies", and it is hardly surprising perhaps that the "psychological" critic tends to understand Joyce's term in a purely psychological sense. The epiphany becomes a moment of mental experience, a brief state of emotion, and *claritas* the subjective reaction to, or the "emotional content" of, the perception of objects. The novelist's task is then envisaged as the recording and communicating of such "moods" or "feelings", so that Symbolism enters art and criticism precisely where Joyce wanted to throw it out: as a means of conveying purely "inner", personal, subjective states of mind by means of purely affective techniques.[32] The net result is that Joyce's theory is completely unbalanced by forcing apart the subject and object he was so concerned to unite: his stream-of-consciousness is taken as "direct quotations" from,[33] or renderings of, the emotions of his characters, which thus provided the material he used "to expand one of his epiphanies into a great picture of a single day in a teeming city".[34] It is no wonder that a critic who reads Joyce's stream-of-consciousness in this way should begin to speculate whether, amid such a chaotic flood of passive mental "impressions" and "associations", he is not *himself* creating the characters and structure of the book.[35]

When the psychological critic does ask why Joyce in particular uses stream-of-consciousness techniques, the answer is usually based on *a priori* assumptions about their Realism—in one or more of the senses we have already noted. Some critics are content (like Virginia Woolf) to take "reality" simply. "One of the striking features of Joyce's style", says Mr R. M. Kain, "is the unusual fluidity with which it turns from the outer to the inner world. It is a style capable of rendering sense-impressions directly as they fall upon the mind and of showing how these impressions give rise to a chain of association within the mind. The ease and clarity with which these two facets of reality are depicted is amazing."[36] Others take the matter further. The stream-of-consciousness novel, says Mr Robert Humphrey, explores the "prespeech levels" of consciousness, which are not censored, not rationally controlled and not logically ordered.[37] The actual processes of the mind at these levels therefore cannot be represented by shaped and directed analyses of states of mind, but only by such devices as will reflect and exemplify the laws of psychological association, compression and multiplicity.[38] Yet, as Mr Humphrey very well realizes, what the mere representation of these levels of consciousness necessarily implies is the reduction of all experiences to the same importance, which is to say, to the same unimportance. Moral values can come into play only with the conscious, reflective *activity* of the personality. And at this point the question of values begins to haunt the discussion of Joyce's method of presenting his characters—for where, on this interpretation of it, can values enter Joyce's world at all?

We are now once again offered Joyce the moral "Realist". By ridding his work of all signs of its author, says Mr Humphrey, he was able to "present life as it *actually is*, without prejudice or direct evaluations. It is, then, the goal of the realist and the naturalist" (my italics). This, we might have supposed, was the goal of most artists whatever their outlook, but Mr Humphrey means it in a special sense for Joyce, and his meaning represents what is perhaps the commonest interpretation of *Ulysses*:

the *Odyssey* pattern is a means for equating the heroic and the ordinary, and the undifferentiated internal monologue is a means for equating the trivial and the profound. Life is depicted by Joyce so minutely that there is no room for any values to stand out. . . . Only within stream of consciousness could the necessary objectivity be attained for making it all convincingly realistic; for the pathos is in the fact that *man* thinks he is special and heroic, not that *Joyce* thinks he is pitiful.[39]

What this means is that the pathos lies in the fact that man is not *really* special and heroic; this surely is what Joyce's technique must mean if we take it as "realistic" in this sense. Realism is the "scientific" negation or "exposure" of all values.

On the other hand, behind this Naturalistic Realist, Mr Kenner offers us Joyce the Metaphysical Realist, who portrays the modern world's vision of *itself* as mere matter and mere subjective impression and so, by his parodic imitation, makes the most devastating criticism of it. When we ask how this criticism is imaginatively validated in the novel, since the positive values by which the whole world of *Ulysses* is judged would necessarily have to be suggested from outside it, Mr Kenner's answer is in effect that it is validated by the very completeness with which those values are *not* imaginatively realized in the book!

In Shakespeare's *Coriolanus*, the vision of the Body Politic, expounded by Menenius in the first scene, is continually present in the imagery and continually denied by the facts. Three centuries later its denial by the facts is so strident that its presence is attested only by rubric and gloss. The genitals of Dublin are gelded, its heart is a graveyard, its lungs inflate and deflate to the rhythm of giant presses, its corpuscular bodies circulate, discrete entities, to the rhythm of the art of mechanics, through an arterial labyrinth of stony streets; all in the sharpest possible contrast to the pulsating universe of *Finnegans Wake*, one level above the *Ulysses*-world of eternal fixity. It is no reproach to the techniques of *Ulysses* that the correspondences are frequently of the most mechanical kind; the more mechanical the better, for Joyce's purposes.[40]

Even leaving aside the perhaps unworthy suspicion that this kind of artistic interpretation could prove anything about anything, we may well wonder if Joyce's moral position is not itself compromised by such imaginative impotence. Why, for example, do his values not need poetic enactment like those in—if not *Coriolanus*—then *The Brothers Karamazov* or *Four Quartets*? Such a total rejection of modern life as Mr Kenner imputes to Joyce raises the problem (no less than does Flaubert's moral Realism) of what basis, what "reality", the author's values possess. There is certainly no possible basis in the reality Joyce is supposed to portray for the existence of any values by which that reality could be ordered and so evaluated. It is hard to see how Mr Kenner's large claims for the "symbolism" and the techniques really establish much relevance for artistic organizations and moral values so extraneously, so mechanically asserted.

Interestingly enough, Mr Humphrey realizes the similar critical consequences of *his* naturalistic interpretation of stream-of-consciousness fiction. Given the kind of material such novels apparently represent, they must be "subject to formlessness and, in a sense, meaninglessness". The individual consciousness has only a subjective importance; it offers no essential meaning to others. It has, moreover, "no specific ordering; it is capricious and fluid; it offers, in short, no basis for analysis and interpretation". But the consequences Mr Humphrey notes raise more than the mere technical problem of how to present the stream of consciousness to the reader; they raise the fundamental question of how naturalistic representation, with its implicit passivity towards its material, can ever achieve meaningful shape from within. When Mr Humphrey goes on to examine the structures of *Ulysses*, however, he seems to confuse these two issues, arguing that the shifting "frames of reference", the "devices for differentiation and variation", the "means for getting lights and shadows", and the whole elaborate "symbolic" scaffolding, do in fact "superimpose form on [Joyce's] formless subject matter".[41] They impose pattern, of course; the inner form, the objective, impersonal articulation, is still to seek—and, on this basis, still impossible.

This is the critical problem that Wyndham Lewis raised from the first when he attacked not only *Ulysses* but all stream-of-consciousness writing for its simplistic naturalism and its consequent lack of "all linear properties whatever, . . . all contour and definition . . . in a jellyfish structure, without articulation of any sort".[42] The usual reply to this, of which Mr Kenner's may be regarded as a more sophisticated version, is to point to the "structures" of extraneous parallels, the "themes", and the recurrent "symbols". Yet these hardly express a structure in and of the material itself. It would not answer Mr Lewis's attack however many times Bloom or Stephen thought of the same objects or felt the same feelings, nor does it make any difference however important we think the objects or feelings are in themselves apart from their rôle in the book: these could never provide an imaginatively meaningful form, never articulate and define moral insight, never make us feel that the action itself possesses a vital, complex significance. The only real reply to Mr Lewis would be to show that *Ulysses* is not simple Naturalism with Symbolism superadded to it. For once we see the force of his objections and critically examine the kinds of approach usually made to *Ulysses*, it is obvious that the supposed significance of the so-called structure of "symbols" is only a function of the supposed significance of the so-called realistic "subject-matter". One emphasis engenders the other, yet neither singly nor together do they answer the real questions the reader wants to ask: *why* does Joyce explore the characters' stream of consciousness in the book? *why* does he organize the book in the way he does? what values is Joyce revealing *in* his material? In the final analysis the issue with both the "symbolism" and the techniques is the same, and arises from the same assumptions. Seeking the meaning and value of the work in its representation of some metaphysical, or material, or even subjective Reality, we inevitably split what the artist tried to unite and express in the one "gesture" or symbol or epiphany.

It may be interesting to see how these correlative categories of "symbolism" and "realism" do emerge once we read Joyce's stream-of-consciousness in the light of such preconceptions about it. A passage from Stephen's consciousness in "Proteus" forms a convenient example:

> They came down the steps from Leahy's terrace prudently, *Frauenzimmer*: and down the shelving shore flabbily their splayed feet sinking in the silted sand. Like me, like Algy, coming down to our mighty mother. Number one swung lourdily her midwife's bag, the other's gamp poked in the beach. From the liberties, out for the day. Mrs Florence MacCabe, relict of the late Patk MacCabe, deeply lamented, of Bride Street. One of her sisterhood lugged me squealing into life. Creation from nothing. What has she in the bag? A misbirth with a trailing navelcord, hushed in ruddy wool. The cords of all link back, strandentwining cable of all flesh. That is why mystic monks. Will you be as gods? Gaze in your omphalos. Hello. Kinch here. Put me on to Edenville. Aleph, alpha: nought, nought, one. (34-5/38-9)

(This, incidentally, immediately follows Stephen's realization that the world exists "there all the time without [him]" whether he is observing it or not.) One "psychological" commentator has made a detailed analysis of the whole paragraph. The first sentence, he says, naturally presents no problem—it is presumably "objective" description or stage-direction from the author. The second sentence "begins the humor of extended association, by giving the midwives' appearance a kind of ritualistic significance". The next sequence "merely serves to acquaint us with certain objective details"—presumably more stage-direction though disguised as Stephen's mental "impressions". Only with the sentence beginning, "A misbirth with a trailing navelcord" does "Stephen's imagination begin to control the development of ideas". The analysis naturally concentrates on the tendencies of Stephen's "subconscious", on his "phantasmagoric image" of a navelcord telephone, and on the way in which various "objects" are "transformed by the vagaries of Stephen's imagination"—even apart from midwives and navelcords there is the sea, and Eden, and so on.[43] In short, the "object" is there, to be glimpsed through Stephen's "impression" of it; but Stephen distorts it; and the result is an example of—the subconscious mind at work? or perhaps of Stephen's moral subjectivism? or perhaps Joyce's use of "poetic" Symbolist devices? or perhaps of his formless naturalism? On the other hand, it might equally be taken as Joyce's citation among the flux of Stephen's "associations" of that powerful symbol, *omphalos*?[44] Or perhaps the citation of a Freudian symbol of fertility? Or does the passage express the mechanistic values of the modern world as suggested, for example, by the umbrella and the telephone?

At first glance perhaps there is no reason to suppose that it is not one, or even all, of these. Yet simply to suppose so is to miss the most obvious meaning of the passage, and consequently to miss the *structural* connection between these so-called random "impressions" or "associations" and the rest of the chapter— that is, with Stephen's developing self-scrutiny, which, as I tried to show in the last chapter, is both the form and content of "Proteus". The truth is that the "objects" are presented to us only as Stephen sees them and they *are* what he sees. We are not given two separate bits of reality—the "real" sea or midwives, and the "real" stream of subjective impressions—but one: Stephen's experience. And the paragraph does not simply record various levels of mental life—passive impressions and associations, subconscious distortions, and imaginative control— but a total action of the mind. Stephen's sensibility, his imagination, is controlling everything in the passage. There is no more reason for supposing that his mind is merely a passive register of impressions or associations (midwives—sea—mother—birth— navelcords—omphalos—Adam—God) than there is for supposing that (say) Macbeth's mind is in his soliloquy, "If it were done when 'tis done" (Duncan—virtues—angels—trumpets—judgment—damnation—pity—babies—wind?—cherubs—rumours—

couriers, and so on). And surely no one has ever supposed that Macbeth was "distorting" Duncan's virtues, for example, by speaking about them in this painfully "subjective" way, or that there was much profit in analysing Shakespeare's mastery of the "subconscious" psychological processes of extreme worry. The speech expresses Macbeth's act, at a specific point in the total action, of apprehending his world, and it thus enables us to apprehend it that way too. If our insight into that world is greater than his, it is not simply because we know more about babies or couriers than he does, or more about how the mind works under intense pressure, but because we can understand his act of understanding itself in the full context of the play. Similarly, the paragraph from Stephen's stream of consciousness expresses his apprehension of the physical, elemental unity of mankind, as it appears to him in the physical grotesqueness of the midwives, the grotesque and even ugly ministrations to physical birth, the grotesquely pretentious speculations raised upon that common fact, and the ineluctable mystery that produces from "nought nought" the irreducible "one". Human oneness is the objective content of his "gesture", his act, just as, in a general sense, a moral problem is the object of Macbeth's. But in both cases only by an attentive response to the tone, the rhythms, the fusions of metaphorical meaning, and the dramatic context, can we grasp the object in its specific quality.

To suppose, moreover, that we could whip "omphalos" out of Stephen's monologue or "babe" out of Macbeth's soliloquy, trace the recurrence of the same "object" or "image" in other passages, and then to identify the meaning of the work with our deeper speculations about navelcords and babies, would be the short way to poetic and critical vacuity. The most we can say is that the mere repetition of words or images of a similar meaning (for in different contexts they hardly retain the *same* meaning) may evoke a general, usually indefinable, mood or atmosphere, may suggest a kind of uncrystallized richness, a mysterious sense of another order always on the fringe of what form or order we do apprehend in the action as a whole. Simply to note the repetitions however, is nothing in itself, nor does their effect exhaust the meaning of the work. For such repetitions are more obviously and more fundamentally significant for what happens to them in their different contexts—the feelings and insights they bring into a situation, and what the situation does to them in turn. The same applies to characters and setting, of course, since these are also aspects of the total "gesture" of a work. Neither "themes" nor characters can properly be regarded as self-subsistent elements existing prior to the work and possessed of a determinate significance in themselves.

To ignore the force of all this (though I offer it more as a reminder than a theoretical persuasion) is to be tempted into those assumptions that encourage us to look for the meaning and value of a work of art in the wrong place, and (in the case of *Ulysses*) that inevitably invite Wyndham Lewis's objections to the whole book. The interpretation and criticism of *Ulysses* are often bedevilled by the confusion between such words, objects, experiences, "themes" as seem important to the meaning of the book simply because they recur and the critic thinks them significant in themselves, and those experiences that are important because their meaning is created—imaginatively and concretely realized—in the book itself. Such "themes" as "omphalos", the Mass, and paternity are cases in point; Dublin's classical values, on Mr Kenner's argument, another; or the *Odyssey*; or the colour orange.[45] Similarly with the characters. The extravagances of nineteenth-century "character studies" of Shakespeare are now universally and properly repudiated, yet Joyce is still occasionally criticized for distorting characters he really knew in 1904, and the meaning of the book still sought in what happens outside it—will Bloom get his breakfast in bed? will this change his relations with Molly? did Stephen really come back to the Blooms? did he have an affair with Molly? Similarly with the Freudian "symbols" and Myth. No doubt the world is full of Freudian symbols and echoes of one myth or another, and a tower or a sceptre mentioned in a work of art may be regarded as a symbol as readily as any in the artist's dreams or in an anonymous myth. Nevertheless there is a vital difference between its significance as a "real" symbol to the psychoanalyst or anthropologist and its significance in its artistic context to the reader of the work.[46] This is not to say that the literary critic is better off without any knowledge of psychology or anthropology, or of the setting of a work, or the circumstances of its author and composition, or any other kind of knowledge, but only that he needs, even more, a responsive devotion to the work as it is and not another thing.

SYMBOLISM AND REALISM: A DIGRESSION

Perhaps it is ungraciously labouring the obvious to insist on such critical misdirections, yet they seem to arise so frequently with Joyce that I believe they obscure not only his real achievement but also the light that exegetical commentary can cast on it. His symbolism in *Ulysses*, for example, can easily be misread and over-valued by bringing to it the same idealist, allegorizing, or psychological assumptions that his theories repudiate; the realism of his art can likewise be confused by trying to split subject and object where he was concerned to unit them; and such values as his art expresses can be mistaken, or even entirely missed, by accepting the consequent dichotomy of Naturalistic "matter" and a Symbolist "structure" imposed on it by a feat of mechanical organization. The conclusions his theories really suggest are more convincing than this. The significance of the artist's symbols, the value of his art, are created by his art *in* and *of* the "reality" it presents; the epiphany or "structural rhythm" exists only as it is both perceived and felt in the work, not as a superimposed pattern derived from "truths" known outside it. Such "rhythms" ought not to emerge too obtrusively or they *will* seem imposed; on the other hand, their presence must be felt or the presented "reality" will appear mere mechanical transcription. The artist's gesture must create its content, yet be resisted by it, and yet not be swallowed up by it—which is only to say again that the various "rhythms" or informing principles or "quiddities" of a work have to be apprehended *in* its represented "reality". The commentator must therefore beware of discovering patterns that are not really to be felt, or of concentrating so much on the "reality" presented that he neglects its significance, the gesture of the mind actively in-forming it even while projecting it. And this applies to the *characters*' gestures as well as the artist's. For if Joyce *is* a Realist, the world he pictures is not the simplistic mechanical nightmare it is commonly assumed to be, a world in which people merely register passively "objective" impressions and "subjective" associations, but one in which action, the moral action of the individual spirit, is not only possible but fundamental. Implicit in his theory, I believe, we may find figured the central concern of the book, as well as the most profitable guide to its techniques and, what is ultimately inseparable from that, to its structures.

247

Chapter VII

STRUCTURES AND VALUES

JOYCE'S stream-of-consciousness techniques undoubtedly represent the mental life of his characters no less than the internal analyses of older novelists represent the mental life of theirs. Equally, his treatment of Bloom and Stephen clearly owes a great deal to the psychological discoveries of the last century and to the technical devices of novelists and poets over the same period. Freud, Frazer and Flaubert obviously stand behind *Ulysses*. But it is necessary to distinguish the central critical issues. To the reader of *Ulysses* the centre of interest is neither the accuracy of its psychological representations nor its technical devices in themselves. As with any novelist, what most interests us about Joyce is the *quality* of the consciousness he represents—his conception of human life. We want to know, for example, whether he really does see it as he is commonly supposed to, as the purely "subjective", passive, associative, undifferentiated flux of "impressions", in which any experience is as any other and all values are reduced to insignificance. *Is* his "stream-of-consciousness" writing merely the realistic representation of a world incapable of any values, and hence of any form, other than what the individual artist may care to impose upon it by a purely personal assertion?

To attempt a general answer to what is finally the most important question about *Ulysses* would involve examining the nature and significance of all Joyce's methods of organization, but I have selected what seem to me to be the four most important: I. his use of the stream-of-consciousness; II. his methods of dramatic organization (particularly within the individual chapter); III. his unusual narrative techniques and their relation to the dramatic action; IV. the development of the mythic vision and, in particular, the rôle of "Penelope". Of course no such selection (or commentary) can pretend to be exhaustive, but I hope it may offer at least a working cross-section of the book as a whole.

I

When William James first used the phrase, "stream of consciousness", he was thinking less of a continuous, even flow of mental "impressions" than of the individual's sense of personal identity and continuity, and he pointed out, with an obvious truth, that "consciousness . . . does not appear to itself chopped up in bits".[1] Yet what is perhaps a mere truism about real people may serve to underline the first relevant fact about the consciousness of Bloom and Stephen (if not of Molly)—namely, that it *is* chopped up in bits. Whether we agree or not that Joyce is exploring the "prespeech level" of the mind, he does represent it by means of words, and his representation is inevitably divided and organized, at the primary level, in linguistic terms: phrase, sentence, paragraph, and—we might also add—chapter. The mental life of the characters is at least actively structured by the author according to the rules of conscious, articulate syntax, however loosely applied.

Regarded as representation, such "bits"—and particularly the paragraphed bits—may appear to be simply eddies, or temporary whirlpools, in the stream of thoughts or "impressions", or perhaps (as is usually the case in the novels of Dorothy Richardson and even sometimes in Virginia Woolf's) merely the casual blockages and redirections produced by an "objective" event impinging on the "inner" attention. In fact, this is quite often what they are in *Ulysses* too. As Bloom walks about Dublin, new objects provide continual stimuli to new thoughts about them, and the reader catches a sense of the object from its reflection in the character's thoughts:

He slipped card and letter into his sidepocket, reviewing again the soldiers on parade. Where's old Tweedy's regiment? Castoff soldier. There: bearskin cap and hackle plume. No, he's a grenadier. Pointed cuffs. There he is: royal Dublin fusiliers. Redcoats. Too showy. That must be why the women go after them. Uniform. Easier to enlist and drill. Maud Gonne's letter about taking them off O'Connell street at night: disgrace to our Irish capital. Griffith's paper is on the same tack now: an army rotten with venereal disease: overseas or halfseasover empire. Half baked they look: hypnotized like. Eyes front. Mark time. Table: able. Bed: ed. The King's own. Never see him dressed up as a fireman or a bobby. A mason, yes.
He strolled out of the postoffice and turned to the right. (64-5/71-2)

The whole of the Dublin scene is apparently evoked and suggested by its effects rather than by description. Joyce himself said that he wanted the reader "to understand always through suggestion rather than direct statement", and as a number of his critics have pointed out, he conveys the thick, surrounding detail of the scene largely in this way.[2]

Although this most elementary kind of division in Bloom's (and Stephen's) thoughts seems necessarily accidental and therefore artistically meaningless, it is by no means the only, nor even the most characteristic, principle of organization. The paragraphs have a unity and a relationship to each other far more significant than such casual coincidences of "objective" events. A paragraph like that from "Proteus" discussed in the last chapter has, as I have already suggested, a greater coherence than a simple mixture of casual "objects" and subjective "reactions" to them. For a more extended example of Joyce's stream of-consciousness, however, we may take a passage from the same chapter Virginia Woolf mentioned in her essay on "Modern Fiction":—"Hades".

After the service for the departed Paddy Dignam is over, the mourners talk with John O'Connell, the cemetery caretaker. He cracks a joke with them, and Martin Cunningham observes that the joke was told with a purpose: "to cheer a fellow up. It's pure goodheartedness: damn the thing else." This little interchange directs Bloom's private meditative thoughts for four paragraphs (99-101/106-7); but it does so only because it embodies another relevant aspect of the subject he has been probing and scrutinizing all through the chapter: the theme of death. The "outer" event, the conversation, is not the real object to which his subsequent meditation is the reaction and by which it is organized. Rather, the event is assimilated to the main theme and its primary meaning lies in what Bloom *makes* of it. The organizing principle of his meditation is in fact two-fold. In the first place, it is Bloom's own character, the principle or "structural rhythm" that relates these four paragraphs not only to the rest of the chapter but to all those other places where his characteristic preoccupations and outlook are expressed in similar reflections. In the second place, however, the principle is the kind of reality that forms the content of Bloom's gesture of mind, the subject that is projected in and by his speculative *activity*.

The first of these four paragraphs begins with a conventional summary of his present state of mind: "Mr Bloom admired the caretaker's prosperous bulk" (a point dramatically realized in the course of his monologue). From then on we are presented with Bloom's own gestures, his activity of mind. He proceeds to recall various earlier thoughts—represented by verbal echoes—which he brings gradually to focus on a present speculation about the caretaker: "fancy being his wife". This radiates out further into consideration of love among the tombstones and the kind of person that might find it attractive: "spice of pleasure . . . tantalising for the poor dead . . . desire to grig people". The underlying pity for the dead, and the moral implications of that pity, obviously form one "structural rhythm" here. The basic theme of these meditations—as of the whole chapter—appears in the seemingly casual and spontaneous phrases that weave together the fragments just quoted: "in the midst of death we are in life. Both ends meet." However much this seems a cliché in abstract, it is very far from a cliché in its total context. As we shall see, it represents the theme that the whole chapter realizes and qualifies in dramatic terms; in other words, it is the meaning revealed in "reality", in life itself, by Bloom's mental gesture. Finally, Bloom returns to the caretaker again. One remembered fact about him clinches Bloom's apprehension of the various experiences he has brought together, and in turn throws new light on the caretaker himself: "eight children he has anyway". The sardonic enjoyment of that vital statistic is Bloom's as well as ours.

In the second paragraph, Bloom moves (and I use the active verb deliberately) to another aspect of the basic theme, and reveals to us another aspect of himself. He considers the renewal of life from the earth; his focus is now "Holy fields. . . . It's the blood sinking in the earth gives new life. Same idea those jews they said killed the christian boy"; and the paragraph concludes with a characteristic Bloom joke about the earth taking delivery of good fat corpses "with thanks". The third paragraph shifts to yet another aspect: the decomposition of the body while yet "the cells or whatever they are go on living. Changing about. Live for ever practically. Nothing to feed on feed on themselves." During all this, verbal echoes are reminding us, as well as Bloom, of related thoughts and experiences, or preparing us for them. Thus the whole context of Bloom's meditation is widened and its structural rhythms engage with other parts of the book: the meeting of Bloom and Stephen in "Ithaca", for example, when christian and jew confront one another, or Bloom's reflection in the following chapter, "Aeolus", when he concludes that "justice it means but its everybody eating everyone else. That's what life is after all." (114/121)

The fourth paragraph begins with an echo of an association of ideas established earlier (59-60/66-7), a song by which, in this context, Bloom connects his thoughts and feelings about Milly to his present graveyard meditation. He has pondered the connection between sexual activity and death, the alternation of life and death, the growth of life out of death, and now he feels both life and death as aspects of the one cosmic dance in which both ends meet: "But they must breed a devil of a lot of maggots. Soil must be simply swirling with them. Your head it simply swurls. Those pretty little seaside gurls." Bloom now turns to the joking and fun associated with graves and gravediggers (inevitably with a reference to *Hamlet*), and finally to the joke of reading one's own obituary notice, which is supposed, as he recalls, to give one "second wind. New lease of life." And as the whole range of experience Bloom contemplates is crystallized in this phrase, he returns to his earlier starting-point, the caretaker, the prosperous bulk he so much admires. At that, another passage of conversation interrupts his thoughts; but we could well say that in effect his activity of mind has reached a natural point of rest.

Clearly this is far from the random, unorganized chaos it was once thought to be. It is certainly no mere record of a stream of passively registered "impressions" or "associations". The verbal echoes, the juxtaposition of images, the loose and flexible syntax, and the other devices of suggestion, are all subordinate to the shaping, relating, interfusing process of the imagination: Bloom's primary imagination, as it were, and Joyce's secondary imagination, moving behind (but through) the other in a different rhythm. The passage gives an appearance of the random, spontaneous movement of thought (as indeed it must, just as the dramatist must give an appearance of spontaneous freedom to his action), but it is very far from an exact reproduction of a mind simply reflecting impressions, or casually drifting at the mercy of "objective reality", or even of the false starts, dead ends, irrelevancies, incomprehensible fragments and stupidities, we are all familiar with in our own experience. It is quite deliberately and artistically shaped and rendered. And the basis of organization is clearly the unit of the paragraph, and the paragraph in turn the expression of a separate mental act of apprehension. In short, the real artistic (and dramatic) unit of Joyce's "stream-of-consciousness" writing is the epiphany. What he renders dramatically are minds engaged in the apprehension of epiphanies—the elements of meaning apprehended in life. By apparently getting down to "raw" experience, he discovers the attitudes and values that give it form even as it *is* experienced. In this passage from "Hades", as in that from "Proteus" discussed earlier, the paragraph forms the imaginative integer: it expresses both a single "structural rhythm" or quiddity in the world as the character contemplates it, and at the same time it renders a single act of the character's personality. It is an integral active gesture of Bloom-Joyce.

What we may call "reality" in a novel or a play is always twofold: it is what the characters apprehend, the content of their acts of understanding, so to speak; and it is the content of the artist's creative gesture, in which he too expresses his understanding of his world—that is to say, what is represented by the characters and their actions themselves. Symbols are likewise two-fold: in the first place, objects, events, phrases, that are meaningful to the characters in the context of their personal preoccupations and which (for them and so for us) recall those preoccupations and which therefore (for us alone) evoke the personalities partly defined by them. In the second place, we may refer to the preoccupations and the personalities themselves as dramatic symbols by which the artist expresses his total meaning. Thus epiphanies, in the sense I have used the term, are at one level acts of apprehension made by the characters—not rare and special moments of mysterious insight (such as Virginia Woolf's novels often turn upon), but common acts of understanding in everyday life. But they are also, at a higher power, as it were, the artist's apprehensions of the significance of those acts (their forms or "quiddities" perhaps). The characters perceive meanings in life; we are shown further meanings in their perceptions. The twofold organizing principle of Bloom's graveyard meditation is simply what we should expect to find in *any* dramatic work: there is nothing fundamentally odd or unique about Joyce's methods. Even though the distinction between the characters' apprehensions and the author's (or ours) sometimes, for a moment, seems to disappear, Joyce maintains sufficient artistic detachment from his action, preserves the "dramatic" integrity of his aesthetic symbol, to make the distinction sharp and significant enough.

A great many of the symbolic "themes" in *Ulysses* are really devices to help create the characters themselves, not dark emblems to suggest mysterious significances in any reality supposedly common to the characters and to us. Presenting his characters' acts to the immediate witness of the reader with a minimum of editorial comment, Joyce inevitably had to create the illusion of a continuous identity abiding in and beyond the separate acts of apprehension: in other words, what William James tried to analyse as the continuous "stream of thought" *underlying* the mind's static "perchings" or "substantive conclusions".[3] To achieve a recognizably authentic portrayal of his characters Joyce had to suggest the continuity of their personalities, the presence of memories and preoccupations, in the present tense of his action. As the "psychological" critics have pointed out, one of his methods was to disperse fragments of epiphanies apprehended by the characters as "themes" or "motifs" recurring in other epiphanies, and so, together with the more conventional devices of characterization—dialogue, physical action, direct description, internal analysis, stylistic variation—to create a sense of the characters' individual presence. There are scores of such "themes" as this, and they form the largest and most obvious group of "symbols" (so-called) in the book: "agenbite of inwit", "parallax", the "seaside girls", drowning, *Hamlet*, and so on.[4] Each of these assumes a slightly different meaning as it reappears in different contexts. The "seaside girls" motif becomes part of Bloom's complex attitude to Milly and of his attitude to Boylan too; part of those feelings becomes part of his attitude to death; and they both in turn become involved in the issues of "Circe". Such motifs do not really serve, as is sometimes suggested, to identify the character whose interior thoughts we are witnessing—I doubt if there is any place in the book where we can confuse, accidentally, one stream of consciousness with another, and the motifs are often harder to remember than the various styles are to distinguish. Nor are the motifs signposts to what is "really" going on,[5] nor do they, of course, provide an artistic structure for the "jellyfish" reality of modern life. They are a means of characterization, more specifically, a means of representing and defining the individual character by expressing the personal centres from which his feelings and thoughts radiate and to which they are constantly returning. The jingle of Boylan's carriage becomes a symbol to Bloom for that "conquering hero", for the adultery he commits with Molly, and so for all the pain and nostalgia and struggle towards acceptance that Bloom's marriage habitually evokes in him. Similarly "Plumtree's Potted Meat" expresses some of his preoccupations as the phrase, or the object, recurs in his experience: it is an advertisement read casually while talking about his wife; it is an irritating example of a poorer advertisement than he (man of many devices) feels he could invent; an empty tin of the stuff is a mute reminder of Molly's activities during the day. Its significance in each case arises from the immediate context of his thoughts. The name of Martha, his potato talisman, "Sweets of Sin", a phrase from *Don Giovanni*, and scores of such personal symbols, like his memories, hopes, actions and words, help—by their shifting significance in scores of different contexts—to specify and crystallize him as a character and hence as an artistic symbol in the proper sense.

So with Stephen also. When, for example, he perceives the sea, "hailed as a great sweet mother by the wellfed voice" of Mulligan (3/7), as a bowl holding "a dull green mass of liquid" like that brought up by his dying mother, and then compares Mulligan's shaving-bowl with the boat of incense he carried at Clongowes school ("I am another now and yet the same. A servant too. A server of a servant" (9/13)), the point of all this is not any special meanings real bowls have in themselves, but the way in which it defines Stephen's trapped, obsessive state of mind. Even Mulligan's bowl in the very first sentence ("on which a mirror and a razor lay crossed"), whose significance Stephen does not ponder, adds no mysterious significance to bowls. It serves to set off, and so to crystallize for the reader, Mulligan's easy blasphemy; perhaps, too, the mirror and the razor may suggest something of his egotism and moral destructiveness; and, beside Stephen's responses to bowls, it helps place dramatically the superficial carelessness of one young man against the deeper struggle of the other. But once again the thematic "symbol" has no meaning apart from its dramatic function.

These motifs have been conveniently listed together and indexed by Mr R. M. Kain, and, as we might expect, those in Bloom's mind are both more numerous and more varied than those in Stephen's. Stephen's are mostly verbal: phrases from his philosophical and theological reading, from Blake and Dante, and especially from *Hamlet*, predominate over objects apprehended in the world about him. As Mr Kain comments, "though Stephen's mind may be more profound in the generally accepted sense of the word, it is not more interesting. His thought is complex, but the complexity rests on one level, that of metaphysical speculation. Bloom's is ever alert, ranging over the whole of experience."[6] And that precisely is the dramatically significant difference between the two characters. Such motifs or "themes" may be formed from any object, of course. Some are completely within the fictitious world of *Ulysses* (like Boylan's jingle); some possess a public and complex significance outside it (like *Hamlet*). In either case, however, the significance of the "symbol" is, primarily, the significance it has for the characters, and, more generally, the significance it has in relation to all the other aspects of the book. Given our ordinary ways of understanding character and the degree of attention Joyce has every right to expect from the reader, they need no elaborate commentary to explain them. The size—the sheer bulk—of *Ulysses* may make our apprehension of the characters difficult, especially as we normally expect the novelist to give the reader more explicit editorial help than Joyce does; nevertheless, we apprehend characters in real life or in drama from similarly immediate acts and feel ourselves competent enough. What needs critical interpretation, therefore, is less the significance of these thematic objects and phrases themselves, for they are only *fragments* of symbols, than the genuine symbols: the characters and their predicaments, the centres from which these motifs arise and which they serve to evoke.

Motifs of this kind depend for their artistic validity on the *consonantia* they exhibit, that is to say, on their coherence or *probability*. No matter how profound we think "parallax", for example, as a symbol of Relativity, or "paternity" as a symbol

256

of Man's proper relationship to his True Self or God, or "Agendath Netaim" (53-2/59-60) as a symbol of Primal Innocence or the Jewish Heritage, unless we are convinced that these things hang together with the rest of the book, that Bloom would really think and feel about them as he does, they would remain inert and pointless. And I think there is very little question that we are so convinced in nearly every case. Joyce's first and fundamental artistic achievement, the enabling condition of all the rest, is just this firm establishment of his characters as credible human beings. We expect as much from any novelist, of course, and usually take it for granted, but given the highly magnified focus at which Joyce presents his figures, together with his widely varied raids on "reality", his success represents a considerable technical feat.

One indication of his success was pointed out long ago by Ezra Pound and Edmund Wilson—the way in which the various streams-of-consciousness are clearly distinguished stylistically, and distinguished, moreover, through a wide variety of situations and areas of consciousness.[7] We can immediately detect the difference between Bloom's consciousness when we first meet him in "Calypso" from Stephen's in "Proteus", but we can also detect the significant difference between Bloom's and that of the other commercial-traveller, Mr Kernan. Moreover, we recognize the characteristic style and tempo and mood of Bloom or Stephen in conversations, reveries, and even in the fantasia of the unconscious: Bloom at the end of "Nausicaa" is still recognizable as the Bloom of (say) "Aeolus", and both he and Stephen are quite clearly differentiated in "Circe". More fundamentally, however, Joyce preserves the probability of detail that necessarily underpins every other effect. As the passage from "Hades" may illustrate, almost every phrase of Bloom's meditation (and Stephen's too) is coherent within the structure of his character as well as within the dramatic context in which his acts are placed by the artist.

This is not to say that Joyce succeeds in every detail. Indeed, his general success has so much overshadowed his occasional failures that it is worth suggesting one or two qualifications. "Eumaeus", for instance, seems to me one of the weakest sections of the book, though not only for the reason usually given—that it is too boring a way of expressing boredom. As well as that, as

I have suggested earlier, it seems to distort Bloom's character. His constant recourse to cliché throughout the book certainly expresses one aspect of him; the observations and feelings with which they are interfused and the values by which they are shaped express another. In "Eumaeus" he seems to shrink only to the former aspect. However tired he may be supposed, however much Joyce is concerned with the stale dregs and Hollow Men of modern life, Bloom seems a rather different character from what he has been: less responsible, acute and complex, and more like his parody, Mr Kernan. He is meant to dwindle at this stage of the book, of course, as our angle of vision widens, but he seems in the event less to dwindle than to be debased.

Some of the details of his earlier actions also seem a little contrived. One example is perhaps the "Agendath Netaim" motif, which first appears as an advertisement he picks up from the butcher's counter. It is quite in character that he should be attracted to it, and yet the advertisement itself is perhaps a little too obviously placed there by the author and the address of the advertising company ("Bleibtreustrasse"), a shade too convenient for a not-very-converted Jew like Bloom. A more obvious case in the same chapter is "metempsychosis". We first meet the word when Molly, having stumbled over it in *Ruby: Pride of the Ring*, asks Bloom what it means. Once again, quite apart from whether the word appears in a real book or not, it seems too pat, and its symbolic relevance somewhat too obviously underlined:

—Metempsychosis, he said, frowning. It's Greek: from the Greek. That means the transmigration of souls.

—O, rocks! she said. Tell us in plain words. . . .

—Some people believe, he said, that we go on living in another body after death, that we lived before. They call it reincarnation. That we all lived before on the earth thousands of years ago or some other planet. They say we have forgotten it. Some say they remember their past lives.

The sluggish cream wound curdling spirals through her tea. Better remind her of the word: metempsychosis. An example would be better. An example?

The *Bath of the Nymph* over the bed. Given away with the Easter number of *Photo Bits*: Splendid masterpiece in art colours. Tea before you put milk in. Not unlike her with her hair down: slimmer. Three and six I gave for the frame. She said it would look nice over the bed.

Naked nymphs: Greece: and for instance all the people that lived then. (57-8/64-5)

Even though this particular detail may not worry every reader, Joyce's meticulous notation of reality does nevertheless involve the continual problem of making such details seem at once both natural and meaningful—or rather, of finding the resource to *vary* the degree and kind of significance the details possess from point to point. The reader almost inevitably looks for consistency, especially once he has learned that there is a significance to be discovered. Allegory, for instance, is much easier to grasp than the shifting emphases and local dramatic significances charac-teristic of *Ulysses*, and the history of its criticism perhaps suggests that Joyce's method runs twin dangers: on the one hand, of altogether concealing the informing activity within the mass of apparent naturalism, and on the other of producing a nightmare in which everything seems insistently to signify something, a supercharged meaningfulness contrived by a ubiquitous author forever with a finger on his nose and a mysterious look in his eye. In short, the danger of Joyce's elaborate artifice is not merely that it leads the reader to make either too little of the book or too much, but also that the artifice may completely obscure his view of the art.

Similar problems arise with the characterization of Stephen, but are rather more obvious and acute. The fact that Stephen is so often taken as a young man completely and eternally locked in his sterile frustration, although not in itself an adequate reading, does nevertheless, register a weakness in Joyce's present-ation of him. Wyndham Lewis put his finger on a relevant half-truth when he called Stephen a stage poet. The trouble is not quite that Stephen is a dramatic cliché, any more than Bloom is; it is rather that his underlying strength and vitality—in com-parison with which Mulligan's ebullience seems febrile and incapable of real growth—cannot be anything but suggested. The only contexts in which Stephen can come to life are private, solitary ones. The nature of his growth still requires rejection of his circumstances and of the people about him. As yet, it affects positively only his inner relations with himself. It is for this reason, as I suggested earlier, that "Proteus" is the key-chapter for our sympathetic understanding of him, for without that progressive self-scrutiny and his saving touch of ironic self-criticism, Stephen does indeed seem a poor sack even by the side of Mulligan, and merely the cold, egotistical, pretentious, and unpleasant young man he appears to many readers. Perhaps in his desire not to let him off lightly, Joyce was a little too savage with him.[8] In any case it is easy to see Joyce's problem. Given the extremely *potential* positives Stephen represents and the personal nature of his problems, Joyce had to present his character's spiritual crisis within as dramatically as possible while at the same time maintaining the difficult balance between the reader's sympathy and impatience. Many of Stephen's attitudes to the world about him are undeniably flat, almost mechanical, in effect; some of the "agenbites of inwit" are particularly unconvincing—that in "Wandering Rocks", for example, where he meets his sister Dilly buying a French primer in a pathetic attempt to improve her mind:

> Show no surprise. Quite natural.
> —Here, Stephen said. It's all right. Mind Maggy doesn't pawn it on you. I suppose all my books are gone.
> —Some, Dilly said. We had to.
> She is drowning. Agenbite. Save her. Agenbite. All against us. She will drown me with her, eyes and hair. Lank coils of seaweed hair around me, my heart, my soul. Salt green death.
> We.
> Agenbite of inwit. Inwit's agenbite.
> Misery! Misery! (230/240)

This is the kind of thing to which Stephen is only too prone, and which makes it difficult to take him as seriously as he takes himself—even, at times, to take him seriously as a dramatic figure at all. To understand him as a whole, we must set the *kinesis* against the potentialities, for neither Stephen nor Bloom is to be summed up in terms only of their clichés and limitations. The real problem, however, is that we cannot always be quite sure how much of a theatrical cliché Stephen is meant to be, or precisely what degree of flatness or inertness in characterization his adolescence and his symbolic function in the novel require. And yet, we should also notice, one of the major sources of Joyce's pervasive irony is precisely this ambiguity in Stephen: behind the clichés of the writing flits the shadow of Joyce's satirical grin.

At least we can say that neither Bloom nor Stephen degenerates into a symbolist's dummy, though there are occasions on which they come close to it: in "Eumaeus", or in "Oxen of the Sun", or in parts of "Nausicaa" or "Circe" perhaps (but not in "Circe" as a whole, I believe, nor in "Ithaca", where their dramatic integrity changes in nature but is not destroyed). So too, we may feel, with other details like those I have quoted from the earlier chapters. Yet whether we do feel such details are probable or not in the created reality of the book (and decisions of this kind probably depend as much on taste as on judgment), and for the moment leaving aside Molly, who is a much more minor figure and a much more problematical success, Joyce's achievement is solid enough to establish his two main characters in their settings beyond all real question. We need not go to the extremes of some critics who claim that we know Bloom better than any other character of fiction. We learn a lot *more* about him than we do with other characters, perhaps, which is only fitting for a "complete hero", but Joyce's encyclopaedic details represent no necessary advance on the kind or the depth of knowledge we have of the characters of (say) George Eliot or Tolstoy or James. (A glance at some of the critical dossiers compiled about Bloom may even provoke the suspicion that the mass of information we are given *about* him may occasionally obscure our understanding *of* him.) What we do require of the novelist is that he make the experience of his characters immediate and coherent enough to engage our participating feelings and values, which are the material in and by which he creates his order. And this Joyce does.

Even at the risk of labouring the obvious, however, it is worth repeating that this could not occur were the protagonists the spiritual nonentities they are sometimes supposed to be. To achieve any significance, they must act. What Aristotle observed of Greek tragedy is just as true of the modern novel, or indeed of any dramatic form however complex or "poetic" its organization, however urgent seem its archetypal references. If Bloom and Stephen were merely symbols of a spiritual state of predeterminable significance, or merely tracks on which trains of "impressions" and associations clanked wearily by from a foreknown viewpoint to a foregone conclusion, they might possess some meaning as philosophical *exempla* or provide interesting texts for critical eloquence; they could hardly realize any imaginative meaning in life as we know it. Such a meaning would violate our common sense of what human beings are like, our knowledge of their moral activity, even though we may expect an author to inform his actors' activity with a significance greater than any they can perceive themselves. But if Bloom and Stephen are not simply the victims of Joyce's cosmic irony, or the *exempla* of some philosophical attitude, or the passive reflectors of "objective reality", in what sense are they *actors*? Or to put it another way, in what sense are Joyce's structures, the symbolic forms of his meaning, supported by the reality he renders in the novel? How does Joyce's total gesture emerge from, while at the same time it informs, his world?

The clue to the answer, I have suggested, lies both in his aesthetic theory and in his use of the stream-of-consciousness; specifically, in the term common to both—the epiphany. Both the theory and the technique arise from, and point to, the central theme of the work itself: the activity of the human spirit through which, in which, life continually seeks to understand itself and, understanding, to re-create.

Bloom is the protagonist of the book quite simply because he is so thoroughly representative of humanity, not merely as *l'homme moyen sensuel*, but also in his ineluctable isolation, his humble courage, and his unselfconscious aspirations to moral integrity. In this he is like Ulysses; but he is also a peculiarly modern representative in his *social* isolation and in his consciousness of *time*. The former marks the atomization of his society and its distance from the moral values Bloom himself brings to bear upon it even while he embodies it; the latter marks the burden of history by which the effort at self-understanding, personal or social, is immensely complicated and enlarged. While his limitations are therefore as representative as his virtues, they also deny him any absolute heroic stature. He requires qualification and placing in a context he can only dimly and intermittently perceive. This is partly the function of Stephen and of Molly. They qualify and place him, but he qualifies and places them in turn. To his necessary humility Stephen adds a necessary pride; to his acceptance, rejection; to his easy curiosity, a potential depth and intensity of vision; but neither is completely human without the other. And to complete the humanity of both, in Joyce's view, is required one more aspect: the elemental, disturbing, even turbulent material force below all moral life, the figure of Molly. In the total design all three are complementary, each suggesting an appropriate comment on the other. But there is also a fourth person as well, whose presence is continually suggested or implied and who is necessary to qualify and place the moral potentialities of the others—the artist himself, the poetic personality whose presence is felt, and unmistakably insisted upon, in the continual commentary of shifting styles, juxtapositions, points of view, and in the emergent perspectives of the actions performed by the other three. Indeed, as I have tried to show, the artistic realization of the author's vision *is* the action in its broadest sense and constitutes the context by which the meaning of the other three characters and the world they inhabit is given definition. But equally they define that total vision and qualify it. The fourth character is, very largely, the sum of the other three—but spiritually *actual* where they are only *potential*. And his ironic omnicompetence, the product of that achieved actuality of moral vision, is qualified and sweetened by the limitations of the humanity he represents—"represents" in both senses, active and passive. For if Bloom, Stephen and Molly are surrogates for the author, so he is for them, and all for the creative, mythopoeic spirit of humanity which is necessarily shown as free and universal and yet conditioned by its local time and place. In other words, the "now and here" of *Ulysses* and the actuality of spirit achieved by the author, from the plenitude of which the *Ulysses*-world is viewed, cannot be understood as absolute. Like any such symbolistic vision, its ironies regress infinitely into the void.

Once we ask why Joyce presents his characters' streams of consciousness, on what plane of activity their presented gestures cohere, and what symbolic relationships are established between them and other aspects of the book—particularly with the elaborately suggested temporal perspectives past and future—it becomes impossible to take *Ulysses* simply as the representation of social, cultural, psychological or metaphysical reality as we know it already. The characters are not merely social representatives, embodying a particular ethos at a particular point in history, nor merely the representatives of significant moral or spiritual predicaments. They do have these functions, but they are presented, ultimately, at a different level too: as agents, as well as reagents, engaged as best they can in understanding their world and themselves, and expressing that understanding in their gestures—that is to say, in deeds of the personality by which their worlds and their selves are actually realized. Rejection, acceptance, criticism, sympathy, revolt, aspiration—each attitude is coeval with and informs their very apprehensions. To regard their monologues as simply the representation of a passive receptivity to the "objective" world or of "subjective" reactions to it, is to see only their function as representatives of predetermined reality and to miss their crucial activity altogether. For the monologues also, as the brief example from "Hades" may serve to suggest, express their acts of understanding—including their focal acts of self-understanding—in which the enacting personality expresses its own life while the reality it confronts is at the same time also revealed and defined. *Ulysses* portrays, as well as objective reality as we all may see it more or less, the symbolizing power that, under its given circumstances and conditions, projects its own reality: what we may call the Bloomworld, the Stephenworld, the Mollyworld and finally the Joyceworld. Thus the deeper encompassing vision of the author is in one sense external to his dramatic action, and in another its natural product—and measure. The pervasive irony generated in the gap between is not the savage irony that an ideal Reality casts on Appearance, but the kinder, more humorous and tolerant irony that Achievement casts on Potentiality. What meanings are enacted by *Ulysses* are rooted in the life enacted in it, the activity by which humanity apprehends its world and so informs it with significance. Its symbolic structures are founded in its presented reality as the epiphanies apprehended by the characters ripple out, deepen, and are enriched and interrelated in the apprehensions of the author.

It may well seem that Joyce's final value is Art itself, and so in a sense it is. Not, however, in the sense that Art is Stephen's final value in the *Portrait*, where he conceives it as (somehow) a pure, unconditioned expression by the artist of "Life", yet never relates it to any specific aspect of the artist's life and supposes it discussable in purely formal—and so ultimately meaningless— terms. In *Ulysses* art is no longer viewed so idealistically even by Stephen. The book insists, through and through, upon the limits within which the primary imagination, the daily perceptions of such a man as Bloom, are contained (limits which are the *given* realities of society and of language) no less than upon its freedom. And as Stephen's treatment of Shakespeare and Joyce's treatment of Stephen imply, those limits cannot be ignored by the secondary imagination of the artist, for they constitute part of the moral experience whose meaning he seeks to know in the process of ordering and refashioning it. In effect, Art becomes not so much any final value in itself as a symbol of that value, a symbol that partakes of the reality it signifies and expresses it as articulately as it can be expressed. In the *Portrait*, art is a symbol of what makes for life: "all that nourishes art is living", it has been observed, "all that stifles art is dead".[9] What *Ulysses* does is give that proposition a deeper meaning by insisting upon *all* the conditions of art—obscure and difficult as they may seem to the young potential artist—and upon *all* the significance of the vitality art expresses. We may call that significance plenitude of vision, or the self-knowledge of life, or *stasis*, but this is to say very little and to mislead even in saying so much. For the meaning and validity of such phrases, whatever these may be—and it is clear, I hope, that these are not of a formal, philosophical kind—are definable only in terms of what the book itself realizes. To develop them any further in abstract terms would only be further to divagate. Nevertheless, they may perhaps direct us to the central imaginative organizations of the work.

II

The organizations depend, as I have suggested in Chapter VI, upon Joyce's use of two main devices: juxtaposition and the deployment of "point of view". Neither is original to Joyce of course, and he uses neither modishly for its own sake. In his hands, they are the expression of a subtle and complex vision of life, the artistic conventions signifying a moral meaning, and what we must try to understand is the way in which he uses them as means to his proper aesthetic ends.

Juxtaposition is the means by which the dramatic symbol or epiphany is constituted. The meaning of such a symbol is an unseen current that leaps between the elements brought together and unites them into an otherwise inexpressible unity. Ideally, the symbol eschews any syntax that might limit the possibilities of connection between its elements or might commit it to the *directed* patterns of connection found in ordinary discursive speech. It prefers silent juxtaposition. We can see this in Joyce's monologues for example. Although the sentences of which they are composed do observe the rules of syntax rather than the structure (whatever it may be) of the "prespeech levels" of mind, and the sentences in turn are organized into integers of paragraph-epiphany, the relationships between the sentences—that is, between the elements brought together in the epiphany—and the relationships between the epiphanies themselves, are generally not overtly expressed at all. Such syntax as the writing possesses is important precisely because it is the *minimum* linguistic connection necessary to meet the requirements of general probability of character and local specification and at the same time to express these particular symbolic elements. What further relates the elements, like what constitutes the probability of character, we must ourselves imaginatively work to understand. This deliberate looseness of syntax is one of the obvious characteristics of symbolistic poetry, where (whether for loss or gain), the energy of a channelled syntax is replaced by the energy of suggestive juxtaposition; and in this respect *Ulysses* is clearly symbolistic in method. The stream-of-consciousness techniques, by permitting the maximum play between the elements of experience juxtaposed by the characters, enlarge the possible ways in which we may view that experience. The relative thinness of plot in the ordinary sense can be regarded as the avoidance of any over-committed syntax of event, which thus permits the maximum play of meanings in the relationships of characters, setting, and events. The elaborate but unsystematic repetitions of words and images constitutes no syntax of esoteric or metaphysical meanings, but rather a pervasive suggestion of an *un*apprehensible order beyond any actually perceived: a suggestion that, like the unfolding mythical vision, palliates and transmutes what would otherwise be an over-deliberation, a too *knowing* consciousness, in the book as a whole. Just because of its very lack of commitment, juxtaposition is a constructive method eminently suited to "dramatic" art, art devoted to the responsive scrutiny of the now and here. It preserves the apparent spontaneity of the life presented and yet permits the artist the subtlest and most far-reaching expressive activity within it—so far-reaching, indeed, that it inevitably invites the kind of over-ingenious interpretations from which *Ulysses*, like many symbolistic works, has suffered. But underlying all this, juxtaposition is also the expression and medium of a particular view of life. In the broadest sense, its capacity to mean as much or as little as we wish it too (and "we", in this context, refers to author and reader alike), its shifting multivalence, the very pervasiveness and ambiguity of the energy it generates, reflect a deeply ironical response to a universe of ambiguity. To mention these two key terms of modern criticism is at once to suggest the familiarity of the method in poetry; in the novel, *Ulysses* exploits it about as far as it will go (and *Finnegans Wake* perhaps further).

A great deal of the irony in which Bloom is immersed derives from such sly juxtapositions of events or values. These include not only the Homeric parallels and the sharp disparities between events and the style in which they are rendered, but also the intercalations of "Wandering Rocks", for instance, and such dramatic moments as Bloom's sudden bolt into "the Greek architecture" or his loss of a trouser-button. In each case, juxtaposition is the instrument of a commentary at once critical and dramatic whereby the event, which has one meaning for the actors, is given another for the reader. It is tempting to talk of "levels" of meaning, but the effect is more flexible, more suggestive, than "levels" may imply. Thus the jingle of Boylan's carriage becomes for us an echo of the notorious jingle of Bloom's bed; Stephen's realization that he devours "a urinous offal from all dead" (47/51) is placed for us against Bloom's relish for the inner organs of beasts and fowls. Stephen's laugh at the end of his lecture on Shakespeare (200/209), or Bloom's appearance in the same chapter (206/214), possesses the same multiplicity of significance. So with hundreds of the details. Even "Plumtree's Potted Meat" becomes to us a sidelong metaphor for Molly herself as a consequence of its position:

—Wife well, I suppose? M'Coy's changed voice said.
—O yes, Mr Bloom said. Tiptop, thanks.
He unrolled the newspaper baton idly and read idly:

> *What is home without*
> *Plumtree's Potted Meat?*
> *Incomplete.*
> *With it an abode of bliss.* (67/73-4)

It is hardly a metaphor that calls for the analytic apparatus of mediaeval Rhetoric. What is rather more interesting about it, like those of which it is a typical example, is that we need not take it as a metaphor for Molly at all if we do not wish to. It commits Joyce to nothing. On the other hand, we may once again seek a significance in *every* juxtaposition, rather in the manner of Mr Gilbert, and be tempted into finding one where none exists—or rather, where nobody else can find any: being committed to nothing, juxtaposition, like life, can be very unfair to critics. (What possibilities yet unexplicated lurk, for example, in the three books Stephen turns over on the bookcart (229/239): *The Irish Beekeeper, Life and Miracles of the Curé of Ars* and *Pocket Guide to Killarney*?) Yet such juxtapositions are the very stuff of *Ulysses*, the artistic manipulations by which the preoccupations and perceptions of the characters are made into symbols for the reader and which give such manifold meaning to Stephen's metaphors of Christ and God, the *Hamlet* symbolism, and the whole central relationship of paternity.

Just as the irony is not simply directed against the characters or the world they inhabit, so not all the symbolic juxtapositions are ironic. Some are more like signposts, if we wish to follow them, to "themes" or motifs and significances established more vitally elsewhere. A good example is the episode in "Aeolus" where two epiphanies are placed side by side: against the kinetic success of the journalist, lauded by the Dubliners gathered in the newspaper office, Stephen places the eternal rhymes of Dante (and his own callow attempts in the same direction):

He saw them three by three, approaching girls, in green, in rose, in russet, entwining, *per l'aer perso* in mauve, in purple, *quella pacifica oriafiamma*, in gold of oriflamme, *di rimirar fé piú ardenti*. But I old men, penitent, leadenfooted, underdarkneath the night: mouth south: tomb womb.

—Speak up for yourself, Mr O'Madden Burke said. (129/137)

Although Burke's casual sentence has an obvious ironic bearing on Stephen's case, we may easily suppose that Stephen sees it that way too, and this very largely neutralizes the irony and subordinates it to a more general effect of emphasis: Burke's remark merely underlines the relevant fact, of which Stephen himself is quite well aware, that as yet he lacks the mastery and freedom of Dante. Other juxtapositions go beyond both irony and emphasis and serve actively to endorse. As Bloom, agitated by thoughts of Molly's infidelity, pulls his mind up short—"Stop. Stop. If it was it was. Must"—he passes by "Adam court" (156/165). The incident of John Henry Menton's hat (107/114) is another instance. The two most striking examples, however, occur at the end of "Proteus" and at the end of "Cyclops": the homing ship revealed to Stephen's "rere regardant" gaze, and the metaphoric ascent to heaven of ben Bloom Elijah. Neither of these images has much force in itself; in each case the impact derives from its position, its relations with what precedes it, and the more distant contexts of significance it actively relates to one another. Towards the end of "Wandering Rocks" Stephen's ship is mentioned once again, though this time in conjunction with another traveller on the river, Elijah Bloom's "light crumbled throwaway", which is already linked for us with the sacrificial and prophetic aspects he has revealed in "Lestygonians" (139 ff./149 ff.). Yet again the mere mention, or even the conjunction, means very little in itself apart from its devastating position in the dramatic context. Coming directly upon Mulligan's condemnation of Stephen and Haines's complacent superiority to all things Irish (235-6/244-6), the image conveys so sharp and positive an endorsement of Stephen and Bloom that it is hard to resist calling it authorial comment.

In one of the most suggestive accounts of Joyce's dramatic methods, Irene Hendry has remarked that all his work is "a tissue of epiphanies, great and small, from fleeting images to whole books, from the briefest revelation in his lyrics to the epiphany that occupies one gigantic, enduring 'moment' in *Finnegans Wake*". She begins her discussion with what she takes as the simplest form of Joyce's narrative epiphanies, that exhibited in *Dubliners*. Here, as she says, Joyce employs a method already familiar in the short-story. The *quidditas* of the material is revealed by some event or detail that, added to the rest, suddenly illuminates, integrates, and gives them all symbolic meaning. It acts rather like the final block that completes a child's design. "Such stories", as she observes, "are usually considered to be 'objective' because the author offers no overt interpretation of his material but merely arranges it so that its meaning is 'revealed' directly to the reader."[10] But although Miss Hendry assumes Joyce more or less abandoned this kind of juxtaposition after *Dubliners* it is in fact very common in *Ulysses*. The only difference is in the range and complexity of the design, for it is not simply a device whereby the real state of affairs is revealed to a character (as the commonly cited example of Gerty MacDowell's limp may suggest); it applies to the symbolic meanings revealed to the reader. Every chapter of *Ulysses* contains such a final "block" epiphany, similar in structural position if not in effect to those at the end of "Proteus" and "Cyclops", and, like them, both giving its imaginative force to and taking it from the total context of the chapter. The most frequently mentioned case is perhaps the last episode of "Wandering Rocks" where the vice-regal procession serves to recapitulate the social decomposition of modern society much as Fr. Conmee's journey in the first episode served to adumbrate its spiritual decomposition. But this is only one of the weakest examples of a general technique, sharing with the endings of "Oxen of the Sun" and "Penelope" a certain obviousness and flatness. Even in "Telemachus", where the action has gathered far less significance and momentum, Stephen's silent "Usurper" (21/24) brings the preceding action to a sharper dramatic focus. Similarly in those episodes I have already discussed earlier: Bloom's bath in "Lotuseaters", for example, which crystallizes both the drift of his perceptions and our perception of his moral activity; or Stephen's quotation from *Cymbeline* at the end of "Scylla and Charybdis"; or the "Cuckoo" at the end of "Nausicaa", which again both places and is placed by Bloom's moral attitudes developed in the chapter; and so on, indeed, right through the whole book. The last "block" of each chapter only completes a design already composed of "blocks", of intricately interconnected epiphanies.

To speak of juxtaposition merely in these terms, however, is to over-simplify the ways in which Joyce deploys his material, and especially the consciousness of his characters. This is where we must turn to his use of the narrative "point of view". As with most novels, the artist's vision of life is sometimes implicit in the very stance of the "objective" narration; more often it is expressed through the characters' "subjective" consciousness of life; and as a whole, of course, it is expressed by the complex interconnections of the two, in their variable, shifting convergences and separations. In other words, we must recognize that the texture of the writing does not allow any rigid division of "subjective" and "objective", and that the mere recurrence of motifs and images is imaginatively impotent in itself. Only if we get rid of the misconceptions can we begin to perceive the complexity of the *dramatic* organizations, of which both the representational naturalism and the thematic "symbolism" are but aspects. And although the kinds of organization vary from chapter to chapter, as the discussion of "Lestygonians" and "Wandering Rocks" (in Chapter IV) and "Proteus" and "Circe" (in Chapter V) has perhaps suggested, we may well continue with "Hades" as a convenient if not exhaustive example of Joyce's art.[11]

The most obvious kind of organization in "Hades" is the representational: the sequence of time and place, from the first departure of Paddy Dignam's funeral at about 11 o'clock to the final departure of the mourners from the cemetery about an hour later. The carriage takes Simon Dedalus, Martin Cunningham, Jack Power and Mr Bloom along a clearly defined route which is registered partly in Bloom's thoughts, partly in direct narration. It is quite easy to distinguish between "objective" places and events and Bloom's "subjective" thoughts about them—at any rate, at first—and undoubtedly we are meant to:

> Mr Bloom put his head out of the window.
> —The grand canal, he said.
> Gasworks. Whooping cough they say it cures. Good job Milly never got it. Poor children! Doubles them up black and blue in convulsions. Shame really. Got off lightly with illness compared. Only measles. Flaxseed tea. Scarlatina, influenza epidemics. Canvassing for death. Don't miss this chance. Dog's home over there. Poor old Athos! Be good to Athos, Leopold, is my last wish. Thy will be done. We obey them in the grave. A dying scrawl. He took it to heart, pined away. Quiet brute. Old men's dogs usually are. (82/89)

Yet such details of scene and circumstance are simply inert information, without imaginative logic or relevance except in as much as they are felt as the given context, ultimately the given *material*, of further insight and organization. Similarly with Bloom's subjective reactions. Gasworks and dogs' home, streets, passers-by, graveyard, monuments, mourners are observed in a context of private experience and by a mind preoccupied with jealousy, loneliness, compassion, and so on. The passage just quoted, for example, reveals far more about Bloom than about the objects he is supposedly looking at, so that even in this apparently simple case, the subjective-objective distinction is much more precarious than it may seem at first sight. But infused with the representational sequence of the chapter is another kind of organization, which overlays the gap between objective details and subjective thoughts by bringing both together in a common pattern of images and themes.

The central, interrelated themes of the chapter—the cycle of life and death (and the rôle of womankind in both), the forms of death, the state of Ireland, the universal isolation of the individual—ramify into almost all the details. Bloom sees an old woman peeping through her curtain at the funeral: "glad to see us go we give them so much trouble coming" (79/86); Mr Dedalus, his age "beginning to tell on him now" is "full of his son" (81/87); Bloom reflects on "how life begins" (81/88); the others tell Dedalus the story of the Jewish moneylender, Reuben J. Dodd, and his florin's worth of gratitude for his son's rescue (87/93); Bloom notes the deadness of a passing street (88/94); his father's suicide is evoked (88, 93/95, 100); they pass cattle on the way to the slaughter—"emigrants" (90/96)—and the house where Childs was murdered (92/98-9); and in the cemetery, as we have seen, Bloom's thoughts constantly turn upon the cycle of death and life. Each of the men in the carriage is separated from the others by private troubles and each is also separated from a normal family life: Bloom's pain and loneliness we know; Cunningham has a drunken wife; Power has formed an odd, rather pathetic, liaison with a barmaid; and Dedalus's drinking and alienation from his children are part of the present action. Bloom is further isolated from the others by his race, by his father's suicide, by his notorious cuckoldry. Old Virag's desperate isolation is recalled in Bloom's thoughts (89/95); later, over Dignam's grave, he returns at length to the same theme. "The Irishman's house is his coffin", he reflects (102/108), and Ireland's hopes, like her streets and canals, are seen as decaying. Parnell is a dying memory. Even grief itself seems frozen in deadly immutability. The rat Bloom observes in the cemetery seems more vital than anything the cemetery represents. The word "heart"—the "symbolic" organ for this chapter according to Joyce's scheme[12]—recurs in one context after another; so does "home", "grave", "blood".

Yet the mere presence of these themes would be nothing

without the dynamic interplay by which they are given real depth and meaning. Merely to note that "heart" recurs, for example, is of little significance without also noting how its ambiguities are dramatically explored and played off against one another: "heart" as the physical organ of life (Paddy Dignam's); "heart" as the symbol of social life (old Ireland's Sacred Heart); "heart" as the seat of affective life (old Ireland wearing its Sacred Heart on its sleeve; Bloom's sympathy and compassion; the love that kills; warm fullblooded life; etc.). When Bloom, in the midst of his meditations by Dignam's grave, suddenly notices Ned Lambert's suit, recalls that Lambert used to be a dressy fellow ("used to change three suits in the day"), and then observes that the suit is dyed (102/108), the motifs involved—time, the dance of the hours in different colours, "dyed", etc.—however closely related verbally to the rest of the chapter, remain merely verbal. Similarly with Bloom's observation of Dignam's arrival at the cemetery before the mourners (93, 95/99, 102), or the explicit mention of the canals over which they pass: the Homeric parallels they represent are purely nominal.[13] Just as the themes require dramatic enactment so do the characters. Bloom, for example, is played off against Dedalus even though each is involved in the same themes. The difference is drawn early and very sharply. Dedalus reacts possessively, kinetically, when the carriage passes Stephen, his "son and heir". As he snarls abuse at his son's activities and "lowdown" associates, Bloom sits silently watching and judging: "noisy selfwilled man. Full of his son. He is right . . ." (81/87-8). So Bloom's act of mind begins, but it really centres on the ideas of "life" and "independence". He recognizes the futility of trying to possess or dominate the processes of life, the growth of son or daughter, and in so doing he not only places Dedalus's "selfwill" but also realizes dramatically (in the sense that includes *exhibiting*) one sense of vitality of the heart. Where Bloom is the outsider, made to feel a little uncomfortable by the story of Reuben Dodd, the moneylender, and his son, Dedalus is the crony of cronies, the wit, whose savagely dry comment on the story nevertheless reveals his own deep imprisonment in frustration (87/93). Bloom's compassion for children, animals, people down on their luck, suicides, for the Dignam family and for Dignam himself, plays, with increasing consciousness and force, against the conventionalities of the situation. And as we perceive this, the static pattern of interwoven themes becomes visibly inadequate to describe the dynamic organization of the chapter. At the beginning and at the end of it Bloom is equally snubbed: he is the last invited into the carriage, he is "Bloom" where the others are addressed by Christian names; so his courtesy to Menton is snubbed at the end. But now he has the last word—"Thank you. How grand we are this morning" (107/114). The similarity of the situation only underlines the difference: the devastating finality with which Bloom's small silent comment places Menton and all he represents. It is a dramatic authority Bloom has accumulated during the course of the chapter; and it vividly suggests the extent to which the structure of the chapter is basically a development of moral awareness—Bloom's in the first instance, ours in the last: an *action* in which setting, characters and themes are all finally absorbed. We may well compare its organization with that of a poem—but it is a *dramatic* poem we must have in mind.

The unit is the epiphany, of course, but there are different kinds of epiphany. Some are purely "objective", presented to us immediately by unostentatious narration without reference to Bloom's consciousness at all. The little episode at the beginning is an example of this kind; so is that in which Dedalus is told about Reuben Dodd and his son and reveals so much about his own paternal feelings; so is the final episode with Menton. Most of the epiphanies, however, do engage Bloom, and it is important to notice how they do so. In the early part of the chapter, during the actual journey to the cemetery, he seems very largely a *passive* reflector of the casual, passing scene: he notices the gasworks and dogs' home, glances over the deaths column in the newspaper, hears a street organ, notes Dumphy's pub, and so on, his mind all the while bringing associated experiences to bear, roughly and readily but with unconscious "thematic" significance, upon the given object. In such moments he remains very largely an exhibit himself, his drifting thoughts revealing characteristic attitudes, values and preoccupations, which are juxtaposed with or against his immediate setting. At other times, however, he becomes a reflector more conscious, more alert, than in cases like that of the gasworks. He penetrates further into the given object and focusses perceptions of value. Thus the raindrops are reflected by his consciousness not because the fact of rain needs subjective notation, but because it is relevant that *he* should perceive their formation: "Apart" (82/89). After Cunningham has mentioned the cause of Dignam's death—"Breakdown. . . . Heart"—Bloom observes

Dead side of the street this. Dull business by day, land agents, temperance hotel, Falconer's railway guide, civil service college, Gill's, catholic club, the industrious blind. Why? Some reason. Sun or wind. At night too. Chummies and slaveys. Under the patronage of the late Father Mathew. Foundation stone for Parnell. Breakdown. Heart. (88/94)

As the mourners enter the cemetery, Bloom notes a wretched mother and daughter coming out, and again it is his mind that registers the significance of its object (93/100). Although such registrations are very far from merely passive reflections of "objective" reality, his insight is still restricted to the single object given, as it were; his understanding is not at its most freely searching and connective. Epiphanies of that deeper kind are very carefully placed, crowding to a climax near the end of the chapter. And they are typically the points at which the writing is most complexly alive, for it is these acts of Bloom's mind, which are really acts of his whole being, from which the themes and images radiate and on which the fundamental dramatic structure rests.

The first of these we have already noticed: the epiphany (81/88) in which Dedalus's selfwill is placed, and in which are crystallized some of the themes lightly suggested in the opening pages: the initial snub, the old woman peeping at the funeral; the silent community of isolation in the carriage as "all wait", Dedalus's alienation from his son. The experiences that Bloom brings together—Molly's remembered cry, "Give us a touch Poldy. God, I'm dying for it", Rudy's and Milly's growth, the now hopeless dream of making his son "independent", and all the rest—give complex but precise definition to the tone of his final "Life. Life", while his act, juxtaposed with its setting, gives preliminary definition to the themes as well as to his moral status in relation to them.

The second of these crucial acts is that in which, while suicide is discussed, Bloom realizes, and we realize even more, what the desperation of isolation means. The epiphany opens with a childish rhyme running in Bloom's thoughts: "Rattle his bones. Over the stones. Only a pauper. Nobody owns" (88/95). This functions as a refrain whose meaning is explored in the different contexts of experience brought together by Bloom: the general social hostility to suicide, the heartbreak and loneliness that cause it, the private hell from which it springs, Cunningham's sympathy for Bloom, their mutual but unspoken knowledge about each other, old Virag's pathetic desolation, the individual's rights that "nobody owns" but himself, and his ultimate aloneness. The themes of isolation and kinship, verbal motifs like "heart" and "blood", are "cashed", so to speak, in the moral situation and its enactment. Whether the *verbal* motifs are explicitly used or not is irrelevant. Suicide and the mutual isolation of Cunningham and Bloom become active symbols of each other; so do their common sympathy of heart, their common pain, and their common silence. Cunningham perceives little of this perhaps, but Bloom certainly does—partly, indeed, because he also understands Cunningham's case. So, in the same proportion, do we, outside Bloom and understanding him in a way he cannot, perceive most.

By intermittently moving our point of view outside Bloom's, Joyce preserves the distance necessary for us to perceive the sad ironies of the case. Once Bloom's situation and acts have been placed in relation to the others', however, and we have begun to feel the quality of his moral engagement, the "objective" narrative can fade away for longer stretches and Bloom's activity increase. This begins to occur, roughly speaking, once the funeral reaches the cemetery. More and more of the themes are picked up, developed and enacted in Bloom's consciousness. The funeral service itself is rendered in a series of epiphanies—the priest, the chapel, the actual service—in which it is quite impossible to differentiate between "objective" narrative and "subjective" monologue (95-6/102-3). What seems simple description—"The whitesmocked priest came after him tidying his stole with one hand, balancing with the other a little book against his toad's belly"—appears something rather different when *Bloom* thinks, "Eyes of a toad too" (96/102). In effect the narrative point of view has shifted entirely behind Bloom's and serves as a tacit endorsement of it.

Bloom's view is critical and naturalistic. The priest seems toad-like, poisoned; the chapel "full of bad gas"; the service almost meaningless in its listless conventionality. Yet Bloom also recognizes that, however empty the priest's gestures are, "he has to say something" (96/103). Death requires more than "shovelling them under by the cartload doublequick" (93/100). On the other hand, "once you are dead you are dead"—the heart, "seat of affections" is truly broken (98/104). Both for Bloom and in him, real vitality is the vitality of the heart, although not—as the whole chapter demonstrates—in any merely sentimental sense. It is in the context of these epiphanies that we catch him, as he catches himself, unconsciously lilting (97/103); Dedalus breaks down in sentimental grief for his wife(97/103); and Bloom, as we have already seen, meditates the cosmic dance of life and death (99-101/106-7). The epiphanies that follow (101-2/108) are still Bloom's and focus other aspects of the human condition—man's isolation and subjection to time, for example, and his desire for burial—but so complexly relating them that the result defies brief analysis. At the centre is the genuine note of compassion—"Poor Dignam!"—which, in its context after a fragment of a song about Robinson Crusoe and Bloom's realization that "every Friday buries a Thursday if you come to look at it", also expresses, for Bloom and for us, the universal case Dignam so unconsciously, almost indeed wryly, represents. Perhaps even here we perceive that it is also the case Bloom himself represents; in any case, the conversation about names and the mysterious thirteenth man in the mackintosh recall the universal application to mind.

Whatever we think of Bloom's values—and certainly they are not those of a devout Christian, Roman Catholic or otherwise— they are not quite as simple as some critics have supposed. True, the "frying pan of life"—the "gentle sweet air" that whispers about the mourners—is for him sharply opposed to the "fire of purgatory", and he shows no sign of belief in the importance or even existence of religious "realities". Nevertheless, it is no stupid or superficial man who senses, for example, Molly's view of Boylan, "after: thinking alone" (84/91), or places such widowed grief as Queen Victoria's: "but in the end she put a few violets in her bonnet. Vain in her heart of hearts. All for a shadow. Consort not even a king. Her son was the substance. Something new to hope for not like the past she wanted back, waiting. It never comes. One must go first: alone under the ground: and lie no more in her warm bed" (94/101). This is the kind of awareness that gives meaning to his response while the coffin is laid in its grave:

> The coffin dived out of sight, eased down by the men straddled on the gravetrestles. They struggled up and out: and all uncovered. Twenty.
> Pause.
> If we were all suddenly somebody else.
> Far away a donkey brayed. Rain. No such ass. Never see a dead one, they say. Shame of death. They hide. Also poor papa went away.
> Gentle sweet air blew round the bared heads in a whisper. Whisper. The boy by the gravehead held his wreath with both hands staring quietly in the black open space. . . . (102/109)

The meaning of the symbolic juxtapositions in this last sentence or two derives from, though it also extends and endorses, the juxtapositions made by Bloom himself. Perhaps an even clearer example of the same process and effect occurs in the epiphany partly concerned with Parnell, the symbol of Irish national aspiration. Hynes and Power agree to visit his grave. Power mentions the belief that Parnell will come again; Hynes shakes his head—" 'Parnell will never come again,' he said. 'He's there, all that was mortal of him. Peace to his ashes.' " Placed sharply beside this is a composite epiphany which is worth quoting at length:

> Mr Bloom walked unheeded along his grove by saddened angels, crosses, broken pillars, family vaults, stone hopes praying with upcast eyes, old Ireland's hearts and hands. More sensible to spend the money on some charity for the living. Pray for the repose of the soul of. Does anybody really? Plant him and have done with him. Like down a coalshoot. Then lump them together to save time. All souls' day. Twentyseventh I'll be at his grave. Ten shillings for the gardener. He keeps it free of weeds. Old man himself. Bent down double with his shears clipping. Near death's door. Who passed away. Who departed this life. As if they did it of their own accord. Got the shove, all of them. Who kicked the bucket. More interesting if they told you what they were. So and so, wheelwright. I travelled for cork lino. I paid five shillings in the pound. Or a woman's with her saucepan. I cooked good Irish stew. Eulogy in a country churchyard it ought to be that poem of whose is it Wordsworth or Thomas Campbell. Entered into rest the protestants put it. Old Dr Murren's. The great physician called him home. Well it's God's acre for them. Nice country residence. Newly plastered and painted. Ideal spot to have a quiet smoke

and read the *Church Times*. Marriage ads they never try to beautify. Rusty wreaths hung on knobs, garlands of bronzefoil. Better value that for the money. Still, the flowers are more poetical. The other gets rather tiresome, never withering. Expresses nothing. Immortelles. (105/111-2)

To omit any of this characteristic epiphany is to miss part of its complex significance. There is no opposition between the "objectivity" of the first sentence and the "subjectivity" of what follows; in fact, the ease with which our view of Bloom and of the miserable marble around him slides into his view of it indicates how far the critically intelligent feelings are his, how subtly sympathetic the irony directed towards him has become. Against the insidious sentimentality of Hynes and Power and the funeral monuments, his insight is sharp and antiseptic. Surrounded by "stone hopes", hearts and hands frozen in useless grief, he perceives that garlands of bronzefoil express nothing, that the transience of human grief is the condition of its value.[14] The substance of life is the son, "not the past she wanted back, waiting".

The climax of the chapter is preceded by Bloom's sight of a rat among the graves—the main significance of which I take to be the unnerving horror Bloom does *not* feel (and which some of his critics do). His "acceptance of life" means just those clear, firm recognitions of the natural condition embodied in his various epiphanies, and the rat has a kind of final demonstrative necessity. Bloom looks it fairly in the face. The real climax of the chapter, however, is the epiphany immediately after, from which I have quoted in an earlier chapter:

The gates glimmered in front: still open. Back to the world again. Enough of this place. Brings you a bit nearer every time. Last time I was here was Mrs Sinico's funeral. Poor papa too. The love that kills. And even scraping up the earth at night with a lantern like that case I read of to get at fresh buried females or even putrefied with running gravesores. Give you the creeps after a bit. I will appear to you after death. You will see my ghost after death. My ghost will haunt you after death. There is another world after death named hell. I do not like that other world she wrote. No more do I. Plenty to see and hear and feel yet. Feel live warm beings near you. Let them sleep in their maggoty beds. They are not going to get me this innings. Warm beds: warm fullblooded life. (106-7/113)

At this stage it is perhaps enough to note that to analyze the full significance of this—especially of "the love that kills"—would be to analyse the total meaning of the chapter itself, including the accumulating significance of woman as wife, widow, mother; of unity and isolation in the family; of the sense of time and the conventionalities of death; of all those values, spiritual though not perhaps Christian, engaged and realized by Bloom himself; and including, finally, Menton's "hate at first sight" and the silent, humble human authority Bloom has now assumed.

The complete absence of a specifically religious dimension to Bloom may seem to some readers the most damaging criticism of him possible—so damaging, in fact, as to suggest a wholesale irony on Joyce's part. But even though Bloom signally fails to achieve "warm fullblooded life", "Hades" surely contains no annihilating irony. On the contrary, the adjustments of our vision it performs are sympathetic, not hostile, to Bloom, and underline his positive vitality. Ironies elsewhere, as we have seen, suggest his spiritual and social limitations sharply enough; his ideals are divided and confused; certainly, for good or bad, he is incorrigibly secular and naturalistic. Yet if he is somewhat vulgar, he is not mean, not hostile to life. To take one chapter in isolation is to circumscribe its significance of course, but what it enacts is to that extent relevant. Whatever else he lacks, Bloom is not without compassion, dignity, courage and even wit; and the basic structure of the chapter is precisely the dramatic realization of this. As for the "structural" scheme of organ (heart), art (theology), colour (white, black), symbol (caretaker), technic (incubism), this has a certain biographical interest as an example of Joyce's working-notes, but very little else. So too with the detailed Homeric parallels: whether we notice them or not, they certainly possess no structural importance. The effective organization of the material lies partly in the rendering of setting and events, the characters and plot. More fundamentally, however, it lies in the verbal texture and inter-relations of the epiphanies, in their juxtaposition and sequence, and ultimately in the developing moral insight they achieve.

III

If the formal values of "Hades" are *created* in the represented reality they are also felt as *revealed* in that reality as well. The art achieves the impersonality wherein the artist and his world, at times separated by a gap of irony, also appear to merge, until the total activity of the one becomes the meaning of the other. The juxtapositions and sequence of the epiphanies assume symbolic significance easily, without strain. There is none of the obvious manipulation, the external adducement of significance, characteristic of some of the other chapters from "Cyclops" onwards. In those, the gap between the formal values implicit in the techniques and organization and the values enacted by the characters progressively widens. The relation between the two is never broken completely: as we have seen with the over-all Homeric parallel and "Ithaca", the formal values originate in those enacted and take their imaginative justification from that fact. They develop and project the potentialities of "reality" as it is established in the early chapters (of which "Hades" is a rich example), though as they do so the view they enforce upon us becomes increasingly distant from life as we ordinarily know it. The organization of the book is the progressive enlargement of our vision, indeed our conception of "reality".

But the process is not uniformly realized, not without its irritating lapses and downright failures. The weakness begins to germinate in "Wandering Rocks", where the irony widens the subject-matter though at no very great depth of insight. The following chapter, "Sirens", begins to exhibit even more of that precarious intellectualization of structure under which some of the later writing collapses completely. The attempt at a *fuga per canonem* form, for example, is not only unsuccessful in practice; more fundamentally, it is meaningless in conception.[15] Apart from its place in Joyce's total scheme—consideration of which we may postpone for a moment—the only kind of effect it could achieve is a purely specious *patterning* of the material, an extrinsic imposition of casual shape. Its relations to the action likewise exist at no great depth of insight. Both form and action are connected with music, and the aesthetic *stasis* Bloom receives from the song he overhears is indeed engaged with his agitated *kinesis* over Molly and Boylan: the effect of aesthetic beauty is clear enough[16]—

He bore no hate.
Hate. Love. Those are names. Rudy. Soon I am old. (270/280)

What saves the chapter from mere ingenuity is just this dramatic conflict in Bloom—overlaid though it is by the gothic encrustations of the style—and the use of the musical conceits, partly at least, as a self-parodying, ironic device for placing Bloom's compensatory substitutes for his impotent relations with Molly, the weaknesses of his isolation and frustration:

By rose, by satiny bosom, by the fondling hand, by slops, by empties, by popped corks, greeting in going, past eyes and maidenhair, bronze and faint gold in deepseashadow, went Bloom, soft Bloom, I feel so lonely Bloom.
Tap. Tap. Tap.
Pray for him, prayed the bass of Dollard. You who hear in peace. Breathe a prayer, drop a tear, good men, good people. He was the croppy boy. (272/282)

Probably the best of these self-ironical "musical" jokes is the conclusion of the chapter, where the tap of a blind man's stick, Robert Emmet's rhetoric, Bloom's digestive criticism of it, and the harsh mechanical clamour of the city, all coincide just when Boylan (blazin' and boilin') is at last consummating his visit to Molly (276/286).

At first sight, the disharmony between the dramatic and technical form in "Cyclops" and "Nausicaa" seems less acute than in "Sirens". The action—which includes the anonymous Narrator in the former and Gerty MacDowell in the latter as "reflectors"—enacts such spiritual clichés as invite the satiric parodies by which they are placed. Thus in "Cyclops" one kind of verbiage is juxtaposed with another to illuminate the values implicit in each:

—Ay, says Joe. He paid the debt of nature, God be merciful to him.
—Good Christ! says Alf.
Begob he was what you might call flabbergasted.
In the darkness spirit hands were felt to flutter and when prayer by tantras had been directed to the proper quarter a faint but increasing luminosity of ruby light became gradually visible, the apparition of the etheric double being particularly lifelike owing to the discharge of jivic rays from the crown of the head and face. . . . (286/296)

On this aspect of Joyce's work, Mr Kenner's analysis is unsurpassed: the language and mind of Dublin is indeed the subject, though it is also important to notice how Bloom's social, racial and moral isolation from the others in Barney Kiernan's pub largely protects him (as it is meant to do) from the impact of the critical irony. Even while his talkativeness and scientific "knowledge" are properly placed, and his assumption of the prophetic mantle glossed with humour by the ending, his real stature remains quite firmly established. But as I suggested in an earlier chapter with respect to "Nausicaa", however appropriate the satiric rendering may be, there seems a touch of self-indulgence about it. The criticism implicit in the wildly vivacious comic parodies is not so subtle as to demand the elaboration it receives, an elaboration that is in fact little else than repetition or variation of the same simple formula.

The dramatic structure of "Cyclops" is one of the simplest in the book: Bloom is exhibited rather than rendered so that the hostility and incomprehension he receives from his society may be placed against *our* knowledge of what he means—both in what he says and what he is. That of "Nausicaa" is more complex. Bloom has his characteristic double rôle—expressing Gerty's significance, for example, both by his responsive masturbation and by his critical understanding of her at the same time. His painful loneliness, figured in his fantasies about Gerty and Molly; his limitations of insight, figured in the flitting bat, in his inability to express himself in words on the sand; his lassitude, figured in his slower, more jumbled epiphanies; combine with the unquenchable activity that still informs his acts of understanding—of womankind, of the Citizen, and above all, of the natural processes of which everyone is part. The total effect, however, is to distance him, solitary, "cuckoo", cut off, as he himself partly realizes, from the vital processes represented by sexual love, a complexly pathetic figure of a condition more widespread than he knows:

Then you have a beautiful calm without a cloud, smooth sea, placid, crew and cargo in smithereens, Davy Jones' locker. Moon looking down. Not my fault, old cockalorum. (361/372)

It would be perhaps tedious to analyse the effect of the last pages of the chapter in full, but one aspect of it does demand notice: the similarity of the viewpoint it achieves to that of "Cyclops". The complication of the earlier chapter does not lie in anything the characters say or do, but in the critical values implicit in its technique. "Cyclops" develops from what goes before it only in making our detached evaluation of the immediate scene more explicit than it has been (and, in effect, more simple). In other words, the development it exhibits is intellectual rather than imaginative. There is still a connection between the represented and the formal values, but the emphasis has now decisively shifted to the latter, which are more sophisticated, more thought out, than any the represented reality can bear of itself. In "Nausicaa" the same is still true, though less markedly. The attitude expressed in the technique of the chapter as a whole—that is, including both Gerty MacDowell's section and Bloom's—is more general, more "philosophic", more distant, than any enacted by the characters. They are viewed less as morally engaged individuals than as universally representative cases; the natural processes of which Bloom is partly aware are expressed at a much higher level of abstraction than any he is capable of, and they overshadow and absorb the characters themselves. Therein, indeed, lies much of Bloom's pathos, and the vantage-point from which the spiritual waste represented by Gerty appears relevant to the chapter as a whole. The technique and structure once again enforce an intellectually conceived view of reality, and the generally admitted failure of the next chapter, "Oxen of the Sun", only continues to its logical conclusion a process already well under way.

"Oxen of the Sun" is an interesting failure in that it sharpens to acute relevance a number of critical questions already looming over earlier chapters. Here the connection between the represented and the formal values can only be described as *cerebral*, and we may well begin to consider how far the same term applies to other aspects of the book. For instance, once this intellectualizing process is set in motion, what are we to say of the structural relations between one chapter and another? The first chapters of the book carry us forward dramatically; the last bring the temporal perspectives of the whole to a final focus; but these central chapters—from "Wandering Rocks" to "Oxen of the Sun"—seem as a group merely to elaborate rather than develop, to be organized in no way more vital than the chart Mr Gilbert prints of organs, arts, colours, symbols and techniques: the kind of organization, in fact, suggested by Joyce's own declaration of intention:

It is an epic of two races (Israelite-Irish) and at the same time the cycle of the human body as well as a little story of a day (life). The character of Ulysses always fascinated me—even when a boy. . . . It is also a sort of encyclopaedia. My intention is to transpose the myth *sub specie temporis nostri*. Each adventure (that is, every hour, every organ, every art being interconnected and interrelated in the structural scheme of the whole) should not only condition but even create its own technique. Each adventure is so to say one person although it is composed of persons—as Aquinas relates of the angelic hosts.[17]

This kind of scheme can be profitably ignored through large sections of the book, but these five chapters provoke its consideration. Clearly it is a presupposed, pre-meditated scheme, very much like the alphabetical or other extrinsic arrangement on which an ordinary encyclopaedia is composed.[18] The "chaffering allincluding most farraginous chronicle" demanded control, and this, as Joyce's commentators have pointed out many times, his Homeric parallel and his "symbolic" scheme provided. But such control is only pattern, not form; it must infuse and shape the reality it helps represent or it means nothing. The Homeric parallel developed as a whole, as I have suggested, does do this, but such an effect is hardly achieved in these middle chapters. So conceptual, so external, and so arbitrary does the pattern of their "symbolic" and technical devices appear that we may begin to wonder if Joyce realized quite fully the limitations of Stephen's account of *consonantia* in the *Portrait*. Indeed, the kind of intellection implicit in his deployment of such "symbols" may make us wonder, more fundamentally, what Joyce meant by *thinking*.

The thematic patterning of *Ulysses* has received far too much attention—or perhaps the wrong kind of attention—and the vivacity of the writing far too little.[19] The parodies of "Cyclops", for example, for all their serious intentions and qualified success, constantly fizz and crackle and explode in comic absurdities like the "Celtic" lyric of Garryowen, the Citizen's dog:

The metrical system of the canine original, which recalls the intricate alliterative and isosyllabic rules of the Welsh englyn, is infinitely more complicated but we believe our readers will agree that the spirit has been well caught. Perhaps it should be added that the effect is greatly increased if Owen's verse be spoken somewhat slowly and indistinctly in a tone suggestive of suppressed rancour.

> *The curse of my curses*
> *Seven days every day*

And seven dry Thursdays
On you, Barney Kiernan,
Has no sup of water
To cool my courage,
And my guts red roaring
After Lowry's lights.[20] (296-7/307)

Even in "Oxen of the Sun" and "Eumaeus", where our reservations go further, there is still the same comic inventiveness; it appears again in the pedantic precision of "Ithaca" or in the hectic, swirling movement of "Circe", where the episodes of the Black Mass and the drunken soldiers, for instance, despite the heavy thematic importance they bear, carry their meaning lightly on a wave of ludicrous wit. In the long run, it is the verbal dexterity, the inventiveness, the comic verve—a mixture of "conceited" wit and sheer blarney—that keeps the reader reading when the dramatic intensity dies down. The passages that are meant to be dull are often ingeniously dull; there is usually a tough lyric grace beneath the slight reasonableness of the boredom. Certainly if no *realized* pattern composed of these arts, organs, colours, and the rest, emerges with any assurance, whatever Joyce put there or his commentators discover, it is nevertheless well to remember these primary facts especially when considering these middle chapters and the more dubious aspects of the others.

As many readers have found, the weight of the "symbolic" scheme does oppress.[21] The details of its pattern and techniques are elaborated ruthlessly, and while the reader would be glad to forget them, their presence is insisted upon. What is wrong, both in these chapters and elsewhere, is not so much that the details are too many as that the formal structures are too weak: not always meaningful enough, not sufficiently subtle and rich, to give the material they support more than a general, almost abstract, relevance. And this applies to the elaborations of the parodies, of the Homeric parallels, and even of the setting, just as much as to the "symbolic" scheme. Their *raisons d'être* (the cycle of the body, the parallel myth, the circle of the arts, the re-creation of Dublin, and so on) are in themselves too simple even to be called ideas, too mechanical even to achieve imaginative suggestiveness. Not enough happens to them intellectually or dramatically. With the exception of the Homeric parallel (considered as a whole), and occasional vitality in its parts (as with "heart" in "Hades"), the "symbolic" scheme remains stillborn, remarkable more for its pretentiousness than its intelligence.[22]

In a letter to Frank Budgen outlining his conception of "Oxen of the Sun", Joyce wrote of his plans almost as if he were one of his own commentators:

> This procession [of stylistic imitations] is also linked back at each part subtly with some foregoing episode of the day and, besides this, with the natural stages of development in the embryo and the periods of formal evolution in general. The double-thudding Anglo-Saxon motive recurs from time to time . . . to give the sense of the hoofs of oxen. Bloom is the spermatozoon, the hospital the womb, the nurse the ovum, Stephen the embryo.

Unlike some of his commentators, however, he adds a further remark:—"How's that for High?"[23] Even without reference to the actual result, the self-criticism seems more penetrating than the serious intention—unless (and it is possible) the intention is not serious at all—though it is hardly likely that what is part of a whole encyclopaedic pattern affecting not only the one chapter but also the very divisions and relations of many chapters should be an idle practical joke. Indeed, it is Joyce's intense desire for *total* pattern, his encyclopaedic ambition, from which spring these weakly cerebral tendencies of his art.

Joyce's problem was to range over the whole of modern life without having to express large areas of it only by explicit analysis or debate as, for example, Thomas Mann does in *The Magic Mountain*. His solution was a brave but futile attempt to employ an encyclopaedic symbolism like that of mediaeval Catholicism in order to dramatize these aspects of life—at least to the extent that mere technique *can* dramatize. The insuperable difficulty was not merely that a symbolism once truly encyclopaedic was no longer so, but that his symbols could not form, as they did for a mediaeval poet or even for Phineas Fletcher in the seventeenth century, an exoteric language of manifold but ordered meanings disposable by the poet with un-selfconscious conviction. The result is that Joyce's encyclopaedic symbols can make an intelligible pattern only of the most superficial kind— especially since the words (or things: the difference here is immaterial) he employs as conceptual keys in the texture of these chapters not merely possess no public authority but are never *given* any. "No more orderly book of fiction was ever written", Mr R. P. Blackmur has said, "and no book in which the principles of order, unless taken aesthetically, seemed so frivolous or impotent. Dante is casual in comparison, for Dante tried to put things in order only within reason and tradition, whereas Joyce went ahead anyway, presenting a kind of nihilism of unreasonable order. He had an overmastering predilection for order and a cultivated knowledge of many kinds of order, and their heresies, within the Graeco-Christian tradition, catholic, classic, historical, and aesthetic, but he had to treat them all, in fact, as if they were aesthetic, images or stresses rather than summaries or concepts of the actual."[24] With Joyce, as I have tried to show, "aesthetic" means a good deal more than this criticism suggests, and among its meanings is the moral imagination Mr Blackmur also demands. Even so, any attempt like Joyce's to encompass a universal range of experience unquestionably breaks down once it is divorced from a prior universality of belief or the universality of imaginative realiza-tion. The "symbolic" scheme so violently obtruded into these chapters from "Wandering Rocks" to "Oxen of the Sun" attempts much the same effect as the Homeric parallel, but without its foundation and enactment in the characters' own lives and in the reader's belief in the abiding poetic truth of the original myth. The trouble with these chapters in short is that their order is not "aesthetic" enough.

Perhaps this is the necessary price for the attempt Joyce makes to shift our attention from the represented reality to the shaping activity of the artist. Given the strategic need to bring himself, as artist, into the action of his book, Joyce could hardly use the old tactic of direct authorial commentary. That would draw attention to him, but not as a *dramatis persona* and certainly not as an unmoved mover suggested within yet beyond the action. What he did, however, is in its way very like intruded authorial comment. It does markedly shift our view of the action by splitting form and content, for instance, and it does try to bring critical, intellectual considerations to bear upon the enactments of the story; the difference is that Joyce, with his technical sophistication, probably reckoned the cost involved by his urgent strategy. This does not lessen the cost, of course, and perhaps it only underlines the weakness of the intellectual resources he could throw into the balance. Nevertheless, the weakness of these chapters is not utterly devastating to the work as a whole. All the various points of view projected in the book are meant "aesthetically", to *compose* a whole, not to derive from a total encyclopaedic view already in existence, and if some do not contribute—seem, in fact, to *be* so derived—this does not destroy what is established. And if we must dismiss their attempt at a purely "symbolic" structure, there are nevertheless other structures traceable in these chapters holding bits and aspects together with the rest of the book. Bloom's conflicts develop; ironies accumulate; he and Stephen meet and are played off against each other and against their respective circles; our vision drifts toward a longer, more distant view of them; natural process begins to absorb them in a wider context; and Joyce does manage to prepare the action for its purgative climax in "Circe" and at the same time to prepare our vision of it for the ironic climax of "Ithaca".

These two chapters carry the two clear and firmly established structures of the book as a whole. At the end of "Circe", the figure of Bloom, "secret master", looks back to Stephen at the end of "Proteus" and forward to Molly at the end of "Penelope". The central structure of the book is not the "tonal" pattern of moods appropriate to the time-scheme, the "dance of the hours"[25]; nor is it the pattern of arts, organs, colours, and the rest. It is rather the strong, firm double-arch supported on the columns of the three main characters in "Proteus", "Circe" and "Penelope", a structure that stretches even through the wastes of dulness. The less obtrusive, more easily recognizable dramatic technique of "Circe" itself, the rich expressiveness of its hectic swirl crystallizing the sense of disorder and collapse already developing in "Nausicaa" and "Oxen of the Sun", its brilliant comedy and sudden arrest and illumination, the resumption of moral activity by the characters, all finally clarify and knit together the whole tripartite order.

The other structure—the development of the "mythic" vision —is like an intersecting plane on to which we are imperceptibly moved not only by the range of styles[26] but by the whole substance of the writing. At the end of "Circe" we have left the characters' consciousness altogether and are no longer concerned with them as moral agents. Our attention is now directed to the significance they have accumulated over fifteen chapters. They have become *cases*—complexly meaningful and moving cases—but now finally absorbed by the wider forces of which they are part. This process of withdrawal has already begun in the five middle chapters. The two structures have begun to draw apart. Our point of view has been progressively shifted from the characters', moved now to one side, now to another, from the political slant of "Cyclops" to the literary gynaecology of "Oxen of the Sun", but developing towards the dramatic detachment of "Circe" and beyond that to the further detachment of "Eumaeus" and "Ithaca". The last three chapters, in fact, complete the action by working its symbolic significance out to the uttermost limits. Yet they also demand critical inspection just as much as the five middle chapters, not in this case because of their failure to realize their intention but because of the kind of vision they do express.

IV

The detachment of these final chapters is really a disengagement from social activity, a disengagement from purely ethical considerations. Their subject is no longer the characters and their world but the meaning they possess in the widest, most general context. The natural processes of growth and decay, the universal elements of nature (and not only human nature) are now the themes evoked, and the relations between the earlier action and the vision that actually completes it constitute the real interest. As we have seen, critics have sometimes supposed that the meaning of the book depends on whether Molly will get Bloom's breakfast on the following morning, or whether the Blooms' relationships will change for the better or not, or whether Stephen will return, and occasionally they have criticized Joyce for leaving such issues obscure.[27] But he leaves them open or obscure not, as William Empson suggests, because *Ulysses* is a "problem novel", but because, by "Penelope", they do not matter; they have no bearing on the central themes except as marginal possibilities in a "reality" already transcended. The developments that do matter—Bloom's and Stephen's dim realization of their own and each other's plight, and the foreshadowed presence of the mature artist contemplating his world of experience—*are* established. Beyond that, events lose their immediate importance as events and become only representative symbols, the characters dilate into myth,[28] our view circles over the whole landscape, which loses its detailed particulars. Life appears less of an activity experienced than a spectacle contemplated: we turn, in these final chapters, from its arithmetic to its algebra. Though Stephen did not foresee it when he spoke of the God-like artist, Joyce's art does seem finally to reach a kind of *abstractionism*.[29] The term is almost unavoidable; and it suggests something of the self-conscious, ironic, geometric spirit to which Senor Ortega y Gasset once ascribed the "dehumanization" of modern art.

The three final chapters are like a recapitulation, though in a new key. "Eumaeus" circles back over the political and social emptiness of Dublin, the dimension in which Bloom is most isolated and diminished, though in doing so it seems to diminish him too much, to deny more than has been *shown* to be there. This is largely because the social dimension is itself isolated. The characters and especially their lack of contact and vitality are only an abstracted text on which "Eumaeus" expatiates at large: the social condition of modern man is an empty boredom. The balance is somewhat restored in "Ithaca", where Bloom's and Stephen's positive vitality and possibilities are also taken into account. From its even more distant vantage-point at the very limit of objective detachment, they are seen to merit compassion and honour as well. The catechism is in fact a dialogue of one— the artist who pares his fingernails interrogating the artist within his creation, the "artistic" temperament interrogating the "scientific", the world the book portrays seeking the certainty of its own truth. The final irony of the chapter is that by its critical, cold objectivity it does the worst that can be done to the characters and yet in doing so reveals their human validity. It guarantees, as it were, and so protects the source of genuine emotion.[30] Which is why, for all its rather boring "scientific" appurtenances, it is one of the most moving sections of the book.

Of course, neither chapter deserves to be called "dehumanized". Both at least preserve the characters and the world in which they are immersed as their object of discourse, and even while the writing transmutes them into symbols, it can do so only because their symbolic meaning has been already established dramatically. They are *human* symbols. With "Penelope", however, there is a definite problem. Joyce himself said that "in conception and technique" he tried "to depict the earth which is prehuman and presumably posthuman",[31] and though this clearly does not account for everything about the chapter, it does bring the issue of Joyce's values to a crisis. How far does "Penelope" represent a retreat from life disguised as a descent to its elements?

For one of the most sensitive and sensible accounts of Molly's rôle—as of so much in the book—we may turn once again to Mr R. P. Blackmur, for he puts as persuasively as is possible, and without the usual unnecessary sentimentality, the case Joyce evidently had in mind. The two "postscriptive" chapters ("Eumaeus" and "Ithaca"), as he says, "send us back into the body of the book which they formalize in cliché and catechism, the exhausting material out of which inexhaustible symbol can be made. Of this the proof is Penelope, which is not a postscript or appendix, but the symbolic declaration of all that has gone before so far as it can be resumed by Molly Bloom. She it is who waited, and she who was waited for, a kind of underthought or other thought underlying even Bloom. She comes after the theological inquisition, after the summa, all fire inside, an act of grace. Molly is necessary to any culture but not as its foundation; she is rather the basic building material: the problem that first *and* last must be controlled. . . . Molly sees, excuses, cultivates herself to herself. She casts neither light nor darkness: she is the self before it understands itself. . . . Molly is of the unloving underworld: the *demimonde sensuel*. She is ploughed, penetrated, seeded like the earth in spring and heaves Yes to what happens to herself, Yes to variation and repetition, gestation and parturition, Yes Yes, Yes to Yes. She bears: Bloom is being born. She is the object of rites, the answerer. He is the maker of rites, the questioner. Her many lovers bring her nothing; who knows what they take away?—Nothing, so long as the procession does not stop. . . . So, in her monologue, she judges, *is herself*, the periodicity to which all the phantoms of love and intellect are condemned. She is the 'coarsened' or verbalized mystery to which men return as they came from it."[32]

This is certainly more persuasive than vague talk about the

Great Mother, or the Virgin and "unity, reconciliation, and peace", or "the eternal Paradise of Dream", or a "soul bestialized by mortal sin".[33] She is meant as a simple, shrewd, elemental figure, a spokesman and symbol of the processes of Nature. Her own Naturalism is appropriately simple and direct, quite innocent of issues that might worry her husband and Stephen: "it didnt make me blush why should it either its only nature . . . what else were we given all those desires for Id like to know" (736/762). The more sophisticated (and aggressive) meaning *we* may give her question is well outside her range of comprehension. So, too, are the implications of what we may call her "natural piety":

God of heaven theres nothing like nature the wild mountains then the sea and the waves rushing then the beautiful country with fields of oats and wheat and all kinds of things and all the fine cattle going about that would do your heart good to see rivers and lakes and flowers all sorts of shapes and smells and colours springing up even out of the ditches primroses and violets nature it is as for them saying theres no God I wouldnt give a snap of my two fingers for all their learning why dont they go and create something I often asked him atheists or whatever they call themselves go and wash the cobbles off themselves first then they go howling for the priest and they dying and why why because theyre afraid of hell on account of their bad conscience ah yes I know them well who was the first person in the universe before there was anybody that made it all who ah that they dont know neither do I so there you are they might as well try to stop the sun from rising tomorrow (740-1/767)

Her understanding of herself is likewise simple and elemental: she is a woman, valuing her beauty, her sexual attractiveness, her capacity for physical pleasure: "yes he said I was a flower of the mountain yes so we are flowers all a womans body yes that was one true thing he said in his life and the sun shines for you today yes that was why I liked him because I saw he understood or felt what a woman is and I knew I could always get round him" (741/767). She judges everybody and everything, with unconscious comedy, at the level of her sensual shrewdness. Her attitude to Bloom is a mixture of respect, contempt, good-humoured wonder, hostility, admiration and acceptance. She sees through his subterfuges, but understands nothing of his ideas. She has all his inadequacies as a man and a husband catalogued, intends to go on cuckolding him, even contemplates the possibility of divorce, knows him inside out, as she thinks, yet (as the beginning of her monologue shows) she is still capable of being surprised by him, and returns (at the end) with pleasure and wonder in her mind to his proposal of marriage. But for all her comic, multitudinous voracity, she can hardly be said to think or to act in her long soliloquy; she merely exists as herself. Her stream-of-consciousness does not consist, like Bloom's or Stephen's, of separate epiphanies, but simply recollects experiences, jumbles them together without differentiation, and absorbs them all. As she is presented, she is the element, the raw material, the ever-unfulfilled potentiality of Life; her stream-of-consciousness is essentially *passive*—which is why it is so different from the others in the book and does so easily fit the categories of the psychological critics and the "jellyfish" attack of Wyndham Lewis.

Passivity, simplicity, the comically reductive view of the senses: hardly the formula for a really convincing personality who has to combine the Wife of Bath, Penelope, Gea-Tellus, Mme Bovary, and a dash of Wordsworthian peasantry. It is no wonder that some readers have felt Molly lacked the dramatic reality of Bloom or Stephen[34]; the wonder, indeed, considering the very *conceptual* nature of her significance, is that Joyce manages to present her so vividly.

Despite the fact that she has been called a "masterpiece of comic portrayal"[35] and is portrayed from "within", she seems, in a more important sense, constructed from outside, a projection of an idea previously conceived; and it is the idea, I suspect, that stirs the critics' eloquence more than the actual character. Joyce's women are never really women—a fact on which his female critics have sometimes remarked.[36] Stanislaus, his brother, thought he suffered from a typical "Irish paradox"— "faithfulness to one woman and at the same time a profound hostility to women in general", a combination of "desire and disdain" that is given its "most pitiless expression in the last chapter of *Ulysses*, in which Joyce reveals the soul of a woman".[37] But the question is whether it *is* the soul of a woman revealed there. To one reader at least, Molly is less a woman than Woman, a portrait decked with individual details, all of which nevertheless illustrate a few, basic, conventionally female traits: a happy ignorance and inconsistency, cattiness, warmth, maternal instincts, the assumption of superiority to the male and all his activities, and of course a consuming interest in "love": "true or not it fills up your whole day and life always something to think about every moment and see it round you like a new world" (718/743). This is neatly done as far as it goes. Yet she surely lacks the odd, unpredictable moral contours of an individual, male or female, which *action* would necessarily require. She is evidently conceived at a level, and for a context, in which the specific quality of her life matters less than the mere elemental fact of her sex. Joyce's own account of the chapter is quite revealing here:

Penelope is the clou of the book. . . . It turns like the huge earthball slowly surely and evenly round and round spinning. Its four cardinal points being the female breasts, arse, womb and . . . expressed by the words *because, bottom* (in all senses, bottom, button, bottom of the glass, bottom of the sea, bottom of his heart) *woman, yes.* Though probably more obscene than any preceding episode it seems to me to be perfectly sane full amoral fertilisable untrustworthy engaging shrewd limited prudent indifferent *Weib. Ich bin das Fleisch das stets bejaht.*[38]

His interest is focused on the kind of writing, and on the abstractions it is to suggest, rather than the individual personality. And if only for this reason, she—or rather, the Flesh and *Weiblichkeit* she represents—is a dramatic symbol of far less power than Bloom or Stephen. Their significance lies in what they are as individuals acting in a particular way in a particular context: all their wider meaning derives from that. To the extent that Molly is less realized, her significance seems more putative. She is the Jungian Anima, the mystery of animate Flesh, the Earth, Nature, the ever-renewing potentiality of Life ever indifferent to its moral developments, and to become all this in the scope of one chapter she has to be divested of the individual, human qualities that would limit her pure potentiality but which would also give her an interest—essentially a moral interest—greater than that of the Flesh, or Woman, or any abstract prehuman or posthuman force. To carry this symbolism, she has to be reduced to a simplicity that contrasts sharply with the dense portraits of the two men and which is saved from our immediate rejection only by Joyce's abundant comic detail. Thus the first problem she presents is that if we think of her as a human being (*Christiana naturaliter animal*), we inevitably begin to wonder what *her* yea-saying can mean. Is any affirmation meaningful spoken or represented by such a self-consciously conceived figure?

Even the famous affirmation at the end of the chapter seems itself a little contrived in relation to the rest. The way in which critics usually speak of the monologue obviously owes a good deal to the idea she is taken to represent: "unpunctuated flow", "unbroken", "torrent", and similar words suggest profound forces moving irresistibly or heaving like the sea. But as Mr Philip Toynbee has very justly observed, the monologue is in fact written in the "rather weary language of the English lower middle class", the mere lack of punctuation does not produce an unbroken rhythm at all, and there is simply too much of the same "rather muddy liquid".[39] There is one passage, however, where the coyly ambiguous syntax and the absence of punctuation, unsuccessfully masquerading as the flux of consciousness, do not distract the reader's attention and he is not slightly bored by the sheer monotony of Molly's mind. This is the passage in which Joyce's conception is most clearly realized (and from which most critics quote): the last two pages or so, beginning with Molly's praise of Nature (mountains, sea, fields, cattle, "and all kinds of things") and ending with the final "Yes". Whereas the rest of the monologue has an effect rather like that ascribed to Milton— you have to read it once (supplying punctuation) for the sense and a second time (taking the punctuation out again) for the sound—the last pages do flow more easily. Though the sentences are longer, they seem to need little punctuation to run easily: the recurrent "O" and "yes" help distinguish the sense, and the syntax is little more than simple accumulation. Hence the effect of gathering speed, and the sense of the activity and rich- ness of life as attention turns to natural scenery, flowers, sunshine, distant Gibraltar, the nostalgia of youthful love, and all the recollections Molly again recollects from the moment she decided whether to accept Bloom's proposal:

and the poor donkeys slipping half asleep and the vague fellows in the cloaks asleep in the shade on the steps and the big wheels of the carts of the bulls and the old castle thousands of years old yes and those handsome Moors all in white and turbans like kings asking you to sit down in their little bit of a shop and Ronda with the old windows

of the posadas glancing eyes a lattice hid for her lover to kiss the iron
and the wineshops half open at night and the castanets and the night
we missed the boat at Algeciras the watchman going about serene
with his lamp and O that awful deepdown torrent O and the sea the
sea crimson sometimes like fire and the glorious sunsets and the
figtrees in the Alameda gardens yes and all the queer little streets and
pink and blue and yellow houses and the rosegardens and the jessa-
mine and geraniums and cactuses and Gibraltar as a girl where I was
a Flower of the mountain yes when I put the rose in my hair like the
Andalusian girls used or shall I wear a red yes and how he kissed me
under the Moorish wall and I thought well as well him as another
and then I asked him with my eyes to ask again yes and then he asked
me would I yes to say yes my mountain flower and first I put my arms
around him yes and drew him down to me so he could feel my breasts
all perfume yes and his heart was going like mad and yes I said yes I
will Yes. (741-2/767-8)

The simplicity, speed, and rhetorical power of these pages are
the real basis of Molly's symbolic force (though it is worth noting
how narrowly the writing escapes vagueness and sentimentality
by deliberately hinting that these belong to Molly). The intention is like that of "Ithaca" on a smaller scale: to reveal at last
a genuine vitality even from within what seemed only dull
monotony and comic earthiness. But where the effect of "Ithaca"
grows out of what precedes it, this affirmation seems more
artificial, more like a conclusion attached, by an effort of will,
to a discourse of rather different meaning.

This pervasive hint of self-conscious contrivance in the chapter
manifests itself in a number of ways provoking unease. Even
apart from the rather self-conscious obscenity,[40] we are expected
to take Molly, the sane, full, fertilizable, engaging, shrewd,
prudent *Weib*, at her own valuation as the flower of life, when
Molly, the amoral, untrustworthy, limited and indifferent
Fleisch, suggests, to say the least, reservations about the "life" she
represents. Her Naturalism is so crude that the only kind of
vitality she can be said to embody is an impersonal, unconscious,
undifferentiating animation. In one way, her acceptance of
Bloom, like her interest in Stephen, must be taken as an endorsement of their essential humanity: Bloom was the one man she
knew who "understood or felt what a woman is"; he has more
"spunk" in him than Boylan (702/727); while Stephen's superior
intelligence and education are his largest attractions (734 ff./
759 ff.). As Joyce put it, she is "the indispensable countersign to

Bloom's passport to eternity"[41]; or as Edmund Wilson put it, despite her indiscriminate sexuality, "she will tend to breed from the highest type of life she knows: she turns to Bloom, and, beyond him, toward Stephen. This gross body, the body of humanity, upon which the whole structure of 'Ulysses' rests— still throbbing with so strong a rhythm amid obscenity, commonness and squalor—is laboring to throw up some knowledge and beauty by which it may transcend itself."[42] And yet what does her endorsement, her "yes", really amount to?—"and I thought well as well him as another and then I asked him with my eyes to ask again yes and . . . drew him down to me . . ." (742/768). The apparent inconsistency in Molly's attitude is not itself the point; I only draw attention to it because it helps pin down the sense of emotional falsity in "Penelope". The last pages strongly suggest that her acceptance of Bloom is a kind of endorsement of him, partly moral, partly almost divine; yet the fact is that such a figure as she can only respond with equal generosity, and equal indifference, to Bloom and to Boylan.[43] She declares everything that has gone before, as Mr Blackmur rightly says, "so far as it can be resumed by Molly Bloom"; but how far is that? Another critic has tried to draw an analogy between her and Dante's Virgin,[44] but the evident falsity of the analogy underlines the same difficulty. Ultimately, I suppose, Molly exhibits a religious problem that Joyce never quite satisfactorily met. She is a symbol in which all human experience can be absorbed, but in the absorption it necessarily loses its meaning as experience. She declares everything at the cost of all the discriminations so patiently and securely realized in the rest of the book.

In its sheer all-inclusiveness, "Penelope" does offer a magnificent conclusion to the whole design. Looking back at the modes of irony generated in the book, at the wide historical and cultural perspectives, the apparent relativism or "montage", finally stabilized and held in the mythic contemplation of "Ithaca", and at the moral activity expressed by the characters and placed by the encompassing activity of the techniques, the last chapter arrives almost as an act of humility. It is as if the artist, in the consummation of his self-knowledge, acknowledges that his total act of contemplation is, after all, conditional. His total act represents life at its fullest because most fully in possession of itself, but, so "Penelope" seems to say, it actualizes only one of the inexhaustible potentialities of life; in turning to Molly it celebrates at once its ultimate source, material and possible supersession. In "Penelope" the book rejects all claims to finality: Molly's "yes" means "come what may, what can, as all this did". The humility is also proud, of course. Such a gesture implies the sovereignty of the imagination in which life, the content of the "yes", has flowered. And it is just here that the affirmation seems most ambiguous. For Molly's "yes" is not just the first word but the last. We must take it as an affirmation not merely of possibility but of fact, and in this sense it means too little because, we might say, it includes too much. Molly lacks the authority to affirm or to deny; only the imagination can do that in the degree to which it realizes itself in its contemplation of life. Molly's "yes" seems to say, "instinctive wonder and delight lie at the heart of life, and are my gift to all", yet for *Molly* to say this, with all her monotonous and petty sexuality, apparently far removed from the instinctive joy of the living body, is to blur the real and irremovable difference in vitality of spirit between Bloom and (say) Menton or Boylan or Mulligan. Her openness to all, her wholesale acceptance, is necessary, but not her reduction of all to the same level. It is hardly surprising that the mood of the chapter has been sometimes compared with Hardy's cosmic indifference,[45] or that Molly's "yes" has sometimes been taken as "no", the last triumphant exclamation of spiritual death.

The vitality of Bloom and Stephen, limited though it is, rightly belongs to them and is sealed in the completer vision of "Ithaca". "Penelope" seems to represent a change in that vision, a deliberate and self-conscious turn; and the self-consciousness betrays. What ought to be intuitive life vividly there before us is too much mere knowledge, mere imputation, of intuitive life. And we may well begin to wonder how far the all-inclusiveness of the chapter really represents a sentimental greed of mind, a desire to reject nothing, to include all, and cook it, as Lawrence said of Whitman, in the "awful pudding of One Identity".[46] For all its earthiness and overt affirmation of life, much of "Penelope" (far more than "Ithaca") paradoxically suggests a retreat in Joyce from living human beings towards dehumanized abstractions like Life and Humanity.[47]

Nevertheless, however ambiguous, Molly's "yes" is an affirmation, and its ambiguity hardly destroys the far more impressive affirmations realized elsewhere in the book. The real effect of the chapter, I believe, is to remind us of the further manifold possibilities of life, thus making more explicit what was already contained in "Ithaca", and to direct us, finally, back to the flux from which the imaginative understanding and ordering of the artist arose and to which they are directed. It is impossible to put the achievement any less vaguely, however, and it is less than what the chapter pretends to. On the other hand, its gesture is effective enough, perhaps, for us to recognize the humility and modesty it intends.

V

Looking at the structures of *Ulysses* as a whole, we must inevitably grant, I think, that its flaws and limitations are both deep and serious. The most obvious perhaps is Joyce's trust in ingenuity to fill out his basic design instead of imaginatively penetrating his material and informing it through and through. The busy ant-like industry with which he piles in detail, his inability always to select the necessary from the available,[48] the itch to get *everything* in, produce some maddening exhibitions of misdirected elaboration. He seems to worry his material almost obsessively at times. The painstaking verisimilitude of the Dublin setting, for instance, and the closely woven net of physical details, or the intensive teazing of the Homeric parallel and the schematic "symbolism", or the vast catalogues in "Cyclops", "Oxen of the Sun", "Eumaeus" and "Ithaca", all have their function; yet they seem to have mattered to Joyce far more than their function warrants. Their treatment is, in one sense of the term, still "epical", projected from some unease in the author himself, rather than completely "dramatic". So too with his evident love of pattern for its own sake, and in particular his tendency to rely on purely verbal arrangements of his material, which so weakens his encyclopaedic scheme that it often remains little more than an arbitrary and empty ordering gesture.

Although this kind of limitation has been often remarked on by his critics,[49] the mechanical "symbolism" has sometimes been claimed (for example by Mr Kenner and more sensitively by Mr Blackmur) as a deliberate device, an important part of the total meaning. On this view, the very arbitrariness and mechanical application of the "symbolism" are taken to suggest, like a metaphor, the spiritual order so conspicuously missing from the modern world; the empty, formal patterns are supposed, by their very impotence to control experience, to evoke the values that would control it or have done so in the past: in other words, we are to take *Ulysses* as a direct grandchild of Flaubert. One cannot say categorically that Joyce had no such notion in mind, and certainly his outlined scheme does, *in itself*, have this kind of representative social significance. Yet to grant that he might have meant it is not to grant that his failure is therefore a success. It is hard to see how automatism could ever be a symbol of vitality, or artifice perform the labour of art; if the implication of this view is true, that although Joyce's correspondences are often quite mechanical "the more mechanical the better, for Joyce's purposes",[50] then we may as well apply the whole of Henry James's criticism of Flaubert to Joyce too: "if it be objected that the images in question were addressed to his purpose better than others would have been . . . the purpose itself then shows as inferior".[51] But the question is whether any such critical purposes as this are realized in *Ulysses*; and I think the answer is that they are not. On the contrary, where Joyce's criticism of life is realized, it is in a manner requiring no simple-minded imitation of the emptiness it nominally rejects and no such narrow definition of its nature. It is enacted by the vitality that actually discriminates and evaluates its experience as it bodies it forth, by the activity that encompasses and reveals what is alive in the world of which it is part. "It is art that *makes* life", James insisted, "makes interest, makes importance, for our consideration and application of these things, and I know of no substitute whatever for the force and beauty of its process."[52] And since the whole of Joyce's aesthetic is founded upon the same belief, and only in its practice can we feel his achieved apprehension of life, we may perhaps conclude that his encyclopaedic schema is not in itself especially critical nor perhaps, as Mr Levin has suggested,[53] so centrally important as it has sometimes seemed since Mr Gilbert first revealed its existence.

The truth is not that Joyce's peculiar purposes make his failures into success but rather that they may seem almost the condition of his success; as Mr Levin puts it, "his very failures are the outcome of that state of cultural disintegration which he so

keenly sensed and so comprehensively rendered".[54] The exile
and egotism that made his achievement possible and formed part
of its central subject also had another side. Deliberately rejecting
the values of his native society in order to preserve his moral
integrity and detachment, he had to rely on his own capacity to
comprehend his society whole and to judge it. All he had in
common with it, in the end, was a history, a language, and such
values, implicit in both, as he was forced to discover in the fullest
scrutiny of his own case. There was nothing unique in his case, of
course: not merely was he the artist who exiled himself from a
corrupting society, he was also every citizen from whom the
living reality of Society itself seems to be exiled, and ultimately
every human being in his irremediable isolation. Faced with the
absolute and comprehensive claims of Roman Catholicism—
claims the force of which he had experienced in the very mould-
ing of his sensibility—he had to work out the grounds for his own
moral activity as a man and an artist with a compensating
absoluteness and comprehensiveness. The charge that he tried
to make a religion of Art is not true in the ordinary sense that he
used art as a substitute for moral and religious values; rather, it
was for him the engagement, discovery and enactment of those
values; but the context in which he was forced to establish his
attitude led him to take all life as his personal province, to aspire
to contain more than he could in fact actually and fully grasp,
and to employ artistic methods that falsified his own proper
insights. There is an unhappy, if partial, truth in the observation
of one of his critics that his conception of the symbol is close to
that of the mediaeval Church[55]; too often he did think of it
simply as a flat verbal or emblematic counter standing for some
meaning outside itself. But his exile, the search for self-knowledge
it imposed, and the universality of his predicament—painfully
exacerbated in the modern world—constituted his major problem
as an artist. He had to resist the "nets" of his society and yet
understand their necessity and power; what is more, he had to
extract the widest significance from his understanding at the
same time as he explored it in depth. The moral pivot of his
work, as he came to conceive it in *Ulysses*, was the *imaginative*
universality of his understanding, the dramatic image of the
individual who, exiled and alone, comes by time and effort to
understand his human community with all men at all times; its

moral range was the *encyclopaedic* and *historical* universality of his understanding. And this was smaller than he supposed.

The problem he faced with the first—the dramatic action—was to provide the necessary temporal and moral depth without a conventional plot. Instead, the gradual establishment of the Homeric parallel, the progressive shift from the characters' consciousness to our detached consciousness of them, the comprehension finally completed in "Ithaca" (and "Penelope"), carry the values upon which the whole book rests. The characters and their world are continuously revealed from, and evaluated by, the full understanding which in them is still only potential, realized only in part. That life is always like this, however, always in process, values always decaying and struggling to realization, is Joyce's very theme. The play of his irony arises from his confrontation of a point of time, one day, not with an ideal world it can never touch but with the still half-formed values it nevertheless contains in itself. That he himself did not realize and embody them as fully as he thought does not invalidate his relative maturity and insight, and in any case his imaginative grasp of the action is more important than his intellectual grasp of its total context. But apart from the intellectual purposes of his techniques, he had to establish their dramatic, and hence their moral, authority, and this he could do only by insisting on his presence in and behind the action as the end to which his creation moved. If his techniques increased the range of his material, they could make imaginative sense only if they were always seen to depend on the transcendent artist as their point of reference. To establish that figure he had the resource neither of explicit commentary nor of a single style: the complete immanence of his suggested presence forbade the one, and his sense of the diversity and complexity of the world he contained forbade the other. Up to a point he could simply use his characters' thoughts to help him—Stephen's theory of Shakespeare and his views on history, for example, with their echoes in Bloom's attitudes to time and art; but actually to exhibit his own activity he had to employ variety—or more accurately perhaps, change—of dramatic technique. The risk he ran was to allow mere analysis, arrangement and device to replace understanding, dramatic form, and moral penetration, to allow technique to fall apart from its dramatic meaning, to evaluate reality without also creating its presence: in short, to let his structures appear mere subjective patterns arbitrarily imposed upon a meaningless, chaotic "reality". And although his action and the sense of his own dramatic presence do survive the occasional lapses, the encyclopaedic universality of his work suffers far greater attrition.

The only method by which he could command the whole panorama of modern life was by placing about his central symbols—Bloom, Stephen, and their relationships to each other and to the author who contained them both—many diverse contexts, and in those aspects of human life exploring the significances they might reveal. The difficulty here was that the inevitable limitations of his symbols would prevent their activitating, or being activated by, the given context, that his dramatic action would not support his encyclopaedic intention. Although the protagonists could reflect in the full implications of their consciousness the typical predicaments of modern society and the predicaments of life at any time—partial creativity, understanding and freedom, combined with partial blindness, alienation and bondage—they could not in themselves reflect the whole of the world they inhabit either in its temporal or its social range. A tremendous amount had to be adduced—by parody, technical "point of view", and "symbolic" correspondences—of which they are necessarily either completely or partly unconscious (for it is a mark of their significance that they *are* unconscious of it). As well as being adduced, however, it had to be explored in its relations to them. The Homeric parallel taken as a whole, together with the other mythical parallels, is largely successful, I believe, in bringing a large sweep of history within the book and giving it significance in this way. It *is* dramatically related to the characters; but it succeeds less by the ingenious detailed correspondences Joyce draws than by the broad dramatic correspondence insinuated by the techniques and structures. The various arts of life are similarly adduced— rhetoric in "Aeolus", for example, or mechanics ("Wandering Rocks"), music ("Sirens"), politics ("Cyclops"), painting ("Nausicaa"), navigation ("Eumaeus"), and so on—yet too often these remain very imperfectly dramatized, related to the central symbolism of the action only by strained or verbal analogies. The result is that these aspects of life lie inertly *beside* the action without the dramatic presence and evaluation it ought to provide them, and the level of critical intelligence at which Joyce "symbolizes" them—once divorced from his deeply felt action—is too superficial to carry its own separate conviction.

This, I would suggest, despite the claims made for his savage intellectual irony, is really one of the gravest of Joyce's limitations. Compared with some of his contemporaries—Lawrence, Mann, Eliot even—his grasp of the underlying conditions and causes of the twentieth-century nightmare of history is not particularly impressive.[56] Those aspects of it he does evaluate derive from his dramatic action: the morass of cliché, sentimentality, violence, scientism, religiosity, social and cultural alienation, together with a groping for self-understanding and moral realization. To render all this is a large achievement; but it is as well to recognize that it represents no encyclopaedic criticism of our present age. It would be truer to say that it is a criticism, a necessary and mature correction, of the romantic assumptions underlying Flaubert's criticism of *his* age. Despite Joyce's use of modern psychology and the historical circumstance of 1904, it is worth recalling how much of twentieth-century life, the "now and here" actually about him, is not within his orbit. "Aeolus" and "Cyclops", for example, can hardly be supposed to express the deeper currents of modern politics, nor the satire on scientism the full significance of modern science. Apart from Bloom as the representative of the lower middle-class, there is no treatment of class relationships, presumably because Dublin could not provide the material. For all the critics' talk about Industrial Man, we may notice that Industrialism, both in its direct impact and in its monopolistic and imperialist developments about the turn of the century, is notably untreated. Its effects are reflected in the Dublin scene, of course, but only indirectly and unspecifically, and even "Lestrygonians", "Ithaca' and the rootlessness of Bloom and Stephen do not carry the analysis to the end—once again, Dublin in 1904 could hardly afford the opportunity. As for the mechanization of life expressed in "Wandering Rocks" and "Eumaeus", we need only cite Lawrence's treatment (admittedly with far richer material at his disposal) to feel the simplicity of Joyce's insights into the circumstances of our age. The same applies to sexual relationships even more obviously: although Joyce's treatment of women—Mrs. Purefoy, Gerty MacDowell, Molly Bloom—seems to cover all the possible aspects of sex, it is again far too abstract to render its specific human meanings.

All this is not to deny what Joyce does achieve; it is only to deny its universal range, to insist in fact upon the restrictions imposed by his subject-matter and the artistic straits to which he was brought in trying to see all round and through his world. We may grant that the very scope of his ambitions precluded their complete achievement (after all, even in his own terms, the artist is only *like* God); but, we must also add, although his material could yield some of its implications by the methods of adducement and schematizing with which he sought them, it could certainly not yield all. His mistake lay not so much in his theoretical understanding of his art as in the practical application he sometimes gave to his understanding. Style, technique, dramatic image or symbol, do indeed "*make* life" in one sense, and one can understand Joyce's reply when his brother tried to discuss Fascism with him: "Don't talk to me about politics. I'm only interested in style."[57] Yet to recall Henry James once more, although no one would have understood Joyce's retort better than he, one wonders if Joyce would have understood the full force of James's remark that "style itself . . . never *totally* beguiles; since even when we are so queerly constituted as to be ninety-nine parts literary we are still a hundredth part something else. This hundredth part may, once we possess the book —or the book possesses us—make us imperfect as readers, and yet without it should we want or get the book at all?"[58] The tenuousness of his grasp on that pragmatic truth is the price Joyce paid for his upbringing, his exile, and his rigid devotion to his art.

Our evaluation of that price is largely a matter of critical emphasis, but critical emphases on Joyce have too seldom been free of polemical motive or inadequate readings of his work. Mr Kenner, for example, can almost disregard the price altogether, and T. S. Eliot, finding Joyce's work "penetrated with Christian feeling", can use his "orthodox" sensibility and "trained mind" as sticks to beat D. H. Lawrence with.[59] For all the obvious truth in such a view of Joyce's sensibility, it is a view that demands further qualification, to say the least. Quite apart from the absurd falsity to Lawrence in Eliot's remarks, the judgment on Joyce hardly meets all the actual facts. The meaning of his art is wholly "orthodox" neither in Eliot's sense nor in Mr Kenner's, and his sensibility is not comprehended by those elements they would presumably approve. If it is true that Joyce uses the categories of his native religion, we have also to recognize that he changes their meaning and moral import. He uses Aristotelian and Thomist terms to work out an aesthetic neither Aristotelian nor Thomist; he uses the symbolism of the Mass to express a very different Incarnation; if he can quote scripture to his purpose, Homer and Shakespeare are even more apposite to that purpose; he admired Blake as well as Dante; and while he shared many values with the Church, there were others he did not. We could surmise that Goethe, for example, would have understood him better than Augustine. As for his "trained" mind, we have to remember his ingenious tomfooleries with Homer, myths, and "symbolism", the uncertainty of his critical and social insight, the ambiguity of "Penelope", and the whole enterprise of *Finnegans Wake*. His selection and use of European culture, and the values he expressed in his art, are at once too idiosyncratic and too free to be called "orthodox" in any restrictive sense. In the loosest sense of the word they are "traditional" perhaps: Bloom's virtues and Stephen's legitimate aspirations, together with the criticisms directed by and at both men, embody no original or prophetic gospel. Nevertheless, Bloom is no "orthodox" hero, and Joyce's art is orthodox only in that it recognizes the contribution, among others, of orthodoxy to its values. But it is also radical and original in its exploration of the viability, the possible *bases*, of traditional values in the modern world, and in its discovery of them in (so we must conclude) unorthodox places.

The opposite point of view puts the cost of Joyce's personal history at the extreme. Thus Mr D. S. Savage sees him as a super-Aesthete who, having cut himself off from all belief, was led to solipsism, moral bankruptcy, a passive "realism", and finally to attempt to create in his art a comprehensive, magical substitute for life. "Meaning implies selectivity, discrimination, which in turn are dependent upon an initial act of faith. By the abandonment of faith, discrimination is rendered impossible, and there must ensue a surrender to the indifferentiated flux of being: it is this which is presented in *Ulysses*." Mr Savage does recognize some of the effect of Joyce's early "over-indocrination" and the connection between Catholicism and Aestheticism, but his judgment places a tendentiously restricted meaning on "faith".[60] He leaves little room for those of us who, as Dr Leavis has put it, "find[ing] no such approach to tradition and orthodoxy possible can only cultivate the sense of health we have."[61] And once again, despite Mr Savage's genuine insights, his view is inadequate to the actual facts of *Ulysses*: it is revealing that he can rely upon Mr. Gilbert's account of it and suppose Joyce was not fully aware of the *Hamlet* theme. He is certainly right in attacking Joyce's abstract pantheism, especially as it appears in "Penelope" and *Finnegans Wake*; what he misses in *Ulysses*, as does Mr Kenner, is the firm but subtle poise of Joyce's irony and his shaping, evaluating activity.

Many of Joyce's troubles arose, I believe, from the combined narrowness and intolerance of his native society. The tradition in which he had to find his sense of vocation appeared to him an ideal one, largely unsupported in his actual environment. The world he knew at first hand had too few means by which the past could enrich *his* present, for it was turned backward, richer in memories, dogma, and talk than in living values potent in social manners or a current of moral and literary intelligence. That, at any rate, was Joyce's own sense of it; and in backing his own moral conscience against it, and so having to discover what he shared with it and where he must reject its conception of life, self-consciousness was inevitably forced upon him—in moral and aesthetic outlook as well as in his awareness of history. This is perhaps too common a fate to require special emphasis, but in addition to the social and cultural disintegration of his age, and the subtle inhibitions of self-consciousness, he also inherited, unwittingly, one of the assumptions of his teachers. Looking at his work as a whole, what is more striking than his use of religious terminology, or even his self-conscious devotion to art, is the mistrust he evidently felt about his moral rights unless he could establish a complete, watertight intellectual justification for them.[62] He understood much of this combination of self-mistrust and self-assertion in himself, of course, projecting his understanding in Stephen Dedalus—the "cursed jesuit strain . . . injected the wrong way" (6/10)—yet it remained all the same. For his own vast schemes in *Ulysses* and *Finnegans Wake* are clearly related to the same radical unease. He could not get away from the sense that he may have been, as he phrases it in *Finnegans Wake*, a "condemned fool, anarch, egoarch, hiresiarch", and so could not escape trying to reflect "from his own individual person life unlivable, transaccidentated through the slow fires of consciousness into a dividual chaos, perilous, potent, common to allflesh, human only, mortal" (*FW* 188, 186). One may say, like Mr Savage in his gloss on this passage, that Joyce's inturned ego was forced, by the "repudiation of faith", to seek meaning in ever-widening circles of abstract inclusiveness, while his internal disintegration always brought his aspirations towards unity to collapse.[63] It seems to me rather that his central impulse to look at life squarely and truthfully (not simply to substitute art in its place) eventually ran foul of his unconscious need to write a personal *Summa*, its force hampered, and in his last work dissipated, as he became intellectually more ambitious and more elaborate, so anxious to protect his insights on every side by fitting everything into their patterns that they finally lost the edges of definition.

Perhaps my sense of his basic limitations can be better suggested in D. H. Lawrence's terms, without any reference to the "repudiation of faith", even though Lawrence's objections to Joyce clearly demand qualification. Thus Lawrence's claim that Joyce's self-consciousness prevents any moral evaluation of his material is obviously not true of *Ulysses* (however relevant it is to *Finnegans Wake*)[64]; but behind that is the objection, implicit in Lawrence's work as a whole, to the damage that self-consciousness, separated from passional and sensuous vitality, may entail for the integral human being, and especially for the quality of his thinking and willing. All abstractions, all dogma, Lawrence maintained, get in the way of a direct reckoning with life in its full complexity and with the effort "to find a new impulse for new things in mankind". What he valued in the novel was just its capacity to deal with life whole, and to inform the reader's sympathetic consciousness, his vital taste, leading it into "new places", away "in recoil from things gone dead".[65] Although he does not state them explicitly, the reasons for his dislike of Joyce are easy enough to see: the lack of emotional spontaneity in Joyce's work, its wilfulness and intellectuality, the revulsion from the flesh (so marked in the abstraction of "Penelope"), its absorption with "what I am", and its concern with the past.

"*What next?*" Lawrence insisted. "That's what interests me. 'What now?' is no fun any more."[66]

In part at least this does prompt some real reservations about Joyce, both about his background as well as about the way he took to command it. Paradoxical as it may seem, the long and apparently profound traditions of religion, art and life that were available to him offered little real nourishment to his sensibility, so that for all his elaborate use of European culture, the roots of his art seem curiously shallow. He could maintain only a highly equivocal attitude to Catholicism; he could assert his Irishness only with an equivocal irony. It would be difficult to say where in the Europe of today he would necessarily have escaped it, but there is a faint hint of a residual provinciality about him.

The provincial spirit [said Arnold] . . . exaggerates the value of its ideas for want of a high standard at hand by which to try them. Or rather, for want of such a standard, it gives one idea too much prominence at the expense of others; it orders its ideas amiss; it is hurried away by fancies. . . .

Arnold went on to cite Ruskin's etymological flights about Shakespeare as an illustration of the provincial mind—flights all too reminiscent of some of Joyce's. Joyce may have found the inspiration for his "symbolic" habits of mind in the mediaeval Church; his use of them has even been called "classical"[67]; but in fact, since he lacked a standard at hand different from any the Church as he knew it could have provided him, they manifest a superficiality, an extravagance, a romantic instability, that mark the limit of his imaginative achievement.

Lawrence serves to underline an even more fundamental limitation in Joyce, however, and one far too little mentioned: the narrowness of his range as a *novelist*. Even including the work outside *Ulysses*, Joyce shows intuitive, sympathetic understanding of very few individual human beings. His characters do not *live* in relation to each other, the variety of *human* relationships he treats is very small. He treats social and moral themes; he concentrates, intensifies, his vision has a hard edge; but such narrowness seems as much a lack of vital outgoing feeling in him as a critical comment on the disintegration and "paralysis" of his society and age. In any case, whether its origins lie in his subject or himself or both, his emotional poverty, with all that goes with it of constriction and aridity, prompts the gravest reservations about his work. It seems impossible not to endorse the perceptive conclusion of Mr Levin, that while the mistrust and evasion of life implicit in his wilful verbal patterning of its organic relations, his unintelligent intellectuality, his growing desire to swallow life whole—characteristics that Lawrence had every right to reject—do not sum up his genius, they are inseparable from it.

*　　*　　*

These reservations must be admitted; and if I have concentrated on those aspects of Joyce's work in which I believe his real achievement lies—the aspects expressive of his "classical temper" —I have done so because he is so often praised for those least able to bear critical scrutiny. One version of his achievement would present him as the "fabulous artificer" who constructed a verbal microcosm in *Ulysses,* and in *Finnegans Wake* embraced the whole of human experience within his art. If this is a view of his work with which Joyce cared to flatter himself at times and which has been assiduously fostered by commentaries on his verbal marvels, nevertheless its disregard of the dramatic contexts from which his "symbolism" derives its only relevant meaning leaves too little grounds for taking his artifice as serious art. Similarly, the combination of simple Naturalism (mainly in "subject") and Symbolism (mainly in "method"), decked out with Mythic or Archetypal profundities—the Super-Aesthete formula—is once again incapable of supporting the status usually assigned to his art. The Flaubertian critic of the modern world, rejecting its corruption in savagely "realistic" art (and inspired, presumably, by the same romantic idealism as Flaubert) is another version open to similar objection; and so too is the sophisticated variation that would substitute neo-Thomist metaphysics for romanticism, and praise the same essentially passive, mechanical "realism" as major art for the values it so brilliantly does *not* exhibit. Then there is Joyce the profoundly wise philosopher—Buddhist, Hermeticist, Jungian, and so forth; or Joyce the Super-Comedian, who reduces everything, by relativity and stream-of-consciousness, to the same level of cosmic indifference; or Molly-Joyce, who affirms everything by saying "Yes" at the end of the book. None of these different accounts of *Ulysses* is impossible. On the contrary, they are those most commonly accepted, and Joyce permitted, encouraged, and no doubt held some of them himself; with more or less distortion, indeed, each of them does face some aspect of the book. Yet however possible or widespread, each one of them, while purporting to show *Ulysses* as a major achievement, seems to me to emphasize precisely those elements of Joyce's work to which hostile criticism has been, and ought to be, directed—but which are nevertheless quite unrepresentative of what is most central in his work and most alive.

To suggest what that is has been my intention in this study—not only by indicating what I take to be the most important aspects of the meaning of *Ulysses*, but also by trying to place each of those aspects in the light cast by the others. Joyce's aesthetic theory, his irony, his concern with time and myth, his use of symbol and the stream-of-consciousness, are so closely inter-related that to try to understand any without reference to the rest is to distort all. His aesthetic cannot be separated from the moral values that animate and direct it. Once his irony is separated from the total context to which the aesthetic points, both its tone and its objects become oversimplified. Once disregard his moral and aesthetic values and the play of his irony, it seems possible to discover the meaning of his work in the meanings of the myths he used instead of the other way round; the proper sense of his symbolism is confused; and his stream-of-consciousness seems merely the passive notation of psychological, or some other, "reality". These are the emphases I have tried to shift, for singly or together they seem to me to obscure the real significance of the book. Not that the aspects of *Ulysses* I would emphasize instead are so stably realized that no other view is possible; nevertheless, it is to the active, the dramatic, that we should look, rather than the passive, the ingenious, and the purely verbal. The significance of any work of art can rest ultimately only on what that view of it reveals. Although my sense of the appropriate view implies (I trust) no wildly new interpretation of the book, it may suggest rather different contours of relevance and evaluation.

With Joyce's aesthetic, therefore, I have concentrated on his conception of the "epiphany" or symbol, on the relation between art and experience, on art as dramatic expression, and on the notion of self-understanding and moral detachment at the heart of the whole theory. Obviously, the theory is something of a personal *apologia*, a justification of Joyce's own right to stand outside the universal and pervasive values of his society; but he does not, as I see it, advocate moral *indifference* as the proper stance for the artist. Detachment is a subtler attitude, and if he himself never held it so completely that he could always distinguish it from its cruder substitute, his effort was a large one and largely, but not perfectly, achieved in *Ulysses*. Even his encyclopaedism, his attempt to survey the whole of life, was, I think, inspired by the desire to see life whole. The two things are not the same of course, but at least Joyce's failure is less frivolous than the success with which he is sometimes credited—that of rejecting (or alternatively, of accepting) the whole of modern life. His Dublin is a dubious place and his criticism of it sharp, but cheerfulness keeps breaking in. There is vitality in it still. As I see it, his irony neither entirely rejects Bloom and Stephen, with all they represent, nor entirely affirms them; it does not indiscriminately level modern life with that of the Homeric or any other age, nor indiscriminately deflate it by comparison. It is dramatically more complex, morally more subtle. Similarly, I have tried to emphasize the connection between the temporal perspectives of his characters on the one hand and his use of myth on the other, for the Homeric (and other) parallels gain significance only from the *dramatic* development of what I have called the "mythic" vision. The gradual realization, by reader and artist, of a sense of the wholeness of life, of its ironical paradoxes, its intermingled decay and vitality, its absurdity and mystery—the implicit view from which both moral criticism and mythic parallels derive, or rather, to which they converge—is an achievement that places the intellectual encyclopaedism, and finally, I think, outweighs it. Joyce's concern with the past is the other side of his concern with the present and future. The traditionalism of *Ulysses* is not mere scavenging among *olla putrida*, nor does its originality lie in mere technical experimentation. (We might recall, when pondering Joyce's "influence" on the novel—or the lack of it—that what can be imitated of any truly original work is often representative of its least original and vital side.) Joyce affirms only the timeless validity of Stephen's struggles towards maturity and of Bloom's suffering, integrity, and superiority to circumstance. In their lives, which represent the social, ethical and historical relations of the present, he searches for their true moral being as the grounds of a complete and secure vision of man. And he turns to the stream-of-consciousness not simply to record the given reality of the present nor to interweave "symbols" of transcendental values nowhere to be found in it: neither purpose accounts for the real structure and effect of the monologues. Rather, they exhibit the activity of his characters apprehending meaning in the given reality, expressing values by giving life shape, evaluating and informing it at the same time. The basic activity of the citizen is the basic activity of the artist. Each properly lives, in Joyce's view, only in his apprehension of value, and values in turn are the expression of the moral order, the detachment or freedom, of the individual. In Stephen, he projects an image of the artist in whom the very force of his desire for freedom has unbalanced his conception of it, and whose achievement of it in the future depends on understanding the meaning of Bloom. In Bloom, he projects an image of what is still alive in the human spirit even among all its most ambiguous manifestations.

Joyce is undeniably limited as a novelist both in the range of his sympathetic insight and by the tendency to intellectualize his vital intuitions. Looking at his situation as a whole, however, we must grant that "What am I?" is no idle or superficial question in his mouth. *Ulysses* is more than a merely personal exploration, art is less than his supreme good. Both are transformed into dramatic symbols of a more universal and humane meaning, a completer kind of self-understanding, which the effective structures of the book enact. And although *Ulysses* is often treated as the modern novel that above all others reduces or destroys moral values or denies their effect in the modern world, it is precisely in the engagement, discrimination, qualification, and affirmation of values that it most succeeds. The one theme that seems to me firmly and richly achieved in *Ulysses* (accompanied though it is by other imperfections) is the vitality of spirit by which both citizen and artist, to the degree to which they possess it, are alike justified. Vitality of this kind has little to do with the "affirmation" of "Penelope"—indeed, the confusion exhibited there only prompts reservations about Joyce's sense of his own values and achievement. It appears rather in the patient scrutiny of Bloom and Stephen, in the stable, dramatic apprehension of their significance and that of their world, and in the disentangling of what makes for sanity and growth in the nightmare of history and its accumulated rubbish in the present. These activities represent the moral and aesthetic values of what the young Joyce already understood as "the classical temper". And in the expression of that temper—despite the romantic infinities and "profundities" towards which he drifted himself and, even more, those saddled upon him since—lies all that is most fundamental, free and vital in his work.

NOTES

Chapter I

1 For the biographical facts, Richard Ellmann's fine biography, *James Joyce*, N.Y., 1959, is now the standard source.

2 Marvin Magalaner and Richard M. Kain's useful book, *Joyce, the Man, the Work, the Reputation*, N.Y. University Press, 1956, includes summaries of scores of such comments, though unfortunately without much discrimination of their critical value.

3 Magalaner and Kain, p. 193.

4 The phrase is T. S. Eliot's; see his "Ulysses, Order, and Myth", reprinted in Seon Givens (ed.), *James Joyce: Two Decades of Criticism*, N.Y., 1948, pp. 198-202.

5 It is well represented in some of the articles in the Joyce number of *Envoy*, V, April 1951. Arland Ussher's lively essay on Joyce in *Three Great Irishmen*, London, 1952, is of a somewhat different calibre, however.

6 E.g. David Daiches, *The Novel and the Modern World*, Univ. of Chicago Press, 1939, and D. S. Savage, *The Withered Branch*, London, 1950.

7 E.g. Stuart Gilbert, *James Joyce's Ulysses*, London, 1930, revised ed. 1952; S. Foster Damon, "The Odyssey in Dublin", esp. "Postscript, 1947", in Seon Givens, pp. 203-42; William York Tindall, *James Joyce, His Way of Interpreting the Modern World*, N.Y., 1950; and in another mode, Hugh Kenner, *Dublin's Joyce*, London, 1955.

8 Donne, *Fifty Sermons* (1649), p. 322, quoted from Helen Gardner's essay on *The Limits of Literary Criticism* (The Riddell Memorial Lectures), O.U.P., 1956, p. 49. The whole of Miss Gardner's essay is very apposite to the Symbolist interpretation of literature as well as of Scripture.

9 Cf. the concern over the limitless possibilities of symbolic interpretation of *Ulysses* expressed by Magalaner and Kain, pp. 159, 205. However, Marvin Magalaner's essay, "The Other Side of James Joyce", *Arizona Quarterly*, IX, 1953, pp. 5-16, seems to me an interesting illustration of how the mere presence of "multiple symbolism" in a literary work, and the artist's intentions in using it may become confused with the question of its artistic effectiveness.

10 See the footnote on p. 101 above for some characteristic examples of this approach.

NOTES

11 In his youthful essay on *When We Dead Awaken* (a play that has a significant relevance to the themes of Joyce's own work, incidentally): see "Ibsen's New Drama", in *The Fortnightly Review*, CCC, N.S., 1 April 1900, p. 589, reprinted in *The Critical Writings of James Joyce*, ed. Ellsworth Mason and Richard Ellmann, London, 1959.

12 Edmund Wilson, *Axel's Castle*, N.Y., 1931, pp. 191-236.

13 Magalaner and Kain, pp. 214-15; cf. p. 152.

14 Tindall, pp. 125-6, 35, 7.

15 *ibid.*, p. 29.

16 *ibid.*, p. 27.

17 T. S. Eliot, "The Three Voices of Poetry", in *On Poetry and Poets*, London, 1957, pp. 87, 100.

18 Frank Budgen, *James Joyce and the Making of Ulysses*, London (1934), 1937, p. 291.

19 See Joyce's own brief but definite rejection of Aestheticism, in *Critical Writings*, p. 43.

20 One of the best discussions of this point is the essay by Jane Jack, "Art and *The Portrait of the Artist*", *Essays in Criticism*, V, 1955, pp. 354-64.

Chapter II

1 For some details of the Literary and Historical Society to which Stephen addressed his paper, and the actual dates on which both his paper on "Drama and Life" (transformed, in *Stephen Hero*, into "Art and Life") and that on Mangan were given, see Kevin Sullivan, *Joyce Among the Jesuits*, N.Y., 1958, chap. 5.

2 See William T. Noon, S.J., *Joyce and Aquinas*, New Haven, 1957, pp. 11, 23. Fr. Noon's study is a useful supplement and corrective to Hugh Kenner's treatment of Joyce's aesthetic in *Dublin's Joyce*, chap. 9.

3 *ibid.*, pp. 9-10. The qualifications added by Sullivan, pp. 165 ff., do not really alter this conclusion.

4 For illuminating backgrounds to Joyce's aesthetic, see A. G. Lehmann, *The Symbolist Aesthetic in France, 1885-1895*, Oxford, 1950; Frank Kermode, *Romantic Image*, London, 1957; and Raymond Williams, *Culture and Society, 1780-1950*, London, 1958. In different ways, each one of these helps

to place both the problems Joyce shared with his age and his individual solutions to them.

5 See Noon, pp. 44-5, for Stephen's confusions at this point.

6 See J. Mitchell Morse, *The Sympathetic Alien*, N.Y., 1959, p. 95, on Joyce's use of Aquinas and Aristotle at this point. Morse also sees some of the same fallacies in Stephen's argument that I have examined below: see his "Personal Postscript", *ibid.*, pp. 124-6.

7 But contrast the views of Noon, pp. 49-51 and, especially, p. 72. Noon *contrasts* the identification of *claritas* and *quidditas* in *Stephen Hero* (a notion which he says is "quite easily interpreted as a Thomist derivative") with the concept in the *Portrait*, which is closer to the Scotist *haecceitas*. He comments that "the specific or universal form rather than the individual form is the inner heart of the object as Thomists view the individual thing. . . . The Thomist would argue too that the Scotist haecceitas, in any case, presupposes the specifying quidditas, and that the haecceitas of itself is ineffable and incommunicable, capable of intuition but in no way capable of conceptualization, whereas the quidditas of the singular is utterable, intelligible in one's own mind, and communicable to the minds of others." It seems to me, however, that even in *Stephen Hero* there is a confusion of aesthetic apprehension—the process of intuitively grasping a non-conceptualized meaning, even perhaps one not capable of conceptualization but only of symbolic expression—and ordinary apprehension; and that consequently a philosophically precise exposition of Stephen's (or Joyce's) meaning is impossible.

8 In his essay on "Joyce and Aquinas: The Theory of Aesthetics", *Philological Quarterly*, XXXVI, 1957, pp. 20-35, Maurice Beebe also draws attention to the emptiness of Stephen's *consonantia*, though he concludes, rather oddly, that in effect this brings Stephen's aesthetic closer to Henry James than to Aquinas (p. 25). The conclusion certainly applies to Joyce's position as a whole, but hardly to Stephen's. Mr Beebe seems willing to take Stephen's *talk* about "life" as a genuine element in his aesthetic. For another criticism of Stephen's *consonantia*, see Noon, p. 48.

We might also notice that the same objections apply to Stephen's description of "rhythm", on pp. 234-5 of the *Portrait*: "Rhythm . . . is the first formal esthetic relation of part to part in any esthetic whole or of an esthetic whole to its part or parts or of any part to the esthetic whole of which it is a part." Stuart Gilbert, p. 36 n., draws attention to the similarity of this to a remark of Coleridge's: "The sense of beauty subsists in simultaneous intuition of the relation of parts, each to each, and of all to a whole: exciting an immediate and absolute complacency, without intervention, therefore, of any interest, sensual or intellectual." The similarity is striking, and it is barely possible that Joyce knew of Coleridge's essay; nevertheless, the objection still remains. Whether or not Beauty be defined in terms of a formal (or geometrical) principle, the harmony of art cannot. It is interesting to notice that Coleridge's editor, Shawcross, makes some of the same objections to Coleridge's arguments here as I have made to Stephen's: in particular, to the implicit separation of form and content, and to the citation of mystical speculations in illicit and confusing support of the argument. See Coleridge's *Biographia Literaria, edited with his Aesthetical Essays*, 2 vols., Oxford, 1907, II, 310 ff., esp. notes to p. 232, l. 5; p. 235, l. 7; p. 238, l. 24; p. 239, l. 14.

9 On the ways in which literature necessarily engages our moral experience and values, and the relevance of this to formal questions, see the interesting essays, M. H. Abrams, "Belief and Suspension of Disbelief", and Cleanth Brooks, "Implications of an Organic Theory of Poetry", both in *Literature and Belief*, ed. M. H. Abrams, English Institute Essays, N.Y., 1958.

10 This, I think, is the objection to the interpretation of the phrase offered by A. D. Hope, "The Esthetic Theory of James Joyce", *Australasian Journal of Psychology and Philosophy*, XXI, 1943, pp. 103-4. The meaning Hope points to belongs rather to *Ulysses* than to anything that the theory in the *Portrait* involves.

11 Cf. Hope, *loc. cit.*, p. 105.

12 In his essay on "James Joyce: Esthetic Freedom and Dramatic Art", *The Western Humanities Review*, V, 1950-51, pp. 29-40, James R. Baker argues that Stephen does intend to relate truth and beauty organically (pp. 35-6). However, I cannot really see that Stephen's intention is realized, especially if once we begin to press certain relevant questions. Stephen's (and the early Joyce's) attempts to define beauty in terms of the sensible, and art in terms of the sensible and the intelligible, are confused by the crucial vagueness about the place of intelligibility in *all* apprehension.

13 One of the best treatments of the aesthetic in *Stephen Hero* is James R. Baker's essay referred to in the note above.

14 *Shelley's Literary and Philosophical Criticism*, ed. John Shawcross, London, 1909, esp. pp. 128-30.

15 The distinction of words ("literature" *vs.* "poetry") Joyce probably derived from Verlaine's "Art Poétique", as Tindall has suggested, p. 109; cf. Joyce's *Critical Writings*, p. 39, n. 2. But the distinction is already present in Shelley's *Defence*, and in substance Stephen's distinction seems closer to Shelley than to Verlaine.

16 See J. Maritain, *Art and Scholasticism*, trans. J. F. Scanlan, London, 1930, pp. 24 ff., 162 ff. But see J. Mitchell Morse, *The Sympathetic Alien*, p. 94, on the difficulties of making Aquinas yield a theory of artistic *creation*.

17 E.g. Kermode, pp. 2, 53 and 64-7. Cf. Kenner and Noon, who also properly concentrate on the epiphany as the key to Joyce's own aesthetic

thinking. (Irene Hendry, in her essay on "Joyce's Epiphanies", in Givens, pp. 27-46, was perhaps the first critic to make real use of the concept as a guide to the forms of Joyce's imagination.)

18 E.g. Rudd Fleming, "*Quidditas* in the Tragi-Comedy of Joyce", *University of Kansas City Review*, XV, 1949, pp. 288-96. Cf. Tindall's comment, p. 122, that Kenneth Burke's theory of form as a "pattern of psychological responses does not account for all Joyce meant by harmony". It certainly accounts for more than *Stephen* seems to mean, though I agree that Joyce's views are not to be reduced to Stephen's. Nevertheless, I do not see that Mr Tindall's "musical organization and development" necessarily amounts to more than a pattern of psychological responses either; applied to literature, it would seem to mean even less.

19 See, for example, Kenner, p. 148; cf. the revealing remark, p. 146, n. 1, about "the only metaphysic in which the theory of epiphanies is meaningful". It is interesting to note the kind of conclusion to which Mr Kenner's understanding of the matter leads him. He seems to suggest (pp. 139-40) that art is either engaged in "objective" registration (e.g. "distant trains move slowly") or in "subjective" self-expression (e.g. "distant trains crawl doubtfully")! In short, his notion of *claritas* as objective impersonal Truth —a Truth which he assumes may be verified elsewhere (and which bears a strong likeness to Dogma)—all too easily becomes *claritas* as depersonalized Truth. Nowhere does Mr Kenner suggest what the artist as an individual has to do with the creation of art; the artist seems to be no more than a catalyst—in the most non-vital sense of that highly equivocal term.

A. D. Hope, *loc. cit.*, pp. 111-12, also takes *claritas* in a Thomist sense, seeing it as the *judgment* of coherence in the work, the assessment of its congruence with our knowledge of reality—in other words, as artistic truth. This is what I think Stephen ought to have meant, and perhaps what Joyce tried to get at in *Stephen Hero*; but I do not see how Stephen's theory in the *Portrait* can bear this interpretation. Fr. Noon, it is interesting to notice, speaks of Stephen's "romantic version of the neo-Thomist aesthetic", and comments that it "sounds at times like a plea for the refined essence of poetry, pure and distilled" (*op. cit.*, p. 53).

20 David Daiches, *Literary Essays*, Edinburgh and London, 1956, p. 173.

21 Cf. the conclusions of Mr Kenner (*loc. cit.*), and Haskell M. Block, "The Critical Theory of James Joyce", *Journal of Aesthetics and Art Criticism*, VIII, 1950, pp. 172-84.

22 Cf. Noon, pp. 38-9, on the similarity of Kantian and Thomist aesthetics on these matters.

23 See, for example, Joyce's *Critical Writings*, pp. 41, 43. It was because he equated Joyce's attitudes with Stephen's that Paul Elmer More was led to attack his art: see *On Being Human* (*New Shelburne Essays*, vol. 3), Princeton

and London, 1936, pp. 69-96. More's general interpretation of *Ulysses* is hardly tenable, but he does point to some of Stephen's limitations.

Chapter III

1 Giambattista Vico, *The New Science*, trans. by Thomas Goddard Bergin and Max Harold Fisch, N.Y., 1948, para. 205, p. 66. There is also a relevant hint in Bloom's use of Shakespeare for the solution of "difficult problems in imaginary or real life"—"in spite of careful and repeated reading of certain classical passages, aided by a glossary, he had derived imperfect conviction from the text, the answers not bearing on all points" (638/661).

2 Gilbert, p. 48, takes this as an allusion to Buddhism and reincarnation. This may be so, but the more obvious reference is clearly to Aristotle.

3 E. Gilson, *The Philosophy of St Thomas Aquinas*, trans. E. Bullough, Cambridge, 1929, p. 254.

4 Kenner throws a good deal of light on this aspect of Stephen, and the parallels between *Hamlet* and the *Odyssey*, in *Dublin's Joyce*, chap. 11.

5 This point may recall a possible source for Stephen's metaphor: Jonson's elegy on Shakespeare—"Looke how the fathers face/Lives in his issue . . ."

6 For the parallels between Stephen's Shakespeare and Joyce's Bloom, see William M. Schutte, *Joyce and Shakespeare*, New Haven, 1957, pp. 127ff.

7 Cf. Stephen's more immature remark about his own growth in the *Portrait*, p. 273. Mr Richard Ellmann has noted an echo in this passage from *Ulysses* of Croce writing on Vico: "Man creates the human world, creates it by transforming himself into the facts of society: by thinking it he re-creates his own creations, traverses over again the paths he has already traversed, reconstructs the whole ideally, and thus knows it with full and true knowledge." See his *James Joyce*, p. 351.

Whether Joyce did actually use Croce or not, this passage is very apposite to the general tenor of his aesthetic and his techniques (see Chapters VI and VII below). It also has an obvious bearing on his possible use of Vico in *Ulysses*: see note 13 to Chapter V below.

8 Kristian Smidt, *James Joyce and the Cultic Use of Fiction*, Oslo and Oxford, 1955.

9 I have not developed the obvious similarities between Joyce's aesthetic and some of T. S. Eliot's views (even in the interpretation of *Hamlet*), but it is perhaps worth remarking that the similarities go with some very important differences—especially on the nature of poetic impersonality and

its relation to the artist's own personal maturity. As far as I know, Joyce's possible influence on Eliot—in poetry as well as theory—has never been really explored.

10 But cf. the relevant discussion in Schutte, pp. 87 ff., though I cannot altogether agree with his conclusions that Stephen means that "dramatic" art is impossible unless the artist free himself from all fathers, material and spiritual (pp. 93-4), or that Stephen's thoughts on paternity have only "a peripheral relationship to his main argument" (p. 90), or that there is little more to Stephen than *kinesis* and Aestheticism (chap. 7).

11 Noon, esp. chap. 6, "Sabellian Subtleties: The Trinitarian Theme", pp. 105-25.

12 Noon, pp. 105-6, has also noted this proximity. Aquinas's account of the heresies of Arius and Sabellius occurs at Ia, xxxi, 2; the Holy Ghost is discussed at xxxvi; and the three qualities of beauty are mentioned shortly afterwards at xxxix, 8.

13 Noon, pp. 118-19. I am much indebted to Fr. Noon's clear, convenient exposition of the Trinitarian issues. The fact that Stephen uses God as an analogy for Shakespeare and the artist, and not vice versa, is one necessary qualification to Edward Duncan's useful analysis of the Shakespeare-God parallel in "Unsubstantial Father: A Study of the *Hamlet* Symbolism in Joyce's *Ulysses*", *University of Toronto Quarterly*, XIX, 1950, pp. 126-40, see esp. p. 135.

14 Noon, pp. 111-12.

15 *ibid.*, p. 110.

16 *ibid.*, pp. 114, 117.

17 *ibid.*, p. 125.

18 See O. A. Silverman (ed.), James Joyce, *Epiphanies*, Lockwood Memorial Library, University of Buffalo, 1956.

19 Noon, p. 70. Fr. Noon does not place as much emphasis as I do upon the dramatic aspect of the epiphany, nor does he regard the difference between the aesthetic of *Ulysses* and the earlier theories as sharply or of such importance. His chapter on the epiphany, however, is the most thorough examination of the matter, and indispensable to any further discussion. Probably the best general context in which to place Joyce's mature conception of the epiphany is provided by Lehmann's *The Symbolist Aesthetic in France, 1885-1895*, esp. chap. 6.

20 Charles Feidelson, Jr., *Symbolism and American Literature*, University of Chicago Press, 1953, pp. 70-2.

NOTES

21 The symbolism of Stephen as Christ (sacrifice, redeemer, priest) in the *Portrait* is explored—rather solemnly—by C. G. Anderson, "The Sacrificial Butter", *Accent*, XII, 1952, pp. 3-13.

22 Allen Tate, "The Symbolic Imagination" and "The Angelic Imagination", both in *The Man of Letters in the Modern World*, N.Y., 1955, pp. 115, 97, 112.

Chapter IV

1 D. J. Enright, "Cormac's Ruined House, A Survey of the Modern Irish Novel", *Scrutiny*, XI, 1943, pp. 187 n., 188.

2 Wyndham Lewis, *Time and Western Man*, London, 1927, Book 1, chap. XVI, "An Analysis of the Mind of James Joyce". For a discussion of the Lewis-Joyce controversy, see Geoffrey Wagner, *Wyndham Lewis, A Portrait of the Artist as the Enemy*, London, 1957, chap. 11.

3 Frank Budgen, "Further Recollections of James Joyce", *Partisan Review*, XXXIII, 1956, p. 539.

4 The vagueness of this supposed process is one of the grounds on which Mr Maurice Beebe attacked Mr Kenner in his review of *Dublin's Joyce* in *Kenyon Review*, XVIII, 1956, pp. 649-54. Mr Beebe also makes some of the same criticisms as I have developed. See also Richard M. Kain's "Joyce: Aquinas or Dedalus?", *Sewanee Review*, LXIV, 1956, pp. 675-83.

5 See *Letters of James Joyce*, ed. Stuart Gilbert, London, 1957, p. 170.

6 Others, we might note, have thought of Molly's "yes" more simply as the expression of "blind biological impulse". See, for example, Daiches, pp. 141-2, and Savage, p. 189.

7 Joyce himself is reported to have said in 1923, "Life is suspended in doubt like the world in the void. You might find this in some sense treated in *Exiles*" (Ellmann, *James Joyce*, p. 568). Cf. the interpretation of the play offered by Roland van Weber, in Maria Jolas (ed.), *A James Joyce Yearbook*, Paris, 1949, pp. 58-9.

8 For the personal background to the play, see Richard Ellmann's illuminating essay, "A Portrait of the Artist as Friend", *Kenyon Review*, XVIII, 1956, pp. 53-67.

9 Cf. the remark by Padraic Colum: "It was as though there were two projections of Joyce in those days, one his own person and the other the comic *persona* with which Gogarty invested him"—See Mary and Padraic Colum, *Our Friend James Joyce*, London, 1959, p. 37. On Mulligan's values, see J. Mitchell Morse, "Augustine, *Ayenbite*, and *Ulysses*", *Publica-*

tions of the Modern Language Association of America, LXX, 1955, pp. 1145-6, 1151 (now reprinted as chap. 2 of his book, *The Sympathetic Alien*); and Schutte, pp. 96 ff. Incidentally, Mr Schutte seems to miss the point of Mulligan's "insult" to Stephen: "O, it's only Dedalus whose mother is beastly dead" (*Ulysses* 7/10). The offence, as Stephen sees it, surely lies not in "beastly" but in "only".

10 Frank Budgen, *James Joyce and the Making of Ulysses*, pp. 17-18; and see p. 191 for Joyce's views on the limitations of Christ as a perfect man. Cf. Lionel Trilling's remarks on the absence of Evil in *Ulysses* and on Bloom's unmilitant virtue and humble innocence in *The Opposing Self*, London, 1955, pp. 149-50.

11 Stanislaus Joyce, *Recollections of James Joyce*, N.Y., 1950, p. 16; cf. Mary and Padraic Colum, p. 184.

12 St Augustine, *Confessions*, Book VII, chap. 12. Cf. J. Mitchell Morse, "Augustine, *Ayenbite*, and *Ulysses*", *loc. cit.*, and "Augustine's Theodicy and Joyce's Aesthetics", *ELH*, XXIV, 1957, p. 40, which now form chapters 2 and 8 of his *The Sympathetic Alien*.

13 Cf. Harry Levin, *James Joyce, A Critical Introduction*, London, 1944, pp. 91, 152; Richard M. Kain, *Fabulous Voyager*, Univ. of Chicago Press, 1947, esp. chaps. 12 and 13.

14 Richard Ellmann (*James Joyce*, p. 28) reveals that it was Joyce himself who supplied Herbert Gorman with the description of the real Fr. Conmee as "a bland and courtly humanist". Stuart Gilbert (p. 235) describes the musings of the character in *Ulysses* as "those of a kindly humanist", and he is followed by Sullivan (p. 16 ff.), who is obviously thinking of the real man. No simple equation between the man and the character in the novel is possible, however, and while Joyce's phrase is probably no more than the truth about the one, it is hardly applicable to the text of his book without considerable irony.

15 Douglas Knight, "The Reading of Ulysses", *ELH*, XIX, 1952, p. 64.

16 Knight, *ibid.*, p. 78. Cf. Kain, pp. 167, 181, though Mr Kain hardly develops the full implications of his insights. On p. 181, for instance, he points out that it is Bloom "who expresses the most important criticisms of the place of the church in the modern social order"; on p. 182 he claims that Bloom's "real religion . . . is money"! This same opinion is echoed again in Schutte, p. 145: "Bloom cannot commit his life to the practice of an all-embracing love and charity, because his mind is constantly absorbed in schemes for material gain." One might well wish that what ails Bloom and the society he represents *were* as simple as that.

17 The reference to "druid's altars" is of course meant to be related to Stephen's quotation from *Cymbeline* at the end of "Scylla and Charybdis" (206/215). The two moods obviously qualify each other.

18 Stanislaus Joyce, *My Brother's Keeper*, London, 1958, p. 174. Stanislaus describes how he tried to argue his brother out of his socialism by recalling to him the duty of remaining proudly aloof from the multitude! Cf. Ellmann, *James Joyce*, p. 247.

19 Bloom has been criticized because "he constantly meditates sociological and economic improvements—a gigantic public soup kitchen or a new sewage disposal system" (Knight, *loc. cit.*, p. 78). In fact he is very far from considering gigantic soup kitchens as any kind of improvement.

20 Kain, p. 211; cf. p. 173. The Chaplinesque flavour of Mr Kain's phrase, "the little man", is no doubt unintentional; in any case, it is quite inappropriate to Bloom.

21 For Joyce's attitude, see Stanislaus Joyce, *My Brother's Keeper*, p. 174, Ellmann, *James Joyce*, p. 247, and the articles Joyce wrote for the Trieste newspaper, *Il Piccolo della Sera*, 1907-12, translated by Ellsworth Mason in "James Joyce's Shrill Note", *Twentieth Century Literature*, II, 1956, pp. 115-39, now included in *Critical Writings*. Even as a journalist, however, Joyce obviously remained more of a moralist than a politician.

22 See Kain, pp. 205 ff., and Kenner, pp. 255-6. To the latter, Bloom is "not entitled to any sentimental regard as the champion of the plain man. He is the most inadequate Messiah imaginable." There have been other "Messiahs", however, whose inadequacies suggest that even historical fact can beggar some imaginations. But of course Joyce does not offer Bloom as a Messiah at all.

23 *Letters of James Joyce*, p. 152.

24 R. P. Blackmur, "The Jew in Search of a Son", *The Virginia Quarterly Review*, XXIV, 1948, pp. 109-12. Cf. Tindall, pp. 33 ff.; Ellsworth Mason, "James Joyce, Moralist", *Twentieth Century Literature*, I, 1956, pp. 196-206; and Richard Ellmann, *James Joyce*, chap. XXII.

25 Joyce's various essays and book reviews gathered in his *Critical Writings* and the rather more interesting letters quoted by Ellmann, *James Joyce*, pp. 217, 241 ff., may suggest a qualification to this, but for all their interest they hardly amount to a significant critical achievement of the kind I suggest.

26 *Letters of James Joyce*, p. 135.

27 Arnold, in his essay on Tolstoi in *Essays in Criticism, Second Series*.

28 Cf. Ellmann's sensible comments on the difference between Joyce's outlook and Eliot's in the chapter mentioned above.

Chapter V

1 For some of the differences in detail between the *Odyssey* and *Ulysses*, see W. B. Stanford, *The Ulysses Theme*, Oxford, 1954, chap. XV, and Joseph Prescott, "Homer's *Odyssey* and Joyce's *Ulysses*", *Modern Language Quarterly*, III, 1942, pp. 427-44.

2 Levin, pp. 53-8.

3 Much of the controversy about the parallels arises, I believe, from a failure to distinguish the effects of different kinds of parallel. See, for example, Rudolph Von Abele, "*Ulysses*: The Myth of Myth", *Publications of the Modern Language Association of America*, LXIX, 1954, pp. 358-64; Philip Edwards, "*Ulysses* and the Legends", *Essays in Criticism*, V, 1955, pp. 118-28; Andrew Rutherford, "Joyce's Use of Correspondences", *Essays in Criticism*, VI, 1956, pp. 123-5; and the earlier article by Vivienne Koch, "An Approach to the Homeric Content of *Ulysses*", *Maryland Quarterly*, I, 1944, pp. 119-30.

4 The phrase is L. A. G. Strong's; see *The Sacred River*, London, 1949, p. 156.

5 Edwards, "*Ulysses* and the Legends", *loc. cit.*, p. 123. I hasten to add, however, that I use Mr Edwards's phrase only for its convenient ambiguity. Despite his apparent belief that by pointing to "the sameness of all ages" Joyce "[enlarges] his characters from the local and particular" (pp. 123-4) his essay is one of the few comments on the parallels that combine perception with critical common sense.

6 W. Y. Tindall, "Dante and Mrs Bloom", *Accent*, XI, 1951, pp. 86-7.

7 Kenner, pp. 181 ff., discusses this variation of effect.

8 Cf. W. B. Stanford, "The Mysticism That Pleased Him", *Envoy*, V, April 1951, pp. 62-9, as well as his *The Ulysses Theme*, p. 213.

9 Kenner, p. 177.

10 Cf. Joyce's view of *Dubliners* as "a chapter of the moral history of my country"—a chapter that could, he thought, affect the rest of the story (*Letters of James Joyce*, pp. 62-3). We might also note a passage in *Stephen Hero*: "This suggestion of relativity [in love poetry], he [i.e. Stephen] said, mingling itself with so immune a passion is a modern note: we cannot swear or expect eternal fealty because we recognize too accurately the limits of every human energy. . . . Cranly would not hear of this: for him

a distinction between ancient and modern was a trick of words because he had in his own mind reduced past and present to a level of studious ignobility. Stephen tried to sustain against him that though humanity may not change beyond recognition during the short eras known as the ages of man yet these ages are the preys of different ideas in accordance with which every activity, even the least, which they engender is conceived and directed. The distinction, he argued, between the feudal spirit and the spirit of humanity at present is not a phrase of the men of letters". (p. 155). What is perhaps most interesting about this is less Stephen's insistence on historical differences than his rejection of Cranly's attitude— an attitude often ascribed to Joyce himself.

11 The phrase is Levin's, p. 57.

12 For the use of Irish myth, see H. E. Rogers, "Irish Myth and the Plot of *Ulysses*", *ELH*, XV, 1948, pp. 306-27; for Don Giovanni, Vernon Hall, "Joyce's Use of Da Ponte and Mozart's *Don Giovanni*", *Publications of the Modern Language Association of America*, LXVI, 1951, pp. 78-84. Another parallel sometimes mentioned is *Don Quixote*.

13 It is interesting to note that there are some oblique references to Vico's *New Science* (which Joyce used for *Finnegans Wake*) even in *Ulysses*: Vico Road is mentioned in "Nestor", Stephen's history lesson; the clap of thunder in "Oxen of the Sun" is a Vicchian symbol; and the general notion of cycles of history is common to both books too. Joyce had evidently begun reading Vico in Trieste (see Ellmann, *James Joyce*, p. 351), so it is quite possible that the Neapolitan's theories about history, myth and the Homeric epics may have affected Joyce's conception of *Ulysses*. Ellsworth Mason, in a doctoral dissertation on "James Joyce's *Ulysses* and Vico's Cycle" (Yale, 1948), has attempted to trace parallels between Vico and *Ulysses*, but his argument for direct influence is not really decisive.

If there were any such influence, however, it is Vico's theories about Homeric myth and his teleology that would seem to me to bear on *Ulysses* rather than, as Mr Mason argues, his less important and original theory of historical cycles, which may have more relevance to *Finnegans Wake*.

The notion that history moves to one great goal of historical understanding is the heart of Vico's whole outlook. He conceives his New Science as the rational, sophisticated equivalent of such works as the Homeric epics wherein man attempted to express his consciousness of his own nature in earlier ages still dominated by mythopoeic "thinking". In Vico's history of the human spirit, Reason and intellectual analysis have grown from, have been moulded by, but have gradually replaced, the only means by which primitive and then Heroic societies were able to understand their world and themselves—imagination and myth. His own rational, philosophic New Science, therefore, represented the last modification of the human mind, when man, having grown through his theological and social-mythical projections, finally stands in full self-knowledge—and therefore in freedom. Thus Vico develops a teleology very like that underlying *Ulysses*, and implicitly suggests a similar use of Homeric myth as a basis for the comparative definition of the present "Human" age. The cycle of history, which Mr Mason explores, plays a much less obvious part in Vico's work—and, despite some ingenious arguments and interpretations by Mr Mason, in *Ulysses* as well, I believe.

Nevertheless, the ways in which Joyce's passionate interest in Vico affected his conception of *Ulysses* (if it affected it at all) must still be left for further investigation. It is worth noting, however, that Mr Ellmann's citation of Croce on Vico (a passage Joyce most probably knew) lends support to the emphasis I have suggested above.

14 Cf. Gilbert, p. 107, though Mr Gilbert seems to imply that Stephen is presenting his true personality to Mulligan and Haines.

15 Cf. Tindall, *James Joyce*, p. 30: "water means reality". Professor Curtius and Mr Gilbert take the sea as the "primordial element, giver and taker of life" (Gilbert p. 128). Mr Kenner, on the other hand, takes it as "matter" (p. 211), with the implication, which I think unjustified, of *mere* matter. Of course the sea is a traditional Neo-Platonic symbol for matter or the amorphous substance in which natural forms are embodied, but, as with all such symbols, its meaning in *Ulysses* is what the work *makes* of it. The most thorough discussion of Joyce's related symbols of woman, moon, water and life, together with Stephen's fear of drowning, is Maurice Beebe, "James Joyce: Barnacle Goose and Lapwing", *Publications of the Modern Language Association of America*, LXXI, 1956, pp. 302-20.

16 See Joseph E. Duncan, "The Modality of the Audible in Joyce's *Ulysses*", *Publications of the Modern Language Association of America*, LXXII, 1957, pp. 286-95, for an exposition of the Aristotelian terminology Stephen uses here.

17 Cf. Stephen's language here with that in "Scylla and Charybdis", pp. 179/189; 187/196.

18 From "Who will drive with Fergus now", which Joyce himself set and used to sing, and which was one of his mother's favourites: see Stanislaus Joyce, *My Brother's Keeper*, p. 143, and Patricia Hutchins, *James Joyce's World*, London, 1957, pp. 186-7.

19 For a brief discussion of the passages of Dante Stephen recalls, see Tindall, "Dante and Mrs Bloom", *loc. cit.*

20 Kenner, p. 196.

21 See *Letters of James Joyce*, pp. 138-9: "the idea being the crime committed against fecundity by sterilizing the act of coition".

22 A. M. Klein, "The Black Panther: A Study in Technique", *Accent*, X, 1950, pp. 139-55, traces the pattern of a Black Mass in "Telemachus". Some of Mr Klein's details seem very strained, but he may be right in suggesting one means by which Joyce places Mulligan and Haines and suggests the metaphor of God—(or Christ—) artist.

23 But contrast Kenner's comment on this passage, p. 213.

24 In his article on "Dante and Mrs Bloom", *loc. cit.*, p. 89, Mr Tindall briefly discusses the symbolism of urine, which he takes as water: "to Joyce water meant life and making water was not only creating life but, by extension, creating art". This seems questionable, both physiologically and poetically. Making water in this sense is to eliminate waste-matter; urine is not the same as water; and Stephen creates neither life nor art.

25 The dark turn of Bloom's thoughts is apparently caused by the same cloud that provoked Stephen to recall his mother's death (7/11). This detail of organization is of no importance in itself, of course; it is only a way of underlining the relations between the two men. It would not matter if we missed the cloud altogether.

26 J. Mitchell Morse also warns against over-estimating Bloom's passivity; see "The Disobedient Artist: Joyce and Loyola", *Publications of the Modern Language Association of America*, LXXII, 1957, pp. 1018-35, now chapter 6 of *The Sympathetic Alien*. As Mr Morse points out, it is Bloom's moral *activity* that is the most striking thing about him, and he is in some ways set off, as predominantly a moralist, against the ambivalent and relativistic imagination of Stephen.

27 William Empson, "The Theme of *Ulysses*", *Kenyon Review*, XVIII, 1956, pp. 26-52.

28 This *is* the view taken by Knight, "The Reading of *Ulysses*", *loc. cit.*, pp. 72-3, 65-6. But Stanford, pp. 218-19, seems to me to be closer to the truth in his description and evaluation of this part of the story.

29 For the identification of the black panther with Christ, see Klein, *op. cit.*

30 J. Prescott has collected and annotated many of these fragments in his articles in the *Modern Language Quarterly*, XIII, 1952, pp. 149-62; and *Modern Language Notes*, LXVII, 1952, pp. 334-6.

31 Stanford, *The Ulysses Theme*, p. 216, notes the connection between Bloom's political fantasies and the Ulysses of the *Iliad*.

32 This ballad and its dramatic significance are briefly examined by Vernon Hall in *Explicator*, XII, 1954, no. 25.

33 *Letters of James Joyce*, pp. 159-60.

L*

34 For similar views of *Ulysses*, though reached by different approaches, see Jackson I. Cope, "James Joyce: Test Case for a Theory of Style", *ELH*, XXI, 1954, p. 234; and Stanley Poss, "*Ulysses* and the Comedy of the Immobilized Act", *ELH*, XXIV, 1957, pp. 65-83, which discusses the way Joyce's techniques produce the sense of historical identity and simultaneity. These, and my views, owe an obvious debt to Joseph Frank's concept of "Spatial Form in Modern Literature" (in R. W. Stallman (ed.), *Critiques and Essays in Criticism, 1920-1948*, N.Y., 1949, pp. 315-28).

35 For an interesting sidelight on this problem, see the discussion of Thoreau's difficulties in Feidelson, pp. 137 ff.

36 Cf. the views of Richard Ellmann in *James Joyce*, chapter XXII, on the dynamic relations between naturalism and myth in *Ulysses*.

37 E.g. Gilbert, p. 144, n. 2, or Kenner, p. 181, although Mr Kenner rightly stresses (but only in rather general terms) the analogies with the Homeric *situation*.

38 At times we may wonder whether the details are always discovered in *Ulysses*: see, for example, the names of Molly's family, p. 144.

39 Gilbert, pp. 265, 293, though admittedly these are extreme examples.

40 See Levin, pp. 57-8; Kain, pp. 42 ff.

41 Joyce's comparison is cited in Stanford, p. 223.

42 See Gilbert, p. 172.

43 *ibid.*, pp. 351-2.

44 The "mythic" approach has obvious affinities with such beliefs as Arnold's, for instance, that poetry can provide a kind of substitute religion.
    Some examples of critics who have treated *Ulysses* in this way are listed by Von Abele, "*Ulysses*: The Myth of Myth", *loc. cit.*—they include S. Foster Damon, A. M. Klein, W. Y. Tindall and Edward Duncan, among others. T. S. Eliot's essay on "*Ulysses*, Order, and Myth", is concerned only with the use of myth as a kind of intellectual control; characteristically, Eliot does not raise questions about the "truth" of the myth so employed.

45 Stuart Gilbert is perhaps the prime example of this tendency, with his suggestions about reincarnation and historical cycles, and his citation of Buddhist doctrine. These, as Harry Levin rightly observed, are no more than metaphors in *Ulysses*; and even if Joyce believed they were more than that, the reader of his work need not. Yet W. Y. Tindall thinks that

Molly's concern with "metempsychosis" "supports the Homeric parallel by suggesting that Joyce's characters are the reincarnation of Homer's" (*James Joyce*, p. 97); and the term "reincarnation", with all its misleading implications, is still liable to crop up in commentaries (e.g. William Peery, "The Hamlet of Stephen Dedalus", *Univ. of Texas Studies in English*, XXXI, 1952, p. 109). There is all the difference in the world between suggesting that Stephen *is* Hamlet, or Bloom *is* Ulysses, literally, and suggesting how and why they are identified metaphorically. The former, with all due respects to honest believers in reincarnation, would be mere crankiness in Joyce in Europe in the present century; the latter demands proper exploration by the critic. But perhaps nobody really takes the reincarnation view of the parallels very seriously; on the other hand, the similar "re-enactment" notion is still a popular explanation of the relationship between *Ulysses* and the *Odyssey*. Thus Stanford, p. 212: "Joyce, as is well known, constructed [*Ulysses*] to the pattern of Homer's *Odyssey*.... Dedalus and Bloom ... re-enact the experiences of Telemachus and Odysseus among modern equivalents of Odyssean places and characters." It is natural that Stanford should regard the structure in such over-simple terms, approaching it, as he does, in the manner of an iconographer. Using Joyce's own comparison between much of his work and the Book of Kells, Stanford comments: "just as those Irish illuminators did not interfere with the canon of the Gospels, so Joyce kept faithfully to outlines of the Ulysses myth as described in the *Odyssey*. But, like the Irish monks, on this accepted, familiar foundation, he wove an astonishing structure of erudition, imagination, and symbolism" (p. 223). Of course, Stanford does also recognize that Bloom is no mere Ulysses in modern dress (see p. 214 for example), and clearly his appreciation of the book is deeper than his description of it sometimes seems to imply.

46 See Jung's celebrated essay "On the Relation of Analytical Psychology to Poetic Art", printed in his *Contributions to Analytical Psychology*, London, 1928, pp. 225-49: "The creative process, in so far as we are able to follow it at all, consists in an unconscious animation of the archetype, and in a development and shaping of this image till the work is completed. . . . [The artist] brings it into relation with conscious values, thereby transforming its shape..." (p. 248). This has at least the merit of incorrigibility.

47 *Letters of James Joyce*, pp. 146-7.

48 A point amply borne out by Stanford's exploration of this very tradition in *The Ulysses Theme*.

49 See Von Abele, *op. cit.*, who also criticizes this conception of *Ulysses*, though on grounds that seem to me rather too limited.

50 For a list of authors dealing with Ulysses whom Joyce read, see Stanford, p. 276, n. 6.

51 Ortega y Gasset, "The Nature of the Novel", *Hudson Review*, X, 1957, pp. 11-42; the quotations are from p. 33. But cf. Hegel's similar views in *The Philosophy of Fine Art*, transl. F. P. B. Osmaston, 4 vols., London, 1920, IV, 171.

52 Hegel, *loc. cit.* In his book on *The Epic Strain in the English Novel*, London, 1958, chap. 8, E. M. W. Tillyard also denies that *Ulysses* can be regarded as "epic", but for quite different reasons.

53 Cf. R. P. Blackmur's comments in "Parody and Critique: Notes on Thomas Mann's *Dr Faustus*", *Kenyon Review*, XII, 1950, esp. pp. 32-3.

Chapter VI

1 These devices are conveniently listed by David Hayman, *Joyce et Mallarmé*, 2 vols., Paris (Lettres Modernes), 1956, esp. I, 79 ff.

2 Gilbert, p. 53.

3 Cf., for example, Yeats's uncertain grasp of the point in *Ideas of Good and Evil*, London, 1903: cf. pp. 127-8, 230, with the essay on "The Symbolism of Poetry".

4 Tindall, *James Joyce*, p. 112. Cf. Stanislaus Joyce, *My Brother's Keeper*, p. 140: "Theosophy may have been the only intellectual adventure of his nonage that he regarded as pure waste of energy".

5 For Stephen's use of Aristotle in this passage, see Joseph E. Duncan, "The Modality of the Audible in Joyce's *Ulysses*", *loc. cit.*, pp. 286-95.

6 Cf. Stanislaus Joyce, *My Brother's Keeper*, pp. 53-4: "In early youth, my brother had been in love, like all romantic poets, with vast conceptions, and had believed in the supreme importance of the world of ideas. His gods were Blake and Dante. But then the minute life of earth claimed him, and he seems to regard with a kind of compassion his youth deluded by ideals that exacted all his service, 'the big words that make us so unhappy', as he called them. Yet he had believed in them wholeheartedly —in God, in art, or rather in the duty (he would not have called it 'duty') imposed on him by the possession of talent".

7 The most thorough account of Joyce's acquaintance with Hermetic writings is W. Y. Tindall, "James Joyce and the Hermetic Tradition", *The Journal of the History of Ideas*, XV, 1954, pp. 23-39. Mr Tindall seems to me rather to exaggerate Joyce's use of specifically Hermetic ideas and not to distinguish carefully enough between Stephen's attitude to them and Joyce's own; but he is surely right in emphasizing the private, purely executive use Joyce made of Hermetic ideas and symbols in his work.

NOTES

8 Joyce's *theoretical* debts to Mallarmé have not been fully explored as yet. Stephen's reference to Mallarmé's interpretation of *Hamlet* is only a hint of an influence, and a reaction, that go much deeper, I believe. Mr Hayman in his study of the two writers mentions the similarities (I, 55 ff.), but does not press them very far since his study concentrates on the parallels between *Finnegans Wake* and *Un Coup de Dés*. Mr Hayman (I, 27 ff.) also mentions the seminal importance that Arthur Symons's *The Symbolist Movement in Literature* (1899) probably had for Joyce, and it is worth noting that Symons's essay on Mallarmé suggests some of the obvious limitations of his achievement. Herbert Marshall McLuhan's essay on "Joyce, Aquinas, and the Poetic Process", *Renascence*, IV, 1951, pp. 3-11, is also suggestive about Joyce's double relationship to Aquinas and Mallarmé, but does not develop the questions involved.

9 I cannot agree with L. A. G. Strong's emphasis on Blake's influence as he develops it in *The Sacred River*, esp. pp. 83-9. Mr Kenner, p. 146, is, I think, quite right on the radical difference between Joyce and Blake, though he over-simplifies the issue by supposing that Scholasticism is the only possible metaphysics on which the notion of epiphanies can make sense. On the general question of attitudes, it is worth pondering the implications of a passage in *Stephen Hero*: Stephen, we are told, "toyed also with a theory of dualism which would symbolize the twin eternities of spirit and nature in the twin eternities of male and female and even thought of explaining the audacities of his verse as symbolical allusions. It was hard for him to compel his head to preserve the strict temperature of classicism" (pp. 187-8). Cf. the criticism of Blake in *Critical Writings*, p. 215.

10 Lehmann, pp. 229, 242-3, 246.

11 A point also made by Ellsworth Mason, "Joyce's Categories", *Sewanee Review*, LXI, 1953, pp. 427-32. An interesting suggestion about the source of Stephen's terms—viz. Ruskin's *Fors Clavigera*—is made by Charles T. Dougherty, "Joyce and Ruskin", *Notes & Queries*, CXCVIII, 1953, pp. 76-7.

12 Cf. Leon Edel's brief discussion of Stephen's distinction, similar in direction but in more purely psychological terms than I would care to use, in his *The Psychological Novel, 1900-1950*, London, 1955, pp. 119-20.

13 This is the view of Joyce's aesthetic and intentions taken by Paul Elmer More and criticized above, but it is an interpretation strongly encouraged by such interpretations of *Ulysses* as Ezra Pound's.

14 Cf. Levin, p. 38, and, especially, Hayman, I, 63, 67-9.

15 This is one of the implicit assumptions of Mr Kenner's whole approach to Joyce, for example, and it evidently underlies the extraordinary interpretation of the *Portrait* offered by Caroline Gordon in "Some Readings

and Misreadings", *Sewanee Review*, LXI, 1953, pp. 384-407. It is interesting to relate to this line of thought Stephen's sense of the Roman Catholic position in *Stephen Hero*, pp. 181 ff.

16 E.g. Melvin Friedman, *Stream of Consciousness: A Study in Literary Method*, Yale University Press, New Haven, 1955, pp. 7, 23, 239; Robert Humphrey, *Stream of Consciousness in the Modern Novel*, Univ. of California Press, 1954, pp. 15 ff.

17 *Letters of James Joyce*, pp. 63-4.

18 *Stephen Hero*, p. 68; Gorman, p. 97.

19 Flaubert, letter to Mme de Chantepie, 18 March 1857, in his *Correspondence*, 7 vols., Paris, 1926-30, IV, 164-5. (It is interesting to note that Flaubert's last phrase about beauty, the splendour of truth, is echoed in *Stephen Hero*, p. 68.) Stanislaus Joyce, *My Brother's Keeper*, p. 155, n. 2, mentions Flaubert's letter as Joyce's source. Cf. with this letter also III, 61-2; V, 227-8, VII, 280. These references are noted in J. Mitchell Morse, "Augustine, *Ayenbite*, and *Ulysses*", *loc. cit.*, p. 1147, or *The Sympathetic Alien*, p. 144, n. 10.

20 See Edel, pp. 75-6. There are other similarities between Joyce and Bergson, of course, some of which are traced by Shiv. K. Kumar, "Bergson and Stephen Dedalus", *Journal of Aesthetics and Art Criticism*", XVI, 1957, pp. 124-7. Whether they are anything more than general similarities, however, is another question.

21 See Morse, *loc. cit.*, p. 1158, or *The Sympathetic Alien*, pp. 35-6.

22 See, for example, Humphrey, pp. 33, 63, and Norman Friedman, "Point of View in Fiction: The Development of a Critical Concept", *Publications of the Modern Language Association of America*, LXX, 1955, pp. 1160-84, esp. 1161-3, 1184. Useful correctives are E. M. Forster, *Aspects of the Novel*, London, 1927, pp. 107 ff., and W. J. Harvey, "George Eliot and the Omniscient Author Convention", *Nineteenth-Century Fiction*, XIII, 1958, pp. 81-108.

23 Percy Lubbock, *The Craft of Fiction*, London (1921), 1926, chap. XVII, p. 258.

24 Virginia Woolf, *The Common Reader* (1st Series), London (1925), Penguin ed., 1938, pp. 148-51.

25 Dorothy Richardson, Foreword to *Pilgrimage*, London, 1938.

26 The three main books on the subject are those already cited, by Robert Humphrey, Melvin Friedman and Leon Edel.

NOTES

27 See, for example, Edel, chap. i, esp. pp. 23-4.

28 Cf. Edel, p. 24; Humphrey, pp. 15-16.

29 The phrase is Humphrey's, p. 63.

30 In the essay, "How It Strikes a Contemporary", also in *The Common Reader*.

31 Cf. Arnold Kettle, *An Introduction to the English Novel*, vol. 2, London, 1953, p. 106 n., and Savage's essay on Virginia Woolf in *The Withered Branch*.

32 For this interpretation of "epiphany", see Edel, chap. VIII.

33 Cf. Friedman, p. 7. Mr Friedman incidentally notes that interior monologue represents the mind "in the active state", but unfortunately fails to appreciate the full significance of this in his discussion of Joyce, and makes no real distinction between what (say) Dorothy Richardson regards as "the active state" and what Joyce does.

34 Edel, p. 102.

35 See, for example, Edel, chap. VI, Humphrey, pp. 85-6.

36 Kain, p. 131.

37 Humphrey, pp. 2-4.

38 *ibid.*, pp. 63-4.

39 *ibid.*, pp. 15-16.

40 Kenner, pp. 237-8.

41 Humphrey, pp. 86-8.

42 Wyndham Lewis, *Everyman*, 19 March 1931, cited by Strong, p. 101. Lewis had already elaborated the same point, of course, in *Time and Western Man*.

43 Friedman, pp. 223-4, 103. In all fairness, one should add that Mr Friedman's analysis is restricted to the psychological processes involved, and he does not pretend to any symbolic or other general interpretation. I quote his comments, however, because they do reveal explicitly what seems to be the most common approach to Joyce's stream-of-consciousness writing. In so far as it can be analysed psychologically, Mr Friedman is excellent; yet the limitations of such an analysis—indeed, the fundamental ambiguity of an approach that places a pre-formulated "realism" at the centre of enquiry—does make his literary judgments less convincing than his psychological observations.

44 Gilbert does take the passage this way, pp. 60 ff.; cf. the discussion (p. 63, n. 2) of Bloom's supposedly unconscious allusion, which leads Mr Gilbert to comment, with some wonder, on Bloom's "uncanny flair for the esoteric".

45 "As for Orange, suffusing 'Calypso', where the charms of sun-warmed orange-groves of Jaffa impel Mr Bloom's *Drang nach Osten*, the clue is simple. It was the colour of Greek harlots' dresses." Kenner, p. 241. Mr Kenner's analysis of the "meaning" of the first few lines of *Ulysses* (p. 228) is a more extended exercise in the same style.

46 A passage of Freudian interpretation is offered by Tindall, *James Joyce*, pp. 115-16 (italics mine): "There is, for example, the Gold Cup Race, which is both an actual race and a Freudian symbol. In this race, Sceptre, the phallic favorite [*sic*], loses to Throwaway, the outsider, who represents infertility. . . . *Continual allusions* to cattle and their disorders *establish* the foot and mouth disease, the subject of Mr Deasy's letter to the press, as *a significant theme*. In the maternity hospital, cattle *serve* as an obvious symbol of fertility, and foot and mouth disease, the trouble with cows, becomes a symbol of infertility and Dublin's distemper. That foot and mouth also *functions* on a Freudian level (foot as male and mouth as female) *corroborates their meaning* in this context. As ' bullock-befriending bard', Stephen champions fertility or art against the sterility around him." Mr Tindall goes on to discuss the unknown man who first appears as the thirteenth in "Hades" and becomes accidentally called Mackintosh. He reappears (very briefly) at the end of "Oxen of the Sun" (408/420), where he is mentioned as drinking Bovril. Unfortunately, as Mr Tindall notes, amid the general infertility of Dublin "Bovril or the essence of fertile cows does little good"—that is symbolically, of course.

A piece of equally flexible Jungian interpretation is offered by Mr H. E. Rogers, in his article on "Irish Myth and the Plot of *Ulysses*", *ELH*, XV, 1948, pp. 306-27. Mr Rogers argues, among more convincing matter, that Morgan, the son of the god Mananaan MacLir, expresses the search for the personal entelechy or integration in *Ulysses*, and that Irish myth, embodied in the appearance of the spectre of Mananaan MacLir, in "Circe", dressed and bearded as "A. E.", "gives the climactic chapter of *Ulysses* its meaning, and liberates the plot of the book" (p. 322). Despite the real parallels between some aspects of the book and Irish myths which Mr Rogers convincingly reveals, it is difficult to see how an uproarious parody of theosophical mumbo-jumbo (to which Stephen shows consistent hostility) gives the "climactic" chapter such meaning; it seems more like a parodic expression of Stephen's preoccupation with his own futility. When the spectre cries, "Aum! Baum! Pyjaum! I am the light of the homestead, I am the dreamery creamery butter" (484/499) the passage surely expresses Stephen's scorn of Russell's literary ideals and his uneasy envy of Russell's literary success. Mr Rogers (pp. 322-3) comments on the profound meanings of "Aum" in Sanskrit, and moves by imperceptible logic to Hermeticism, theosophy and Jung. By a process more like free-association than textual analysis, however, he arrives at the quite sensible conclusion that Stephen is seeking self-integration. Yet we may wonder why "Aum" is so profoundly discussed and "Baum" is not. The whole process of "interpretation" works, in fact, without the slightest notice of the rude noises the context directs at the theosophico-hermetico-yogibogi-box of mandalas and Psychic Wisdom.

Some timely comments on "hunting the symbol" are also offered by Schutte, p. 6.

Chapter VII

1 William James, *The Principles of Psychology*, 2 vols., London, [1929], I, 239.

2 Budgen, *James Joyce and the Making of Ulysses*, p. 21, for Joyce's remark. The critics referred to include Kain, p. 20, and Richard Ellmann, *James Joyce*, chapter XXII. Mr Kain (pp. 134 ff.) cites some good examples of Bloom's stream-of-consciousness directed by "objective" events.

3 James, I, 243.

4 These verbal "themes" or "symbols" function in relation to the characters like the details that give physical integration and continuity to the setting and action; on these, see Kain, chap. 4.

5 Cf. Friedman, pp. 14, 231-2; and the commonly used analogy with the Wagnerian "leitmotiv".

6 Kain, pp. 277 ff.

7 Ezra Pound, "Ulysses" (1922), in his *Literary Essays*, ed. T. S. Eliot, London, 1954, p. 404; Edmund Wilson, p. 204.

8 See Budgen, p. 52.

9 Jane Jack, *loc. cit.*, p. 356.

10 Irene Hendry, in Givens, pp. 40, 31.

11 Cf. the treatment of similar material in "Hades" and *Stephen Hero*, pp. 148-150. The comparison neatly illustrates the difference between "epical" and "dramatic" art.

12 See Gilbert, p. 41.

13 *ibid.*, pp. 167 ff., where these and other parallels are noted.

14 Contrast Mr Kenner's comments (p. 210) on this passage, however.

15 For a discussion of the fugal structure, see Gilbert, p. 248, and Strong, pp. 33 ff. The criticisms of Joyce's achievement in Levin, pp. 73 ff., and Friedman, chap. 5, though limited, seem to me unanswerable.

16 Bloom's thoughts about the two "joys" (see chap. III), and the beauty of woman and art (see chap. IV), are of course brought into play all through "Sirens".

17 *Letters of James Joyce*, pp. 146-7.

18 Cf. Levin's comments, pp. 57-8.

19 But see Kain, pp. 33-4. But the critical issue is surely not one of naturalistic *vs.* satiric intent, as Mr Kain seems to imply, but of the *dramatic meaning* of Joyce's organization of his material.

20 For some details that add to the joke, see Joseph Prescott, "Local Allusions in Joyce's *Ulysses*", *Publications of the Modern Language Association of America*, LXVIII, 1953, p. 1226.

21 Cf. Levin, *loc. cit.*, Wilson, pp. 213 ff.; Kain, pp. 40 ff.

22 Cf. Philip Toynbee, "A Study of James Joyce's *Ulysses*", in Givens, p. 278.

23 *Letters of James Joyce*, p. 139.

24 R. P. Blackmur, "The Jew in Search of a Son", *loc. cit.*, p. 101.

25 See Kain, chap. 2, for a discussion of this aspect.

26 Cf. Douglas Knight, "The Reading of *Ulysses*", *loc. cit.*, pp. 64-5.

27 See Wilson, pp. 201-2; Levin, p. 96; Enright, "Cormac's Ruined House", *loc. cit.*, and Empson, "The Theme of Ulysses", *loc cit.* There is a balanced summary of the issue in Morse, "The Disobedient Artist: Joyce and Loyola", pp. 1032-3, or *The Sympathetic Alien*, pp. 85-6.

28 Cf. Strong, p. 136, and Toynbee, *loc. cit.*, p. 249.

29 Cf. I. Hendry's discussion of Joyce's abstractionism in the *Portrait* (Givens, pp. 34-6). There is a wide difference, however, between an artist's definition of an "essence" by its aesthetic particulars, which is the effect Miss Hendry is really concerned with, and the "philosophic" distance from all particulars, which is the effect characteristic of *Ulysses*.

30 Cf. Wilson, p. 218.

31 *Letters of James Joyce*, p. 180.

32 Blackmur, *loc. cit.*, pp. 114-15.

NOTES

33 Gilbert, p. 386; Tindall, "Dante and Mrs Bloom", *loc. cit.*, p. 91; Damon, "The Odyssey in Dublin", in Givens, p. 239; Stanislaus Joyce, *Recollections*, p. 27.

34 See, for example, Levin, p. 93, and Edel, p. 90. Others—Edmund Wilson for one—think Molly quite successful.

35 Kain, p. 100.

36 Hendry, *loc. cit.*, p. 36; V. Koch, "The Homeric Content of *Ulysses*", *loc. cit.*, p. 126.

37 Stanislaus Joyce, *Recollections*, p. 26; cf. *My Brother's Keeper*, p. 164.

38 *Letters of James Joyce*, p. 170.

39 Toynbee, *loc. cit.*, pp. 282-4.

40 Cf. Levin, p. 93.

41 *Letters of James Joyce*, p. 160.

42 Wilson, p. 224; cf. Kain, pp. 101-2.

43 Richard Ellmann is right, of course, in pointing out that Molly has not had twenty-five lovers; there have probably been no more than two. He is rather less convincing, however, about the significance of her personal judgments. See *James Joyce*, chapter XXII, esp. pp. 388-9. Cf. Murray Godwin, "Three Wrong Turns in *Ulysses*", *Western Review*, XV, 1951, pp. 222-4. On Molly's attitudes, see Morse, "The Disobedient Artist", *loc. cit.*, pp. 1032-3.

44 Tindall, "Dante and Mrs Bloom", *loc. cit.*

45 See Levin, p. 90; and cf. Daiches, pp. 141 ff.

46 D. H. Lawrence, *Studies in Classic American Literature* (1924), London, 1933, chap. XII, pp. 164-5.

47 Cf. John Peter, "Joyce and the Novel", *Kenyon Review*, XVIII, 1956, pp. 619-32, for a similar criticism directed primarily at *Finnegans Wake*.

48 Cf. Vivian Mercier, who sees this as one of "The Limitations of Flaubert", *Kenyon Review*, XIX, 1957, p. 408. It is interesting that one quality that attracted Stephen to Ibsen was his "minute and wilful energy" (*S.H.* 33).

49 For example, by Wilson, pp. 213 ff.; Levin, pp. 22, 25, 152 ff.; Kain, pp. 46-7; Toynbee, *loc. cit.*

50 Kenner, p. 238.

51 Henry James, "Gustave Flaubert", in *The Art of Fiction*, ed. Morris Roberts, N.Y., 1948, pp. 135-6.

52 James, in a letter to H. G. Wells (10/7/1915), printed by Leon Edel and Gordon N. Ray (eds.), *Henry James and H. G. Wells*, London, 1958, p. 267.

53 Levin, p. 57.

54 *ibid.*, p. 21.

55 Hendry, Givens, p. 45. Miss Hendry does not, however, draw out the full implications of her observation.

56 This is not meant, of course, as an attack on Joyce's lack of social consciousness or Marxist insight, as it is by Alick West in his *Crisis and Criticism*, London, 1937, pp. 143 ff. The real criticism to be made about Joyce is rather more complex than he there supposes.

57 Quoted by Richard Ellmann in his Introduction to Stanislaus Joyce, *My Brother's Keeper*, p. 23.

58 Henry James, *op. cit.*, p. 148.

59 T. S. Eliot, *After Strange Gods*, London, 1934, pp. 38, 48, 58-60.

60 Savage, pp. 158, 163, 161-2. K. Smidt's view of Joyce's "cultic" use of art is very like Savage's.

61 F. R. Leavis, "Mr Eliot, Mr Wyndham Lewis and Lawrence", a comment on *After Strange Gods*, in *The Common Pursuit*, London, 1952, p. 241.

62 Cf. the interesting conclusions of Stanislaus Joyce, *My Brother's Keeper*, p. 120. Both Mr Levin and Mr Kain have also taken a similar view of Joyce's case: for the former, see pp. 25, 28, 45; for the latter, pp. 13, 46-7.

63 Savage, p. 199.

64 For a brief discussion of this point see William Deakin, "D. H. Lawrence's Attacks on Proust and Joyce", *Essays in Criticism*, VII, 1957, pp. 383-403.

65 See *Lady Chatterley's Lover*, chap. IX.

66 Lawrence's explicit criticisms of Joyce are to be found in his *Selected Literary Criticism*, ed. Anthony Beal, London, 1955, pp. 114 ff., 148-9 (on *Finnegans Wake*), 291, 411. The passage quoted is from p. 117.

67 Cf. Gilbert, p. 43.

INDEX

"Appetites" in aesthetic theories of Joyce and Stephen Dedalus, 47-50
Aquinas, Thomas, 44, 48, 61, 69-71, 79, 85, 89, 91
Aristotle, 66, 72-3, 75, 79, 86, 88-9
Arnold, M., 310
Artistic forms in aesthetic theory of Stephen Dedalus, 77

Bergson, H. L., 231
Berkeley, G., 86
Blackmur, R. P., 18, 137, 288, 292, 298
Blake, W., 219
Bloom, Leopold, 25, 28-9, 35-6, 49-50, 92, 96-9, 104-5, 117, 119-37, 250-2, 314
and Ulysses, 196
as Joyce's spokesman, 124
as protagonist of *Ulysses*, 262-3
attitude of to Molly's adultery, 174-6
consciousness of time of, 152-3
in "Calypso", 171-2
in "Circe", 134-5, 180-7
in "Cyclops", 132-4
in "Eumaeus", 258
in "Hades", 125-6, 271-80

in "Ithaca", 135-6, 190-5
in "Lestrygonians", 126-30
in "Lotus-eaters", 124
in "Nausicaa", 283-4
Joyce's description of, 116
presentation of, 170-88
relation of to society, 134-7
relation of to Stephen, 136-137, 167-9, 178-80, 186-8, 190-4
Bloom, Molly, 109, 159
rôle of in *Ulysses*, 292-300
Budgen, Frank, 287

Chamber Music, 16
Chase, Richard, 19, 24
"Circe", 180-7, 289
"*Claritas*":
in aesthetic theory of Stephen Dedalus, 52-4, 89
in psychological criticism, 239
"Classical temper", 31-2, 59, 214, 315
Coleridge, S. T., 230
"*Consonantia*" in aesthetic theory of Stephen Dedalus, 52-4, 70
"Cyclops", 282-4

Dante, 79-80
De Generatione Animalium, 79
de Rougemont, Denis, 89

341